Seeking Liber...
Dr. Bill
February 2012

Breaking the Siege:
Voyages of Free Gaza and the Freedom Flotilla

An Inside Story About the Gaza Civil Rights Movement by Sea

Dr. Bill Dienst

ISBN: 0615447627
ISBN-13: 9780615447629
LCCN: 2011902155
Dr. Bill Dienst, Omak, WA

Dedication:

⌘   ⌘   ⌘

This book is dedicated to the Palestinians of Gaza; as well as those living in present day Israel, the occupied West Bank, and in the Palestinian diaspora. You will never be forgotten!

We look forward to the day all Palestinians will be granted their basic human rights such as to travel freely, go to work and educate their children. Many of these rights are denied to the people of Gaza and much of the occupied West Bank.

Therefore, the majority of Royalties earned from this book will be donated to Gaza-based humanitarian organizations as directed through the Gaza Community Mental Health Programme (GCMHP). By purchasing this book, you will be contributing directly toward helping people living in Gaza. Additionally, a small commission of $5 on book sales will support activists or international organizations promoting civil rights for Palestinians through Sea Efforts.

Preface

⌘ ⌘ ⌘

Breaking the Siege: Voyages of the Free Gaza movement (FG)

This is a story about courage and determination as told by forty-three human rights activists who founded, organized and purchased boats to go to Gaza. On August 23, 2008, they made history, by landing two small Greek fishing boats, the *Free Gaza* and the *Liberty* in Gaza, They were the first internationals to land there in 44 years.

The volunteers managed to secretly repair two old fishing boats in hidden ports around Athens, Greece, and then sail them to Cyprus while remaining vigilantly alert for Israeli spies intent on sabotaging this global effort before it began.

This book details the harrowing thirty-two-hour maiden voyage through choppy seas from Larnaca, Cyprus, to Gaza Port; how the communication systems of both boats were jammed by Israeli intelligence and how Greek authorities feared that *Liberty* and *Free Gaza* had been sunk. But both boats emerged from the communication blackout and triumphantly entered Gaza Port to the cheers of tens of thousands of Palestinians who had gathered spontaneously to welcome them.

Because of this first success at breaking Israel's illegal siege on 1.5 million people, donors stepped up and purchased a yacht we named the *Dignity*, which made four successful voyages to Gaza from October through December 2008. On its fifth voyage, as Israel was committing massacres on the people of Gaza in an attack called Operation Cast Lead, an Israeli warship deliberately rammed the *Dignity* three times while she was still in international waters, severely damaging the vessel and endangering the lives of the sixteen civilians onboard. Fortunately she was able to make it to safety in Sidon, Lebanon, without sinking.

Undeterred, we bought a fourth vessel, the *Spirit of Humanity (Arion) that* was nearly capsized by the Israeli Navy as we sailed in emergency care workers and medical supplies in January 2009. The boat was forced to turn back in rough waters

On June 30, 2009 while making another attempt to reach Gaza, the *Spirit of Humanity* was boarded and hijacked by the Israeli Navy. All twenty-one unarmed civilian passengers were imprisoned in Israel. Two of the passengers who hold Israeli citizenship were released. After about a week, the remaining nineteen *Spirit* passengers were deported to their various host countries.

We organized for almost a year, knowing that sending in only one or two boats would not make a difference to the Palestinians and Israel's draconian siege on them. We determined that the only way for the world to wake up to the collective punishment inflicted on a civilian population was to increase the size of the boats and the number of people going.

May 31, 2010, while clearly in international waters sixty-five miles off the coast of Israel, a small fleet of five vessels known as *the Freedom Flotilla* was lethally attacked and illegally boarded by Israeli commandoes. Eight Turkish nationals and one American were killed aboard the *Mavi Marmara,* the largest ship in the flotilla. On all other ships, the passengers were beaten and tear gassed. Some with broken bones were thrown on the ground and handcuffed.

This act of Israeli aggression provoked worldwide condemnation and raised global awareness about the ongoing illegal siege of Gaza. Five days later, the Israeli Navy seized the sixth ship, *Rachel Corrie,* a cargo ship carrying reconstruction and education supplies for the people of Gaza. Again, the unarmed passengers were forced to the ground, handcuffed, and held on deck in the blazing sun guarded by dogs and heavily armed Israeli commandoes.

Breaking the Siege describes the human drama of what began as a crazy idea and an impossible undertaking. It describes the creation of this now internationally recognized, nonviolent, direct action movement and how an intense media campaign succeeded in putting the siege of Gaza on the map. We have much left to do. If governments will not force Israel into lifting its illegal blockade of Gaza, we, the members of civil society will continue to sail.

The book also gives insights into the hardships suffered by the people of Gaza as a direct result of Israel's comprehensive land, sea, and air blockade, which are now criticized by international human rights organizations as collective punishment of Gaza's 1.5 million residents.

Unfortunately the strangulation of the Palestinians in Gaza continues, therefore, the work of the Free Gaza movement is only beginning.

About the Authors

⌘ ⌘ ⌘

Huwaida Arraf (US, Israel/Palestine)

Huwaida is a Palestinian with American and Israeli citizenship. She received her bachelor's degrees from the University of Michigan, and her juris doctor from American University (2007). In 2001 Huwaida cofounded the International Solidarity Movement (ISM), which has twice been nominated for the Nobel Peace Prize. She is co-author of the book *Peace Under Fire: Israel, Palestine, and the International Solidarity Movement.*

From 2007 to 2008 Huwaida taught in a human rights law clinic at Al-Quds University in Jerusalem, the first legal clinic in the Arab world. She was on the maiden voyage to Gaza in August 2008, and after that led three more successful sea voyages to the Gaza Strip, as well as two voyages that were attacked by Israel. Huwaida is currently the chairperson of the Free Gaza movement.

Vittorio Arrigoni (Italy)

Vittorio (Vik) has wide experience in international charity work and in the battle for human rights in Europe and Eastern Europe and Africa. In 2003, Vittorio made his first visit to Palestine, initially in a work camp managed by International **Palestinian Youth League** in Eastern Jerusalem and later in Nablus in the Balata refugee camp. In 2006, he attempted to return to Palestine, but he was denied entry.

Held in Israeli detention for a week while appealing the decision, he was then expelled from the country. In August 2006, at the request of the European Union, Vittorio attended the first free elections in the Democratic Republic of the Congo as an international observer. After being abducted in Gaza waters by the Israeli Navy and deported, Vik returned to Gaza on a FG boat. He was there during the winter of 2008-2009, and his book, **Gaza: Stay Human** (Kube Publishing, 2010), is his eyewitness testimony of the attack. Vittorio manages one of the most popular blogs in Italy at http://guerrillaradio.iobloggo.com. At the time of this book's publication, Vik returned back to Gaza, volunteering with the International Solidarity Movement (ISM).

Vik was murdered in his beloved Gaza on April 14, 2011 by a little-known faction there. His tragic death has devastated the activist and Palestinian community who knew and loved him for his joy of life. The second Freedom Flotilla has been named STAY HUMAN in his honor.

Eva Bartlett (Canada)

Eva is a Canadian human rights advocate and freelancer who spent eight months in 2007 working with the International Solidarity Movement (ISM) in West Bank communities, documenting Israeli soldier and settler aggressions against Palestinian civilians (see opt2007.wordpress.com). After spending four months trying to enter the Gaza Strip via Egypt, Eva sailed to Gaza with the third Free Gaza movement boat in November 2008 and lived in the strip until June 2010.

Before the Israeli war on Gaza in the winter of 2008-2009, Eva and ISM members accompanied fishermen on the sea while Israeli gunboats opened fire with live ammunition and water cannon on the unarmed fishermen. During the Israeli massacre of Gaza, she and ISM members accompanied ambulances while witnessing and documenting the Israeli air strikes and ground invasion of the Gaza Strip.

Following the war on Gaza, Eva and the ISM continued accompanying farmers to their land in border areas where Israeli soldiers target farmers and other civilians with live ammunition. Eva also participated in the Palestinian-led, nonviolent demonstrations against the Israeli-imposed "buffer zone," in which tens of farmers, civilians, and demonstrators have been killed and injured by Israeli firing and shelling.

Eva blogs about the situation on In Gaza (ingaza.wordpress.com) and is writing a book about her years in Palestine.

Greta Berlin (US and France)

Greta is one of the five co-founders of the Free Gaza movement. Greta has worked for justice for the Palestinians since the early 1960s. She is the mother of two Palestinian-American children whose father was born and raised in Safad, Palestine and was forced to flee there in 1948. She has been an outspoken advocate for the rights of Palestinians, and has spoken and written extensively on the issue.

Greta was in the West Bank three times since 2003 working with the ISM either in the occupied towns of Bi'lin, Jenin or Ramalah or working in the media office. She was wounded in the leg by Israeli gunfire in July 2003 while protesting Israel's apartheid wall. She was on the first boat into Gaza and has either organized or been in charge of the land and media team for most of the other voyages of the Free Gaza movement. When not working for the rights of Palestinians, Greta teaches engineers and scientists how to design and deliver presentations.

Lauren Booth (UK)

A broadcaster and journalist, Lauren Booth first traveled to the West Bank in 2005, and returned in 2007 and 2009. While living in Gaza, she witnessed the daily humiliations suffered by the Palestinian people under occupation. During the first Free Gaza mission, Lauren was aboard one of the two ships to break Israel's sea blockade of the Palestinian coast—an experience she describes as the greatest moment of her life. She presents the groundbreaking program "Remember Palestine" on Press TV, working closely with a variety of groups, committed to ending Israel's illegal occupation and the siege of Gaza.

Bjorn Borg (Sweden)

Bjorn is the president of the Swedish Port Workers Union.

Eva Boss (Sweden)

A journalist, Eva has been covering the Middle East while based in Cyprus since 1991. Cyprus has good communication and good relations with both the Arab world and Israel. She began as a volunteer at Vestmanlands läns tidning. After receiving a bachelor of science degree in political science and sociology, she went to work for the Swedish newspaper *Svenska Dagbladet's Suburban Capital Press*. This was followed by a newspaper job with Stockholm newspapers *Svenska Dagbladet* and *Aftonbladet*, and the now defunct news agency FLT. She came to Cyprus as the Middle East correspondent for the FLT. She now works as a free-lance journalist.

Bill Dienst, M.D. (US)

Bill is a family and emergency room physician from Omak and Tonasket, towns in rural Washington in the Pacific Northwest of the United States. In 1985, after an intensive summer course in Arabic, Bill took an extra year of medical school and spent six months in Egypt, the West Bank, and Gaza volunteering with various Palestinian health care organizations, initially with the Palestine Red Crescent Society, which was headquartered in Egypt. He has been to Palestine a total of six times on trips sponsored by the Gaza Community Mental Health Programme, by Washington Physicians for Social Responsibility, and with the Palestine Medical Relief Society. He was on the maiden voyage of the Free Gaza movement

Mona El Farra' M.D (Gaza, Palestine)

Dr. Mona is a Palestinian from Gaza who wears many hats. She is a physician by trade and a human and women's rights activist by practice. She is currently the chair of Gaza Red Crescent, Heath Care Committee but has also worked with Al Awda Hospital in Jabalya refugee camp and Union of Health Workers Committee. She is also the projects director for Gaza for the Middle East Children's Alliance (MECA).

Petros Giotis (Greece)

Petros Giotis was born in 1956 in Filippiada, a small town of Epirus, Greece. After high school in Filippiada, he went to Salonica and completed a chemical engineering degree at Polytechnic University. Petros has worked as a journalist since his early university years; he eventually became a professional journalist. Today, he is the chief editor for the Greek newspaper *KONTRA*. For many years he has been a pro-Palestinian author and activist.

Jeff Halper, Ph.D. (Israel)

Jeff is an Israeli professor of anthropology and coordinator of the Israeli Committee Against House Demolitions (ICAHD), a nonviolent Israeli peace and human rights organization that resists the Israeli occupation on the ground. In 2006, the American Friends Service Committee nominated Jeff to receive the 2006 Nobel Peace Prize with Palestinian intellectual and activist Ghassan Andoni.

Jeff was on the first boat into Gaza in August 2008

Anis Hamadeh (Germany)

Anis is a writer, musician, journalist, and editor of www.anis-online.de and www.nonkill-ing.de. Born in 1966 in Hamburg, his mother is German and his father is Palestinian. He spent two years in Baghdad and Alexandria, and has a master of arts in Islamic studies, English, and linguistics. He is the author of the book *Islam für Kids* (in German) and the translator of the book *Nonkilling Global Political Science*. Since 2005, he has lived in Mainz, Germany, where he works as a freelance copywriter and artist. From 2006 until 2008, he was the web master for the Free Gaza movement.

Mary Hughes-Thompson (US/UK)

Mary is a retired TV documentarian and a cofounder of the Free Gaza movement. Before helping break the siege of Gaza on board the *Free Gaza*, she visited the West Bank six times during the current intifada. In 2002 she was beaten and robbed by American-Jewish youths from the illegal settlement of Itamar near Nablus. Mary has gone back to the occupied West Bank to work with the ISM and has also worked several times in Cyprus as part of the Free Gaza land team, most recently during the Freedom Flotilla voyage.

She is also a licensed pilot. A long time nonviolent activist for Palestine, she was also a participant in the recent Gaza Freedom March in Cairo.

FATHI JAOUADI (TUNISIA, UK)

Fathi finished a master's degree in documentary filmmaking at Brunel University in London (see www.arabdochouse.org). Fathi was on the first voyage to Gaza, then has been on several of the voyages as one of the delegation leaders and was on board the *Dignity* when Israel rammed it in international waters on December 30, 2008. He is on the board of directors of the Free Gaza movement and has been one of the indefatigable fund-raisers for the voyages.

Ewa Jasiewicz (UK, Poland)

Ewa is an experienced journalist, union organizer, and solidarity worker. She arrived in Gaza on *the Dignity* and stayed. She was Gaza Project cocoordinator for the Free Gaza movement on the ground in Gaza during Israel's 2008-2009 winter massacre of Gaza (Operation Cast Lead). She is one of the primary organizers of the Freedom Flotilla and was on the Challenger 1 when it was illegally boarded on May 31, 2010.

Ramzi Kysia (US)

Ramzi is an Arab-American writer and nonviolence trainer and activist. Since September 11, he has spent almost four years working in the Middle East, including a year in Iraq with Voices in the Wilderness, a year in Lebanon (during the 2006 Israeli bombardment), and several months in Jordan, Syria, Yemen, and Palestine. He was last in Palestine in May-June 2005, before arriving in Gaza on the first voyage of the *Dignity*. He was a major part of the Cyprus land team during the maiden voyage of the *Free Gaza* and the *Liberty*.

Fintan Lane, Ph.D. (Ireland)

Fintan is a Dublin-based member of the Free Gaza movement and the Ireland-Palestine Solidarity Campaign. He participated in the Freedom Flotilla and was aboard *Challenger 1* when the ships were attacked. He is an historian and the author of several books on Irish history.

Paul Larudee, Ph.D. (US)

Paul, a cofounder of the Free Gaza movement, is a San Francisco Bay Area activist on the issue of justice in the region known as Palestine, which includes Israel, the West Bank, the Gaza Strip, and Jerusalem. He was born to an Iranian Presbyterian minister and his American missionary spouse in 1946 and grew up in the American Midwest and has been to the occupied West Bank several times as a member of the ISM.

Iara Lee (US, Brazil)

Iara, an activist and filmmaker, founded the Caipirinha Foundation, which focuses on global solidarity, cultural diversity, and peace with justice. Under the umbrella of CULTURES OF RESISTANCE (www.culturesofresistance.org), Iara is producing several shorts and a full-length documentary promoting conflict prevention and resolution; she is also working on a variety of arts, cultural, and diplomacy projects.

She was on board the Marvi Marmara when it was attacked on May 31, 2010 and smuggled her chips out so the world could see what happened to the passengers. Her footage has now been used around the world to show what happened that terrible morning.

Sharyn Lock, AKA Bella (Australia)

Sharyn is originally from Australia but now lives in the United Kingdom. A veteran ISM activist in the West Bank, and was badly wounded in an Israeli attack there while working with the ISM in the occupied West Bank. She is one of the cofounders of Free Gaza (FG). After making the initial FG trip, she returned on the *Dignity* and was on the ground with other FG/ISM activists who directly witnessed the twenty-two-day Israeli assault on Gaza in December 2008-January 2009 called Operation Cast Lead.

Her book, **Gaza Beneath the Bombs** (2010, Pluto Press, with Sarah Irving), is her eyewitness account of the attacks. For many years, she fit community work around environmental and human rights campaigning. Her time spent in Palestine led her to acquire basic medical skills, and she is currently a student midwife in the United Kingdom.

Henning Mankell (Sweden)

Henning is the author of some of the world's best-selling books, some of which have sold more than thirty million copies. The books in his Kurt Wallander detective series are perhaps his most well-known books. In addition to his Gaza activism, he is committed to the global fight against AIDS. He was on board the Marvi Marmara when it was attacked and has been an outspoken advocate for the flotilla since returning to Sweden.

Mairead Maguire (Ireland)

Mairead Corrigan-Maguire, Nobel Peace Prize laureate, was cofounder of the Community of Peace People for a peaceful resolution of the Northern Ireland conflict. She has been to Palestine several times to defend the human rights. In April 2007 she was wounded by the Israeli army while nonviolently protesting with Palestinians against the wall in the village of Bil'in. She was on board the second voyage to Gaza, then on board the Spirit of Humanity in 2009 when Israelis hijacked the boat. She was also on board the Rachel Corrie when it, too, was hijacked and hauled into Israel.

Lubna Masarwa (Israel-Palestine)

Lubna is a Palestinian *48* living in Israel. She is a political dynamic activist in Jerusalem working for the Alternative Information Center and Al Quds University.

She chooses struggle as her way against the occupation. She believes that activists should take the authority to change the reality and not wait for someone else to do it. It's important for her as a Palestinian from 1948 to break the siege and keep the relationship with her people. She has also built links with the Palestinian community in Cyprus, where she is regularly active as an educator and adviser at Masjid Mosque.

Cynthia McKinney (US)

Cynthia is a former U.S. congresswoman, Green Party presidential candidate, and an outspoken advocate for human rights and social justice. The first African-American woman to represent the state of Georgia in the U.S. House of Representatives, McKinney served six terms from 1993-2003 and from 2005-2007. She was arrested, forcibly abducted, and taken to Israel while attempting to take humanitarian and reconstruction supplies to Gaza on June 30, 2009.

Niamh Moloughney (Ireland)

Niamh is the Irish Free Gaza coordinator, cultural officer of the Irish Palestine Solidarity Campaign, a community arts worker, and mother of three. She worked to get the Rachel Corrie out of Ireland and then worked with the U.N. to get the supplies into Gaza after Israel abducted the ship.

Tun Dr. Mahathir bin Mohamad (Malaysia)

Tun Mahathir was the fourth prime minister of Malaysia. He held the post for twenty-two years (1981 to 2003), making him Malaysia's longest-serving prime minister and one of the longest-serving leaders in Asia. Mahathir's political career spanned almost forty years, from his election as a Malaysian member of parliament in 1964, until his resignation as prime minister in 2003. As prime minister, he was credited with engineering Malaysia's rapid modernization. During his term in office, he was considered by many people as one of Asia's most influential leaders. Mahathir was also widely known as an outspoken critic of Western-style globalization.[1]

Fatima Mohammadi, (US)

Fatima helped organize two land convoys from the United States to Gaza in 2009 and was aboard the Mavi Marmara on the Freedom Flotilla in 2010, an extension of her experiences as a human rights activist, attorney, and educator. Of Iranian and

---

1   Tun Dr. Mahathir bin Mohamad's biography is from Wikipedia.

American descent, she believes that through education and direct action, all can come to understand the struggles, as well as see the beauty of others throughout the world. She believes that there can be no peace without justice and no justice without truth. This makes it imperative that we all place ourselves in situations where we can see and intimately know injustice. From there, we must be compelled to speak truth into every circumstance at every opportunity. She strives to honor this practice on a daily basis through both personal interaction and public speaking, and through a continued commitment to actions challenging the ongoing occupation and colonization of Palestine.

Adie Mormech (UK)

Adie is a human rights advocate based in the Gaza Strip; he arrived through the Rafah border in March 2010, He was abducted by the Israeli Navy while abroad the eighth Free Gaza movement boat, the *Spirit of Humanity*. He continues to volunteer with the International Solidarity Movement (ISM) and document Israel's ongoing attacks on Palestinians in Gaza.

Andrew Muncie (UK-Scotland)

Andrew is from Spean Bridge in the Highlands of Scotland. He has philosophy degrees from Aberdeen and Edinburgh Universities, plays online poker for a living, and has been deported twice from the West Bank by the Israeli government—once while trying to prevent a collective-punishment house demolition in the Balata refugee camp by the Israeli army and the second time while working with the Tel Rumeda project in Hebron. After arriving on the first Free Gaza boats, Andrew became a long-term ISM observer in Gaza. In spite of being abducted at sea by the Israeli Navy and deported, he returned to Gaza and stayed until fall 2009.

Kevin Neish (Canada)

Kevin is a retired vocational school instructor who has been a human rights activist all his life; he acted as a human shield and human rights observer in Guatemala, El Salvador, Colombia, and Bethlehem, Palestine. "I basically just don't like bullies and try to fight them whenever I see them, regardless of their race, religion, color, or nationality." Many of the photos he smuggled out when he was one of the passengers on board the Mavi Marmara have been used around the world.

Physicians for Human Rights-Israel

Physicians for Human Rights-Israel (PHR-Israel) is a nonprofit, nongovernmental organization that strives to promote a more fair and inclusive society in which the right to health is applied equally for all. It is PHR-Israel's view that Israel's prolonged occupation over Palestinian territory is the basis of human rights violations. For this reason they oppose the occupation and endeavor to put an end to it. PHR-Israel stands at the forefront of the struggle for human rights—the right to health particularly—in Israel and the occupie

Yvonne Ridley (UK)

From County Durham in the United Kingdom, Yvonne is a TV presenter, author, and activist. She first came to prominence when arrested and held for ten days by the Taliban in Afghanistan following the 9/11 atrocity. She was released on humanitarian grounds. A founding member of Stop the Wall and the Respect Party, she has been trying to enter Gaza for many years to show solidarity with the people trapped there. After arriving on the initial FG voyage, she has returned to Gaza as part of the Viva Palestina! land convoy.

M.J. Rosenberg (US)

M.J. is senior foreign policy fellow at Media Matters Action Network. Previously, he worked on Capitol Hill for various Democratic members of the House and Senate for fifteen years. He was also a Clinton political appointee at USAID. In the early 1980s, he was editor of the AIPAC weekly newsletter, *Near East Report*. From 1998-2009, he was director of policy at Israel Policy Forum.

Bianca Shanaa (France)

Bianca is the daughter of a Palestinian refugee who was exiled to Lebanon in 1948. She has a master's degree in political sociology and runs a company dealing with educational products for children in Paris. She is also an activist for the Palestinian Right of Return

Gene St. Onge, (US)

Gene, principal of St. Onge and Associates, is a Lebanese-American and a licensed civil/structural engineer who lives and works in Oakland, California. He has over thirty years of experience with all types of structural building systems worldwide.

Most recently, he has been involved with the Qatar Working Group (QWG), which was established by the Qatar Foundation to develop a program for rebuilding Gaza. As part of his work with the QWG, once reaching Gaza with the flotilla, he was planning to meet with the lead UNRWA engineers in charge of reconstruction to better assess needs and resources.

Gene is working with the QWG to explore ways to use appropriate technology, i.e., local materials with green building systems, to substantially reduce cost and increase the use of locally trained labor. Gene is also cofounder of the Middle East Policy Advisory Committee (MEPAC), a consortium of over fifteen peace and justice groups in the San Francisco Bay Area, which work toward transforming U.S. policy in the region to one based on respect for human rights and international law.

Eyad Sarraj, M.D. (Gaza, Palestine)

Dr. Eyad is a psychiatrist and founder of the Gaza Community Mental Health Program and founder of the International Campaign to End the Siege of Gaza. He is also a commissioner of Palestinian Independent Commission for Human Rights and is one of Free Gaza's advisors in Gaza.

Adam Shapiro (US)

Adam is a documentary filmmaker, human rights activist, and Palestinian rights activist. He lived in the occupied Palestinian territory from 1999-2002 and helped found the International Solidarity Movement (ISM). His films include the award-winning documentary film *About Baghdad* (released in spring 2004), *Darfur Diaries: Message from Home* (released in fall 2005), and *Becoming Nadya* (released 2007).

His latest film is a documentary series on Palestinian refugees all over the world called *Chronicles of a Refugee*. Adam previously served as country director in

Afghanistan for the internationally renowned human rights organization Global Rights. He is co-author of the book *Darfur Diaries: Stories of Survival* (Nation Books).

David Schermerhorn (US)

David is a commercial film producer and is eighty one years young. He was part of the crew of the *Free Gaza* on its voyage to Gaza in August and also of the *Dignity* on its voyage in October. He is an explorer, adventurer, and has traveled around the world on boats. He has been part of the crew on almost every voyage and was on the Challenger 1 in May 2010 when Israel attacked the flotilla.

Hillary S. (UK)

Hillary lives in Sheffield, England, and has long been an advocate in Palestinian solidarity work there. She has been involved grassroots organizing, particularly in the initial grant and fund-raising efforts that made the Free Gaza movement possible. She continues to do media support work on behalf of Free Gaza.

Ren Tawil (US)

Ren was born in San Francisco, California (USA) in 1953, as was his mother. His father Afif George Tawil was born and raised in Jerusalem, Palestine, and was visiting the United States in May 1948 and as a result could not freely return and became a 'displaced person'. Ren first became aware of the politics surrounding the 'Palestinian Problem' after the June War of 1967 as an 8th grader, and has maintained an interest ever since. He was on the first voyage to Gaza in August, 2008.

Marianne Torres (US)

Marianne (retired social worker/MSW) spent more than two weeks in Palestine in the summer of 2010 on a delegation with Christian Peacemaker Teams. The delegation visited Palestinian and Israeli organizations involved in nonviolent resistance to Israel's military occupation, visited refugee camps, stayed with Palestinian families in Hebron and provided mosque and school patrols, to provide international protection to children and farmers from routine violence by Israeli settlers.

They visited the Bedouin village of Al Arakib in the Negev just three days before the Israeli army and high school students demolished it. Marianne reports that after working for Palestinian self-determination for twenty-five years, the visit still presented many surprises and was an emotional roller coaster—from sadness and despair to joy and serious reason to hope, and sometimes back again, even in just one day.

Donna Wallach (US)

Donna is an anti-Zionist activist working for social and environmental justice. She lives in San Jose, California (USA), and is of Eastern European-Jewish descent. She lived in occupied Palestine in the Tel Aviv area from 1981 to 1997 and experienced firsthand the impact of the brutal Israeli occupation on Palestinians living inside Israel, as well as the Palestinians in the occupied West Bank and Gaza. She was in Ramallah during the 2002 siege and spent a week in the Gaza Strip at that time. She shares the grief and outrage of the boat crew that all historic Palestine is still occupied by the apartheid state of Israel. After arriving on the first Free Gaza movement boats, she stayed as a long-term volunteer until December 2008

Darlene Wallach (US)

Darlene is an anti-Zionist activist for social and environmental justice. She lives in San Jose, California (USA), and is of Jewish-Eastern European descent. Darlene spent almost two months in Palestine from May to July 2002. She visited Gaza, Ramallah, and then a night at the Balata Refugee camp, where she was detained and arrested with seven other internationals. All eight received deportation orders from the minister of the interior. They had witnessed brutal collective punishment of the Palestinians. Although Darlene fought the deportation order and was the first person to be released from prison on bail, she was eventually deported. Darlene arrived on the first FG boats, stayed in Gaza, and was hijacked from an Israeli fishing boat by the Israeli Navy, and deported, along with Vittorio Arrigoni and Andrew Muncie (see above), in November 2008.

Stephanie Westbrook (US, Italy)

Stephanie is a founding member of U.S. Citizens for Peace & Justice in Rome, Italy, (http://www.peaceandjustice.it). She is active in the peace and social justice movements in Italy and traveled to Gaza in June 2009.abducted, and taken to Israel while attempting to take humanitarian and reconstruction supplies to Gaza on June 30, 2009.

Table of Contents

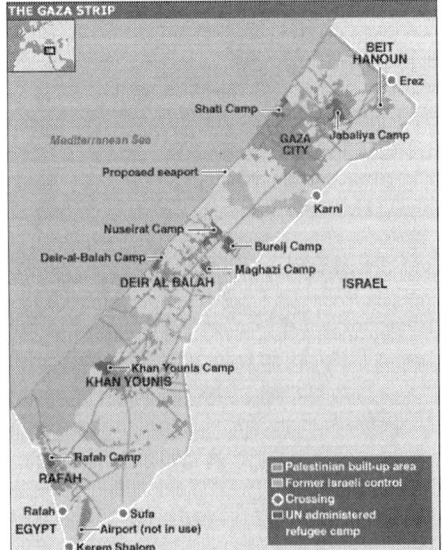

Foreword

By Col. Ann Wright

Ann Wright is a twenty-nine-year veteran of the U.S. Army and U.S. Army Reserves who retired as a colonel. She served sixteen years in the U.S. Diplomatic Corps in U.S. Embassies in Nicaragua, Grenada, Somalia, Uzbekistan, Kyrgyzstan, Sierra Leone, Micronesia, Afghanistan, and Mongolia. She was deputy ambassador in the last four embassies where she served.

You might not expect someone with my background (having served in eight presidential administrations, beginning with Lyndon Johnson and ending with George W. Bush), to be writing a foreword for a book critical of U.S. foreign policy; particularly policies that protect the State of Israel no matter what criminal acts it commits, including many that have been so extraordinarily uneven and harmful to the Palestinians.

In March 2003, after almost four decades of U.S. government service, I resigned from the U.S. State Department in opposition to the Iraq war.

In my three page letter of resignation,

(http://www.govexec.com/dailyfed/0303/032103wright.htm),
I explained my rationale for opposing the Iraq war, but I also took the opportunity to criticize the Bush Administration on other policies, including the Israel-Palestine conflict.

In my resignation letter, I said that I disagreed with the Bush Administration's lack of effort in resolving this conflict and its indifference toward using its influence to resurrect the peace process. I said that "as Palestinian suicide bombers kill Israelis and Israeli military operations kill Palestinians and destroy Palestinian towns and cities, the administration has done little to end the violence. We must exert our considerable financial influence on the Israelis to get them to stop destroying cities and on the Palestinians to curb their youth suicide bombers."

Since my resignation over seven years ago, I have been using my voice from long U.S. government experience to attempt to end the wars on Iraq and Afghanistan, to stop U.S. sponsored torture, and to end unnecessary curtailment of civil liberties as a direct result of the Patriot Act.

It has been in the past two years that I have added my voice and presence to those who have been working so tirelessly to end unjust treatment of the Palestinian people by the United States and Israel.

It was the twenty-two-day Israeli assault on Gaza in December 2008 and January 2009 that jolted me into action. I went to Gaza for the first time in late January 2009, ten days after the brutal Israeli attack ended. As a twenty-nine-year U.S. Army veteran, I was stunned by the amount of destruction. The twenty-two day Israeli attack with American F-16 jets, drones, American Apache attack helicopters, American white phosphorus bombs, and American dense inert metal explosive bombs and killed 1,440 Palestinians including 380 children. The attack also wounded over 5,000 and left 50,000 homeless.

Entire areas had been systematically smashed with American–made weapons. Housing for over 50,000 had been blown up; people were living in tents and piled into family and friends' apartments that were very small and already crowded with their own immediate families. The electrical grid, and water and sewage systems had been destroyed. Schools and hospitals were severely damaged. Ambulances were destroyed. Ambulance crews risked their lives to take injured persons out of destroyed neighborhoods by wheelbarrow.

I decided to help groups get into Gaza and see for themselves the disproportionate force that the Israeli military used against the few people in Gaza who had sent homemade, unguided rockets into areas of Israel along the border with Gaza. In the next six months, I worked alongside many others with CODEPINK: Women for Peace. We were able to get hundreds of international activists into Gaza. These activists returned home to speak of the unbelievable destruction they witnessed there.

They then joined the large group of international citizen activists already challenging the Israeli government's illegal siege of Gaza. Activists are also challenging the complicity of other nations, including the United States, and international organizations, particularly the European Union. These national and international entities participate in the illegal blockade of goods that has resulted in a massive shortage of basic food and materials necessary to keep alive the 1.5 million people who live in Gaza. A narrow strip of land, only twenty-five miles long and between four and seven miles wide, Gaza is considered one of the most densely populated places on earth.

The stated objective of this blockade has been to strangle the Palestinians in Gaza until they overthrow Hamas, a political, militant, and social services group that won the most seats in the 2006 Palestinian Legislative Council elections. Hamas subsequently took over the governance of Gaza. Israel and the United States have put Hamas on their lists of "terrorist" organizations and are doing everything possible to make life so miserable for the people of Gaza that they "overthrow" the government.

The blockade has resulted in the people of Gaza having to dig hundreds of tunnels underneath the border with Egypt to move food and supplies to keep people alive.

Other blockades have previously been used by the United States and other countries in an attempt to effect political change (i.e., overthrow of governments the United States does not like) in Cuba, Iraq, and Iran. But the result of these blockades is that the most vulnerable suffer: women, children, and the elderly. Seldom do the political leaders of the country suffer. None of the blockades have led to the change the blockading country intended. In contrast, citizen-initiated boycotts of goods from apartheid countries, such as South Africa, have been instrumental in effecting political change.

International citizen activists in the International Solidarity Movement (ISM) have protected Palestinian farmers, shepherds, and schoolchildren in the West Bank and Gaza. In the past two years, international citizen activists in five convoys of Viva Palestina have brought hundreds of vehicles and tons of medical supplies to Gaza following the twenty-two-day Israeli assault. In December 2009, the Gaza Freedom March brought 1,350 activists from fifty-five countries to Cairo in an attempt to march in solidarity with the people in Gaza.

But the Free Gaza movement is where a well-coordinated activist challenge to the illegal Israeli siege on Gaza all started. In August 2008, the Free Gaza movement began sailing small vessels into Gaza, directly confronting and bringing international attention to the naval blockade that isolated the port of Gaza from international trade for over forty years. This book is their collective story.

Over the following year, another seven small boats of the Free Gaza movement attempted to bring internationals from around the world, including European Parliamentarians, to see for themselves the devastating results of Israel's policies in Gaza. The boats also brought in Palestinians to reunite with families they had not seen in decades and took out of Gaza Palestinians who needed medical treatment and students with international scholarships who were denied exit visas by the Israeli government.

After the Israeli Navy rammed the DIGNITY and almost capsized the SPIRIT OF HUMANITY, the Free Gaza movement decided on another strategy. The idea of sending not just one or two ships, but six or eight ships to challenge the Israeli blockade moved from concept into reality in May 2010 with the Gaza Freedom Flotilla.

The unnecessary lethal force used by the Israeli Navy, that led to the death of nine passengers on board the *Mavi Marmara* and wounding of more than fifty international activists, resulted in an international firestorm against the Israeli government. The pressure from activists on their governments to not let Israel "get away with murder" had some effect. The Israeli government modified the land blockade, allowing more types of goods and a symbolic increase in the volume of goods that could enter Gaza. However, this is still inadequate. The Israelis did not modify the naval blockade, ban on exports, or the travel restrictions on Palestinians in Gaza that have continued to make the Gaza Strip a large "open-air prison" for its people.

I was honored to be a participant on the 2010 Gaza Freedom Flotilla and to work with the tremendous Free Gaza movement team that pulled the flotilla together.

In face of the Israeli criminal actions of murder, piracy on the high seas, detention, and abuse of hundreds of human rights activists, including theft of personal possessions during the May 2010 Gaza flotilla; at the time of this writing, a second international flotilla is forming to again challenge the Israeli naval blockade.

The steadfast commitment of the Free Gaza movement to challenging the Israeli blockade is one of the great historical nonviolent actions by citizen activists, and I am very proud to be a small part of it.

Chapter 1:

All Aboard the Free Gaza movement

⌘ ⌘ ⌘

Greta Berlin, one of five cofounders of the movement:

Now that we have successfully sailed two small fishing boats into the port of Gaza, people are asking, "How was this idea hatched? Who came up with such a crazy idea to sail boats to Gaza? What were you thinking?"

The idea came from Michael Shaik, a long-time activist from Australia. After Israel invaded Lebanon in 2006, several of us had been tossing ideas around about how to bring to the attention of the world that Israel was locking up Gaza while it attacked Lebanon.

Michael wrote the following to us:

Okay. I have been thinking about this for a long time but am aware that I'm better at ideas than practicalities, so I'll outline what I'd envisaged and let the rest of you do the sanity check.

My plan was this:

- Charter a big boat to sail from New York. Make it clear that its purpose is to: Break the Siege of Gaza (that can be the slogan of the campaign). It is very important that the boat have a big send off, with speeches by important people that will get it as much publicity as possible

- The ship sails to Gaza but stops along the way to pick up supplies from support-ers. This would obviously require liaison with the relevant solidarity groups at the places where it was stopping.

- I was thinking of an itinerary along the lines of New York-Havana-London-Casa-blanca-Barcelona-Marseilles-Rome-Istanbul-Alexandria-Gaza

- The idea would be to build up publicity as we go. If we could get someone like Desmond Tutu to go at least part of the way, that would really help put pressure on other religious leaders to see us and give the boat their blessing.

- The hardest part would obviously be the Alexandria-Gaza leg of the trip. I doubt that the Israeli Defense Force (IOF)would try to sink the boat or anything.

That was my plan. I think it could really bring some serious attention to the hidden violence of economic warfare that Israel is using against Gaza and put pressure on international actors to deal with the issue.

Like I said, it's only an idea, and I don't know how much it would cost to charter a boat. It's a hell of a lot more ambitious than an airport sit-in, but I've been doing solidarity work for Palestine for almost four years now, and the situation on the ground there keeps getting worse and worse. I realize that just about everyone else reading this would probably share my frustration. So my thinking was that maybe it's time to think big, and try to capture people's imaginations to force the issue.

He sent that message in September, 2006 to Mary Hughes Thompson, Huwaida Arraf, Sharyn Lock, Paul Larudee, Donna Wallach, and me.

And thus an idea was hatched, and the Free Gaza movement was born. It turns out that several other people in other areas of the world were thinking the same thing. When we began to publicize that we were going to sail to Gaza—granted a much smaller project than what Michael has envisioned; activists began to add their ideas, asked to join our group, and the beginnings a long two-year project started to take shape.

If we had known it would take two years, 150 people, and eventually close to a million dollars to sail two small fishing boats from Greece to Gaza, I'm not sure how many of us would have signed on to this crazy adventure. But we did. And we made history.

Hillary, a UK Volunteer:

My introduction into the world of the Free Gaza movement came at a public meeting in Sheffield in 2007, where, in spite of ourselves, we became entranced by this crazy idea being presented to us through the ubiquitous PowerPoint.

But this was unlike any other PowerPoint presentation I had seen. However, we are a pretty sensible bunch of activists, and we thought we knew a thing or two about fund-raising for a cause as "controversial" as the Palestinians. So we asked the tough questions: How much is this going to cost? On hearing that it would be a modest (!) $300,000, we protested that it didn't sound anywhere near enough (as if we knew anything about boat buying or sailing across the Mediterranean). And then the killer question—how much have you raised so far? Oh…well….

So it was a great idea—but was it ever going to happen? I'd had a bit of experience getting funding from trusts for relatively "unpopular" causes, and this felt like a challenge I couldn't resist. Like most people though, I was already involved in far too many things…and I still thought it wasn't really realistic.

And then Mushier El Fara, said, "Well, I need to be on that boat!" Mushier, who has lived in Sheffield for many years, is from Gaza and rages silently and not so silently about the way he is forbidden from traveling to his homeland. He is also the inspirational chair of Sheffield Palestine Solidarity Campaign and one of the reasons for my involvement in working with Palestinian people. Well, if he was on board, then I had to be on board too.

Musheir El-Fara' Leaving Sheffied, UK for his Gaza Birthplace

Sharyn and I spent many hours trawling through databases looking for likely trusts to to which we could apply, and along the way we had some fairly tortuous phone calls. Try concisely answering the following: What are the aims of your organization? How are you going to achieve your aims? What are your short- and long-term expected outcomes? The one I liked best was: Who are the likely beneficiaries of your project? If possible, give an estimate of the numbers.

Well, let's see—would one and a half million Palestinians, plus about two million of their relatives throughout the world, be enough for you?

And then, little by little, we got some money! Our first successful grant application was for £5,000 and even better, when we converted it to dollars to let our friends across the Atlantic know, it sounded a lot bigger.

But the long slog of fund-raising was not particularly glamorous, and the number of trusts to which we could apply was pitifully small. Let's face it—most organizations are not interested in ideas about funding small boats sailing across the Mediterranean with the likelihood that they will be stopped and confiscated by the Israeli Navy. Added to that, was the challenge of working with a steering group based in the United States. They didn't seem to understand our need for financial information to make our applications seem even remotely sane.

After all, we were putting in applications for such an off-the-wall idea. The application itself had to come across as 100 percent boringly sensible and thorough. Part of the challenge, of course, was coming to terms with the well-known fact that British English and American English aren't exactly the same language. And while I was fussing, in my terribly British way, about the need for copies of constitutions and accounts, our colleagues in the States were coping with anxieties about so-called antiterror legislation.

One of our leading activists for FG in the United States, Riad Hamad, was literally hounded to death by the FBI. Whether he committed suicide or he was murdered, he became the victim of constant US government harassment.

http://www.austinchronicle.com/news/2008-05-09/621848/

In the end, we raised several thousand pounds from a few trusts, mostly trusts started by good old lefty families with a bit of cash and a conscience. My favorite was the £1,000 we were awarded by the Lipmann Miliband Trust, a fund in the name of socialist intellectual Ralph Miliband. I wonder what his son, the current foreign secretary of the British government, would feel about his father's legacy being spent on the boats that were going to break the siege of Gaza? This was the first of two interesting links between the Free Gaza movement and British politicians.

Calderdale and Manchester Palestine solidarity people put on fund-raiser after fund-raiser, overwhelming Sharyn (whose home region it was) with their enthusiastic work for a plan they could only support from a distance, and a diversity of groups and individuals all over the United Kingdom quietly handed over sums of various sizes.

View from the UK: A Backroom Perspective

As the plans for the boat departure began to seem more and more real, a little bit of e-mail discussion began to take place on how those of us left in Britain, the "backroom team," were going to support those in Cyprus and on the boat. It was also becoming increasingly clear that the backroom team was not so much a team as, well, approximately two of us.

Sharyn was really the lynchpin to much of the planning activity, including publicity, fund-raising, and communication between activists in different countries, but she was heading off to Cyprus or wherever (none of us knew from where the boats would start and that was fine by me). What I didn't know, I couldn't tell Mossad. Likewise Eliza and Osama, both heavily involved, would be either on the boat or the land team, as would Jonny. Other people, who had made contributions in the early days of the project were, for one reason or another, no longer able to give us much time.

So in the last week or two before Sharyn left we tried to set up what we optimistically called the UK support team. We could see two roles for ourselves: first, working to generate publicity and secondly, supporting and campaigning on behalf of the boat crew/ passengers if/when they got stopped or arrested by the Israelis. Since most of us thought this was the likely scenario, much of our attention was focused on this work, including identifying the members of parliament for our UK passengers in order to be ready to bang down their doors if our boat got impounded or the passengers were thrown into an Israeli jail.

We decided to hold a press conference in London and with the help of the London-based Palestine Solidarity Campaign. Jonny (later to join the Cyprus land team) was able to get some "names" who agreed to speak on our behalf.

Getting a press pack together that would attract attention was tricky for all sorts of reasons: basic factual information (like who the passengers were!) kept changing, much of the information was being kept secret, some of our activists did not want any personal publicity, and crucially, we had no photos of anything—not even the boats.

The other problem we faced was that although prospective passengers for the boat had been asked to provide short bios of themselves plus photos, only a minority had done so. This was very frustrating for those of us who were to trying to interest the media.

Of course, in a sense we didn't really want the individuals on the boat to be the story. The endurance and bravery of Palestinians in Gaza was the real story. The passengers didn't see themselves as heroes—but the dilemma was that we needed to make them famous in order to get the publicity that the boats needed in order to shout to the world that Gaza was under siege.

And then…I got a phone call. We had sent out an initial press release alerting media two weeks in advance about our planned press conference, which in turn was to be held about four days in advance of the departure of the boats. The day after the press release went out, the voice at the other end of my mobile said:

"Hello, I'm Lauren Booth, and I want to be on the boat."

Pause…

I sort of felt as though I should know this person, but I didn't, and I made that classic mistake of not saying so straightaway. As the conversation progressed it became clear that she was a journalist and that she was keen—no, not keen, absolutely 110 percent determined to be on our boat to Gaza.

I tried to explain that I thought that the first boat was full, that we had a list of interested people for the second boat, and that, although we were very keen to have some journalists on board, we needed a balance of people with different things to offer.

"Look," she said, in a polite but determined voice. "If I'm on that boat, and I get to Gaza two weeks after Tony Blair didn't, then it's going to be front-page news."

At last, the penny dropped: Blair…Booth…Blair—Booth! I ran upstairs to my computer, to see an e-mail from the Palestine Solidarity Committee office alerting to me to the fact that a journalist was about to phone me and that she was the sister-in-law of Tony Blair, former British prime minister. Blair was now the Middle East envoy for the quartet. He had been in post for over a year and so far had not set foot inside the Gaza Strip. Blair was apparently oblivious to the conditions under which people were living there. Just two weeks previously he had canceled his first proposed visit to Gaza following "security advice" from Israel.

A flurry of e-mails to and from the States and elsewhere followed. Were we or were we not interested in having the sister-in-law of Tony Blair on board? Some rapid googling revealed that Lauren had written some excellent articles about her previous visits to occupied Palestine (good) and that she had also been a contestant on the British reality TV show "I'm a Celebrity: Get Me out of Here" (bad—at least in the eyes of some of us more earnest activists).

There was some anxiety about involving a journalist who wrote pieces for British tabloids, but we were aware that Lauren was, of course, dead right. Her involvement would be a huge publicity coup for Free Gaza and not just in the UK but in the States and across the Arab world.

Vangelis Pissias in Athens:

Finding the *Dimitris K* (the Future *Free Gaza*)

May 2008,

DEAR PAUL, GRETA, DEAR ALL,

WE CAN CELEBRATE. WE ARE SERIOUS.

JUST NOW I CAME BACK HOME FROM A SHIPYARD LITTLE BIT FAR FROM ATHENS...I FOUND IT, AN EXCELLENT BOAT, WOOD BEAMS OF HIGH QUALITY.

DATE OF "BIRTH" 1980: **ALMOST COMPLETELY REHABILITATED.**

VERY CLOSE FRIEND WHO I'D ASKED TO MAKE INVESTIGATIONS IN THAT AREA KNOWS THE STORY OF THIS STRONG AND SAFE BOAT. HE WAS INVOLVED IN REHABILITATION WORKS, AND HE ASSURES FOLLOW-UP FOR SOME MARGINAL ADAPTATIONS. HE KNOWS SOME LOCAL COASTAL AUTHORITY ADMINISTRATORS SO ARRANGEMENTS FOR LEGAL POSSESSION AND EMBARQUEMENT PROCEDURES WILL BE EASIER IN THAT REGION.

THE OWNER ASKED 150,000 EURO. WE TOLD HIM NO MORE THAN 105,000 (IF ALSO ENGAGED TO INSTALL A NEW, SAME TYPE, MOTOR). HE AGREED AFTER MANY HOURS OF NEGOTIATION. **NO NEED FOR SIGNIFICANT ADDITIONAL EXPENSES, ONLY SOME ACCESSORIES AND "COMFORT" EQUIPMENT. I CONSIDER THE PRICE UNEXPECTED FOR THAT KIND OF BOAT, AND I HOPE THAT WITH SOME MORE EFFORT WE CAN AFFORD IT. PERHAPS WE CAN MAKE AN ADDITIONAL EF-FORT FOR COLLECTING SOME MORE MONEY IN GREECE.**

FIRST GENERAL DATA
LENGTH 21 METERS (67 feet long)
WIDTH 6 METERS (21 feet wide)
MOTOR 365 HP, 1700 RPM, TYPE: PENTA VOLVO, VELOC. 9-10 KNOTS,
FUEL TANK 4 CUBIC METER, STRONG HIGH MAST ASSURING EFFICIENT SAILING,
8 CABINS, 4 WC. **POSSIBLE EMBARQUEMENT OF 25 PERSONS** +/- ONE MONTH—
MAY BE 45 DAYS FROM THE STARTING DAY OF THE FINAL STAGE (INCLUDING AD-APTATION WORKS AND LEGAL PROCEDURES) EMBARCQUATION IS POSSIBLE.
SECOND BOAT CARRYING PEOPLE NOT NEEDED, JUST A SMALL ACCOMPANYING ONE (LESS THAN 6 METER LENGTH), VERY LOW PRICE, ONLY FOR CARRYING RE-SERVES AND "SAFETY REASONS."

Preparing the *Agios Nikolaos*
(Soon to become the *SS Liberty*)

Petros Giotis: Notes of a Greek Journalist

It was early in the spring of 2008 when *Vangelis Pissias* asked to meet with me. He told me about a project in which a group, consisting mainly of internationals, had been working on for over a year. The project was based on a simple idea: break the siege of Gaza by sea since no one could access it by land because of the blockade by Israeli and Egyptian authorities. Actually breaking the siege by sea would be a much more complex project.

The Free Gaza movement asked us Greeks to provide mission support: prepare a boat that could reach Gaza but prevent the Zionists spies from learning of the project and trying to sabotage our efforts. Until that time, prior attempts to purchase Free Gaza movement boats had failed. The Zionists had been able to get access to the boats on sale and managed to cancel their purchase. On the other hand, even if a boat could be purchased for FG, it always was at risk of being found and sunk by Zionists.

This means that an absolutely legal action (it is not illegal under international law to sail to Gaza) had to be accomplished in secret, as if it were illegal. So, understandably, for everyone's safety and for the success of the mission, we needed to conduct all our operations in the strictest secrecy every step of the way until and including mooring the two boats clandestinely in separate harbors around Athens. The whereabouts of one boat and crew would not be known to the crew of the other boat. Each one of us involved in this project would function on a need-to-know basis, keeping the overall details as quiet as possible.

I didn't have to give it a lot of thought. I would join the mission at once. The Palestinian cause is a part of our collective conscience as Greeks. We grew up with it. We have always considered the Palestinian revolution our own cause.

We met Palestinian friends and comrades at university. We had helped them before with both open and clandestine activities. Thus, we couldn't say no. When it comes to helping the Palestinian people, who for the last sixty years, have suffered under Israeli aggression and ethnic cleansing, I am completely on board. The Palestinians hold bravely the banner of the fight for freedom, and they are a beacon for all progressive peoples.

Vangelis took up coordinating this indispensable component of the Free Gaza Mission's operations in Greece. Our friends from the FG abroad had already done an excellent job developing the political and financial support for this attempt. There was already an international group that represented seventeen countries that had requested to be on board.

Signatures had been collected in a petition gathering support for the attempt. There were already significant funds, but it was not sufficient. That would be the last of our concerns. We have learned that we must focus on what is most essential to get the job done. If we are to get anywhere with this mission, we must leave secondary matters like adequate financing aside. We must have faith that adequate funding will be dealt with when the time comes.

The main aspect was the preparation of a boat that could take our multinational group to Gaza. As I have already mentioned, our mission had the unique challenge of having to be carried out in secret. If we went forth to the streets and announced that we wanted to buy a boat to break the blockade of Gaza, we would have found many supporters. The Greek people, no matter what their political affiliation, feel very close to the Palestinians. But this open public approach would probably have ended up with a sunken boat.

We had to act cautiously, involving a small number of people who wouldn't ask too many questions. Soon enough, Vangelis found the *Dimitris K.*, an old, but still good simple vessel that, with sufficient repairs, could be rendered seaworthy to carry some twenty-five people. This vessel would become the *SS Free Gaza*.

Then, a network of support was built that would ensure utter secrecy. People like Vangelis and I needed to keep a low profile, since the boat was already under repair in an area where Vangelis carried out research and many people knew him.

Nosy neighbors hanging around the marina would only learn that "the professor is building a boat to go on August holidays with his friends." That is not strange at all in a land like Greece with thousands of small or large private boats. Our network of people worked clandestinely, using methods devised during the fascist dictatorship in Greece (1967-1974). There was expertise as well as a positive social milieu: people have learned not to ask too many questions once they realize you are not willing to answer.

And those directly involved in a clandestine project are well aware that they should not be too curious; they should know only what they need to know in order to accomplish their individual projects within the greater mission. Knowing much beyond the duties of their specific tasks could jeopardize the entire mission. Protecting the mission is of paramount importance. Thus, what is required is maximum secrecy and decentralization, that is, use of a network, most of whose member links are unaware of the other members' specific activities or whereabouts.

When the repairs on *Dimitris K.* had progressed enough, our friends abroad informed us that there were already a high number of participants and that we needed another boat. Time was running extremely short, however.

It is not easy to acquire a boat in late spring nor is it easy to find the people to transform it into a seaworthy vessel. Everyone is too busy on the verge of the new tourist season. Also seeking a boat in the same port area near Athens where *Dimitris K.* was would arouse suspicions instantly. We had to a separate and unrelated place where Vangelis was also well known to the local people because of his university and research activity. A few days later we found a brilliant *trehantiri*, a traditional wooden fishing boat built by *Euboean* ship builders. The vessel was afloat but had been abandoned for four years. The first inspection revealed rotten parts in the wooden framework. The boat needed to be moved to dry dock for repairs.

Thodoris was still one among few traditional craftsmen for wooden boats in Greece. He knew the *Agios Nikolaos* very well. Unknown to him, this boat would become the *SS Liberty* of Free Gaza movement fame. He took great pride in it as he pulled it ashore. "It'll be ready next year, Vangeli," he said. Fair enough for such a busy boat builder looking forward to some rest in the upcoming heat of August.

But not fair enough for the Free Gaza Mission. "Next year sounds too late. I need it ready in a month's time," Vangelis said, while smiling at Thodoris, his boat-building friend. There was no answer on the spot, but we were quite certain Thodoris and his coworkers would curse the Professor and his unreasonable demands.

After the boat accomplished its mission, Thodoris would later describe what exactly happened. "I was lying on the sofa watching TV. There was a news report about boats that had broken the blockade of Gaza. Suddenly, *Agios Nikolaos* was on the screen. I blinked. I couldn't believe my own eyes. I said to my wife, 'That's our boat, ain't it? Our own bloody boat!' Had *Vangelis* told me beforehand, I would've worked more intensely to get it ready earlier. Since it's for the Palestinians, we could have worked all through the night as well."

Many of those people repairing the boat really did work very hard, even late into the night. There were of course some who were used to working rather slowly— taking long breaks for a pint of beer and chitchat at the café. There were moments during this time of secrecy and effort when Vangelis was on the brink of cardiac arrest.

How could you explain to the boatyard repairmen that they had to rush, knowing only that the Professor wanted the boat for a cruise with a bunch of friends from abroad? Could they have worked overtime at night then? But they did work overtime as if they vaguely suspected that *Vangelis* wanted the boat for something more important, although he wouldn't tell them exactly what for.

An E-mail from Bella (Sharyn Lock), somewhere out in the Eastern Mediterranean:

Tue, 22 Jul 2008

Subject: #3: in which I don't tell you very much!

Dear all

Well, I'm in this strange situation that I can't tell you where I am or what I'm doing right now. However I can tell you I'm worn out, got the usual cough I get when I've failed to get enough eating or sleeping done, and I am VERY HAPPY.

Things are going well, and best of all I am working with good, courageous people who I never knew before a few days ago and now would trust with my life.

I feel like I'm in my own personal version of *Land and Freedom*, minus the being shot at. (That might come later!). By the way, Ken Loach, who made that film, endorsed Free Gaza movement a few days ago and sent us a donation, too!

Why humans ever do anything other than passionately work for freedom and justice for all, I can't imagine. Even when it involves the greatest risk, as this project does, it brings the greatest joy.

Love you all,

Bella

Dr. Bill Dienst:
En Route to the Region
Exiting America and Broadening Cultural Horizons

July 26-29 2008

I am on my way out—outside the sphere of influence of the corporate pravda networks who define WHAT THE NEWS IS here in the United States of America. Boarding the plane in Spokane, Washington, I see a young man sporting a DARE T-shirt: Drug Abuse Resistance Education. Many of us need to project a message when we are traveling. No doubt I will project a message, too, when I am inbound.

Right now, while outbound, I wear no messages; I have to be careful. I am joining a movement of international activists who will attempt to break the Israeli-imposed siege of Gaza. We will sail two small wooden boats through international waters and directly into Gaza territorial waters. We'll sail right past the Israeli Navy, which keeps the people of Gaza trapped within their enclave, and into Gaza Port. It sounds crazy, I know. No boats have entered Gaza Port from international waters since Israel began occupying Gaza forty-one years ago as a result of the six-day war in 1967.

This siege against the people of Gaza is supported by the USA and it EU allies; yet few in the West are even aware of this man-made humanitarian catastrophe. The goal of the Free Gaza movement is to raise world awareness of this fact.

I fly on to Denver and then an all-night flight that puts me in Frankfurt, Germany, at noon the following day. From the airport, I take a train. Overloaded with luggage, I stumble out of the *Hauptbahnhof,* the main train station, and into the city

I've got jet lag; my body hurts all over, and I'm stressing out with fear about our mission. I need to chill. I take a tram northwest from the *Hauptbahnhof* to a huge public swimming pool. I love being back in Europe again. Childhood memories of living in Brussels, Belgium, for three years back in the early seventies are bringing back tearful feelings of nostalgia; I am a bit prone to emotionality right now because this may prove to be a dangerous mission.

Anis Hamadeh, Free Gaza movement Webmaster in Frankfurt:

Building the Art Culture and the Free Gaza Song

During the planning of the first Free Gaza voyage, I did not realize that it would be a historic event. You never know such things beforehand; it is too abstract. I had been maintaining the Web site freegaza.org for almost a year—not because of my technical skills, but because I was one of the only ones who maintained a Web site. For months there had been only few things to do with the Web site, but as the date of departure grew closer, I found myself in a kind of nervous anticipation. How could I do more to support the group?

It was August first and my friend Sabine and I were playing badminton in a park when a tune came to me from somewhere. At first I was only humming it, but soon some lyrics came to me: Free Gaza, Free Free Gaza, Free Gaza, sail your boat ashore. The tune did not vanish and as soon as we were home, I grabbed the guitar and a piece of paper and composed as if I were in a trance.

The next day I finished the song and phoned peace worker Rüdiger who plays the mandolin. "Rüdiger, do you have time to come over and play this song with us? I just bought a webcam. Let's record this and post it on YouTube." So we did. To top it off, I announced a song contest in the same video: if you can play your version of this song or if you have another song, join in!

To send the link to the Free Gaza mailing list was very exciting. Would they like it at all? I chose a simple melody and easy chords, so that the song could be sung and played by everyone. It was meant to be a musical good luck charm. Yes, they liked it. Some of the boat passengers even made a video response from Cyprus.

A week later another tune came to me, and I wrote the ballad "Stay with You (from the Cyprus Shore a Boat)" and posted the video link to the group. Someone responded, "Hey, we have these T-shirts that say Gaza on My Mind. Could you write a song with this name? I posted the video link on the same day. In this third song there is the verse:

You say it's all about a security risk
and you don't read no Chomsky, you don't read no Fisk
and I got Gaza on my mind and you tell me why.

Noam even replied to it, writing, "Very glad to see the song, and very pleased to be linked with Fisk, particularly in an endeavor as courageous and necessary as this one."

These were amazing, almost mythical days. All three songs were recorded in a studio before the departure, so that the passengers could download them online and have them in their mp3 players. Up to today, the songs have been downloaded more than 30,000 times. Ofer Golany from Jerusalem won the song contest with his easy, Caribbean-style version of the Free Gaza Song; a rock 'n' roll version by Lars RO from Copenhagen came in second. The song contest developed into the Free Gaza Art Festival, an online exhibition with all kind of art for which I painted some Free Gaza pictures based on photos of the voyages. And I still sing the songs...

FREE GAZA SONG
(Chords: D, A, G, F#)

Free Gaza, Free Free Gaza, Free Gaza, sail your boat ashore Free Gaza, Free Free Gaza, Free Gaza, sail your boat ashore

1) *With a boat to break the siege people waiting on the beach, grab the first one in your reach and teach them the Gaza song:*

Free Gaza, Free Free Gaza, Free Gaza, sail your boat ashore

2) *Bishop Tutu has endorsed, he don't want no violent force"Through the barrel of a gun," he says, "Peace can never be won."*

(F#) Tell me what you think of freedom; tell me what you think of love, love, love

Tell your maza, Free Free Gaza, Free Gaza, sail your boat ashore

3) *Now you learned to sing the song, get on board and sing along, open up and in some time you can add a little rhyme*

Free Gaza, Free Free Gaza, Free Gaza, sail your boat ashore

4) *I want everybody to be free everybody every you and me Sing a song of solidarity, sing the Gaza song:*

Free Gaza, Free Free Gaza, Free Gaza, (G) sail your boat ashore.

Dr. Bill:

July 30, 2008
Larnaca Airport, Cyprus, 9:00 P.M.

At baggage claim, there are arrivals from Frankfurt, Tel Aviv, Beirut, Amman, and the Persian Gulf. Cyprus is a free-wheeling, wide-open, anything-goes island divided into a Greek and a Turkish republic; it's the Bahamas of the eastern Mediterranean and a sort of Switzerland—a neutral party in the wider Middle East. It is also an off-shore tax shelter for the wealthy and fifteenth in GNP among the world's nations.

Cyprus was a former British colony from 1917 until 1960. They drive on the left side of the road here. It still has British bases that are considered *sovereign territory* of the UK; it has been separated by an iron curtain into a Greek side and a Turkish side since 1974. Cyprus's entry into the European Union may make the Turkish and Greek national divisions irrelevant and reunification again possible.

Donna Wallach, a fifty-seven-year-old American of Jewish Eastern European ex-traction meets me at the airport. She is wearing a Palestinian kefiyyeh and holding a sign that says Free Gaza movement. Donna lived in Israel for fifteen years, which she calls Occupied Palestine. She also has Israeli citizenship and is anti-Zionist.

An hour later, Scott Kennedy, from the Resource Center for Creative Nonviolence in Santa Cruz, Californian, arrives. I met Scott for the first time in November 2006 in Gaza while we were witnessing Israeli tanks and Apache assault helicopters attack communities in Northern Gaza, killing scores of people. That November, Scott and I traveled together to the southern border town of Rafah, surrounded by a Palestin-ian authority armed convoy. This convoy's mission was to protect us from the fact that we are from the United States.

After clearing the airport, we make it to an apartment just south of Larnaca Airport. It is hot and sweaty in late July. I attempt a fitful and futile overheated sleep. At 3:00 am Greta Berlin, Hedy Epstein, and Mary Hughes arrive from London. Hedy Epstein is an eighty-four-year-old Holocaust survivor who was born in Germany and es-caped the Nazis as a child. Her entire family was exterminated by the Nazis, yet she is an anti-Zionist, pro-Palestinian supporter.

We talk orientation and logistics. Courtney Sheetz, a young student activist from New York, helps me through the confusion of mobile phones and SIM cards. We prepare coffee and breakfast; my futile attempts at sleep have turned into another all-nighter. At 7:15 A.M. Greta and I return to the airport and take an Olympic Airlines flight from Cyprus to Athens, Greece for a press conference to announce that the boats are on the way, and we are getting ready to go to Gaza.

We fly over the Greek islands. Greece has thousands upon thousands of kilometers of coastline and coves, which is good for us. Our two boats are hiding somewhere down there. The Israeli newspapers *Ha'aretz* and the *Jerusalem Post* are reporting that Israeli government officials are frustrated because they cannot find our boats. They want to find them so they can destroy these vessels of hope and put an end to our mission before it begins.

The Israeli press is describing us as a group of "left wing radicals." Let's see: Greta Berlin works for oil companies. Mary Hughes is a member of the Writer's Guild in Los Angeles, a licensed pilot, and a proud grandmother. David Schermerhorn is a retired NYC advertising executive and an experienced deckhand. In addition to her Holocaust experience, Hedy Epstein worked for the Nuremburg trials after World War II.

A bunch of radicals? Ann Montgomery is a Catholic nun and daughter of a U.S. admiral. I am the son of a U.S. Air Force colonel and a family doctor in a rural, red-neck town in the Okanogan Valley of Washington State. There is much more to our group than Israeli stereotypes would like you to believe

We have civil engineers, attorneys, teachers, electricians, journalists, postal workers, informational technology experts, experienced Greek mariners, a chemist, a member of the Greek Parliament, and more among our passengers. And yes, we have many people with years of experience in nonviolent direct action. We have many who have been tear-gassed, beaten, and shot at by the Israeli occupation forces (IOF) in the West Bank.

Some of us have been to Gaza before and most of us have not. Some of us have volunteered with the International Solidarity Movement (ISM) Some have been arrested and deported by Israel in the past for being human rights activists. Some have been denied entry into Israel—not because we are violent, but because we are nonviolent, which is even more threatening to the Israeli occupiers who want to paint the entire Palestinian resistance movement as violent terrorists. Yep, if we are a bunch of left-wing radicals, we certainly have our share of talented people.

Palestinian-American Monir Deeb, American Greta Berlin and Israeli-American Jeff Halper at Cyprus Press Conference

Chapter 2:

Athenian Spooks

⌘   ⌘   ⌘

From Bella:

Date: Mon, 28 Jul 2008
Subject: #4: Hopefully a Needle in Haystack Experience

Here's how we are being covered in the Israeli newspaper *Ha'aretz*. They and we will know more tomorrow! I like how they (pretend to) think we'd prefer a fight rather than actually to achieve our aims. Like the UK *Daily Mail*'s similarly odd view of the anarchist black bloc—but at sea…

Bella

http://www.haaretz.com/hasen/spages/1006191.html

Last update: 12:29 28/07/2008

Israel fears European ship may sail to Gaza to "break siege"

By Barak Ravid

Israel is worried by reports that a group of left-wing activists from Europe plan to set sail for Gaza from Cyprus on August 5 under the slogan: Breaking the Siege.

The activists will reportedly include three members of the European Parliament. It is still not certain how serious the plans are. However, Israel fears that if the ship does sail, it will create a provocation that would at best cause public relations damage and could even result in violence.

The Free Gaza movement and the International Solidarity Movement are organizing the ship. Many of the latter's members have been barred from entering Israel on security grounds.

The organizers have reportedly raised almost $300,000 to finance the operation and recruited sixty people to sail with the ship. These include activists from several countries as well as journalists.

According to the Free Gaza movement's Web site, the activists will include a Holocaust survivor, a survivor of the Palestinian Nakba, as Palestinians call Israel's creation in 1948, and other members of the Palestinian diaspora, in addition to the European parliamentarians.

According to the Web site, the plan is for the boat to enter Gaza's territorial waters— and, more specifically, the "special security zone" that the Israel Navy has declared off-limits to all boats. The organizers thereby hope to provoke a clash with the navy that will end with them being forcibly arrested.

An Israeli government source said that Israel still has little information about the plan, and it is not clear whether it will ever come off. A year ago, he noted, Israel received reports of a similar plan, but because of logistical difficulties the initiative never got off the ground.

In conversations with their Israeli counterparts, Cypriot officials have expressed concern about the boat departing from their shores but say they can do nothing to prevent it. According to the information that has reached Israel, however, Cyprus is not the only point of departure under consideration; the ship might also sail from Turkey or from Alexandria, Egypt.

Israel is still trying to discover the ship's exact identity and more details about the organizers' intentions. It is also trying to decide how to respond. One option that has been raised in official discussions is to simply allow the ship to reach Gaza and thereby foil the organizers' apparent desire for a clash.

Subject: #5: They're behind you! Boats Located in Greece

Tuesday, 29 July 2008

And so am I (or is it all a cunning bluff?)

> For Immediate Release:

> **Can unarmed seaborne civilians break the siege of Gaza?**

A press conference at 13:00H, Tuesday, July 29
> International Press Center, Athens

> Inaugurating the Free Gaza movement: Sailing to Gaza

In August, unarmed Palestinians, Israelis, and internationals will sail directly to Gaza without going through Israeli territory and without seeking permission from Israeli authorities. They include an eighty-one-year-old Catholic nun, an eighty-three-year-old Holocaust survivor, Palestinians from Gaza, sixteen nationalities, members of at least four major religions, and the international press.

On Tuesday, July 29, 2008, the Free Gaza movement publicly introduces its international team along with the Greek vessels that will take volunteers from Cyprus to Gaza in popular solidarity with Palestinian human rights. From that day, any attempt to damage the project will be considered an act of aggression against a nonviolent international human rights mission.

The boats will stop at Greek ports to receive supporters, and there will be opportunities for the press and public figures to travel part of the way on board and to broadcast from aboard ship with the latest high-speed satellite data systems.

We hope this press conference gives our beautiful boats a little more protection. The last few days, with no one knowing about the project here, felt quite risky. If anything happened, would anyone care much? It was hard to feel the boats were safe if we took our eyes off them for even a moment. Now it's public knowledge, so there will be interest (and perhaps some Greek sense of ownership of the mission), and we think that may give us a little more protection. The press conference was apparently packed! Someone we are working with keeps saying, "If there is an attack on the boats, it should be seen as an act of war against Greece!" The specific location of the boats is still secret though.

Read "The Ship of Return," by Charles Glass about the 1988 Ship of Return attempt - our only precursor that we are aware of. There are many similarities to their story and ours, and as I have been making lots of boat-related lists and plans, I have been very aware that the organizers of that attempt must have been making similar lists and plans, with similar hope in their hearts to that I am carrying. And for this the three Palestinian organizers were killed. For them also, I want this to succeed.

Four and Counting
Wednesday, 30 July 2008

According to my colleague Paul, there've been several attempts to obstruct the project. First, earlier this year, we almost bought a boat. The owner agreed, but then stopped communicating with us, and we were told the boat had been removed from the market. Was this the result of pressure from some hostile source? Maybe.

Next, our Israeli participants were indirectly informed that, should they travel with us, they might be charged with treason; a twenty-year sentence. Some of them understandably decided they would have to choose the land-team role instead of sailing and risking this. However, Jeff Halper from the *Israeli Campaign against House Demolitions*, said, "What the hell. I'm going anyway. Let them try to charge me."

Then there was the *Al Jazeera* ad that wasn't. A donor specifically gave money for us to get an *Al Jazeera* ad produced and aired. This would have probably completely sorted out our funding deficits (currently we're going ahead partly on debt and faith!). *Al Jazeera* at first said they thought the ad was great, that they'd give us bonus airtime, the best slots, and then they didn't invoice us.

When we got them to answer our e-mails, they said new and various random things about how it wasn't quite right for airing, and if we said we'd solve the problems they mentioned, they immediately came up with new ones. The thing is, *Al Jazeera* needs access to Palestine, and you know who gives them that. Apparently there was a point when BBC journalists decided not to cooperate with the vetting Israel requires doing on some of their work, and for six months they weren't allowed into Palestine. Our best guess is this sort of pressure occurred.

Subject: Sailing for Riad
Wednesday, 30 July 2008

The final obstruction is the hardest to tell. Do you recall I told you about Riad Hamad, of Austin, Texas, having his house raided by the FBI, and all his papers and his computer and everything taken? His charity, the Palestinian Children's Welfare Fund, had its bank account frozen; it contained $50,000, a large part of which was Free Gaza money they were holding for us and which we'll probably not see again. (As of the printing of this book, we have never seen any of the money that the FBI confiscated.)

Riad was our boat buyer and passionately supportive of the plan to sail to Gaza. At the time he was raided, he was about two weeks away from buying our first boat using that money as a down payment. None of his contacts were safe after that and the information about the boat was permanently lost.

He'd been aware of low-key FBI surveillance for a long time; he was used to it and made a joke of it. But he'd never been raided, and the results of the raid sent Riad over the edge. He also sold Palestinian products on behalf of many people there, but he'd never gotten one step ahead of himself financially, in terms of being able to pay his suppliers in advance of sale.

So, they sent him the goods, he sold them, and sent the money back. Well, now he couldn't send the current money owed because the account was blocked. This was extremely distressing for him; he hadn't enough money of his own to cover it.

Of course, this could have been worked out somehow, but then it was coupled with the FBI questioning both his son and daughter, causing the family great stress. This was just too much for Riad. I think he felt himself to be a risk and a trouble to the family and Palestinian projects he loved.

He handed personal details and project information over to close friends, drove his car to his local lake, and waded into the water. His hands and feet were taped together, but despite the inevitable speculation, people close to him believe this was suicide; perhaps he was ensuring he would be successful, making a point about being forced into this choice.

Was the FBI raid based on a timely Israeli tip meant as an obstruction to our efforts? If so, we lost much more than a boat. I read the many eulogies from his memorial service; he was doing an impossible number of things for an impossible number of people.

For example, while we were in Lebanon, my friend Eliza was asked by Riad to visit a Palestinian family with two severely disabled children. He wanted to buy them wheelchairs and beds that wouldn't come to them in any other way. And he got them both wheelchairs and beds. He took other people's suffering as something he should personally address.

It was now the end of April, and we had promised people we were sailing in the summer, and we had no boats. That's where the Greeks came in; a contact from one of our activists brought them into the project.

So we are also sailing for Riad. His e-mails are still in my inbox; I can't bring myself to delete them.

My colleague Paul was probably the last to speak to him.

Paul Larudee:

Riad's Last Phone Call?

Written April 19, 2008

Riad Hamad, 1952-2008

"Hi, Riad." I knew it was him from the caller ID, even though the phone had never been in his own name.

"Hey, Bolos. How you doin'?" He used the Arabic translation of my name.

"I'm good. How about you?"

"I'm okay." His voice didn't have the usual energy, but perhaps he was in a place where he couldn't speak loudly. "I sent you a couple of e-mail messages."

"Yes, I saw them." The messages were about helping with his charitable work on behalf of Palestinians. There were a few things I didn't understand about the messages, so Riad cleared them up for me. "Now it makes sense," I said.

"Okay. Well, that's all I wanted to tell you." Typical Riad—always in a hurry to get off the phone.

"Wait, I've got some good news!"

"Oh, yeah? What is it?" He sounded surprised.

"We're finally getting donations here. A check for a thousand came in today." We had set up a nonprofit account to receive donations for Riad's work.

"Was it from _____?"

"Hang on a second."

"Well, it doesn't matter.," . . . still anxious to get off the phone.

"What do you mean it doesn't matter? I've got the name right here. No, it's from _____."

"That's nice. Well, gotta go."

"Oh, Okay. Take care of yourself."

"You, too, Boulos."

Those were apparently Riad's last words, spoken from his car near Ladybird Lake in Austin, Texas. At the time I had thought it slightly odd that Riad was repeating what he had already told me by e-mail. I think he just wanted to hear a familiar voice. The police found the phone and car keys on the seat of the unlocked car. Typical of Riad to think of the person who would find the car.

I wish I had told him that the person who sent the check had also written a letter thanking him for the gifts of handmade Palestinian crafts and other items that Riad had sent as a thank you for a previous donation. He had also included handmade thank-you cards from his two young daughters. The older daughter, age eleven, had written, "Live in peace on the world. Everybody should LOVE! I am sad because people should be nice to you, but they are not." The younger, age eight, had written, "I hope you start to live in peace."

I would have read them to him over the phone if he hadn't been so anxious to end the conversation, but I decided to send them to read later and enjoy the children's drawings. The father's letter was longer and more specific in his praise for Raid's tireless efforts on behalf of Palestinians and their rights.

"I have included two checks for the needs of Palestinian children. It is my hope that you will use it to create hope for those oppressed. As we both see the dollar's value sink, the value of life especially in the eyes of the Creator never loses value. I extend this help to you and these children as if they were my own. We have the misfortune in living in very dark times, but in that darkness hope, love, and peace shine like the sun. To those that plant hope, they shall harvest peace."

Harvest peace, Riad.

SHUKRAN for your work and support. *Salamat*

Paul Larudee

Dr. Bill, around Athens
July 29-August 7

Paul Larudee meets Greta and me at the Athens Airport. Paul and Greta have been cofounders of the Free Gaza movement for the past two years and have been working furiously to get the boats purchased and launched, along with Sharyn and Eliza who live in England, and Mary, who lives in Los Angeles.

A taxi takes us to the International Press Center in Athens, where Paul and Greta launch into a press conference with local Greek colleagues translating in Greek. This is intended as a beginning of an intense burst of a major international media campaign. For this will be our main defense as unarmed civilians going up against the Israeli military and related spy agencies. The Greek press, along with *Al Jazeera*, and the *Independent* of London are all at the conference.

**Inaugural FG Movement Press Conference with Paul Larudee,
Greta Berlin and Maria, Greek Translator, International Press Center, Athens**

We intend to have international media aboard the boats; endorsements from international organizations are accelerating. After a lovely afternoon meal, I feel like death warmed over. I am escorted by our Greek hosts to an apartment just north of downtown Athens, where I collapse because of lack of sleep. Greta flies back to Cyprus the next day to be with the Free Gaza movement passengers who are beginning to assemble at the University of Cyprus.

Later, I meet my roommates—Osama is Palestinian from a village between Qalqilya and Tulkarem in the West Bank. He is separated from his family in the West Bank and is living in exile in London because of his previous political activism on behalf of Palestinian civil rights. He is an accomplished filmmaker and yet is not even thirty years old. He has been the communications director for the Free Gaza movement and a major organizer. He carries about five mobile phones that ring continuously. The requirements of his position keep him in a constant state of mania.

Osama talks on the phone with his young sister in the West Bank, whom he cannot see and cannot visit. The Israelis have forbidden him to return home. He is an intense individual because of his life's experiences and very passionate about this project.

Osama's colleague is Christos, a Greek cameraman from the Macedonian province of Greece, who is also living in London, where he works with Osama. Christos has good information technology skills, and he, along with Darlene Wallach, figure out how to hook up my laptop to the Internet.

Darlene Wallach is Donna Wallach's identical twin sister. She is also an anti-Zionist, who lives in San Jose, California. She has an information technology background. She is sent out with others after the first night to the *SS. Liberty*, which is hidden in an undisclosed port under a Greek name outside Athens.

The Acropolis and Port of Piraeus from Lycabettus Hill-Athens

Now we are living in a secret hideaway in a residential apartment here in Athens, while the tenants are off on vacation in the Greek islands; it will become known affectionately as the Speakeasy also known as the Bat Cave since it is deep inside an apartment block on the far side of a courtyard from the street, and one must pass through three steel doors to reach it.

Another hideaway that shelters fellow activists Paul Larudee and Bella is a few blocks away. I will call it the Safe House. The four-star hotel named *the Zafolia* becomes our meeting place during the following days.

Bella (Sharyn Lock) is a thirty-two-year-old Australian activist who has been living in London. She, too, is a major organizer of the Free Gaza movement. Bella has spent nearly two years doing logistical work for the project, mostly alone with a computer, but other good U.K. people have stepped up with a whole string of fund-raising events.

Now Bella is based in Athens and is traveling back and forth to the boats. The *SS Free Gaza* is hidden away in a different port than the *SS Liberty* for protection. That way, if one boat becomes discovered and sabotaged by the Israeli intelligence, The Mossad, there is always a second boat in a separate undisclosed harbor.

Part of my job involves waiting for things to develop. Needing to be patient and waiting for my Greek intermediaries to arrange local medical contacts. This allows me time to get to know Athens and its incredible wealth of human history and ancient artifacts.

On the following night, we have a general meeting at a restaurant in downtown Athens. We meet with *Vangelis*, who along with several of his Greek colleagues found us the two boats we are using after Riad's suicide meant we had to start all over again. It becomes clear that many have committed their hearts, monies, and souls into this project.

I also meet Ken O'Keefe, who has run a dive shop in Hawaii and worked as a human rights activist both in Iraq and in the West Bank. Ken is a former U.S. marine and has become an Irish citizen in an act of conscious protest of the current predatory U.S. foreign policy. When Bush got reelected in 2004, I was disgusted, too, and thought a while about becoming a Canadian. Ken is newly married to a British-Palestinian woman from London who is visiting with us now but has never been allowed to visit Palestine.

We eat, drink, and talk late into the night below the ancient Acropolis, getting to know each other while addressing logistics about how we might pull off our high-risk, quixotic plan.

If You Can't Bedazzle Them with Brilliance, Just Baffle 'Em

Sent to my friends and family on the 4th of August, 2008:

Anchors Aweigh!

Greetings from aboard the *SS Free Gaza*,

We left the Port of Piraeus in Athens at about noon yesterday along with our sister ship, the *SS Liberty*. We sailed directly east through the archipelago known as the Cycladic Islands where Greek civilization originated more than 6,000 years ago. Then we turned in a southeasterly direction and tonight sometime, we will dock at the island of Rhodes, spend the night, depart for the island of Cyprus in the morning, and then take on more passengers and head for Gaza.

Aboard right now, we have members of the Greek Parliament, members of the European Union Parliament, and a relative of former U.K. Prime Minister Tony Blair. We will take on more dignitaries in Cyprus.

Oh, God, this is so exciting and more worthwhile, I think, than anything I have ever done before in my life!

Please pray for us!

Love,
Bill

Of course, this email was made up. If we were going to play the same game that the Israeli Mosad plays, one of "By way of deception, thou shall go to war" why can't we say, "By way of deception, thou shall seek peace?" It wasn't until two months later, in the form of a baseball analogy that I confessed.

Hey, Friends,

Sorry 'bout the change-up I threw at ya'll. What we got here is a ball game. The problem is ya nevah know whose gonna be reading this here e-mail besides us. We, the Free Gaza Bleeding Hearts Club Band are up against a team that likes to play Hardball—the Spooks from Tel Aviv.

So we been tossin' sinkin' curveballs, knuckleballs, splitters, and sliders—anything we can throw at 'em to keep 'em off kilter.

If we throw'd 'em nuttin' but fastballs, they'ed've hit 'em right over the wall and outta the ballpark. The boats would be dead in the warter, and it would be a rout. The ball game would be over, and we would have to come back next year with a new team.

So like, I was tryin' to pitch'em late into the seventh inning wit' a buncha deception screwballs 'bout where the boats are to keep'em off course; then maybe the relief pitchers can take over before they figure all this out.

My sincere apologies,
Dr. Bill,

***

Actually, we haven't left for Cyprus just yet; we are behind schedule by two weeks. Even though we initially projected a departure from Cyprus on August 7, we are far from being ready. It's always more complicated than it initially seems. Greek maritime inspectors must delare the boats seaworthy, and since they are old fishing vessels, they need a major tune-up before they are shipshape.

Additionally, we have information technology experts who are part of our crew. They are installing a sophisticated communications system capable of broadcasting real-time images to shore via the Internet. That way, if the Israeli Navy tries to play rough with us, a group of unarmed nonviolent human rights activists, the whole world will be watching…we hope.

I am staying in Athens while others go out to the boats. I currently have no idea where the boats are being hidden. *Vangelis* and others want to keep this under wraps, and we are operating strictly on a need-to-know basis, since loose lips can sink ships. We also want to limit the number of people coming and going to the boats.

I spend my time trying to develop liaisons with Greek politicians and health care personnel. My goal is to acquire medical equipment and pharmaceutical supplies in two categories:

1) We will attempt to take medical supplies to the besieged hospitals and health care workers in Gaza. Of course, our efforts are only a small drop in the bucket; our two small boats cannot bring sufficient supplies for 1.5 million people who are under this cruel siege. But we will do what we can.

2) Medical supplies for the boat crew and passengers. Since we face the real possibility of being attacked, we must plan as best we can for the worst while hoping for the best. Of course, we are not the U.S. Navy. We don't have the resources to stock a fully equipped sickbay or a hospital ship. The best we can do is to be prepared to provide first aid for common medical ailments, while stabilizing more seriously ill medical or surgical patients before transferring them by air or boat to shore. We must have supplies to provide trauma first aid in the event that we are attacked. If that happens, we might also have to plan for massive evacuation, which is problematic. The nearest shore for evacuation for most of our journey will be hospitals in Israel, the country most likely to attack us. Other alternatives would be Cyprus, Lebanon, or Egypt. If the Israelis evacuate us, they could then try

to spin this into some kind of a propaganda victory about rescuing "those naïve fools at sea."

We have already required that all of our boat passengers obtain medical evacuation insurance before coming on this voyage. We are told in these insurance policies that our evacuation insurance is not applicable in a war zone. Fortunately neither Gaza nor Israel nor the international waters around them have been classified as a war zone. (This must come as great relief to Gaza residents who have been through numerous assaults from Israeli F-16s, tanks, and Apache attack helicopters over the past several years.)

If we do have a medical emergency, or if we are attacked or have some other disaster at sea, we will have to see if our insurers will honor our policies and pay for our evacuations. Still, this is the best that we can do to mitigate the financial effects of any disaster that might happen to us.

From Bella:
2 August 2008

First, I stayed in Athens, where our main Greek contact's wider political circle had volunteered for the job of hosting us, insisting on paying for anything we might attempt to buy, and seeking out obscure things (like helium canisters for balloons) that we wanted. I immediately felt so very welcome and supported on this mad mission.

There I met our quietly spoken, awesomely on-the-case contact who had put a level of effort into procuring and preparing our boats that I still haven't really got my head round it. We'll buy boats, we said, as if it was like buying shoes. Ha! We had NO IDEA. Thank God our contact did; and instead of telling us how impossible it was to find, buy, renovate, equip, license, and crew two boats in the height of national summer holiday, he simply went about doing it.

These people! I don't dare think of this as "my" project anymore. I am not one of the people who have for weeks begun work daily at 6:00 A.M., labored hard in the Greek summer sun, and skipped the afternoon break that's supposed to prevent you dying of heat exhaustion; people who've literally been unable to sleep for worry about engines, bridges, and the uneven flow of money from us to pay for anything. They didn't even know who the hell we were and didn't care because it was Gaza they were working for anyway. Even now, all I can do is paint bits of boat for them and in between painting things, beam at these good hardworking folks, and buy them the odd beer.

Back to my reward, only half of which is meeting these, my comrades. The other half is that this is all taking place on a small Greek island that doesn't allow cars—only mopeds, one of which we have hired, and I drive gleefully with no helmet (sorry, Dad, I don't think they sell them here). After boat work and computer work, there is the bright sea to dive in and in all of this I am in the company of my tall, dark, handsome Italian colleague.

A few days ago, we sat up with our boat into the early hours, at the whitewashed bar opposite, under the stars. We were counting down the hours until the boats' Greek presence was released, until which they were more vulnerable. I expected this one to disappear in front of my eyes, so I simply sat staring at it, reaching blindly for a series of mojitos thatcould arguably go on surveillance expenses. (No, you people who donated— that was a joke.)

Apart from diving into the sea with my camera and my phone in my pockets (one phone down, two to go), and a cash-flow problem that had me phoning anyone I knew that could maybe lend us something toward a late EU 10,000 that was about to set off a domino effect of delays, everything has been going well. Tomorrow I must go back to Athens to follow up various loose ends and boss people round.

I heard that one of the Athens anarchists has made me an anarchy flag to fly. How sweet is that?

Petros Giotis:

Launching the *Agios Nikolaos*:

Work was in progress and the deadline was drawing near. Then *Vangelis* set the deus ex machina working, as in the ancient Greek tragedies.

There was Markos, a six-foot-ten, half-Greek and half-Norwegian lad: a physicist who had studied in the United States and Norway, a diver, a seaman, a captain, an electronics expert, and an inventor. He had an incredible combination of skills and knowledge. *Vangelis* decided to include him in the mission, and he responded,

"Why didn't you tell me before so that I wasn't so busy in August and could travel with you to Gaza?"

Markos immediately started working. He coordinated the different working groups and worked directly on individual projects, as well. At the same time, we thought that I should appear in the Greek port of *Eretria* outside of Athens, where the boat was being hidden, and be prepared to give a hand. A number of foreign and Greek friends were already working there and guarding the boat. I took on the task of transporting the materials needed from Athens.

Markos would give me the list, and every morning I bought supplies from shops in *Piraeus* and carried them to *Eretria,* sometimes in my car and sometimes using the van of a comrade. It was really a welcome-to-the-madhouse situation. Imagine me, a bearded journalist smoking a pipe, buying boat material in shops, without knowing much of anything of boats and related stuff! The shop owners in *Piraeus* were immediately curious about what I was up to, so I had to make up a story! I told them that I was a writer who was going on a research mission sponsored by the Institute of Underwater Archeological Research. I wanted to write a book and at the same time would be helping them in the preparation of their boat.

In the shops in the small village of *Eretria,* I changed roles. There, I appeared as a polytechnic professor, an associate of Vangelis, whom they already knew. I could have been of some technical help concerning the ship but preferred to be back and forth on the street. I will confess to something: I preferred going back home to Athens, rather than being near the ship and sleeping there.

Still, I was haunted by the thought that something could go wrong, and the boat might not be seaworthy enough in time to make the voyage to Gaza. Each day, early in the afternoon, I would reach *Eretria,* driving a loaded car onto the ferry and hoping to finally see the boat in the water as I crossed. Seeing that it was still under repair in the dry dock day after day, I was growing increasingly uncomfortable.

All that went on until one night when we were finally informed that the next day the boat was to be definitely launched. That following day I arrived early in the afternoon. In my car with me were Courtney and Dr. Bill. I was sure that the boat would have been launched already by the time we arrived.

I was stunned to see it still hadn't yet moved from the spot it had been sitting up on blocks for the weeks it had been under repair. I found *Nikos Bolos,* our captain, swimming with O.J. below the hull of the boat. I was a bit angry.

"You are swimming while the boat is still on land?" I asked. I must have been impossible. Still, Nikos calmly explained that the heat had melted the wooden drivers, which meant that the planned noon launching had failed. So they decided to launch it at six in the evening, when the temperature was lower. Indeed, that evening *Thodoris* and his apprentices arrived, and they initiated the preparations in the usual gregarious Greek way—with a lot of shouting and swearing.

They asked us to board the boat, so that they could launch it properly. I was too anxious to do that. I remained on the shore with Courtney, who would film the launching, and Fatua, Ken's wife, who was pregnant and should not take any chances.

The vessel started smoothly on the launch, sliding down the wooden drivers until it finally splashed the water's edge—a beautiful sight! Costas was in his boat with its rigging guiding the launch from a little farther out at sea, just in case. For a short while we were wondering whether its engine would start. Then suddenly it coughed, and roared into action.

Nikos gestured from the bridge that everything was going swimmingly. The boat turned slowly and headed for the harbor. We were tip-top happy! We jumped into the car and drove around the harbor to meet the boat as it docked at the quay.

Agios Nikolaos (Liberty) after being launched from dry-dock in the Port of Eretria

There was a lot of tension during the next three days. The mechanic attended to the final details. A lot of the electrical work had to be completed. I put on overalls and started working as Markos's helper. We had to call in Lefteris, an electrician and a comrade, who worked late into the night. *Niognomon* carried out the last checks, and it was decided that we would definitely be leaving on the 8th of August.

On the previous day, Takis Politis, a university professor, and Yannis Karipidis, a film director, arrived to join the mission. Everybody was absolutely ready. Markos gathered us all and told us about teamwork onboard the boat. Simple rules, including the food we have, how we stand and work on the deck, and how to react to a distress situation.

A Letter to Israeli Foreign Minister Tzipi Livni from Free Gaza movement:

5 August 2008
Tzipi Livni
Foreign Affairs Minister, Israel

Dear Foreign Minister Livni:

On behalf of the Free Gaza movement, we would like to formally invite you to join us on our upcoming voyage from Cyprus to the Gaza Strip. We feel that your presence on this important mission would help alleviate concerns that have been expressed in the Israeli media about our objectives. More importantly, we believe that it would be extremely helpful for you to see firsthand the horrific effects of Israeli policies on the people of the Gaza Strip, as well as to witness firsthand the effectiveness of nonviolent action in bringing about positive change.

While we disagree with many of the statements and policies you have made as the Israeli Foreign Minister, we wholeheartedly agree with a portion of something you wrote two years ago when you said:

"For too long, the Middle East has been governed by zero-sum logic. One side's loss was seen as the other's gain. This thinking has brought much suffering to our region" (Tzipi Livni, "The Peace Alternative," Asharq Alawsat, 18 June 2007).

This is absolutely correct. We seek an end to this suffering. We find ourselves, and you must be feeling this intensely yourself, in truly difficult times. The one thing that is clear is that violence has not worked for anyone in this conflict. As a group of avowed nonviolent, peace activists, we hope that you will accept this opportunity, move past the zero-sum logic of your government's blockade, and join us on this historic voyage to break the siege of Gaza.

Your government's siege on the people of Gaza has been deemed illegal by numerous human rights organizations, has lead to the death of over 200 patients in the last year as a result of being denied adequate medical care, and has caused a man-made humanitarian catastrophe in the Gaza Strip. Clearly this is not the behavior of a civilized government, nor can these policies ever lead to peace for Israel.

Our voyage may seem to be a quixotic endeavor and therefore easily dismissed, but as a group of individuals who fervently believe that such moves can be vitally transforming and that individuals do indeed have the power to change our world for the better, we hope that you will take our offer seriously. We set sail for Gaza in the next few days. Please join us.

Sincerely Yours,

The Steering Committee for the Free Gaza movement, Cyprus

Comment from Greta Berlin:

Well, all hell broke loose when this email went out. Half the people thought it was a brilliant idea, half thought we were insane and sucking up to the Israelis. It turned out that the Israeli government was more worried about us than we were about them and actually wrote us a letter stating, "We know you are good people, but you are misguided. There is already a process to transfer goods from charities into Israel." When we pointed out that they made a huge mistake by saying there was a process to transfer goods from us to Israel and not Gaza, we all thought it was a marvelous Freudian slip.

Of course, we were not going to Gaza to deliver goods even though a small portion of our cargo was hearing aids and toys for children. We were going to Gaza to break Israel's illegal blockade on the people there.

Dr. Bill:
August 5-7 2008

During my final two days in Greece, I am at last taken to one of the boats, the *SS Liberty*, which is hidden in a harbor that is about a two-hour drive and then a short ferry ride across a cove from Athens. The *SS Liberty* is still in dry dock when I arrive, but several hours later, it is launched and taken around to the end of the marina inside the breakwater; now we can walk to town and the ferry dock, which we can see in the distance.

We don't want the villagers at these hidden ports to become suspicious about what we are planning. Even though the majority of Greeks sympathize with the Palestinian cause, gossip among villagers could wind up being passed along to the wrong people.

We pretend that we are a crew of marine biologists about to embark on a research excursion. We are warned by Vangelis not to talk about our real mission, even among ourselves if others can hear us, as some of the villagers can understand English. For Gaza, we say *Mikono,* a Greek Island and tourist destination. We try our best, but several of us slip up periodically and mention the G word.

I meet members of the crew, including some who I had met in downtown Athens a few days before. I meet Nikos and Georgios from Greece, and O.J., from the UK. They will be part of the crew along with Ken O'Keefe. Additionally I meet Courtney again, and Peter from New York City who are part of the information technology crew along with Darlene.

During the next few days, it will become my job to mediate conflicts between these individuals. Without taking sides, let me just state the obvious: A mission such as the Free Gaza movement attracts folks who are hardheaded, independent-minded, ingenious individuals. With all these attributes comes an ego. We all tend to be opinionated and to no one's surprise, sometimes see the world differently.

It is a very interesting social experiment we have created: you put different kinds of people united by a human rights cause on a couple of boats together and add a bunch of logistical hurdles, different cultures, different nationalities, different languages and customs, and then add deadlines and fear, paranoia, and stress. There is bound to be conflict, the patterns are almost predictable.

Over time, I and others are charged with mediating these multiple conflicts, so that our differences in personality do not overcome our common mission; after all, we can't let these differences degenerate and turn us into ships of fools. I admit that this will result in several of us driving each other nuts over several occasions. I will not get into details; that's not the point. The point is that we are able to make it through intense internal disputes.

At nightfall I wander into town to have dinner and a look around. Walking back to the boat, I wind up getting lost. At the breakwater, where I think the boat is located I can't figure out which boat it is in the dark. As I wander back toward town physically and mentally fatigued, a camper van is parked strategically on the shoreline at the entrance to the causeway on top of the breakwater.

Children are playing around the camper and a woman jumps out and asks if she can help. I explain that I am lost. I walk back to town and find my shipmates, who drive me right back to the boat; in retrospect I discover that I had walked right past the boat, but I just didn't recognize it in the dark.

During the night we sleep in shifts with each person taking turns at a two-hour watch. My shift is between 2:00 and 4:00 A.M. Headlights approach our boat along the quay and fear builds inside me as each car approaches. I suppress the urge to cry wolf as the cars pass by. I don't want to wake up the sleeping crew needlessly. This is repeated several times during my watch.

I fall asleep on a foam mattress above deck listening to soft Carlos Santana ballads beneath the stars while waves gently rock the boat and me to sleep. I end up sleeping deeper on the boat out here in the fresh marine air than I have been able to do for days in Athens.

Ken O'Keefe scuba dives and inspects the bottom of the boat each day to make sure it has not been sabotaged from underneath.

I spend the next two days with my shipmates hauling supplies from town to the boat. As I walk to the junction between the breakwater and the shore, I pass the camper. This same woman, whom I saw before the previous night when I was lost, jumps out and asks me if I found my boat. I respond, "Yes."

"So where is it?" she asks. She is in her early forties or late thirties. She is attractive, with long black hair. She could be Greek or she could be Israeli. "Up the breakwater a ways," I respond vaguely. There is something intriguing about this woman and this camper.

In the ensuing days, I notice that all of the windows of the camper van are always occluded by sun-block reflectors. Of course, it's a hot Greek summer day. So I can't be sure whether my concerns about espionage are legitimate. Maybe they are just trying to keep their camper from overheating in the August sun. Though I try, I can never get a decent look at what's inside the camper when I pass by.

I pass again from the boat walking atop the breakwater. As I pass the camper parked at the shore entrance, the woman jumps out behind me. I turn around and have a good look at her, say nothing, and then walk on. I wonder if I should greet her with "Shalom!" the next time I see her.

The last time Palestinians tried to take a ship back to Palestine from exile was in 1988: The PLO Ship of Return. This attempt to sail exiled Palestinians, international journalists, and clerics into Haifa was thwarted by Israel's spy service, the Mossad, before the boat ever left its port in Limassol, Cyprus. Israeli scuba divers sabotaged the engine by blowing it up from underneath the water. The three main Palestinian organizers were assassinated with a car bomb.

I pass from town carrying supplies and walk back along the breakwater toward the boat. As I pass by, I see a man in scuba gear getting out of the water alongside the camper. This sets off alarms in my head.

The *SS. Liberty* is planning to leave this port for Crete as soon as we pass the Greek maritime inspectors' evaluations. The first evaluation, conducted the previous night, uncovered a few flaws when our captain operated the boat at full throttle. These deficits need to be corrected, so we are stuck here for a few more days.

I am looking forward to sailing to Crete aboard the *SS. Liberty*, the sooner the better. But just then I get a call from Paul Larudee, who is either in Athens or with the *SS Free Gaza*. I can't ask him where he is because someone might be listening to our phone conversation or trying to pinpoint our locations by GPS.

"Bill, you need to fly back to Cyprus tomorrow. The boat passengers staying at the university are going stir-crazy waiting for the boats. They don't understand the problems we're having here. They are about to have a mutiny. So I need you to fly back to give them an update from the perspective of someone who has actually been out to one of the boats. And I need you to teach your trauma fist aid course that you have prepared for them."

"Okay," I answer. I guess I won't be sailing to Crete after all. Before returning to Athens, I discreetly report my suspicions about the Mossad camping van parked at the foot of the breakwater entrance, including my spotting of the scuba diver.

"Are you sure?" Giorgios asks me.

"No, how can I be sure?" I answer. "It looks a little fishy to me. Just keep an eye on them."

When I get back to the boat, I point out the camper on the shoreline to Vangelis.

"I think they are Mossad," I say. I also explain my suspicions to Ken and O.J. the other crewmembers. I don't explain it to others because I don't want to scare everyone. Maybe I am being paranoid. I hope I am not getting my crewmates worked up over nothing. This time period before we go public with the boats in Crete and start taking on more passengers may be the most vulnerable part of the voyage.

If the Israelis can disable the vessels while minimizing human casualties, it would be the best out for them. If they maim or kill unarmed international human rights activists, it becomes more of a public relations disaster. As I take the ferry back across the bay toward Athens, I take pictures of our ship on the dock and the suspected camper/spy-mobile, which, I can fit them both in one picture frame.

View from the Ferry while leaving Eretria

Chapter 3:

Are We There Yet? Waiting for the Boats in Cyprus

⌘   ⌘   ⌘

"While in Cyprus, we were pretty much in hiding because we had very real fears that something could happen to one or more of us that would scuttle the entire project. We were followed by the two hippies who showed up everywhere we went. Strange characters were seen skulking about the campus late at night. We formed a night watch, kept all our doors locked and all our eyes open. There was a lot of apprehension."

Mary Hughes Thompson, A cofounder of Free Gaza movement, reflecting on the long days of waiting at the University of Cyprus in Nicosia

Bella, in Greece with the Boats:
Gin & Tonic at 10:00 A.M.

Dear Cyprus Passengers,

From this, you may deduce

1. I am not in any immediate danger.
2. I am under some stress!

Everything's taking us longer (and high sea winds are playing havoc with the schedule), but the whole thing's just getting bigger.

So you'll have heard about the strong winds that have scuppered the current schedule. You should have seen our expressions when it was explained to us. We were not entirely sure that jumping off something very high was not a better option than phoning Greta at the University of Cyprus and breaking the news to passengers waiting there. I made Paul do it. Now I'm trying to write you some commiserations.

I know some of you have reasons that mean you might have to leave. All very well for me; my next appointment is a midwifery degree on September 22. I guess the reason I blocked out two months of my life is that, in my experience, delays for such complicated arrangements often happen. Ideally we will keep you all; I can't imagine how you will feel if you have to pack up and leave at this stage having not even seen a boat.

You have been part of this with us, and maybe for some people their contribution is to begin the public part of the project, to go home, and continue to look after those of us who stay.

From a two-year perspective in working on this project, the delay is a small blip in a big important plan—not for us but for Gaza. It's bigger than all of us now!

We're sending Dr. Bill back to tell you our beautiful boats DO exist and they DO move! I hope we don't have to lose a single one of you.

Hang in there...
Bella

Dr. Bill, on the way back to Cyprus:
August 8-20

My plane leaves Athens in the evening, and I enjoy the panoramic archipelago of Greek islands below one more time. This time I have a better appreciation for the history and geography of Greece than when I flew toward Athens a week and a half ago. I also have more of a clue about where our boats are and where they are going.

The next day I meet with a Cypriot doctor about acquiring medical supplies for the boats. I had met with his rival and immediate predecessor who had contacted me the night before but has broken away in protest and formed a splinter organization. I am learning that August is not the right time to try and mobilize the acquisition of medical equipment on short notice in Greece or Cyprus. Everyone is either on vacation or about to go on vacation, including this doctor. I had tried to make contacts by e-mail from May until July before I arrived here; but it still takes a personal touch to make things happen. It is becoming hard to make the progress I anticipated, especially when my answers to the question about our departure from Cyprus are, "I don't know exactly, but very soon."

I head inland to Nicosia (Lefkosia) to the University of Cyprus, where FG passengers have been assembling and participating in workshops. We are being put up in college dorms. The University of Cyprus, New Campus is located about ten kilometers to the southeast of downtown Nicosia. It is a futuristic concrete structure spread out over a large desert campus. The passengers are of all ages. They range from Adam Quist, a twenty-two-year-old essayist from Denmark who has been to Palestine twice before, to Hedy Epstein, who also has been to Palestine before, and is celebrating her eighty-fourth birthday this week.

We have different backgrounds; it is fun living in a college dormitory again. Immediately around us are real college students from Germany, Spain, Italy, Albania, Bulgaria, Egypt, and other countries taking summer courses. The campus is relaxed and not crowded this time of year. These students are intrigued to hear about our FG project and pleased to see older folks like us still acting out our ideals in a project like this. The evenings are a real social event, as we compare our perspectives on the world and compete with each others' musical tastes out in the courtyard in front of the main student center where the sound system is located.

In many ways Cyprus is reminiscent of the West Bank, with olive groves scattered about an arid landscape, and hilltops of pine. Cyprus even has a barrier separating its Greek side from its Turkish side. This enforced segregation developed following the 1974 civil war. The Greek Cypriot and Turkish Cypriot guards who man the barrier today do not seem as stressed or as hostile as the Israeli soldiers who control all the walls and checkpoints that suffocate the West Bank. Of course, there have been tougher times in Cyprus in the past.

Upon arrival at the UC campus, I enter a classroom workshop, one of many that have been in session during the previous days. Waiting can be the hardest part. The participants are indeed becoming stir-crazy, and many people are getting on each other's nerves. This workshop is about jail solidarity—what to do if we are all collectively arrested at sea and jailed in Israel. Many of those sharing the classroom with me today are veterans of the International Solidarity Movement and have done many nonviolent direct actions in defense of Palestinian people, mostly in the occupied West Bank, but some in Gaza. Many of my colleagues have jail experience in Israel. Andrew Muncie and Theresa McDermott are both from Scotland and have been arrested and deported from Israel for nonviolent direct action. Mary Hughes, Greta Berlin, and Maria Del Mar have all been seriously assaulted and injured by Israeli occupation forces.

Mary, Theresa, Donna, Huwaida, Courtney, Tom and David at
FG passenger workshop, Univ. of Cyprus, Nicosia

Based on previous experience with Israeli forces in the West Bank, the Israeli Occupation Forces (IOF) typically separates the internationals from the Palestinians/Arabs, deports the internationals, and then imprisons and sometimes tortures the Palestinians. We do not want that to happen to some of our fellow passengers who are vulnerable to this kind of racial profiling. Our objective here is that we must all resist deportation until we have factual evidence that our Palestinian and other Arab members have been released and sent safely out of the country. This needs to happen before we, the non-Arab internationals, allow ourselves to exit. We are given the names and phone numbers of Israeli attorneys who can represent us in these disputes. I write the numbers inside the seam of my pant leg. That way if I get arrested I can contact them. We discuss techniques to avoid getting on that plane from that jail cell.

We spend hours developing contingency plans that we can agree on as a group. This is not easy. Studies of group dynamics show that the optimal number of people for reaching consensus decisions is three to five individuals. Beyond that, discussions can easily deteriorate into tangential sideshows and chaotic diatribes where everyone is talking and no one is listening. Our group dynamics are even trickier, given the opinionated bunch that we are.

Ramzi Kysia, the son of Lebanese parents, who is from Washington, DC, is acting as facilitator at these meetings. Aside from experiences in Lebanon, Ramzi has somehow talked his way into staying inside Kibbutz Barkai in Israel for five days with the family of a friend.

Ramzi Kysia

He has also been in Iraq off and on between the years 2001 and 2003 doing the kind of nonviolent direct action work that he is doing with us now. He has Semitic features that a casual observer could take as being either an Arab or a Jew. Ramzi was planning to be on the boats with us but agreed to be the main land team organizer in Cyprus before, during, and after our first voyage to Gaza. He has an analytical mind that is as sharp as a tack, and he is a stickler for detail.

We have five Jews among our boat passengers, the Wallach sisters and Hedy Epstein whom I have discussed previously, and also Edith Lutz, a former nurse and now educator from Germany. She joined this voyage to help children in Gaza and highlight the core of Jewish religion: love and humanity not force and hatred.

Jeff Halper, who just left us a few days ago for Crete, where he will meet up with the boats, is the only Jewish Israeli on the Free Gaza movement boats who is still living in Israel. He is the director of the Israeli Committee against house demolitions (ICAHD), a nonviolent Israeli peace and human rights organization that resists the Israeli occupation on the ground. In 2006, the American Friends Service Committee nominated Jeff to receive the 2006 Nobel Peace Prize with Palestinian intellectual and activist Ghassan Andoni.

I also just missed Angela Godfrey-Goldstein, who returned to Israel from Cyprus. She is also a member of ICAHD and will be doing invaluable media work on behalf of Free Gaza movement inside Israel.

Just before I arrived, Dr. David Halpin and his wife had left after teaching a sea safety course. Dr. Halpin is a British orthopedic surgeon who operates the Dove and Dolphin, which brings medical and other supplies to Gaza. Because of the siege, his supplies have had to go through the Israeli Port of Ashdod, about thirty kilometers north of the Gaza Strip and are then transported overland to Gaza, which adds expense and delay.

Among the Arab members of our passengers, we have Ren Tawil, a second generation Palestinian-American from Minnesota, Monir Deeb, originally from Gaza and now living in Los Angeles, and Mushir El Farah, a civil engineer, also originally from Gaza but now living in Sheffield, England. We have Huwaida Arraf, a Palestinian-American lawyer who also has Israeli citizenship and teaches in Jerusalem. She is a cofounder of the International Solidarity Movement (ISM). We also have Fathi, a cameraman from Tunis, and Rashid, who works as a journalist for the BBC in London but is originally from Algeria.

We have Christians too, like Sister Anne Montgomery, an eighty-one-year-old Catholic nun who has worked with Christian Peacemaker teams and has been a peace activist for over thirty years.

Activists on the March at the University of Cyprus

Other passengers include: Lauren Booth, the British journalist and sister-in-law of Tony Blair; Eliza Ernshire, a teacher from Australia who now lives in the UK and an original organizer of Free Gaza movement; Jonny from Ireland; and Alice and Michael from the UK. Michael and several other passengers are running out of time and will soon have to return to their homes; their frustration with the boat delays shows and adds to the tension of waiting. Kathy Sheetz, the mother of Courtney, who is currently aboard the *SS. Liberty* back in Greece, is a retired ICU nurse who has done extensive relief work in Haiti; Thomas Nelson a semiretired attorney from Portland, Oregon. After decades of practice as a corporate attorney for Portland's largest firm, Tom is now a sole practitioner who represents individuals facing administrative and criminal charges brought by officials with the U.S. war-on-terror bureaucracy and American Indians in land-use matters on reservations in the West. Tom attended his first ISM campaign in August 2001 He comes often to the Middle East and has made numerous stops in Palestine on his way in or out. Tom's clients are located primarily in Saudi Arabia.

Kathleen O'Conner Wang is a grandmother from the Diamond Bar and Long Beach area of Los Angeles who has been active in Palestinian rights issues since the year 2000, when the second intifada began and more so after 9/11 when long standing discrimination and racism against Arabs and South Asians accelerated in the USA.

As facilitator, it is Ramzi's job to keep us focused on our mission. He must allow everyone a chance to be heard, while keeping the extroverts like me from monopolizing the proceedings. It is a thankless task, but I admit, Ramzi does a pretty good job. Each morning he gives us a typed summary of what we decided the previous day to see if we are still in agreement, and if not, he offers us the opportunity to refine the document further. This seems like endless tinkering with the messages to some, which adds to their stir craziness.

My presentations at these workshops are a little bit less mundane. I must give three one-hour sessions (over three days) in trauma first aid for the boat passengers who are interned here; to transform them from lay people into basic emergency trauma technicians able to cope as best they can with a mass casualty incident. One of my main jobs is to be the disaster planner for Free Gaza movement: plan for the worst while hoping for the best. After all, if the Israeli Navy really wants to, it has the clear capability to put torpedoes through both our boats and kill us all. If we were all Palestinian Arabs, I doubt they would even hesitate to do so. The fact that we represent seventeen different nationalities from around the world makes this a much more difficult option for them. My disaster planning focuses on responses if we are attacked or we have some other disaster at sea, and there are survivors. My instruction to this group is intended to empower them, so that we can increase the likelihood that as many of the short-term survivors as possible can become long-term survivors and live to tell their tales. I also have to prepare them in the event that I and other health care providers are killed or incapacitated to the point where we can't help others who are wounded.

I address the concepts of **triage**, the art of prioritizing the care of multiple injured patients into categories based on the nature of their injuries in order to achieve the best possible outcomes for the greatest number of injured passengers. This involves some very hard choices—like classifying some with the most severe injuries as hopeless, while others who are more salvageable are classified as emergent or urgent or can wait a while based on the pattern and severity of their injuries. Thanks to the Israeli incursion into Beit Hanoun, Gaza, in November 2006, I have multiple graphic digital photographs and DVD movies of Palestinians who have suffered serious traumatic injuries to illustrate my teaching points on how to prioritize and provide first aid for various injuries.

A lot of us from the USA in particular, and the West in general, find these images hard to digest. We live in a strange country. In our media, we have graphic depictions and images of fictitious gratuitous violence combined with stories of evil and heroism all the time to get us used to the idea that violence is somehow okay. A lot of our citizens are then persuaded to join the armed forces based on media fantasies about American heroism and evil abroad. But when it comes to graphic depictions and images of real violence, we are sheltered because these images are considered "in poor taste," and they are not aired. If they were aired in the West, I feel that the average citizen might become more alarmed and might not stand for any more of it. That is why the promoters of "endless war" in the Middle East and elsewhere, i.e., those who profit from war, do not want us to see the real violence because it would undermine their bottom line and expose the humanitarian absurdity of our so-called war on terror. This would cut into their sacred war profits, so they try to treat us as mushrooms and keep us in the dark about the real horror of it all. I am sorry if this sounds overly cynical.

So after scaring the shit out of my colleagues, I must also try and cheer them up. On Saturday evening after dinner, we are scheduled to have the next day off. So, I play disc jockey and set up a dance party out in the courtyard as the sun goes down, the heat of the day dissipates, and the crescent moon rises over the college campus. I also provide a lot of gratuitous and self-deprecating humor as a positive coping mechanism, while shamelessly encouraging joke telling. In order to cope with the extremely serious, we must also promote the extremely silly; we need time to unwind, lighten up, and get to know and nourish each other.

Some of our crew venture off campus and bring back refreshments; some of these refreshments contain forbidden fruit that has become fermented. This kind of behavior turns a few heads, as we had previously agreed to certain norms or principles of unity before joining the Free Gaza movement. Among these principles are: no profanity, no sex, no alcohol, or other vices. But as the boats are delayed for indefinite time periods, it becomes harder for some of us to hold the line as model citizens or saints, which we are not. So these principles become modified to: none of these vices while we are on the boats or in Gaza.

I discover that the Greek spirit called ouzo is something that can really get ahead of you, and you should be very careful about it. It does help to dance a lot and burn off some of these evil spirits. As DJ for a multicultural and multiethnic audience of all different ages, I also discover that Abe Lincoln was right: You can please some of the people all of the time, and all of the people some of the time, but you can't please all of the people all of the time. As we traverse traditional American jazz standards like Billie Holiday, Louis Armstrong, Benny Goodman, and Count Basie; traditional and contemporary Greek music; Cuban son; reggae; and traditional Lebanese standard artists like Fairuz and more contemporary ones like the Four Cats, I am interrupted by international college students who want to play their own music of which I know nothing. One group's cacophony is another group's classic. Somehow we all get through the mix, which proves enjoyable night after night, and we learn more and more about each other. Those who are not inspired filter back to the dorms to pursue other projects or to go to bed early.

Musheir and Donna explain Israel-Palestine to international students at the University of Cyprus

Then there are the night owls who gather outside the basement dorm at the base of apartment four. They spend the wee hours outside on the patio drinking tea, smoking cigarettes, and working on banners that we will hang from the side rails of our boats. We will employ these banners as we leave and enter Cypriot and Gazan ports, and/or if we are confronted by media at sea or Israeli Naval forces. We all bring different skills to this mission and I am amazed by the artistic abilities of some of the night crew. Among this late night/early morning crew are Jonny, Alice, Adam, Eliza, Theresa, Andrew, Donna, Maria, and Musheir.

Night Crew Working-Theresa and Rashid

Early one morning some suspicious individuals are spotted on campus by the late night crew; it was about 3:00 A.M. My friends ask them who they are, and they claim that they are architects, who were driving by from Larnaca and stopped because they "were impressed by the architecture." My colleagues refer them to campus security but they never show up. Some of my friends try to follow them, but they disappear. Israeli spies? I don't know. I was asleep when it happened; your guess is as good as mine. But their behavior was certainly peculiar.

From Hidden Ports on the Greek Mainland, through Aegean Waters, toward International Media Attention in Crete

Petros Giotis:
Friday, 8 August

Today is the day. I have a friend who will drive me to *Eretria* at daybreak and get my car back to Athens. I packed a few things in a small bag but I am feeling anxious that I have forgotten something. Luckily, I didn't forget my laptop, my cassette recorder, or my camera.

Giorgos wants to come and see the boat. On the ferry, we have a chat and arrange communication through the Internet. I'll write a piece every day, and the comrades will upload them on our and other Web sites.

Everybody is asleep on the boat except the night watchman. The crew and passengers have been on continuous watch at this stage, ever since the *Agios Nikolaos (SS Liberty)* was launched from its berth. I introduce Giorgos and Darlene; we talk for a while, then he leaves, and I start working. There are quite a few jobs to be completed—mainly things on deck involved with passenger comfort. On a fishing boat, you cannot expect to have many creature comforts. The day is feverish. Markos and I work on the board and finish installation of lights. Ken deals with the rest of the woodwork. He is a real master of his craft. Darlene has a knack for the nitty-gritty and knows the location of all kinds of screws. We should be leaving today. Ken and I can look after the rest en route to Cyprus.

At noon we load foodstuffs, mainly water. Markos has doubled the quantity of estimated water needed. You can manage without food at sea but never without water. Markos and Nikos inform us, "You aren't sailors. The boat will be topsy-turvy even when the sea is calm, so mind what you are eating. You only need pretzels, cheese, olives, honey, and lots of water." These are Mediterranean products, actually. For more than three thousand years, local people have sailed the seas feeding on such blessed natural products.

Vangelis joins us at noon, smiling. He's got all the paperwork. The boat is legal. No Greek authority can stop us. It's been a real battle against red tape through various Greek governmental regulatory bureaus. Very few people could know what Vangelis has been through until he finally got all the paperwork. The rest had the simpleminded impression that they boarded two boats that were bought as if you were buying a couple of used cars. Our mission owes a lot to Vangelis since he's been the coordinator of the operative aspect, the person who discovered, bought, and changed two simple fishing boats into passenger-carrying vessels. He is the one who took all the risks—financial, political, and legal. Apart from traveling by ferry and in his car, he sometimes had to commute using buses in case he was being followed.

We were all later informed that Mossad spent a pretty penny in attempts to trace the boats; they searched in Cyprus, Turkey, Egypt, and Greece, but they found *nada*. Our boats were well hidden in two territorial shipyards and guarded by trusted people. The Zionists' money was spent in vain.

I would, by the way, like to refer honourably and with lots of gratitude to a few other people (men and women) who worked zealously and with great devotion during all those months of preparation without taking a direct part in the mission as being passengers. These humble people don't want their names to be mentioned as they believe they were only doing their duty.

It was noon when we got the official departure document from the *Eretria* Port Police. Officially, Vangelis would be the captain as the owner of a private "entertainment boat." Vangelis himself had to leave the *Agios Nikolaos* though, to inspect the departure of *Dimitris K (SS Free Gaza)* from *Spetses* Harbor. He will travel to *Chania* on it, where we will make our first stop and officially announce that these are the boats that will be breaking the siege of Gaza. (We can finally brag a bit—can't we?) Even when the boats reach *Chania*, neither Mossad nor the Greek authorities will know about the mission. Our good-old clandestine methods have once again proven fruitful.

At 20:00 hours, when it is getting cooler, *Agios Nikolaos* pulls up anchor and starts out of the Gulf of *Eretria* heading south. Nikos Bolos is the captain, and Ken O' Keefe, the first mate. Markos and Nikos continue our intensive on-the-job training of the crew, as we are finally underway. Many of us, Greek and foreigner, are fast becoming sailors.

We are all exhausted but satisfied. The only things we worry about now are engine problems since this boat is sailing on a long voyage after many years. Not to worry, though. Nikos, a chemist by profession and able sailor, has sufficient knowledge of engine matters to act properly if need be. The route is also full of islands; we may go ashore and carry out further repairs if Nikos is unable fix a problem. The trip to *Chania* would be the final test for the boat and will show us its weak points. Then we can act accordingly. After Crete, we have to sail in the open sea for two days to Cyprus and then it will take another day and a half to Gaza.

We set the work shifts on the wheel. Giannis Karipidis gets night shift. I am too excited and can't sleep, so I take first shift. I haven't steered a boat before in my life. It's nothing like driving a car. Markos joins us. We'll make a short detour and disembark him near his place in *Rafina*, east of Athens. He converses with Ken and Nikos all the time. He gives them instructions.

It is past midnight and we get near the bright lights of *Rafina*. The boat reduces speed, closes in on the pier, and Markos takes a leap onto the pier, without the even having to stop. That looks incredible to us land people; for we are not "sea wolves."

I finally go to bed. The hum of the engine and the gentle rocking of the boat put me into a deep sleep.

Saturday, 9 August

I wake up at six in the morning, make myself a cup of coffee, and go to the bridge. Takis Politis, our best steersman, is at the wheel. He doesn't make too many detours, which shortens of our trip and more importantly lowers our fuel costs. Two hours later, I discover that we aren't getting any power from the engine generator. I wake Nikos.

He sees that the fan belt is broken. We hold a quick meeting and decide not to go ashore for repairs, so that we won't waste time getting to Crete (we are off the coast of *Melos)*. We start up the mobile deck generator and presto! We have power on board again.

In the meantime, the GPS batteries are out, there is a wrong handling of things, and there's no way to steer the boat electronically. Nikos shows me how to sail using the compass—the good old traditional and reliable way of navigation for an experienced seaman. Later on, we radio the GPS manufacturer, and they give us explicit instructions on how to repair the GPS.

We are having lovely weather. There's almost no wind. At times, a light north breeze pushes us on, increasing the speed to ten knots. We only want to use eight knots so as not to dodge the engine. Off the coast of *Serifos* we see some Mediterranean dolphins.Two of them approach the boat swimming playfully. Nikos, who adores ancient Greek mythology, mentions *Amphitrite* dolphins (she was the wife of Poseidon, the Greek god of the sea). He starts whistling and the dolphins gather round the boat, jumping and diving all the time, while our foreign friends frantically take pictures and video them.

Well, the first serious mistake has been made: the deck generator, which was not intended for constant work, is now our primary power source. Two hours before arriving in *Chania,* it and breaks down. Now we can only get power from the batteries, and we definitely must not turn on any lights, since the power supply is sufficient only for the boat dashboard on the bridge.

At 20:45, twenty-four hours after our departure, we reach the old harbor of *Chania,* which is an old Venetian-style harbor, probably the most beautiful one in Greece. We've made arrangements and people are expecting us. I phone Vangelis and I ask, "Do we sneak in, pretending to be unimportant, or do we raise the flag of our mission?" There are people on the shore who have worked in the repairing part of the mission, and up to this moment, don't have a clue about the destination of the boats. The official names for the Free Gaza movement boats were not to be announced and still carry their Greek names, another reason Mossad cannot find them. On the other hand, on the very next day we will be officially announcing that these boats will try to break the siege of Gaza.

We decide to hang the banner of the mission over the back of the boats, thus making a giant leap from a covert operation into an overt proclamation. **Here We Come, you Mossad people!** The sky is the limit.

At this point, an important issue that we'd dared not think about arises—we didn't have captains to sail such heavy wooden vessels. Nikos does the sailing. He has sailed the Mediterranean in light sailing boats. He is qualified to pilot heavier fishing boats with a power engine but just barely. He could handle the situation while the boat was docking in the port of *Eretria* but only with delicate handling. He lacks the confidence of a more experienced power fishing boat pilot. In the case of the harbor of *Chania*, the boat has to enter prow first and manuever between two other boats, just as you would park your car in a crowded parking area. But boats have no brakes. The wheel does not respond well when we approach slowly and the reverse stern propulsion takes some time before it works, producing a frightening moment for everyone on the boat. This kind of a docking procedure does not present a real problem for a fishing boat captain, but for a person whose experience is with a light sailboat, this problem proves to be untenable. As a result, we on the *Agios Nikolaos* became stranded on a shallow reef, just eighteen yards from the dock.

Relief follows our general panic and grief finally. While we are frantically trying to figure things out, our friends on the shore keep phoning us. They can see us, but they cannot understand what is happening. The issue is whether we should abandon the boat. I intervene calmly but decidedly, saying, "We don't abandon ship. We are going for a walk now through one of the most beautiful Greek cities, so everyone just relax. Tomorrow we will fix any problems with the ship." We decide to ferry ourselves to shore using the the small rubber motor boat called a Zodiac. We leave a few people on board to care for the boat; in the morning we'll decide what is to be done to free ourselves from this predicament. I'm informed that there are press people at the dock. I say, "I'll go out first and speak to the press, explaining that there's some kind of engine problem." Ken takes us to the dock in the rubber boat.

There are no Greek or foreign journalists, only Yvonne Ridley and Aki Nawaz of Press TV, who will be boarding our boat. They are more like embedded reporters, who will be with us for the ride to Cyprus and then Gaza. In that way they are not really an outside journalist and cameraman. No press statement is needed.

Journalist Yvonne Ridley

British Musician and Film maker Aki Nawaz

My wife waits for me at the pier. She has traveled 170 miles, along with other comrades to meet me here. They look mightily disappointed, although they're smiling to encourage us. Police appear and ask for the foreigners' passports. I don't give them a chance; they only get the passports of the people who disembark on the first trip of the Zodiac. Ken ferries the rest directly to shore. They haven't caught on yet to "what the beef is" with the boat; they just act like good bureaucrats.

I'm looking for accommodations for our foreign friends who are tired. Once more appears the deus ex machina (this is Greece, after all). Vardis Tsouris, a friend and comrade from old times, informs me of a building that can sleep up to fifteen people. It has a decent bath and a place to get a bite to eat. From then on *Rosa Nera* (meaning black rose), a historical building, once abandoned to the decay of time and recently reborn as a community center, will become part and parcel of our life during our stay in *Chania*.

After taking our foreign friends to *Rosa Nera*, I speak with my wife and my comrades for a while, and then return to the boat and straight to bed. I was really shattered. We have succeeded in overcoming so many difficulties; we've managed to move from *Eretria* only to become shipwrecked in shallow water in the first harbor where we've tried to dock.

Sunday, 10 August

I woke up at a few minutes before seven, and the first thing I see when I get to the dock is the gargantuan figure of Markos smiling at me on the pier. He tells me later that my grumpy look then turned into a grin. When we informed Vangelis about the boat's plight, he asked Markos to come to our aid. Ken brings him to our stranded ship in the rubber boat. They both put on swimsuits, scuba tanks, and masks and then they dive. For ten minutes I watch the two divers below the surface as they search the boat thoroughly. The outcome is pretty encouraging: no damage to the boat- not even a scratch. It is sitting gently on the sandbar and didn't hit any rocks. We only have to wait for the tide.

We return ashore with Markos to get a boat that can pull us off the sandbar. The locals are absolutely certain about one thing—there is no tide here. Markos proves to be a scholar, though. He has done his own research and knows that there will be a tide of just under two inches, which is quite sufficient to get us moving. He even knows the exact time of the tide.

A bit later we experience a magnificent view: Markos and Ken diving again, place their shoulders under the boat and push. The tide is in, and there it is: our boat is moving freely again. Spyros is a local man who has a rubber boat with a strong engine. He tied up to our vessel and is now pulling us toward the dock. There is not even a sign of the slightest current. Greek seamanship has done it again. We landlubbers could not have even thought of managing such a situation. How to steer a heavy fishing boat with no engine was a really perplexing issue for us. The solution sounded quite incredible: Spyros would pull from the front, and Marcos and Ken would push from the right and left side of the stern using our own small rubber boat to help to get our bigger fishing boat off the sandbar and back on course! The boat was safely docked, and the batteries charged.

Early in the afternoon Vangelis informed us they would arrive on *Dimitris K.* They, too, had the same problem: a lack of captains with the right kind of experience to manage the heavy boat. A friend of Vangelis, who had captained tankers, began by taking the wheel to leave the harbor, and immediately chaos ensued. Puzzled, our Irish firt mate, Derek took over, with the same result, and then the problem became clear—the ship's wheel had been installed backward, resulting in the boat doing exactly the opposite of what it's supposed to when you steer! The crowded *Spetses* harbor resounded with verbal abuse from fishermen and luxury boat owners. Once he grasped what had happened, Derek actually managed to safely steer the boat out of the harbor, and they set off to meet us.

When *Dimitris K* reaches the outer harbor, Ken carries Markos back in the rubber boat, and he pilots the larger fishing boat and parks it next to ours, the *Agios Nikolaos*. Now, for the first time, the two Free Gaza movement boats are next to each other in the main harbor, the very heart of the tourist district of *Chania*. Banners wide openly proclaim our mission to the world. Our boats are now labeled with their symbolic names in English and Arabic: **SS/Free Gaza and SS/Liberty [*Ghaza Huriya wa Al Huriya*]**.

The FG boats go public, Chania Harbor, Crete, Greece

On this same night, Vangelis, Paul, Derek, Markos, and I have a meeting. We decide that it is urgent to find two experienced captains for our two boats. It would be detrimental to our mission to continue with our current inexperienced captains. First thing tomorrow morning, we will look for our captains. That might prove difficult because August is part of the high season and everyone has gone on vacation.

Israel is now trying everything they can to stop us. They sent out the following advisory just for our two small boats.

Advisory Notice (Maritime Zone Off The Coast Of Gaza Strip)
Aug. 11 2008

1) The Israeli Navy is operating in the maritime zone off the coast of the Gaza Strip. In light of the security situation, all foreign vessels are advised to remain clear of area A in the attached map, bound by the following coordinates:

	E	N
1.	34.19.02	31.46.08
2.	33.56.44	31.33.48
3.	34.29.28	31.35.42
4.	34.13.06	31.19.23

Delivery of humanitarian supplies to the civilian population in the Gaza Strip is permitted through the land crossings between Israel and the Gaza Strip, subject to prior coordination with the Israeli Authorities.

2) Vessels approaching the maritime zone off the coast of the Gaza Strip are requested to maintain radio contact with Israeli Naval Forces on Channel 16, and will be subject to supervision and inspection.

3) In accordance with the agreements between Israel and the Palestinian Authority, entry of foreign vessels to the maritime zone adjacent to the Gaza Strip is prohibited, due to the security situation and, in light of those agreements, foreign vessels are barred from such entry.

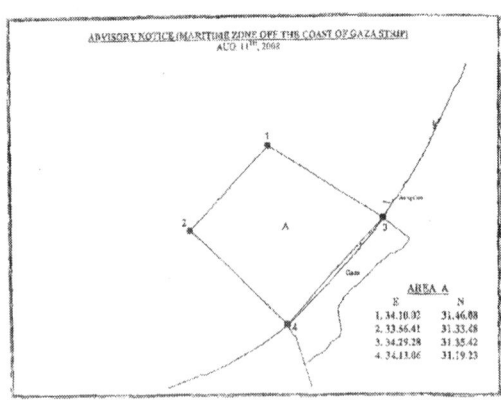

4) This notice is published in order to assure safe navigation and to prevent

vessels from approaching areas in which their safety may be endangered due to the security situation in those areas.

Eliezer Marom, Adm.
Commander in Chief
Israeli Navy

Paul Larudee:
Admiral Marom's Strange Proclamation

The signature of Israeli Navy commander in chief Admiral Eliezer Marom appears on a very odd document. Dated August 11, 2008, it is not written on official stationery or addressed to anyone. The document declares that the Israeli Navy is operating in a maritime zone off the coast of Gaza. Was there any doubt that they have been doing so continuously since 1967? It includes the sketch of a map and a series of coordinates (also attached) to define the zone, which includes all of Gaza coastal waters, and a major slice of international waters as well. It advises all foreign vessels to remain clear of this zone because of a "security situation" that is apparently so obvious that it requires no definition or explanation. The only hint about the "security situation" is a reference to the delivery of humanitarian supplies to the civilian population in the Gaza Strip, which, according to the document, should be done only at the land crossings between Israel and the Gaza Strip (i.e., by Israeli permission only). Why is the Israeli Navy issuing a proclamation regarding the delivery of humanitarian aid by land?

The proclamation goes on to prescribe a set of protocols for vessels approaching the "maritime zone" and to prohibit vessels from entering Gaza because of the undefined "security situation."

Finally, the document pronounces its benevolent intentions to ensure "safe navigation" and its neighborly undertaking to prevent vessels from approaching an area where their safety may be endangered. Endangered? By whom? By what?

There is, of course, an explanation for such a strange document, disseminated (as nearly as can be determined) to a narrow circle of maritime authorities. It is that the document itself is an embarrassment to Israel, which nevertheless feels compelled to issue it in some form, as a disclaimer for any forceful action that they might take against an unnamed threat.

The embarrassment is that the unnamed threat consists of the two converted fishing boats of the Free Gaza movement, bought and refurbished in Greece, and flying the Greek flag. On board is a contingent of forty-four crew and human rights advocates, sworn to nonviolence, as well as a modest cargo of hearing aids for Palestinian children in Gaza. Among their ranks are a Greek member of parliament, an eighty-one-year-old Catholic nun, and the sister-in-law of former British Prime Minister Tony Blair. No wonder Israel is embarrassed. Does Israel seriously consider the delivery of humanitarian aid to be a security crisis? Does the initiative of a small group of harmless people constitute such a threat? If so, what does that say about the kind of state to which Israelis pledge allegiance?

Finally, the declaration's kind words of interest for the safety of vessels traveling in the area hide the threat to use force against the motley flotilla that dares to challenge the entrapment of 1.5 million people in what has become the largest and most permanent concentration camp in the world, and to animate a civil rights movement where others see only a manufactured humanitarian crisis.

Israel's blockade of the Gaza coast is an affront to all peoples, but most especially the seafaring peoples of the Mediterranean, where people have lived, prospered, and built great civilizations through access to the sea since time immemorial, not least in Gaza itself. To deny Palestinians this resource is a human rights obscenity that Greeks, Italians, North Africans, Turks, and other seafaring peoples must unite to condemn.

Admiral's Marom's proclamation shows nothing so much as the desperation and paranoia of a regime that lacks the imagination and courage to embrace a project that harms no one and delivers hope as its primary cargo. It behooves Israel to welcome the Free Gaza initiative as a step toward mutual respect for the human rights of all persons who call the land of Palestine their home.

Petros Giotis, on the *Agios Nikolaos* in Crete:
Monday, 11 August

At about noon Markos has found us a captain. He is from Crete and in three hours time, he joins us. That's Giorgos Klontzas who is as of today the main captain of FG. He comes from my wife's city, *Agios Nikolaos,* here on the island of Crete. It is also coincidentally, the name of our boat. I have never met him. But when Markos introduces us, and we have a cup of coffee together, my first positive impression turns into lasting admiration and enthusiasm.

At thirty-eight, Giorgos has wrought the sea. For years he has worked as a diver and coral fisher. This is a job way more dangerous than sponge fishing, since corals are often found at 130 meters of depth. He now has his own diving ship (one like *Agios Nikolaos)* and has participated in many missions such as archaeological research, wreck salvage, etc). What really counts is the fact that he is straightforward. No ifs, ands, or buts. He is being informed about the mission and the probable danger. He says, "I'll take you to Cyprus, and if I kind of like you, I'll take you down there [to Gaza], too" His criterion was not based on danger resulting from the Zionists, but on the mentality of his shipmates. Later I realized he isn't interested in polite behavior but the willingness to deal with life on a boat. I then remembered F. Engels' words concerning some *Bakunin* followers: "Would these gentlemen go with traveling on a boat on which no one would obey the captain's orders and everyone would act according to their own will?"

Vangelis and Giorgos shake hands. No contracts, no paperwork. Between two honest men, one's word and shaking hands is quite enough. Giorgos gets down to business immediately. The first thing he does is dive and search every inch of the boat's hull.

It's not that he doesn't trust his friend Markos; he wants to shape his own opinion. When I ask him why he would do that, he answers earnestly, "In my lifetime I've been through tough shit, and I know what matters are details." The first detail I could make out was that he pushes three knife blades at three different spots of the ship.

Agios Nikolaos-The Liberty-Al Hurriya in Arabic-coming out of hiding in Greece, with Courtney and Osama

A knife is an important tool for a small boat sailor, since in the case of an emergency he may need to cut the ropes; therefore, he always needs to have a knife handy. He and Markos start checking the engine, the bridge, and the deck, while I make notes of what should be purchased and brought aboard for the necessary repairs.

Meanwhile, Derek informs us that Mathew, a second captain, is on his way here from Cyprus.

Tuesday, 12th August

Our new British captain and I do not share the same sentiments. But I don't pay too much attention to his personality since he is supposed to do his job as a captain, not make friends with me. From the beginning, there is conflict between Mathew and us Greeks: differences in opinion and style, which lead to heated arguments during the next few days. I make sure I calm myself down, convincing myself that it's due to a different cultural mentality.

Mathew gathers the passengers on the deck and delivers a rousing speech, and they clap as if they are just going on a day trip. Giorgos, on the other hand, is very brief when speaking during our boat's meeting: "I want only one thing from you—don't think! When I say something, just do it just as I say!" It's obvious that he doesn't need us as seamen; he needs us to be passengers who for their own safety respect the sea and the knowledge of their boat's captain, and listen when they need to.

Bella on the Boats:
Tuesday, 12 August 2008

I remember a week ago, when we were all less worn out and all our conflicting priorities hadn't driven us quite so crazy. Our so-called "quietly spoken Greek sailing contact" has since done a LOT of shouting, the like of which I have never seen and hope never to see again. I literally feared his heart would give out, but he's still breathing for now.

We have gotten as far as Crete, but challenges before and since have involved such minor things as winds that completely prevent us from moving, captains not working out, having to scour the world for new ones, the satellite technology for live film that might keep us all alive not working properly, and beginning to run out of money. But it's STILL all coming together, and the Gaza folks just await us with even more fervor. We hope to sail today from Crete, into conditions that our experienced sailors tell us will have us all begging for a place on the land team instead of the boats, when we reach Cyprus.

We've just decided to go into debt on faith. This is too important. We would prefer as many as possible of the resources (e.g., the boats and the technical stuff) to remain in the hands of Gaza human rights organizations or Palestine solidarity projects, not to be sold afterwards to repay debts, though this may have to be an option if funds don't come in since otherwise various people who drained their own bank accounts may have to go bankrupt!

Bella

Greta Berlin, Media Team, at University of Cyprus:

Please post this appeal to your lists far and wide. Thank you. We WILL arrive in Gaza.

Two years ago, about a dozen human rights activists devised a plan to sail a boat to Gaza in order to break the siege. We rejected a plan to rent a boat as impractical because a similar venture in 1988 failed when the Israelis disabled the boat before it sailed, and the three organizers were killed. Thus no boat owner would willingly risk his craft. We ultimately decided to purchase two small boats that could carry forty-four passengers, crew, and media.

Each of us contributed what we could, and we also received thousands of dollars from individual supporters. We also held fund-raising events, received a few thousand dollars from small grants, and several angels helped us along the way. Each passenger has paid his/her own way to get here, and many have raised additional money through their groups, worked extra jobs, and asked family and friends to donate. The passengers also paid an additional €700 each for lodging in Cyprus and to cover the cost of supplies and food on land and sea.

Through these efforts we have raised $300,000, which we thought covered our costs. But the eroding dollar-euro exchange rate seriously drained our funds. All of our planning did not anticipate this contingency.

We are now in Cyprus awaiting our boats' arrival from Crete. When they come in, we will fuel up (with very high-cost diesel) and stock necessary food and supplies. We hope to cast off for Gaza this weekend. We are told that of thousands of Gazans will greet us on arrival.

Many people thought we'd never come this far. But here we are, and we firmly intend to set sail regardless of some recent staggering debts. Frankly, we have spent much more than we've raised; here are just a few of our recent expenses:

Two Sailor 250 Fleet Broadband systems to allow us to stay in electronic contact and to send streaming video in real time: $16,000 each, or $32,000;

Repairs required to make the boats seaworthy: $25,000-$30,000;

Electronics, wiring, connections, satellite uplinks, SPOT Trackers to make the system work: $5,000-$8,000. (Most of the labor on the electronics and boats has been donated by the Greek crew and technicians.)

Forty-four life jackets and two hand-held GPS units: $8,000;

Paint & banners for the boats, and balloons & toys for Gaza children: $2,000

Diesel fuel for both boats, both ways, $15,000 to $25,000.

Except for part of the diesel fuel, we have already paid these costs by running our personal credit cards to the limit, borrowing money, and asking some of the Greek crew to help. Frankly, we're tapped out. We need your help so that we sail on the Mediterranean Sea and not on a sea of debt.

Please, donate through the PayPal account on our Web site (www.freegaza.org), send a tax-deductible check to the U.S. address on the Web site, and/or send a check to the address in the UAE. Every donation, large or small, will help keep us afloat.

And, finally, thanks for your interest, support, and prayers!

The Passengers and Crew on FREE GAZA and LIBERTY

Yvonne Ridley, aboard the SS Free Gaza:

Dicing with Death for Gaza
Wed, 13 August 2008

By the time you read this, our two boats, the *Free Gaza* and *SS Liberty* should be sailing from Chania's old port in Crete despite a gloomy forecast of storms ahead. Our captains have decided it is time to quit our dock for security reasons, and so we are heading along the Cretan coastline on our way to pick up the rest of our passengers who have been waiting patiently in Larnaca, Cyprus. We could be in for a rough ride, but we would probably be more at risk by not moving. Israel has a history of using Mossad and Kidon to sabotage and destroy peaceful operations designed to help or show solidarity with Palestinians.

Media interest is once again gathering momentum and there are those who want to join us on board while others are considering hiring their own boats. Wouldn't it be great if we had a huge flotilla? The more the merrier. However, there are concerns from the media because Israel has a history of shooting, killing, and arresting journalists who try to report the truth about the brutal occupation of Palestine. I was reminded of this only this morning as I read a release from **Reporters without Borders**. The human rights group was condemning today's announcement by the IOF to detain Ibrahim Hamad, a soundman employed by the Palestinian news agency *Ramattan*, for six months without bringing charges and without taking him before any court. Israeli soldiers arrested Hamad at his home in Qalandia, near the West Bank city of Ramallah, on July 15. "The Israeli military may not under any circumstances arrest journalists or media assistants without giving a reason," Reporters without Borders said. "If they think a journalist has done something wrong, they must say what it is and they must explain why they are arresting him. We call for Hamad's immediate release." When reached by Reporters without Borders, the management of *Ramattan* firmly condemned his arrest and called for his release. They also-called on the Israeli authorities to explain why they are holding him. "This is not the first time that one of our employees has been arrested by the Israeli military," the agency said.

Israel boasts it is a democracy—these are not the actions of a democratic state. These are the actions of a brutal state that tries to crush those dedicated to telling the truth about the full horrors of the Zionist regime and its determination to see through its deliberate and slow genocide of the Palestinian people.

We will be able to see in a few days time exactly how the Israelis react to a group of peaceful activists who want to sail into Gaza armed with nothing more than love and support for their Palestinian brothers and sisters. If Israel is really a free and open democracy then its navy will let us past, Mossad will stop trying to sabotage our journey, and all of the journalists on board, including me, will be able to report the truth about what is happening in the world's largest open-air prison—Gaza. In the meantime, I would urge the IOF to release our brother Ibrahim Hamad and allow him to continue his media work.

Dr. Bill, back at the University of Cyprus:

Back home, I am usually an early-to-sleep and early-to-rise kind of guy. Here, I try to do both because the night and the early morning are the most tolerable times of the day here in Cyprus, in terms of temperature, and we have no air conditioning in any of the rooms where we sleep, just in the room where we meet. When I can, I spend the late afternoon sleeping in my dorm room with the fan on or hiking a couple kilometers away with other FG passengers to cool off in an outdoor community swimming pool.

Twice I try jogging in the park at 6:00 A.M. One morning, Rashid joins me. He is as sleek as a greyhound while I'm more like a tank. Fortunately, this is social jogging, and Rashid mercifully decides not to leave me in the dust. We jog at my pace and end up talking about what we might do while we are waiting for the boats to arrive.

Our boats continue to be delayed and this is frustrating; they are in Crete, where they have gone public. Now there are photographs of the *SS Free Gaza* and the *SS Liberty* out there on the World Wide Web. Lauren Booth, Huwaida Arraf, and Jeff Halper have all joined the boats in Greece, and have held a press conference with Paul Larudee and other organizers.

But there is also bad news like cost overruns; we all need to dig deeper into our own pockets and give more, and those of us who can, do. To make matters worse, the boats can't cross the straits between the Greek islands and Cyprus first because of equipment needs, and then high waves. The locations of the ships continue to be kept secret.

Lauren Booth and Osama, my Palestinian roommate when I was in Athens, have both received death threats. Someone called Lauren Booth's family in France to tell her children to "Say good-bye to Mummy because Mummy's not coming home from the sea." Osama's family in the West Bank was directly threatened with physical violence by the IOF, and his own life has been threatened as well. Most of us to various degrees are running scared.

Tom Nelson is heading off to Saudi Arabia to visit a few clients. Some of our passengers are thinking of going to Lebanon for a few days. After all, Beirut is only a twenty-minute flight from Larnaca; the drive from here to the airport takes longer. My passport has a stamp from Ben Gurion Airport in Israel, so that probably won't work for me.

Rashid is thinking about flying to Tel Aviv and then making his way to the West Bank, since he has never been there before. As a veteran traveler to the West Bank and Israel, and with experience passing through Ben Gurion airport more than once, I try to give him advice. The main problem is that Ben Gurion usually does not allow Muslim Arabs to pass through the airport. Rashid is from Algeria but has spent most of his life in the UK and has a British accent and a British passport. As we jog through the park and past the waterfowl along the lake behind the reservoir, we try to decide whether he should try and use his BBC press pass. "I know!" he says. "I can pass myself off as an Arab Jew." "Yeah," I pant back. "You look like many Sephardic Jews I have seen in Israel. You could claim that you left Algeria for London because you were part of a persecuted minority…pant….You were raised as an agnostic Jew. Now you are coming to Israel to get in touch with your Jewish heritage…pant…pant…Once you get past customs, you can take a group taxi to Jerusalem, and I can put you in touch with contacts who work for the International Solidarity Movement. They can put you in touch with contacts in the West Bank. Once you are inside, you can do whatever you want."

Rashid is estatic at the prospect. We finish our jog and shower down in the dorm. We wind up in the kitchen for breakfast and explain our elaborate plan to Tom. "It sounds interesting," he remarks. "The only problem with your plan is that your passport gives your name as Rashid. What kind of a Jewish name is that?" Rashid decides to rethink this whole plan and ends up not flying to Tel Aviv. He winds up exploring the Turkish side of Cyprus for a few days instead. I can't go too far because I need to spend the better part of this week stocking the boat with medical supplies to be able to treat ourselves in case we are attacked.

The only good part about this delay is that we get to watch some of the Beijing Olympics, which we would have missed entirely had our mission been on schedule. I enjoy the Greek language coverage from Cyprus. We get to see a balance of the world's best athletes from around the world, not just the Americans, which is more typical when you watch Olympic coverage in the USA.

One person who doesn't have enough time to watch much of the Olympics is Greta Berlin. One of the main original organizers, Greta is now head of the media team. Like Osama, Paul, and Bella back in Greece, she is becoming exhausted from not getting enough sleep. Her phone is ringing incessantly, and she still receives anonymous death threats that unsettle the nerves.

Her dorm room is like Grand Central Station since she has one of the few laptops that is hooked up to the Internet. The college campus technicians who arrange Internet hookup here at the university are all on their August vacation, so late arrivals like me are stuck. Greta tries to take fitful naps in her dorm room while others are taking turns at her desk working off her laptop at all hours of the night and day checking their e-mail accounts.

Greta, along with Hedy and others, is doing multiple press conferences and radio interviews every day and arranging other interviews for the rest of us. The temperature is over 40 degrees C, (over 100 degrees F), and there is no air conditioning. She is in an awkward spot in terms of maintaining her credibility with the media because the world press wants accurate, specific information about when the Free Gaza movement boats will be leaving Cyprus for Gaza, but this is precisely the kind of information that must be kept fuzzy for a variety of logistical and security reasons.

Hedy Epstein is also working overtime, with wall-to-wall press interviews, keeping up a very hectic pace for an almost eighty-four-year-old woman I don't think she is getting enough rest, though. But as a holocaust survivor who worked at the Nuremburg trials, with longstanding public record promoting human rights, she is an obvious media focus for our campaign.

Mary Hughes has been burning the midnight oil working as the chief financial officer among the boat passengers in the middle of the current financial crisis of the Free Gaza movement. She has been at her laptop for hours helping Greta write urgent appeals for financial help and circulating them far and wide. After a lot of airplane rides, classroom workshops and sitting in front of computers, she has developed swelling in her legs that she has never had before. I am helping her address that from a medical standpoint.

On Hedy's eighty-fourth birthday, we finally declare a day off for Greta, Hedy, Mary, and Kathleen Wang. I agree to go with them into central Nicosia and then cross the barrier to the Turkish side. We will try to make it all the way to the northern coast to take a swim and then make it back across the barrier to the Greek side before sunset, so we can celebrate Hedy's birthday at the university with the rest of our passenger colleagues.

What these women don't fully realize is that I am the world's champion for wild goose chases. I am a travel junkie who relishes finding my way amidst disorientation and confusion; I love traveling on the edge, and I don't know when to stop. I am traveling with four older women who move at various speeds. None of us has really explored the Turkish Cypriot side before beyond immediate downtown Nicosia, and none of us speaks a word of Turkish.

It's a good thing these four don't talk to my wife, because she would warn of winter adventures in remote areas of Montana in futile pursuit of ghost towns; she could recount the time I got the SUV stuck in the snow with the sun setting, the temperature dropping, and no one around to help. It was just an unfortunate coincidence that happened twice in a week. Some would claim I don't learn. I am sure that we don't need to worry about snow here in Cyprus in August.

We make it to downtown Nicosia by taxi. We see ancient walls of the Old City, built by the Crusaders and later the Ottomans in the 1500s with moat and all. They look just like the stone walls around old Jerusalem. It's quiet because everything is closed in observance of a Christian holiday honoring the date of Virgin Mary's death. Within the walls of the Old City, we approach another more ominous and modern barrier that looks like the old Berlin Wall. It has spooky, largely abandoned neighborhoods on both the Greek and Turkish sides, where artillery exchanges have occurred, and people have died in the not too distant past.

We take pictures until we reach the signs that say No photographs. We stop for soft drinks at a café on the Greek side with the wall behind it. It is aptly named Checkpoint Charlie Two in reference to its Berlin Wall namesake, but it's more relaxed. I don't know how it works for the Greek and the Turk Cypriots, but it is easy for tourists to cross back and forth through the main checkpoint at the end of the main pedestrian shopping street on the Greek side of Old Nicosia. At the crossing, we show our passports to the Turkish guards, fill out a form, which is stamped, and— *voila!* We pass through the barrier and enter the northern Turkish part of Nicosia. All the signs are in Turkish and the Turkish flag is flying.

On the Muslim Turkish side there is no holiday, and it is business as usual. We walk up to the main mosque with its giant minaret. There is something very familiar about the architecture of this mosque. It has high Gothic arches, gargoyles, and posts for statues. This is not exactly typical of Islamic architecture. This mosque was once a Catholic cathedral built by the Venetians and then converted into a mosque by the Ottoman Turks when they took over in the 1500s. This kind of Christian architecture is distinct from the Eastern Orthodox churches that we see all over the southern part of the city. Cyprus has long been a crossroads and battleground for competing influences over the years; it is at the interface between two continents. In these respects, it is quite similar to Gaza, just more prosperous in these modern times, less crowded, and more endowed with natural beauty. We have lunch near the mosque, in air-conditioned surroundings where we can rehydrate.

Now it's time to find the bus station so we can get to the coast for a swim. We have our tourist map and our know-how. We ask our waiter, who shows us the initial directions on our map. We venture out and after several blocks, we ask for directions again several times and get several explanations in Turklish (a mixture of Turkish and English). We finally find the bus station, though we have walked much farther than some of us had anticipated. After a short wait, we board an overcrowded bus and are on our way to the coastal town of *Keryneia*. I am loving it! I fear the four with me are starting to wonder if they made the right decision. We cross over the northern coastal mountains, which separate the central Cypriot basin from the coast and then head down to the beach. After another bus change, we think we are on our way to a beautiful beach that we have never heard of before.

The bus winds its way through coastal neighborhoods, and I am not so sure we are on the right track. First we head east and then head west. The bus driver lets us off at the luxury tourist resort beach, which is just short of the public beach where we wanted to go. But we are confused and don't know better, so we get off. It costs twenty euros each to gain access to the beach. We have been trying to keep our costs down, which is why we took the buses instead of a taxi. But we also are tired, overheated, and need to swim, so we negotiate a lower price since it is late in the day. The swimming is divine with aquamarine waters and an island with coral reefs that you can swim around.

Hedy recently took swimming lessons back in St. Louis, so she would be ready to be on the FG boats. She gets to practice more here. On the peak above us, there is a giant memorial that looks like the nationalistic style of similar memorials of the former Soviet empire. But this one commemorates where forces from the Turkish mainland hit this beach for the first time during the 1974 Cypriot Civil War. After about nineteen minutes on the beach, we take the bus back to *Keryneia*, and then take another bus back to Nicosia. Hedy receives a call from our colleagues back in

Nicosia who are wondering about our whereabouts, and she reassures them that we all are okay.

The bus back to Nicosia is not as crowded. We cross the coastal mountain pass and down the south-facing mountainside toward the Greek side of Cyprus. This mountainside sports a huge illuminated Turkish Cypriot Flag that seems intended to taunt the Greeks who can see it every night. Our bus driver drops us off in a neighborhood that is closer to the crossing than the main bus station. Unfortunately, we have never been here before, and we are lost. We ask for directions to the crossing in our English-Turkish pantomime. One boy directs us to the west. Another man directs us to the east. Now what? Now the sun is going down, and it is becoming dark. "Well the sun sets in the west, so let's go south and we are sure to run into the barrier," I say.

After negotiating through a few poor and crowded Turkish neighborhoods, we find the barrier. There is a wide swath of no man's land, and we can see neon signs in Greek on the other side. Now what? Where is the crossing? We have differences of opinion within our group about whether we should proceed east or west. I run ahead to the east and run into a guard post staffed by nervous Turkish Cypriot soldiers, who after determining that I am not a threat to them, direct me to the west. After more walking, we finally find a crossing, but it is not the same crossing we used this afternoon. Once we finally get back to the Greek side, we call a taxi that gets us back to the University of Cyprus a full two hours behind schedule. Dinner has already been served, but we are just in time for Hedy's birthday cake.

Happy birthday, Hedy! You have just survived one of Dr. Bill's wild adventures!

Petros Giotis:
Aboard *Agios Nikolaos* somewhere along the north coast of Crete
Wednesday, 13 August

Today we really need to get going. No reason for any further delay. There's been a very good press conference at the pier, right in front of the two boats, which turned into a political solidarity event, in which dozens of progressive people from *Chania*, as well as many Arab immigrants, participated. The boats are ready.

The captains are both professional. And the most important reason for moving now is that we've been informed that the Greek Foreign Ministry, which doesn't hesitate to show its pro-American, pro-Israeli face, has intervened with the Ministry of Maritime Affairs, asking it to sabotage our journey. It can use a very simple way: a technical check of the boats can keep us in Limbo in *Chania* for up to two weeks, meaning that the already delayed mission will get way out of schedule. That would increase the chance of it being canceled or weakened to such a degree that the Zionists could stop us somewhere between Cyprus and Gaza.

The weather seems to be an obstacle to our cause, too. At this time of the year, the westerly and northwesterly winds blow. The forecast shows increasing gale force winds in the southern Aegean for the next few days. Giorgos, Markos, and Vangelis, who also have maritime experience, believe that we really have to leave *Chania* just in case a problem of check and delay comes up. We are at the western end of Crete, and we must reach the eastern end where we then turn on a southeastern heading toward Cyprus. Why waste time then? Let's travel along the northern Cretan coast all the way to *Sitia* (the far eastern city of Crete). There, we can reconsider the weather and, when given the chance, we can sail to Cyprus. Yes, we can.

Mathew looks hesitant, avoiding a direct expression of his opinion. He talks about harsh weather, but, mind you, it's only a wind level of four on the Beaufort scale. This sounds silly to me. We need to get going, even if means a few rough seas. This is not a pleasure cruise that we are going on. It is a holy mission to be accomplished. He has to agree, so it's late at night, and we are leaving *Chania*.

Vangelis has looked after the sail permit; we are supposedly heading to Rhodes. In this way, the ministry people will go there and won't be able to stop us. We have secretly decided not to sail to Rhodes at all. Let the bureaucrats and inspectors who want to tie us up in red tape wait for us there. I deliberately misinform our people in *Sitia* that we have changed our mind and will go to Rhodes after all. If my phone has been bugged (which is quite certainly the case), the bureaucratic inspectors will get the wrong information, allowing us to keep moving out into international waters toward Cyprus.

Thursday, 14 August

I wake up at 6:00 A.M. and go to the bridge to find out if Giorgos wants me to steer. He is outraged. "I'm looking for *Dimitris K* and can't see it anywhere. We specifically told Mathew to be right behind us, and he's just disappeared!" The weather goes swimmingly, only two to three on the Beaufort scale.

I call Vangelis aboard the *Dimitris K* on his mobile and wake him up. "We've lost you!" Giorgos gives him our position and describes it according to the nearest bearings on the Cretan coast. Vangelis calls me back; he is really pissed. Mathew has led them to Iraklion. Vangelis asked him to continue on the same route behind the Agios Nikolaos and he replied, "You can steer if you like."

Well, now we have to make a stop at *Iraklion;* at first we're in the middle of the harbor and then at a remote dock. At our meeting, tension is mounting. The issue is partly a cultural one. Some of the British and Americans who have some sailing experience have more confidence in Matthew's views, and Giorgos' local experience inspires the Greeks and other passengers with more confidence. Matthew probably thinks we are all crazy anyway.

What we have here is a failure to communicate. Ships such as ours have been traveling in a lot worse weather all round the Mediterranean. Rarely have they ever overturned or sunk. Greek sponge divers and fishermen reached Gibraltar many a time paddling.

Paul is cool, calm, and diplomatic with the idea of continuing on. "We've got Captain Giorgos with us, and he is also very experienced in these waters. Who will not take his advice?" I, on the other hand, am furious. I plead to our friends to trust the Greeks; after all, they know this sea thoroughly. Giorgos can give you the position of every single island, even of every rock and small reef. Our boats are not yachts, but they are sturdy. They still rock and pitch a lot and with the smallest of waves. We'll have a hard trip; that's for sure . . . especially further south, where the sea gets rougher. But, these are safe vessels. Don't forget, they're expecting us in Cyprus. Don't forget our mission. We think the boat passengers who are frightened should fly to Cyprus, and then those who remain can sail the boats to Cyprus in peace.

Friday, 15 August

Having wasted a whole day, we aboard the *Agios Nikolaos* decide to leave at noon. It's quite simple—we'll just push on; the other boat will have to follow us. We inform them of our intentions. At about 6:00 P.M., we reach *Sitia.* Just before we enter the harbor, I call our friends to say we are about to arrive in their port in *Sitia.* I'd deliberately misled them—and anyone bugging the phone—about our iternary. They are mighty surprised. Today is one of the three greatest festivals in Greece. Our local friends Theodosius and Dimitris join us within a few minutes of our arrival. More people come until nightfall. Having made a list that settles the night watch duty shifts, we gather at a café to have the much needed shots of *raki.*

Saturday, 16 August

At noon, lots of our friends from *Sitia* come to the boat, bringing us fruit and food. They have invited the local media, and we organise a new press conference. In the afternoon *Dimitris K* finally arrives and now Ken is the captain.

Mathew just left them and went back to Cyprus. I'm at the pier with Giorgos, who watches every detail, encouraging Ken through his docking procedure, a partially lit cigarette butt hanging from his mouth. "Good job, Ken! That's the stuff!" He is the first to shake hands with Ken as he steps onto the pier. Giorgos' teamwork makes me regard him with even higher esteem!

We have decided to get us a second captain who holds a Greek license to sail *Dimitris K* to *Larnaka*. After that we'll see what to do. Giorgos has called an acquaintance of his, who will soon join us after settling some personal business.

During the night, as Giannis and I take a stroll down the waterfront of this little harbor, we come across Giorgos. He wants to buy us a drink. We make small talk for quite a while. I'm really impressed by his stories. "Last year I went to *Kalymnos* to attend a local diving festival. When I saw the sponge divers dancing their dance, I was really touched, and wept. Everybody else applauded, but I wept." What did Giorgos know? *Kalymnos* is the island of the sponge divers. Quite a few of them are struck by the bends and end up crippled. Their dance involves the first dancer pretending to be a crippled sponge diver who's trying to get up and dance, bending on a walking stick. There's one more thing that Giorgos tells me and impresses on me. "I've been through lots of difficulties, and I learned not to allow myself to get desperate. Cause there's always a solution to any one problem."

Dr. Bill at the University of Cyprus in Nicosia:

Now we are hearing that our boats are only a couple days away from Larnaca Port, and our excitement grows. Derek Graham is sent to talk to us still waiting in Nicosia and to brief us about security issues. He is an Irish electrician living in Limassol, Cyprus, and also has seamanship skills. He is also streetwise about Cyprus. He has been with the boats and is here to urge caution as we enter another vulnerable period.

"Look," Derek explains. "Cyprus is famous for two things: its prostitutes and its spies. With Greeks, Turks, Russians, Armenians, Israelis, Arabs, Brits, Americans, and others passing in and out of here, there is espionage from every direction. Be very careful.

The last thing we need now is to have one of us 'disappeared.' No one should go anywhere alone. Travel in pairs or in multiples. Avoid hassles and walk away from large crowds. We don't need someone shot or stabbed in a large crowd by some unknown assailant.

"Stop using cell phones when you get to Larnaca. Israeli mobile phone technology is among the most advanced in the world. They can use GPS to pinpoint your location. Use calling cards and local pay phones instead. Those are more anonymous. Use different SIM cards to create secure networks of friends. Call only other secure phones with fresh SIM cards from within your select network of friends who also have new secure SIM cards, which have never been used to call other phone numbers outside your small network. Otherwise your new number is no longer secure.

"When we get to the boats, we will maintain close watch, with a land-based person, and a boat person who has previously traveled with the boats from Greece. We will provide continuous night watch for each boat at all times."

Some of us were planning to attend a music festival in Plakos, Cyprus, during the final weekend before leaving. We have already bought our tickets. But in consideration of what we have heard from Derek, we reluctantly decide that we better stay put at the university. A mosh pit at some music festival is probably not the best place to be hanging out right now because we have little control over what could happen in that situation.

Petros Giotis: Across the Carpathian Sea to Cyprus

Sunday, 17 August

Captain Zacharias is an able seaman who's worked on merchant ships for years. He arrives in the morning and, after a short conversation with Vangelis, agrees to pilot *Dimitris K* all the way to *Larnaka*. He also talks with Giorgos and they decide we should not go straight to Cyprus, but follow a course near the islands, even if that means wasting half a day. We will be crash testing the boats in the open sea and need to be off the coast in case any serious damage develops.

At 1030, we sail and we are lucky. The *Carpathian,* the roughest Greek sea, is absolutely calm. Not a wave to worry about. On the VHF, we hear people on ships sailing nearby: "Never seen this sea so calm in my life" says a captain. Giorgos catches a tuna around 7 kilos. He pulls it up slowly and everybody applauds as he brings it on the deck. What about cooking it, then? We've got gas but no cooking utensils!

Vangelis suggests that we have it raw. Sushi time! He undertakes the task to cut off some pieces around the fish's head. We dip them in lemon and, in a few minutes, yummy sushi is ready to be served. I've never tasted such a delicacy in all my life!

As the daylight wanes, our ships smoothly sail on a really calm sea. The sun goes down behind the mountains of *Karpathos*. An amazing wonderful view! Then, the full moon of August rises, reflecting its gold on the seawater.

Giorgos and Nikos do not share these moments of peace. There's been an oil leak. They repair the damage temporarily until we reach land and fix it properly.

Monday, 18 August

I wake up early in the morning only to see *Dimitris K* tied behind our boat. Their engine is shut off, and we are towing them. What happened? There's been a problem with steering, and so we tow them in order to avoid further delay until Captain Zacharias and Ken fix the damage. After the repair, we untie the boat, and we all sail on while remaining in visual contact.

A short while before noon, we reach *Kastelorizo*, the last Greek island, next to the Turkish coast. Takis and Giannis recollect that they have an old mate (and a comrade, too), Andreas, from university who lives on the island. They get in touch with him and brief him. While getting closer to the island, a rubber boat with *Andreas* and the mayor of the island approaches us. They escort us to the center of the small harbor, where the mayor receives us warmly and makes arrangements for a lunch for all of us.

The people of *Kastelorizo* have their own historical bonds with Gaza. During the Second World War, the island was under Italian occupation. The British wanted to bomb it, so all its inhabitants had to leave and take refuge in Gaza. The mayor's maternal aunt was born in Gaza. And now two Greek boats are paying their last Greek port of call to their island. They are part of an international mission to sail on to Gaza to break the siege.

It is night and our captains discuss the issue of our departure as the forecast doesn't sound too good. Giorgos suggests we leave in the morning. Zacharias insists we leave immediately. The locals tell us that bad weather doesn't last long. Then, both captains agree.

We set sail an hour before midnight. Two rubber boats escort us to the open sea. Heading to the south, the weather is fine again. Not even a breeze. Only the swell, the silent wave of the Mediterranean Sea, makes its presence clear. We have gotten used to it by now.

Letter to Free Gaza from Israel's Foreign Ministry Office:

We finally hear from Israel's Foreign Ministry Office after our letter to Tzipi Livney.

At first, they send the email saying "We would like to bring to your attention that the transfer of humanitarian aid to Israel is affected, at present, through agreed-upon channels." When we gleefully pointed out that we were sailing to Gaza and bringing in only a small amount of aid to GAZA and not to ISRAEL, they sent the corrected version below.

From: Israel MFA Online <feedback@mofa.gov.il>

Date: Mon, August 18, 2008 at 4:53 A.M.

Subject: Reply to Your Letter to FM Livni - Corrected version

To: "FriendsofGaza@gmail.com" <FriendsofGaza@gmail.com>

Information and Internet Department

Ministry of Foreign Affairs, Jerusalem

18 August 2008

The Steering Committee for the Free Gaza movement, Cyprus

 Dear Committee Members:

Your letter to Vice Prime Minister and Minister of Foreign Affairs Tzipi Livni as published on your Web site has been brought to our attention. We assume that your intentions are good but, in fact, the result of your action is that you are supporting the regime of a terrorist organization in Gaza, an organization dedicated to nonrecognition of the State of Israel and its right to exist; an organization that sends women and children to commit suicide in order to hurt others; an organization that has committed dozens of terrorist acts against Israeli civilians, including massive attacks of rockets and mortar bombs on Israeli communities in the heart of Israel's sovereign territory.

It is this organization that does not allow the Israelis and Palestinians to live in peace. In 2005, Israel withdrew all of its forces and all of its citizens from the Gaza Strip so that the Palestinians could manage their own lives; in return, innocent Israeli citizens were the targets of repeated attacks launched from within Palestinian civilian population centers, turning the Palestinian population into hostages of the terrorist organizations and the Hamas regime. The attacks from the Gaza Strip against Israeli communities continue to this day.

In June 2007, Hamas led a violent coup in Gaza and seized the government illegally, a fact which led to an international boycott and isolation of its government. The international community also set clear conditions that Hamas must fulfill in order to be regarded as a partner for diplomatic contacts and normal economic relations. Hamas is the central player in the Gaza Strip and the address to which you should direct your complaints concerning the situation there. In this protest voyage to Gaza, you seek to remove legitimate pressure on the Hamas government and to violate the conditions of the international community; therefore we cannot cooperate with your efforts.

Your claim that the residents of the Gaza Strip are suffering from hunger is groundless considering the amount of food that passes every day from Israel to the Gaza Strip. There isn't another conflict in the world in which one side supplies all the needs of the other side – food, medicines, water, fuel and electricity. Thousands of Palestinians have crossed into Israel from the Gaza Strip to receive medical treatment at Israeli hospitals.

We would like to point out that the area to which you are planning to sail is the subject of an advisory notice that has been published by the Israeli Navy, which warns all foreign vessels to remain clear of the designated maritime zone off the coast of Gaza in light of the current security situation.

We have received information that you are planning to bring humanitarian aid to the Gaza Strip. **We would like to bring to your attention that the transfer of humanitarian aid to Gaza is affected**, at present, through agreed-upon channels, and the Israeli authorities will ensure that the shipment reaches its destination via the land crossing points. We will be happy to assist you in this endeavor.

If your intentions are good, please choose this way; if you do not intend to deliver the humanitarian aid via Israel, this proves that your goal is political and constitutes the legitimization of a terrorist organization.

Sincerely,

Noam Katz

Director, Public Relations Department

Ministry of Foreign Affairs

Of course, it became irrestible. We had to answer and pick the part of the letter where they said our intentions were good. We ignored the rest of the 'boilerplate PR" that Israel always sent out, and answered Mr Katz right away, highlighting the untruths in the original response by providing factual information backed up by international bodies. And then we sent out a press release to everyone. Our impatience to leave was actually helping our own public relations campaign against Israel's illegal blockade on Gaza.

18 August 2008

Noam Katz

Director, Public Relations Department

Ministry of Foreign Affairs, Israel

Dear Mr. Katz,

The Free Gaza movement thanks Foreign Minister Livni for your response regarding our efforts to break the siege of Gaza. We appreciate Israel's formal recognition of our human rights mission, as well as its acknowledgement that our "intentions are good."

However, several factual errors in your letter need to be addressed. You wrote,

"Your claim that the residents of the Gaza Strip are suffering from hunger is groundless…" According to the United Nations' Office for the Coordination of Humanitarian Affairs (OCHA), "only 43.5 percent of basic commercial food import needs were met during the period between 3 and 30 December 2007."

Furthermore, in May 2008, several international aid organizations, including CARE International UK, CAFOD, Christian Aid, Oxfam, and Medecins du Monde UK, stated that "the stranglehold on Gaza's borders has made...the work of the UN and other humanitarian agencies...virtually impossible. Only a trickle of medicine, food, fuel, and other goods is being allowed in. [The Israeli blockade of Gaza] has made people highly dependent on food aid, and brought the health system and basic services such as water and sanitation near to collapse."

Although, we appreciate your offer to deliver humanitarian supplies for us, Israel's deplorable track record of delivering supplies is, in fact, the very reason for our mission.

Your offer also slights our human-rights mission, which is to break your siege of Gaza. We intend to raise international awareness about the open-air prison called Gaza, where Israel collectively punishes 1.5 million Palestinians. We want to pressure the international community to review its sanctions policy and end its support for Israel's continued occupation. Finally, we want to uphold Palestine's right to welcome internationals as visitors, human rights observers, humanitarian aid workers, and journalists.

We would like to, once again, invite Foreign Minister Tzipi Livni to join us on our historic voyage to end the siege of Gaza, and to see firsthand the devastating effects of Israeli policies on the men, women, and children of the Gaza Strip.

Sincerely,

Greta Berlin, Ramzi Kysia, Tom Nelson

Free Gaza movement, Cyprus

FOR IMMEDIATE RELEASE

Israeli Government Recognizes "Humanitarian" Mission to Break the Siege of

Gaza

Greta Berlin, Cyprus

Angela Godfry-Goldstein, Israel

NICOSIA, CYPRUS (18 Aug. 2008) - In a letter today to the Free Gaza movement, the Israeli Ministry of Foreign Affairs acknowledged that the group of international human rights activists attempting to break the siege of Gaza were "humanitarian," and stated that the Israeli government "assume[s] that your intentions are good."

Greta Berlin, one of the organizers of the Free Gaza movement stated that, "Since the foreign minister's office responded to our invitation to join us and said that we have good intentions, we now fully expect to reach Gaza.

According to recent reports in the Israeli media however, the Israeli military is preparing to use force to stop the nonviolent campaigners from reaching Gaza. It's not clear if the letter from the Ministry of Foreign Affairs signals a change of policy or is simply an attempt to open up an official dialogue between the state of Israel and the Free Gaza movement regarding the current blockade.

The Free Gaza movement is preparing to sail two ships into Gaza carrying forty human rights workers from seventeen different countries. They will also deliver hearing aids for children who have lost some or all of their hearing due to Israeli sound bombs and sonic booms.

The ships have been named the *SS Free Gaza*, and the *SS Liberty* in recognition of the *USS Liberty*, a U.S. Navy ship, carrying 340, that was attacked by Israeli fighter planes and torpedo boats on 8 June 1967, assassinating thirty-four American sailors and wounding 170.

The Free Gaza movement hopes to draw attention to the devastating consequences of the Israeli blockade by actively demonstrating the power of nonviolent direct action to change inhumane governmental policies.

Needless to say, we heard no more from the Israeli authorities.

Dr. Bill in Nicosia, Cyprus:

This afternoon, we are hosted at the high-rise apartment of Nora, a Palestinian living in Cyprus, who grew up in Beirut, Lebanon. We are each given the book *Life at the Crossroads: a History of Gaza* by British author Gerald Butt.

The view from Nora's apartment is breathtaking. We can see all of Nicosia, both the Greek and Turkish sides, and far off into the countryside. We are interviewed by Greek Cypriot television. The next day, people on the street are starting to recognize us, saying they have seen us on TV.

My attempts at acquiring medical supplies for the boats have not produced many results yet. As time gets short, it calls for more desperate measures. I appeal to my fellow passengers to pool the pharmaceuticals we have for the general good. I spend the final mornings with Sr. Anne Montgomery inventorying our stock, and afternoons at a downtown Nicosia pharmacy purchasing the stocks of bandages, bedpans, and other supplies that we don't have, at my own expense. Bella also donated a medical kit that is quite helpful, but it is not enough. Of course "having enough" is a relative term, as we can never have absolutely everything we might need given the wide range of potential degrees of disaster that could happen but hopefully won't.

I purchase medic bags as well. We are throwing things together at the last moment. We are washing all of our dirty laundry for the final time in preparation for departure.

We finally get the word that the *SS Free Gaza* and *SS Liberty* have arrived in the Port of Larnaca. I spend the final afternoon before we leave for Larnaca Port with Kathy Sheetz, the retired ICU nurse, organizing our medical stockpiles for each ship.

Her brother John arrived yesterday. He is an able sea captain who flew here from the Bay Area of California to pilot the *Free Gaza*. John is tense, wanting to get down to the boat, and I am tense, trying to work with his sister to finalize the medical inventory. For a moment, our tensions collide. The tension and excitement are building again. It's getting time to cast our fate to the wind. Our dreams of sailing to Gaza to break the siege are becoming reality.

Chapter 4:

The Spies Who Didn't Love Us

⌘ ⌘ ⌘

Petros Giotis, Aboard *Agios Nikolaos (SS Liberty):*

Tuesday, 19 August

It's morning. Everybody wakes up. The weather is still fine, and we travel smoothly to Cyprus. A little later, one of the side protective balloons falls into the sea. Captain Giorgos doesn't share our disappointment. He idles the engine, dives into the sea, and recovers the balloon. Everybody claps.

Late at night, we approach the city lights of *Pafos*. The Cypriot Coast Guard calls us through the ship's radio that we must shut off all the boats lights, so they can escort us in under cover. It's obvious that they are worried about our safety. (Each boat could become the target of Zionist commandos).

They tell us that the two boats should keep close to each other. Captain *Zacharias* steers a bit away: it's time for him to have a cup of tea so he doesn't want to be near the coast.

Wednesday, 20 August

We reach Larnaka at eight in the morning. We are asked to head to the guarded harbor, not the small marina. We are received as VIPs by the harbor authorities. They assure us they will be at our disposal at any time. An armed sentry is positioned by our boats. Two Cypriot Coast Guard divers search thoroughly under the boats, and there's an underwater camera installed, which is connected with a van on the pier.

Captain Giorgos has now committed himself to joining us all the way to Gaza as a member of the mission.

Dr. Bill reporting from Nicosia and Larnaca, Cyprus:
August 20-22

This Impossible Dream now seems like it could actually come to fruition. The *SS Free Gaza* and *SS Liberty* are in Larnaca Port now under Cypriot Coast Guard protection. It looks like we could get out to sea toward Gaza; but we are still not sure we can actually get in. The Israeli government has made several proclamations to the effect that they will intercept our boats and not let us pass into Gaza.

For the past few weeks, both the Greek and Cypriot governments have been under intense pressure at the highest levels from Israeli government officials and their diplomats, who are trying to stop us. Greece and Cyprus have stood firm with the majority of their citizens who support Palestinian civil rights. "They haven't broken any laws," they say to Israeli officials. We have to be certain that this remains the case.

We must move our supplies inland from the University of Cyprus to the Port of Larnaca in stages because we have limited car space. Our baggage is first piled up high behind locked doors within our dorms so we can keep an eye on it. When cars are ready, the luggage is brought to the curb. We each take turns providing continuous watch of our bags near the curb. The last thing we need right now is to have some Mossad agent posing as a college student walking past our bags and slipping drugs, weapons or other contraband inside our suitcases. This could then be discovered by Cypriot Coast Guard authorities who are charged with assuring safety and clearing of customs, and really mess up our operation. We cram the entire luggage as tight as we can into the first group of cars, and the first group of passengers departs for the port. We in the second group are detailed to do cleanup.

Before leaving Nicosia, we head downtown to the pharmacy to pick up the final list of trauma and other medical supplies. I still can't get everything I wanted. Due to complicated international regulations about controlled substances crossing international boundaries, I have been unable to secure supplies of narcotic pain relievers to use in the event we experience serious injuries. We will just have to tough it out if things get bad and hope for the best. I have a license to prescribe controlled substances in the state of Washington, where I practice, but that does not help me here in Greece or Cyprus. Furthermore, taking prescription narcotics out into international waters and into Gaza presents more legal dilemmas that we have been unable to figure out. I am only a doctor; I have very limited knowledge about international regulations concerning controlled substances and how to correctly address them. There must be a way, as I am sure cruise liners who travel in international waters have them under lock and key in their sickbays. I can only hope nothing really bad happens to us on the Free Gaza movement boats. It could get really horrible if we have to care for folks, who have become close friends, with serious trauma, and we have minimal means to alleviate severe pain.

We cruise in Eliza's rental car along Cypriot superhighways. Eliza has already figured out how not to get lost on previous trips between Nicosia and Larnaca. So this voyage is very quick, and I am content to sit back and listen to the compilation of theme songs we have created for the voyage playing on the rental car's CD player.

We are all dropped off at a hotel that Eliza arranged within walking distance to the boats. We are late to a mandatory meeting of all FG passengers. We enter an overcrowded hotel room to reunite with our colleagues who have been on the boats from Greece. They are tired; some have recently enjoyed their first showers in over a week. They need a couple more days on shore before we are ready to set sail for Gaza.

Osama and Christos, my previous roommates back in Athens, want to room with me, which is fine. Osama makes it clear he doesn't want it known where he is staying, since he is still receiving death threats. I sleep in the bed by the window. The thought that I am between Osama and any prospective attackers keeps me awake for a while.

When we leave the hotel, a hippie dude and his girlfriend try to follow us everywhere we go. Fortunately, these hippies have not yet figured out a way to get into the guarded port. As far as the hotel goes, all they or their associates have to do is just walk in. I am told that this hippie duo was in Crete with our boats and have followed us here. He is barefoot, has blond dreadlocks, and speaks English with an eastern European accent. She is a brunette who dresses more like a conventional summer tourist. I haven't heard her speak. They push around a shopping cart full of their belongings. They look like they would fit in well among the homeless who inhabit warm water ports around the world. I can't see it, but I'll bet that hidden in their junk within the depths of their shopping cart is a sophisticated spy camera. Maybe we are being bugged as well! In their presence, we all revert back to speaking in code words. We try and titrate the dialogue between ourselves to the appropriate level of caution for this occasion: between being careful but not overly paranoid.

One morning, several of us are outside the port gate at a coffee shop. We are all waiting with our passports for clearance by Cypriot port authorities to get our credentials so we can enter and leave the guarded portion of the port. The hippie couple is right in there amongst us. The surreal begins to become normal. We will not allow them to intimidate us. We will instead try to intimidate them.

We take turns taking pictures of this couple. I start serenading them with the old Louie Prima song:

When you're smiling
When you're smiling
The whole world smiles with you

Paul Larudee walks right up to the man, says "Good Morning," and shakes hands with him. The whole scene becomes quite comical. We caution each other to be careful what we say. It could be that the hippies are the diversion, and the more normal looking group of Greek Cypriot men sitting right behind us might be the real spies.

With our credentials we can now pass through the checkpoint that gets us inside the secure area of Larnaca port. Huge cargo ships are being loaded and unloaded on the dock toward the shore from our boats. The *SS Liberty* and *SS Free Gaza* are docked adjacent to each other in their entire splendor with flags from various nations flying aloft. There are armed Cypriot Coast Guard security men milling about. All night long, we keep a minimum of two of our own passengers aboard each ship standing guard in two-hour shifts to watch for any unusual events. The bottoms of each our boats are again checked periodically by scuba divers to assure our safety.

Bella, decompressing in Larnaca:
Date: Thursday, 21 August 2008
Subject: Setting Sail in the Morning

I can't say much more because the Internet man is about to throw us out. I am so tired and just rang my good friend to cry at him for a while about various internal group difficulties I might once have had the capacity to fix but don't any more. Coupled with this decreased ability to solve conflicts is an increased capacity to empathize beyond any reasonable amount with what everyone in the conflict is feeling, and to feel very compassionate for individuals while simultaneously feeling alienated with people generally. Argh!

Our boats are covered with flags, and they look beautiful. Not being a flag type person I never thought to bring the Aboriginal flag I was given last time I was in Oz (Australia), which I feel sad about. On the other hand, the Port Authorities don't seem to like any flags they don't recognize.

We had a press link with Gaza today... Israeli prison would be a pleasant rest after all this work and stress, but we have friends waiting for us.

Petros:
Thursday, 21 August

At 13:30, there's a press conference and a ceremony for fourteen murdered Palestinian fishermen. Greek MP Tasos Kourakis is in Cyprus with a parliamentary delegation. Takis contacts him. He visits the boats, asks to join us, and he is joyously received, thus reinforcing the mission.

Meanwhile, two Mossad agents are pretending to be hippies. They have been stalking us from Athens and at every Cretan port where we have stopped. Now they appear in *Larnaka*. They can't get in the port, since security measures are tough, but they move around the hotel where members of our mission are staying and at an Internet café where our passengers have been hanging out. Takis Politis is pissed and launches verbal abuse at them. They are experienced agents, and they remain calm, as expected.

Dr. Bill:

On the final afternoon and evening before departure, we hold press conferences on the dock next to the boats. We hold memorials with international cameras rolling for fourteen Gaza fishermen, who were killed since 2005 by the Israeli Navy. We also hold a memorial for thirty-four American sailors of the *USS Liberty* who were killed by the Israeli Air Force just off the Gazan Coast during the six-day war in 1967 and ignored by the world.

Huwaida Arraf throwing Roses into the Water

Final Larnaca Press Conference prior to Gaza Departure

We do our best to command the world's attention, hoping that this will raise world awareness and also protect us. Both boats are equipped with camera crews, satellite phones, and news agencies like the Palestinian *Ramattan,* which are capable of real-time streaming television coverage on the Internet. Our story is now being broadcast to networks around the world.

Late at night, some of us are having dinner on the patio of a restaurant across from our hotel. All of a sudden, there is a scuffle right in front of us out in the street. Apparently one man had been robbed by others. We remind each other to stand back. This is not the right time to be a Good Samaritan. Maybe this whole scuffle is being staged to suck us in. We all stay within the confines of the restaurant and off the street. Eventually the Larnaca police show up, and all the fighting settles down without our involvement.

I spend the final half hour before midnight with many of my shipmates inside the Internet café alongside the hotel right before closing time. I am e-mailing my friends and family to say good-bye. There is Huwaida, Eliza, Jeff, and many others there doing the same thing. The hippie dude and his girlfriend are there with us inside the Internet café too.

I lie down on my bed by the window inside my hotel room. I am regressing toward the simplemindedness and internal comfort of my childhood. The old Doris Day tune that I haven't thought of in years since back when I was five years old keeps playing over and over again in my head as I try to fall off to sleep:

Que sera, sera
Whatever will be, will be
The future's not ours to see
Que sera, sera

The Universal Declaration of Human Rights

Chapter 5:

Terror and Sea Sickness

⌘   ⌘   ⌘

"Before sailing, we were told that if any one of us was unwilling to drown at sea or be shot or arrested, or dragged to Israel and thrown in jail—all of which we knew were real possibilities— then we mustn't get on the boat. (Everyone got on the boat.)"

Mary Hughes-Thompson,
A Co-founder of Free Gaza movement

Dr. Bill in Larnaca and Aboard the SS Liberty:
Friday, August 22, 2008

We are all up early before sunrise getting breakfast and doing our final packing before moving out to the boats. Derek, the first mate of the *SS Free Gaza,* says our departure will be at eight o'clock sharp, GMT.

"GMT?" I ask. "Yeah, Greek maybe time." We are back and forth, on and off the boats several times. Dr. Papadoupolous, the Cypriot head of Medecins du Monde has come through with some medical supplies from his office yesterday at the last moment. These are office pharmaceuticals that I spend time labeling as "medical cargo" and stowing below deck on the *SS Liberty*. Things get frantic with last minute details immediately before our departure.

Time ran out for Alice, Michael, and Rashid, who had to return to the UK before the boats were ready to leave Cyprus.

Osama, who traveled with the boats from their hidden harbors around Athens, to Crete, and on to Cyprus, will now stay ashore with Ramzi and be part of the land crew. As a West Bank Palestinian who has been threatened the whole way, he risks too much if we get boarded at sea by the Israeli Navy.

Hedy Epstein had a medical event just a few days before the departure of the two boats from Cyprus to Gaza. In deference to the concerns expressed by me and other boat passengers, Hedy decides not to board the ship. Hedy will later say that she will regret this decision the rest of her life.

Petros:

Today is the big day. Starting at 05:00, the passengers begin gathering at the pier inside the guarded checkpoint. (We Greeks slept on the boat, our home.) There are international media people at the dock. Cypriot authorities perform the last formal checks. You can see that they welcome our mission wholeheartedly. "We are with you," one of them whispers in my ear.

**Greek Crew and Paul Larudee aboard *Agios Nikolaos (Liberty)*;
Petros Giotis is on the viewer's right with Paul to his right. Vangelis is behind.**

Captain Giorgos and Nikos aboard *Agios Nikolaos* are seriously dealing with a broken gas line. That means a bit more delay. We ask *Dimitris K* (SS Free Gaza) to move out first. There's a new captain aboard: Captain John from the USA. Zacharias took the plane back home to Crete.

Leaving Larnaca for Gaza, Vik says goodbye to Osama

Dr. Bill:

Good-byes are bid between those staying ashore and those going aboard several times. Finally at about 10:30 A.M. the lines are pulled in and the *SS Free Gaza* and *SS Liberty* head out. The vessels make a half circle inside the marina with final send off from cheering supporters on the shore, and then head out past the yellow Cypriot submarine at the end of the quay, and then out to open sea.

For our own safety, our vessels are being formally escorted into international waters by the Cypriot Coast Guard. We can only hope that maritime law will be respected, and that we will not be touched by the Israeli Navy in international waters.

Petros aboard *Agios Nikolaos (SS Liberty):*

Then Nikos and Giorgos are done with the repair, and they start the engine. We come out of the harbor at a low speed. The Cypriot patrol vessel escorts us out to a distance of six miles within Cypriot territorial waters. The weather is slightly worse than when we set sail from Greece. It is around four on the Beayfort scale, westerly, and it causes our boats to rock, making the new passengers rather seasick. They lie down, and we tell them what to do. No one is whining, though, and that's a good start. Dr. Bill just barfed all over the stern, and looks pale and weak. So I have to mop up after him.

Dr. Bill aboard *SS Liberty (Agios Nikolaos):*

First there is widespread euphoria aboard the *SS Liberty,* but as the sea gets deeper and rougher this evolves into widespread queasiness. *SS Free Gaza* is within eyesight of us on the *SS Liberty* at all times, though we are never close enough to see how its passengers are faring. We are told to eat small quantities of food frequently to curb seasickness. Many of us end up heaving our cookies anyway.

Dr. Anastasios Kourakis is a university pediatrician and a member of the Greek Parliament. He is certainly one of most important VIPs among on our boats en route to Gaza. Right now, he is showing more of his human frailty as he, too, succumbs to seasickness.

We are all wearing life vests. And we have lines fastened to the boat for just this situation, so we can hook onto someone's life vest, so he or she won't inadvertently fall overboard while heaving his or her guts out. I hook Dr. Anastasios's vest to the line. When he is done being sick, I outfit him with a Transderm Scopolamine patch and he takes a nap. Before leaving the US, I had my family practice partner in my office write a prescription for me for ten of these patches to treat seasickness. We have five aboard the *SS Gaza* and five aboard here on the *Liberty*.

You would think that the eastern Mediterranean would be a boater's paradise in August. Not necessarily so, especially if you are out here in open waters, where there are no islands to buffer the waves. The Greek islands are one thing, but out here, hot air blowing up off the Sinai desert like Santa Ana winds in California can whip up the choppy seas and cause commotion with your inner being. I am starting to feel a bit queasy myself. Perhaps I can distract myself by staying busy.

I am at the stern of the boat, sorting through medical supplies with Edith Lutz from Germany, who has a nursing background and who will be my assistant if we have medical or trauma casualties on *SS Liberty*. Kathy Sheetz, RN, has similar responsibilities on *SS Free Gaza*.

My queasiness seems manageable for a while, but then it overwhelms me quite suddenly, and I barf all over the back of the boat. Fortunately, our medical supplies are spared, but the deck on the stern is a mess. Petros Giotis, a Greek organizer for our Free Gaza movement has better sea legs than I. I am as weak as a kitten. He comments about how I look pale and escorts me to a mattress at mid ship to where the pitch of the seas is minimal. Petros grabs the mop and cleans up after me. Physician, treat thyself. I can't help others if I can't cope with the elements myself. I peel the plastic off the second seasick patch in our stock and put it on.

Dimitris K-Free Gaza photographed from *Agios Nikolaos-Liberty* in choppy seas

Just keep your eye on the horizon. Watch and feel the boat see-saw back and forth and to and fro like a bucking bronco and just pretend you are on some kind of amusement park ride for an extended period of time; say, 30 hours or so of stomach churning excitement. And take lots of naps. That's important.

Eventually I am able to get a handle on my seasickness, but the seas keep getting rougher and rougher. Fortunately, seasickness is the only thing I have had to treat on this boat so far. The sun sets in the west as we continue to bounce through whitecaps heading south.

Now we have southern Lebanon abeam on the portside. We can see nothing, not even city lights, because we are far out at sea, making sure we stay in international waters. For a while, other boats cross our path in and out of the ports of Beirut and other cities in southern Lebanon. Soon the border with northern Israel is abeam.

Paul Larudee is trying to contact Cyprus by satellite phone. The phones worked earlier today, but now neither one is working. We still have contact by walkie-talkie with the *SS Free Gaza*. They tell us that their phones are also down. "So what does that tell you?" Paul asks. "The Israelis have all of our communications systems jammed, and now we are cut off from the world." This is a real disappointment, since we have invested tens of thousands of dollars in sophisticated, real-time Internet streaming equipment in order to stay in touch with the world, and now none of it is working. The Israeli's seem to be acing us in the technology-tennis match.

Electronic warfare from Israel. The GPS sytems for both ships are knocked out

We settle in and try to sleep through a long night of choppy seas. The sight of the lights of *SS Free Gaza* following us is reassuring; otherwise it could be quite lonely out here. We see the lights of other ships coming and going in and out of the Port of Haifa. We keep a close eye on them to make sure that none are trying to approach us. Nikos Bollos, the Greek first mate says the sea forecast is for things to continue getting worse before they get better.

By midnight, things are getting so rough that it becomes dangerous to move about. I nearly get tossed trying to make it back to mid ship from the stern. "Sit down!" Yianis Karapidious screams at me, "Or we will put you below deck!" No time to be polite right now. This real and present danger finally penetrates my muddled consciousness. I sit down. We are at serious risk of being thrown overboard in the darkness if we move about. "I am sorry," I shout back in order to be heard in high winds.

We all fully expect that the Israeli Navy will show up in the next few hours, latch on to our boats, haul us all in to one of their ports, and arrest us. We feel resigned to this probability, but are too tired by the long day's events to feel scared. I drift in and out of short fits of sleep waiting for the sun to rise.

Petros:
Saturday, 23 August

The Zionists have cut off our satellite communications. Only one satellite phone works on *Dimitris K.* We ask them, through the VHF, to approach. We have written a passage for our people in Greece, I dictate it through the loudspeaker to Christos on the other boat. He takes it down and then gives it through the one working satellite phone. That was the last passage sent from our boats, the last communication with the world out there.

Mary Hughes-Thompson, Aboard Free Gaza:

When communication was lost, Lauren got on the one satellite phone we had working and put a message out to the world that we were two small boats; we had elderly people on board. We had sick people onboard and that in an emergency we would not be able to send out an SOS.

During the dark hours of that long, cold thirty-plus-hour voyage, we expected at any moment that masked, armed frogmen would swarm the boat. At one point we were all told to gather one small piece of important baggage and assemble on deck because we had reason to think we would be boarded within twenty minutes. We stood on deck, destroying phone numbers, hiding memory cards, in anticipation of the arrival of Israeli Navy frogmen.

Dr. Bill:

The sun finally rises and still, we see no warships on the horizon. The sea calms a bit. Now, Tel Aviv is abeam, then later, cities like Ashdod and finally Ashkelon. The *SS Free Gaza* reports that the **Ramattan** news crewmembers aboard now have a satellite phone that is working. They have found out that the Cypriot and Greek governments have launched formal protests demanding to know the status and whereabouts of the FG boats, which are registered as Greek vessels. The Arab League has launched a formal protest and is getting involved on our behalf as well. This is all good news.

We are told that a boat full of international journalists is sailing out to meet us from the Israeli port of Ashkelon. We hear that CNN will be sending a helicopter from Israel that will fly overhead to cover our efforts to reach Gaza. We wait for hours but neither boat full of journalists nor chopper from the sky show up. Still no Israeli warships on the horizon either; only us: two synchronous sailing vessels out here on the wide blue horizon. Maybe no news is good news or maybe not. We will have to keep on moving, and see.

Now we are just outside of Gaza's territorial waters at twenty nautical miles. It is 3:30 P.M., and we could be in Gaza port in just over two hours if we go for it. That is, if we are not intercepted. On one hand, Israel may claim that the Oslo process in the 1990s still allows them to control these waters. On the other hand, Israel's former prime minister Ariel Sharon declared in 2002 that "Oslo doesn't exist anymore." One would think that they shouldn't be able to have it both ways, but they often do. So which will it be? We are about to find out.

Our two boats circle each other slowly while we have a pow-wow out here at sea by radio with each other. **Ramattan** on board the *SS Free Gaza* is in touch by satellite phone with members of the Popular Committee against the Siege in Gaza City. Large crowds are beginning to assemble in the port, and they want us to come in right now. Command members aboard *SS Liberty* think we should stay out at sea overnight until tomorrow morning because if Israel apprehends us now as the sun is going down, there will be less news coverage available to us in the dark, and we will be more vulnerable if we go now as a result. The debate goes back and forth between the two boats for another half hour and tensions rise.

Finally, the *SS Free Gaza* crew declares, "We have got seasick passengers, and we are going in!" We see its stern getting smaller as it heads away from us toward the port. We continue to debate amongst ourselves whether we should follow them.

"What about divide and conquer?" I ask. We finally conclude that we're sitting ducks out here by ourselves, and with trepidation, we head full speed ahead into Gaza territorial waters, hoping for the best. Fortunately, the *SS Liberty* is a faster vessel than the *SS Free Gaza*. We are able to catch up and close ranks with them over the next hour.

We are told that Gaza fishing vessels have left Gaza port to come out and escort us in. Later we hear they have been turned back by Israeli warships.

Soon we are ten nautical miles from the shoreline, well within Gaza territorial waters. Still, no warships on our horizons. Where are they? Finally we get a call from *Free Gaza*. **Ramattan** is reporting that Israeli foreign minister Tzipi Livni has just issued an official statement declaring that Israel will not intercept the boats. The growing international pressure from around the world has broken the siege for the first time in forty-one years! The seas grow calmer and euphoria again builds among our passengers.

Ren Tawil aboard the SS Free Gaza:

I was used to thinking that the Mediterranean Sea was so much smaller than the Atlantic Ocean that one could appreciate the difference once setting sail on the smaller body; yet the Mediterranean is indeed an ocean in its own right both in terms of size and tempest, and within one hour I was vomiting what little I had in my stomach as the vessel rocked and pitched without end, and with the setting sun I was retching my empty innards over the side. But we all faithfully took care of each other, making sure to keep some solid food in our tummies at all times, to getting enough water, and keep our life jackets on when not going below. The rolling motion was bad enough to force the sickest to tether them selves before leaning over the rail.

As was the case on land, the deck bristled with electronics—cell phones continually charging, laptops being used to monitor media signals, and anything that pertained to our voyage, in addition to more standard equipment for the crew to navigate and keep an ear to all other passing traffic. The high point of all this monitoring came with word that the Israeli Ministry of Information, after repeated warning that Israeli forces will never permit our landing in Palestine, announced that now they will leave us alone, ostensibly due to the nature of our action being "humanitarian" and "peaceful." The real reason for this 180-degree decision had much more to do with anticipated world criticism of Israel if they had tried to stop us.

Earlier, a formal letter addressed to Free Gaza movement from their information minister concluded that, because our shipment of aid and our intent to carry back Arab passengers was being carried out directly between FG and Gaza's "outlawed" Hamas government, our actions must be deemed as support of terrorism. Their reversal of position on this was clearly a public relations-oriented contradiction of a very longstanding policy.

As we came within twenty nautical miles off the Gaza coast, our radio contacts on board the *SS Liberty* insisted that we wait. Fed up with roughing it, all the sickness and unrequited anticipation of landing, Greta Berlin, me, and others aboard *SS Free Gaza* committed virtual mutiny by way of hand-held communicators, first by arguing on the efficacy of waiting any longer, then by drawing from the consensus on our boat that we will continue without the *Liberty* if they choose to remain and wait. More than one thousand yards separated us before *Liberty* turned about and followed.

Two to three hours, the coastline at last appeared after we spotted an imposing smokestack to the north—Ashkelon, Israel. Just as we began to make out the harbor's opening at Gaza City, a speedboat with four men raced toward us, frantically waving, and all smiles; another soon followed, then the welcoming committees' watercraft grew bigger and bigger, each one bristling with the natives, circling our vessels, weaving in and out.

The emotional climax came with the sighting of the breakwater's endless masses of cheering Gazans 40,000 strong. Children dove from the boats into the polluted water, far from shore, eagerly grabbing for the balloons that we started blowing up an hour earlier and tossed into the bay. Then, as if to seal the two-year promise by FG to close the gap and make Palestine's sea route open once and for all, the boats sidled up to Free Gaza and Liberty and spilled their teary-eyed passengers onto our deck, who then embraced us as if we were liberating soldiers.

Dr. Bill's Account of the Arrival from Aboard the Liberty:

"Land ahoy!" Someone shouts. We scan the shore with our binoculars. We are now inside three nautical miles, and then the Gaza City skyline gradually enlarges in front of us. In spite of all the hardships during the past few years, Gaza shines like an emerald at this moment from the bow as we head in. As we get closer, the reality becomes clearer.

Gaza is overcrowded. To the north, we see the coal-fired power plant across the border in Ashkelon, Israel, then the crowded cinderblock buildings of Beach Refugee Camp, then more sturdy high-rise buildings and towering minarets in the Rimal district of Gaza City, and then wall-to-wall inhabitation all the way south as far as we can see beyond the town and refugee camp of Deir Al Balah. Now we can pick out the marina. And there are fishing boats packed with Gazans coming out to greet us! The breakwater is packed wall-to wall with people cheering.

As we enter the port it is sheer joy, jubilation and pandemonium! It is if we were astronauts returning from the moon. After all, each and every one of the Apollo astronauts has been to the moon and back, and an additional three and a half decades have passed since the last humans have arrived from international waters into Gaza Port. The only possible exception might be hostile Israeli commandos, courtesy of their navy. We are much more friendly visitors than that.

Hundreds of boys are swimming out to our boats from the shore, as local fishing boats encircle us. It looks chaotic and dangerous, especially for the fearless young boys in the water. I am hoping no one gets hit and injured by a vessel or its propeller. Several dignitaries come aboard our vessels via the fishing boats, and we are served tea and coffee while we attach a ladder to the sides of our boats to accept those who have swam out to us from shore. A Boy Scout band plays for us from an adjacent boat. Pretty soon, both boats are jam-packed with people all over the deck and on the roof above. There has to be a limit. We haven't even docked yet, and it is difficult to see how we will get through all the crowds in the water to do so.

Finally, the police detail starts coming aboard our vessels to do crowd control and limit further boarding of our boats. Our vessels ease their way through the local fishing boats and people in the water and finally reach their moorings. We slowly disembark and are escorted through the dense crowds and onto buses that will take us a couple blocks up the beach to the *El Deira Hotel,* our new home while we are in Gaza. We are pressing the flesh like crazy and hugging all the children all the way to the bus. A woman gives me a sash made of green fabric with Arabic writing and places it over my head like I am some sort of war hero. I say, *"Shukran"* [thank uou]. We all gain insight about what it must be like to be famous politicians, rock musicians, or members of a sports team.

Bella, after disembarking from the SS Free Gaza[2]:

Dear Everyone,

How can I possibly begin to coherently tell you anything of the last twenty-four hours?

I can't even comprehend any of it right now, let alone communicate it. You'll just have to get it in scraps of thoughts.

Yvonne and I are sitting here right now trying to think of the date yesterday. "We've made history and neither of us even knows what day we did it on," says Yvonne. "Just as well that it wasn't us running the Battle of Hastings. We'd be saying ten sixty-three or was it ten sixty-five?" We've now agreed it was August 23 yesterday, and I am very much hoping this finally gets me into the Housman's Peace Diary (without dying) even if just for next year.

We left Cyprus August 22, in the morning, and were very lucky to have it and the following day be the only two slightly cloudy days I've experienced onboard. Because normally, there simply wasn't enough shade for twenty-five of us above deck on the *Free Gaza,* and below was steaming hot. The sea was good in sailors' terms but enough so that most people were a little sick and about eight were

---

2   Reprinted from, Sharyn Lock, *Gaza Beneath the Bombs,* (London: Pluto Press, 2010), 12-14

very sick. Working as a medic with former nurse Kathy turned out to be the perfect job for me.

I spent most of the night feeling a little queasy unless lying flat on the deck, but one of my comrades was so ill all night that we had to give her dialoryte at fifteen-minute intervals most of the night. I simply lay down beside her, drowsing in between dosing her, observing our fantastic crew (including the wondrous O.J., and Vik who along with me learned the basics of piloting) as they stepped over me and Donna to keep the *Free Gaza* going through the night in two-hour watches. The sense of being in a great randomly-rocking cradle was intensified by watching the unchanging stars above me. Sometimes I could get up for a little while and gaze at the horizon, sea edged in all directions, watching lights of the occasional other ship (which always unnerved us a little) as well the red port light of the *Liberty* moving parallel with us. In the day, the sun was harsh, but in the sea at night there is just beauty.

By early evening, we were getting what I considered the best quality Channel 16 harassment of the trip. Channel 16 is the emergency channel that must always be kept unobstructed. But ever since sailing from Greece there'd been regular strange messages in Hebrew, Arabic music being played to us, etc. This time, someone was just repeating "They're lost. They're lost." Simple yet very sinister under the circumstances! Who was lost? Us…the *Liberty*? But we could see their lights. Or could we? Was that really the *Liberty*? And if it was, did it still have people aboard? How could we be sure? Because for long stretches at a time, we couldn't contact each other. Never trust technology, I tell you we had it all—satellite phones, radios, and extremely expensive satellite Internet and video streaming—to little benefit. The video streaming had apparently been sabotaged pretty thoroughly from long distances before we even set sail, though we had some capability sometimes; everything else stopped working on both boats shortly after the "they are lost" broadcast.

We were no longer able to use the normal sea communication systems even for SOS messages. We heard later that the Greek government, wondering how the MP they sent with us was doing, had tried every method to contact us, and eventually decided we must have been sunk. Before the communications system went down however, we'd heard that media coverage had taken off and that the Arab League had announced its support of us, and stated that Israel must act in every way to protect our peaceful mission. Then there was silence.

But we had two secret weapons: our walkie-talkies, apparently too low tech to be sabotaged, that allowed us to talk between boats, and the two journalists onboard (Mr. Ramattan and Mr. Aljazeerah) had a working satellite phone. Using this, we put out a press release announcing the apparent sabotage and calling particularly on the Greek government to protect us as we were sailing under Greek flags. (Actually we were sailing under about fifty flags, including a Free Leonard Peltier one, but you know what I mean.)

Morning was a blessing. Everyone cheered up, I felt fine again, and the sick people attempted some dry Greek bread. The amazingly cheerful Lauren stopped juggling walkie-talkies, and made yet another round of tea. (Let me apologize now for thinking her most useful role was going to be being related to Tony Blair.)

The working satellite phone began ringing and didn't stop: Musheir giving interviews in Arabic, Vik in Italian, and Jeff in Hebrew. We began to put up more flags. Messages came in about whether a media boat was coming or not coming from Israel to meet up with us. We kept grabbing passing crew and asking them how many hours until we left international waters? Two…one…

Then, having established contact again with the *Liberty*, we had an argument with them, miles out from Gaza territorial waters. Paul and Vangelis wanted to stop, postpone entering Gaza waters— our most dangerous stretch to cross in terms of potential Israeli attack—until the next morning, so we'd avoid the greater risk of attack at night.

But we on SS *Free Gaza* weren't interested. If we weren't stopped, we'd reach Gaza in three hours, and there would still be three hours until dusk. We called our Gaza hosts. "*Yalla!*" [Come now], they said. Technically we had a steering committee of three on our boat; Greta, Musheir and Jeff, and two on the Liberty. But the "discussion" was happening on walkie-talkie, which made it impossible. We'd created an odd numbered steering committee to vote if they had to, and as I saw it (clinging to some semblance of process) that's what we'd just defaulted to, i.e., our entire boat including three steerers wanted to go ahead. The *Liberty* asked for an hour to talk. No, said the *Free Gaza*, that hour's daylight can't be wasted—we're off. And we did the boat equivalent of stomping off. I don't dare imagine what the *Liberty* thought of us at that point, as we watched them get smaller and smaller.

Twenty minutes later, we got a call from the Israeli media. The foreign minister had just stated, "We are not going to stop the boats." We weren't going to prison.

Vik wasn't going to be climbing the mast. I wasn't going to be shot for refusing to co-operate with the Israeli Navy. We weren't going to get to eat our siege supply of vine leaves. Lauren wasn't going to get to sing "Israeli men" to the tune of "It's raining men" as we were boarded, which was just as well since we hadn't worked out the dance routine yet. None of that was happening. The impossible was happening instead. We were going to go to Gaza.

So there we were, with Derek, our first mate, shouting at us to tidy up our boat for its imminent achievement of the impossible: arrival to Gaza. We lurched about, picking up roll mats and empty water bottles, and putting them down again to go and stand in the bow, gazing at a hazy horizon. Derek climbed the mast. I don't know how much time passed; all I was doing was beaming at everybody in turn. Then we heard Derek shout, "LAND HO!" I still couldn't see a thing, but we all began to cheer.

Land Ho! shouts Derek

Approaching the Gaza Skyline and preparing for Gaza arrival on board Free Gaza

"Do it again for the camera," said Mr. Al Jazeera.

"LAND HO!" shouted Derek again.

"Didn't quite get that…"

"LAND –"

I looked for Hani, "Mr. Ramattan," hoping for the sake of Derek's voice that he was filming too. But Mr. Ramattan was collapsed in the lifeboat, sobbing out a lifetime of Palestinian tears. And then I could see buildings, I really could, and then I could see a boat. We'd heard the fishermen had come out in the morning hoping to meet us but had gone back when Israeli ships shot at them as usual. This yellow boat had a handful of flag waving men in it, and as soon as it reached us, we spotted a wildly lurching kayak behind it, powered by a wildly lurching young man . . . and then another boat overflowing with cheering women, as well as men, waving flags and almost spilling into the sea. And then we were surrounded, wooden boats dipping and turning and not quite crashing into each other as they circled us, carrying us into port on a wave of jubilation. Osama had promised us thousands waiting on the beach, but Osama thinks big, and I never quite understood what the reality would look like.

Free Gaza and local fishing boats

It really was thousands shouting, waving, and attempting to board our boats and shake our hands. Cameras were everywhere, held by smiling people who no doubt were supposed to be asking the usual daft questions like, "how do you feel to be here?", but who kept interrupting themselves to repeat "Welcome to Gaza! [*Ahlan wa sahlan*!] Thank you so much for coming, thank you, thank you! Now the world knows anyone can try to come to help us, if they wish to try."

Quickly overwhelmed, I retreated below deck and hid until security people came to extract us, rushing us through the rocking crowds like film stars, throwing us into a minibus, and taking us along the shore to a five-star hotel that they seemed to feel was the least they could do or more to the point—the safest place for these first crazy days.

Here, in a restaurant overlooking crumbling shacks on the beach, we exchanged greetings with our hosts in such a daze that I still don't know most of their names. But the important thing was we had all of them. Every group with which we'd worked was united in their support of our accomplishment. The Popular Committee against the Siege and the International Campaign to End the Siege on Gaza, the Gaza Medical Relief Society folks, the Gaza Community Mental Health Program, and other nonpartisan groups, Hamas and Fatah reps, and PFLP were present. Huwaida even got a congratulatory call from Mahmoud Abbas, the head of government in the West Bank (not particularly legitimate, but the only one the United States talks to). For at least an hour or two, we had achieved Palestinian national unity.

The next day, just as I thought the dreamlike quality of things might at least start to disperse, some of my comrades came back from an unofficial lunch with the

Hamas prime minister. Many of us chose not to attend to remain clearly politically separate from any faction. My comrades announced that we would be given Palestinian citizenship. And for the first time I began to cry.

Agios Nikolaos waiting to dock safely

The Gaza boyscout band serenades us upon our arrival

Triumph on the Gaza pier

Dr. Bill's Account of the Arrival Reception:

All forty-four of us are taken to the El Deira Hotel and are assigned rooms. I am advised by fellow passengers who are fluent in Arabic that maybe I should take off the green sash, which was given to me by the elderly lady on the shore, since it is promotes Hamas. I must confess that I don't know enough Arabic to realize this. Free Gaza movement is neutral when it comes to taking sides in internal Palestinian political matters. Our intension is simply to provide international solidarity with the besieged people of Gaza. It is up to the people of Gaza and the rest of Palestine to work out their internal political differences between themselves. Still, Hamas is now the dominant political power in Gaza, so it becomes necessary to interact with Hamas on multiple levels, just as it would be if another Palestinian political party were to be the dominant power here.

Our baggage arrives later, taken off the two boats by the police after we had negotiated the chaos of dense and giant crowds in the marina. The two bags I stowed on the *Liberty* full of office pharmaceuticals from Dr. Papadopoulos and from Musheir are missing. I will have to get back to the boats in the next few days to find them. After settling in, we are hosted for a dinner reception out on the hotel veranda overlooking the beach. We can see our boats docked to the south about a half a kilometer away.

Mr. Khoudary is the chairman of Popular Committee Against the Siege, and a member of the Palestinian Legislative Council. He heads one of two local groups in Gaza here to formally greet us. Members of other political factions (Fateh and others) are also among the crowd. The board members of the Palestinian International Campaign to End the Siege on Gaza are also here to formally greet us: Dr. Eyad Sarraj, Dr. Mona El Farra' and Raja Sourani are here, along with members of their staff and hundreds of others. They represent nonpartisan, "civil-society" movements largely consisting of non-governmental organizations (NGOs). There are also media and cameras all around. We are being broadcast all throughout the world, except among the corporate networks in the USA who are largely censoring this event. As for the breaking of the forty-one-year-old siege by the Sea of Gaza? They don't want Americans to ask why such a cruel siege has been in effect for so long.

I first met Dr. Eyad Sarraj back in 1985. He has been founder and chairman of Gaza Community Mental Health Programme for over thirty years and has been instrumental in the development of mental health services in the Gaza Strip. He is also a writer and internationally recognized human rights activist. He has the reputation of being a nonpartisan and pragmatic community leader in Gaza. Dr. Mona El Farra' wears many hats. She is a physician by trade and a human and women's rights activist by practice. She is currently the chair of Gaza Red Crescent but has also worked with Al Awda Hospital in Jabalya refugee camp and Union of Health Workers Committee. Raja Sourani is probably the Gaza Strip's most prominent human rights lawyer. He is head of Palestinian Center for Human Rights.

We talk out on the veranda at El Deira Hotel until late into the night.

Chapter 6:

Getting to Know the Lay of the Land in Gaza

⌘ ⌘ ⌘

Dr. Bill: Background of the crisis in Gaza

Mr. Haniyeh came to power in a democratic process in January 2006, after Hamas earned a plurality of representatives elected to the Palestine Legislative Council. The PLC is the Palestinian Authority's Parliament. This mandate resulted directly from democratic elections that were carefully observed by international monitors, including Jimmy Carter and his organization. These January 2006 elections were deemed fair, in spite of the Israeli Occupation Authorities, who interfered with Palestinian political campaigns, especially in East Jerusalem. Weeks after the election, Israel summarily imprisoned elected West Bank PLC members who are also members of Hamas. The Israeli's have since put a suffocating chokehold on the entire Gaza Strip.

In spite of their rhetoric about wanting to promote democracy in the Middle East, the US, Israel, the UK, and the EU did not respect the democratic mandate among the Palestinians. Instead, under Israel's insistence, the West has done everything it can to undermine the democratic process. When a Palestinian national unity government for the Palestinian Authority was carefully negotiated with the help of the Saudis in early 2007, Israel and the Bush Administration worked tirelessly to undermine it.

In Gaza, covert actions against Hamas occurred relentlessly through the offices of Elliot Abrams, the National Security Agency, and the CIA. Abrams has supported renegade militias, like those controlled by Fateh strongman Mahmoud Dahlan. These militias were encouraged by the Americans and the Israelis to incite a Palestinian civil war in Gaza to take out Hamas. In June 2007, internecine warfare started and Hamas prevailed in Gaza, while Fateh prevailed in the West Bank. Israel and the neo-cons in America succeeded again in a ruthless, cunning, and cruel division-and-conquest of Palestine.

This cruel siege of the Gaza Strip, which has been going on to some extent for years, became intensified, especially after September 2007 when Israel declared Gaza a "hostile entity." Collective punishment of the entire population of Gaza for having the nerve to voice their democratic choice has been put in place in a misguided attempt to limit the power and influence of Hamas.

Efforts by Israel and American to undermine the democratic process in Palestine leaves a bitter taste for so-called democracy and other western values in the mouths of most Gazans. There is now widespread alienation away from these values, allowing those with more fundamental and authoritarian methods of governance to take hold. I notice these changes compared to when I last visited Gaza in 2006. This is largely what is behind the move toward Hamas. It was a protest vote against the lack of tangible progress in Palestinian human rights and a perceived corruption and incompetence in the existing Palestinian Authority (PA) and political party, FATEH. (Of course, it has been American and Israeli officials who did most of the corrupting of the PA and Fateh.)

Israel has been unwilling to negotiate with Hamas, just as they were unwilling to negotiate with the more secular PLO twenty years ago. They keep playing this game of finding endless reasons why they can't negotiate, because the Israeli government prefers full-spectrum dominance over negotiation and fairness. We all know the current precondition that we hear all the time in our media for Israel's negotiating with Hamas: That they need to "renounce violence and recognize Israel's right to exist." Sounds reasonable; let's look at this little further. How about another precondition that we never hear in our media that is equally valid like "Not one more dime for Israel until they renounce violence and recognize Palestine's right to exist?" This seems reasonable, too.

There are roughly six million Jews and six million Christian, Druze, and Muslim Palestinian Arabs living between the Jordan River and the Mediterranean Sea—not to mention an additional six million Palestinians living in exile. Israel and the US are always looking for excuses not to negotiate with Palestinian leaders and other powers that be in the region that try and stand up for their rights and against to neocolonialism; the Israelis and Americans like to bully the situation and try to create quislings within the Palestinian leadership that they can "negotiate" with in bad faith. Superficial frames around "Israel's right to exist" seem reasonable to the majority of Israelis and Americans. We are encouraged to indifference and apathy by our mainstream media. They don't really want us to know the full dimension of suffering among the Palestinians, in particular the current deliberate man made catastrophe in Gaza or our deep financial role in all of it.

Israel and the US took the same approach with the PLO until twenty years ago. In those days the Israeli occupation authorities encouraged the growing Hamas movement in Gaza while shunning the PLO. This was also divide-and-rule in the opposite direction than it is run now. Finally Arafat was forced to recognize Israel and renounce the Palestinians right to exist on 78 percent of their historic homeland. He did this in 1988, and again in 1993. Arafat was a civil engineer, not a lawyer. He assumed his concession would mean that 22 percent of historic Palestine, including East Jerusalem, would become the Palestinian homeland. He did not fully understand how the game was being played. What did Arafat get for the Palestinian people in exchange for Israeli recognition? He got virtually nothing. Only further loss of his credibility among Palestinians. His loss of credibility resulted from subsequent worsening of internal corruption and favoritism within his organization, which was encouraged by the Israelis and the Americans.

The weak and subservient PA followed, including the disaster that resulted from the endless so-called Oslo Peace Process, whereby the remnants of Palestine continued to be divided by checkpoints and Israeli settler highways into smaller pieces. Arafat wound up under house arrest the last two and one-half years of his life. Abu Mazen (Mahmood Abbas), the current prime minister in the West Bank, has gotten very little for all his reconciliatory remarks. Now the Palestinian population is either exiled or warehoused between walls. The overall situation for Palestinians is now much worse than when the PLO recognized Israel twenty years ago.

The point is that **people** have a right to exist. Israeli Jews and Palestinian Arabs each have a right to exist. But nation-states don't necessarily have a right to exist, especially if the foundation of their existence is based on underlying injustice. Apartheid in South Africa did not have an inherent right to exist nor did the Confederate States of America. Imagine if talks between Nixon and Brezhnev back in the 1970s, or Reagan and Gorbachev in the 1980s were preconditioned on the USA's recognizing the Soviet Union's right to exist as a communist state? We would still be fighting the cold war. Well guess what? The Russian people still exist, but the Soviet Union does not. Why does Israel's right to exist as a state for Jews only go unquestioned by the rest of the world?

Dr Bill:

I have stayed at the El Deira Hotel before. It has a different flavor this time. It has become the collective compound for the Free Gaza movement here in Gaza. We fill the hotel beyond capacity.

Outside, the main road is barricaded and off limits to the general public. We are protected by police officers and security men, who monitor those walking in and out of the hotel. They do all this for our safety; they are trying to make sure that we are not infiltrated by Israeli collaborators or disgruntled locals, who might be alienated by the West's affiliation with Israel. We are being treated extremely well by our hosts so far. It becomes clear very quickly that most of the people of Gaza are quite joyful that we are here. Still, we have to do our best to prevent an adverse security event like abduction, kidnapping, or killing. Here in Gaza, something like this could very well be one thing made to look like another. During the next few days we will wonder how much protection is enough and how much is stifling and too much. I want to walk down to the boats in the marina where I have walked before by myself on previous trips. This time I need an escort of bodyguards to drive me there and back.

I return to the *Liberty* and can't find the bags from Medecins du Monde, Cyprus, or the bag from Mushier. I know exactly where I had put them. They must have been unloaded with the other bags, but they weren't at the hotel. They may have gone to the militia's health services. I hope that does not get me in trouble when I get home for providing material support, (i.e., medical supplies), to Hamas.

After breakfast out on the Veranda, we have a general meeting of FG to discuss our itinerary while here. Ismail Haniyeh, the prime minister in Gaza, would like to meet with us.

It is our first morning after arrival in Gaza. Right now, Free Gaza movement needs to decide how our organization will respond to the demonization of Hamas and intimidation against meeting with their leaders by Israel, the USA, and EU. These Western powers with external control over Gaza have justified cruel collective punishment of the entire population because they consider Hamas a "terrorist organization."

After debating what to do amongst ourselves, I am proud to say that Free Gaza movement refuses to buy into this kind of intimidation and demonization against simply talking with Hamas. We will not fall for this tactic to silence dialog. We are here in Gaza to listen to the full spectrum of Palestinian opinion. We are willing to talk to any Palestinians who want to talk with us. At the same time, we resent how Israel meddles in internal American politics. We don't intend to meddle here. We are here to show that talking is preferable to endless war, the alternative to not talking. Consequently, it would be ludicrous for us not to meet with members of Hamas, the dominant political power right now in Gaza.

This doesn't mean that individuals within our group cannot make their own decisions. Jeff Halper, the Israeli member of our delegation, decides not to meet with Hamas. He doesn't want the entire discourse among the media back in Israel to be dominated by the headline "Jeff Halper meets with Hamas." He wants the humanitarian hardships due directly to the siege in Gaza covered instead.

Our first visit this morning is to *Al Shifa* Hospital, the largest medical center in the Gaza Strip. It takes us up several city blocks; a luxury of space as far as Gaza is concerned. Shifa is a large teaching hospital and has had the full spectrum of primary care and specialty services, which are starting to fall apart. But like other hospitals in Gaza, the problem in not lack of knowledge. Gaza physicians have been trained all over the world. Since the siege, further training abroad is drying up because it is becoming more difficult for medical students and residents from Gaza to come and go. In Gaza, the current problem is deterioration of the medical infrastructure due largely to the tightening siege.

We are taken to the medical oncology unit, where they have fully trained oncologists, but now a markedly limited stock of cancer chemotherapy drugs, which are rationed by Israel from outside. For example, when there are several patients with similar cancer diagnoses who need a particular course of chemotherapy, the doctors must choose between giving one patient a full course of treatment and denying it to others or giving all patients incomplete courses of treatment limited by the on-again-off-again interruption in supplies coming in through Israel.

Over in the dialysis unit there are similar stories of deteriorating infrastructure. Patients who previously received dialysis three times per week are now limited to once per week. They are getting weaker because they have to wait longer for limited dialysis machines to purge the normal metabolic poisons from their bodies. This leads to further medical complications that could be mitigated through more frequent dialysis. Meanwhile, there are dialysis machines sitting up against the wall that are dormant because of a lack of reagents and repair parts to maintain them. In the surgical unit the breakdown of the system is similar. There are not enough anesthetic and surgical supplies to keep up with demand. Even though there are surgeons capable of doing the operations, the operations are not getting done because of the lack of essential supplies.

The breakdown of medical services due to the siege increased the need for Gazans with certain medical problems to travel abroad. Efforts to travel abroad for medical services are being blocked by the Israelis. According to the Gaza Ministry of Health, as of August, 2008, over 250 Palestinians have died while waiting through endless Israeli bureaucratic delays denying them exit to Egypt, Israel, Jordan, or other places for subspecialty care currently not available in Gaza. There are thousands of medical patients with time-sensitive illnesses whose lives are being directly threatened by the siege. There are also thousands of Gazan students whose hopes and future livelihoods are being destroyed by the siege.

After visiting *Shifa*, most of us take a bus north to a large assembly hall in the middle of *Shati* (Beach) refugee camp. The hall is surrounded by cinderblock apartments, with windows filled by the faces of local residents. They look down from their windows on us in the assembly hall and the proceedings begin. There are abundant still and movie cameras capturing our event with the prime minister.

Ismail Haniyeh speaks to us through his English interpreter. He describes our arrival as "heroic." He bestows medals and embraces each of us. Up close he appears to be a very charismatic teddy bear. Even those in Gaza who dislike Hamas speak fondly of this prime minister. He does not live in a mansion, like the other prime minister in the West Bank. He lives among the people right here in Beach camp. After our meeting, he takes us on a walking tour of the neighborhood so we can all gain a deeper appreciation of the reality of life here in Gaza.

We visit family after family in overcrowded apartments, where people are packed to more than ten to a room. There extremely limited room in Beach Camp for gardens or other vegetation.

Gone Fishin: Greta Berlin:
August 25, 2008

I sat at the front of the fishing boat, one of six that went out this morning. They are old wooden boats, outfitted with bits and pieces of mechanical parts, rope twisted together and fishing nets. Israel has refused to let Palestinians fish in their own waters for the past 15 months. Even before that, they restricted Palestinian fishermen to around 6 miles. Now, they shoot holes in the boats and in the fishermen if they are caught farther out than about a kilometer.

So today, 19 of us were going along to break a different kind of siege… the denial of Palestinian rights to fish, something every other country bordering the Mediterranean has. Only Palestinians are told they can't fish for their livelihood, provide for their families and contribute to their own economy. We decided that, since we sailed into Gaza (one fisherman told us we were the first boats to come into the port in 41 years; they have been forced to buy everything from Israel, who charges them exhorbitant fees to buy their own fish back).

We arrived at the port about 4:30 am, sleepy and stumbling about amid the dozens of security men standing there guarding us. We were told we'd have to wait, because the fishermen were afraid to go out to sea with us, uncertain whether they would be shot at or worse. Finally, four hours later, six boats showed up, and we boarded, two or three to a boat. The port is small but perfectly adequate for these boats plus our own two that were on the dock front to back. The media climbed into one of them, escorting us out.

All the Palestinians said they wanted to go out past the six-mile limit. They were as eager as we were to test the noose hanging around their necks. At eight miles, three Israeli patrol boats showed up, buzzing up and down in front of us, a man on a machine gun at the back of each one. Six cousins, the youngest 15, owned the boat I was on and they were, at first, nervous when the patrol boats showed up. I'm sure the Israelis were having a coronary wondering what to do with us, but they left us alone. I'm sure their media will now say they 'escorted us' out to sea, but that would be a lie.

Six hours later, the men had caught more fish in their nets than they had in four years. They were ecstatic, and I got to watch them haul the tons of fish up and over the back of the boat, sort them, water them down, they pick out the best 8 inch shrimp to cook for my friend, Moussa, and me. By the time we pulled back into port twelve hours later, my skin was bright pink from the sun, they were overjoyed with their catch, and the boats that went out would provide an income for over 16 families for a month.

"Will you come tomorrow? Will you come and fish again?" And, of course, we can't. They had challenged Israel's horrible siege on them, and, today, they won. But without us, will the Israeli come back tomorrow and get even?

We can hope that these men will be able to go out once more and do what generations of men have done… go fishing.

Chapter 7:

Gaza Is More than a Prison

⌘ ⌘ ⌘

Lauren Booth:

The most common metaphor used to describe life for the 1.5 million inhabitants of the Gaza Strip in Palestine is that of a prison. Having been trapped in Gaza by Israel's forces at Erez on one side and the Egyptian border police on the other side at Rafah for some time, I am able to report conclusively that this metaphor is inaccurate. I appeal to those with an interest in honest reporting to stop using this term to describe conditions here. For Gaza, besides having fixed parameters patrolled by armed forces, has little in common with a prison. For a start, prisoners in Europe receive three meals a day. While the taste and quality of these meals varies, each day's food allowance is nutritionally balanced to ensure that prisoners receive the optimum vitamins and minerals appropriate for their age group. No one goes hungry in a British jail.

Palestinians in Gaza are eating less. Parents are forced by the ever-tightening Israeli restrictions at the border, forcing them to reduce their children's daily intake merely to ensure that they can survive day by day. A study by the World Food Programme and UNRWA in May of 2008 found that 89 percent of the surveyed population had reduced the quality of food they have bought, while 75 percent, had reduced the quantity they ate since January 2008. The food that packs the shelves here is largely made up of biscuits, sweets, crisps, and fizzy drinks—empty carbs, sugar, and fat-laden junk. Local medical experts report that in Gaza, a diabetes time bomb is about to explode as a result of the siege. Almost all families have reduced their consumption of fresh fruit and vegetables to save money and very few Palestinians now eat fresh (red) meat. Families cannot afford to compensate for the lack of protein and vitamins. Considering the high prevalence of anaemia and other micronutrient deficiencies, this will have health consequences in the long term, especially for children.

I walked through Beach Camp, the refugee camp where Ismail Haniyeh, the prime minister, lives with his family. We were immediately surrounded by many of the camp's curious children. Many of the children's eyes seemed oddly flat and dull; a milky mist covers the cornea in many cases. Dr. Khamis El Essi, a rehabilitation specialist, randomly inspected the skin, teeth, and eyes of the barefoot children crowding around us on the muddy paths running between their impoverished homes.

Children of Beach Camp with Dr. Khamis El Essi

"This boy's eyes are dull—lack of minerals," he said of one eight-year-old boy. Another child, whom I estimated to be roughly the same as my eldest daughter Alex (seven), was smiling at us and waving "hello." His mouth revealed five or more partially formed uneven stumps. I presumed his milk teeth had just fallen out. After a brief interview with the boy, Dr. Khamis told me "This boy is small for his age. He is twelve. The lack of vitamins in his diet has affected his bones. His poor diet has already ruined his teeth." Signs were clearly visible in all the children of varying degrees of anaemia, poor growth, and malnutrition.

One of my first invitations was to meet the Hamas prime minister, Ismail Haniyeh. A group of us from the peace boat had been asked to dinner at his home, an apartment in the heart of a refugee camp. The entrance to the dining area is unpaved and broken. There are pools of muddy water, which I had to step through to get to the door.

I was quickly surrounded by Hanieyeh's special guards, a group of boys all looking too young to be carrying such big guns. I would have been tenser, but I have gotten used to the casual way guns are carried by the police force. They scowled at us as we walked in, perhaps trying to portray weighty authority, an air somewhat undermined by their propensity to grin and giggle when spoken to. For all their geniality, discipline and control were their bywords.

Increasingly on the streets, women not wearing the hijab receive disapproving glances. Rumors abound in the Shisha restaurants, places with outdoor space to smoke Arabic hubbly-bubbly pipes, of beatings meted out to those found with alcohol. We ate in a bombed-out ground-floor hall, open to the elements save for uneven sheets of corrugated iron. Simple trestle tables had been placed in lines and covered in plastic cloths.

Haniyeh is a giant of a man but with a "Hey guys, trust me" demeanor that disarms his critics; he's the Tony Blair of Hamas. After we had eaten, we walked the tight, rubbish-strewn alleyways of the refugee camp. There were skinny children everywhere making games out of the trash lying around. The main one seemed to entail crouching in the dirt and donkey dung, and flicking stones at tin cans.

Dr. Khamis, Lauren and Yasser with Beach Camp children

Israel has now restricted entry of food items like fruit, milk and other dairy products, wheat, flour, rice, sugar, salt, cooking oil, and frozen foods. All the key elements of vulnerability in the population have their roots in the military and administrative measures imposed by the Israeli occupation. This is no natural disaster. This is deliberate man-made malnutrition. Gazans are faced with regimented border closures and the destruction of assets, such as acres of orchards, like in the town of Beit Hanoun and many other communities. This rationing of imported food supplies, and destruction of domestic food production has lead to soaring food prices, falling incomes and growing unemployment; elements which combine to jeopardize the livelihoods of Palestinians, leading to heavy debt and changes in family eating habits. Previously self-reliant families are falling into the poverty trap: unable to escape from their situation.

I repeat, Gaza is not a prison. It is much more than that.

Since September 19, 2007, almost 1.5 million Gazans have been tortured emotionally, physically and psychologically by crippling sanctions. Movement beyond this forty-by-ten kilometer enclave has been made not merely difficult, but (since the Rafah crossing has been open to the public just eight days this year), largely impossible.

Yesterday, I met with Dr. Basem N. Naim, the minister of Health in Gaza. His office was experiencing a black out, and there was no lighting. We sat in dimness to talk about the current situation for hospitals and patients.

With the international refusal of governments to cooperate with Hamas, even on social issues such as health and education, it is impossible for the ministry of health to have any forward planning for patient care. Dr. Basem gave the example of many cancer patients who receive the first two treatments for their life threatening condition. When the date for the third treatment arrives, the drugs are unavailable. Their condition worsens. At some unknown stage in the future, treatment will have to recommence from the start.

Over 240 patients in Gaza have died as a direct result of the siege conditions since autumn 2007. Health care is in a constant state of crisis now due to deteriorating infrastructure. Before June 2007 some 9,000 essential items were reaching the Gaza Strip; since then only nine groups of items are allowed in. This summer, between fifty and one hundred and fifty different essential supplies of medicine have been reduced to zero stock. Another 100 to 120 items of disposable essentials such as syringes have also reached zero stock. Elevator parts for lifts have been recently banned by Israel, too. Without spare parts from the outside world, hospital lifts are breaking down. Dr. Basem cites the case of a hospital where patients have needed to be carried on the shoulders of orderlies up four flights of stairs between a ward and an operating theater. Since July 2008, the ministry of health has had NO surgical alcohol. Today the health ministry has NO chlorine for cleaning.

Gaza is no prison. Prisoners in the UK receive high quality health care as needed. In a prison, the inmates have access to clean water, good, clean sanitation, and a twenty-four/seven supply of electricity. Here in Gaza, electricity, fuel, and gas have been drastically reduced and are now intermittently cut off due to a lack of fuel. Things are bad here and getting worse.

The fuel situation is a catastrophe. Power is in short supply, affecting hospitals, fresh water availability, sanitation, and the functioning of daily life here under conditions of extreme duress. I have visited hovels in Beach Camp, whose paltry stoves can no longer be used to prepare a single hot meal each day for families of ten and more, who are confined together in very small spaces.

There is no access to fuel. Wood is in sparse supply in this increasingly dusty, barren land, yet increasingly open fires are the only available method of cooking for the mothers of Gaza. Shops are short of everything, and even basic materials have spotty availability. Banned items that are hard to find here but available in western prisons include: clothing, books, computers, telephones, and even shoes.

During our meeting with John Ging (the director of UNWRA), the difficulties faced by aid agencies in getting the raw materials of life through the checkpoints that handle cargo were outlined. For example, it has taken UNRWA many months of wrangling with the Israeli authorities in order to have paper, needed to print books for the agency's many schools, allowed through. The unwarranted, unreasonable delays meant tens of thousands of Gazan school children faced the 2009 school year without essential textbooks.

In the UK, the notorious child killer Ian Huntley relaxes in Frankland Maximum security prison in county Durham. Officers guarding Huntley have reportedly been told to play games with him, including Scrabble and chess. He is allowed special sports clothes, has a cell to himself, with a television, CD player, and a Nintendo Game Cube console inside. It has also been claimed that guards must address him as Mr. Huntley, presumably to boost his self-esteem. Depression amongst prisoners in the UK is high, but there are numerous channels through which effective treatment and support can be provided. In British prisons, the mental health and comfort, not to mention the rehabilitation of prisoners, is taken seriously. Their rights are protected by law. In UK prisons, inmates are offered a range of activities including access to college and university courses.

Gaza is not a prison. Families (including spouses) are cut off from one another for unlimited periods of time. Life here is one of relentless interruption after another. I attended a candlelit vigil in the Gardens of the Unknown Soldier in Gaza City. This ceremony was held by mothers who had been separated by the IOF from their families in the West Bank and also abroad, and are unable to reach their children because of the siege.

Nisreen is twenty-seven, a stunning beauty with a quiet grace. Candle shaking in her hand, she could hardly restrain her emotional pain as she told me her story. In 2006 she went on a visit from her home in the West Bank town of Qalqilya to relatives in a neighboring village. On her return, a temporary Israeli check-point blocked her route home. Born in Gaza, her papers for Qalqilya were ig-nored; her permit to live there disregarded. Her place of birth was Gaza, and the Israeli guards insisted that back to Gaza she must return. She was driven, crying for mercy, to Erez, accompanied by a female IOF soldier who spoke no Arabic. "I was roughly forced to cross Erez," she told me, "then left here to rot." Nisreen has seen neither her ten-year-old nor her three-year-old son for "fourteen months and two days."

Nisreen is stuck in Gaza, seperated from her childen and husband, who are in the West Bank. Mona El Farra' has a daughter suck in Jordan trying to get home to Gaza

There are many parents in a similar situation encased in this overcrowded Gazan internment camp. They have been suffering the emotional effects of an enforced separation (of unknown length) from their children, their partners, and their homes in the West Bank, Israel, Egypt, and beyond.

Just this morning my good friend Dr. Mona Al Farra', a highly respected physician and author of the award-winning blog From Gaza from Love, was shaking after a call from her sixteen-year-old daughter. *Sondos* has been visiting family in Jordan; her school year started this week here in Gaza, but for two weeks permission for her return home to her mother has been confounded and refused without expla-nation by Israel's border authority.

Why and on what legal grounds would a schoolchild be refused return to her parental home? No one here can explain. If this policy of refused permits and enforced incarceration or exile is not Israel's intention, then the closure policy is an utter failure. If the intention is to punish the innocent, as must be suspected when one witnesses the daily, hourly monotony of the cruel, permit/no permit process, then it is a very effective and emotionally devastating policy indeed.

Family unification has been denied further after the Israeli Knesset passed the Nationality and Entry into Israel Law (July 2003). This bars Palestinians in the occupied territories with an Israeli spouse from getting citizenship or residency status in Israel. The net result is that these families are not allowed to live together. Thousands of married couples and their children are forced to remain apart or leave both Israel and the occupied territories and move abroad. The new law solely targets Palestinians. Besides this law, Israeli Arabs married to Gazans are barred from entering Gaza to visit their families. Meanwhile, Jewish prisoners in Israel are permitted conjugal visits from spouses under law. Wives regularly get pregnant during these 'compassionate' visits. Prisoners around the world may have regular contact with friends and relatives.

The most psychologically punishing element of all under this cruel siege is that Palestinians in Gaza have no idea and certainly no say in when it will end. In a prison, inmates have a fixed release date they can look forward to, a time in the near (or distant) future when they know they will be reunited with loved ones. The people I have met, since arriving here with the Free Gaza Boats are denied this hope. They live devoid of self-determination, adrift from the rest of the world on a sea of imposed uncertainty. In short, they dare not hope at all.

Gaza is not a prison. Someone who is imprisoned is closely confined as a punishment for a crime after due process of law. Is this a concentration camp? This definition of an enclosed space where innocent victims (usually of one race and including children held against their will) collectively suffer punishment because of their ethnicity or creed is one that should be familiar to every Israeli soldier, politician and citizen.

For Palestinians in Gaza, a UK prison with access visits from family members, three square meals a day, rehabilitation and education programs, good sanitary conditions and health care would be an improvement over life here.

Gaza 2008 is not a prison. It is the largest internment camp, slowly becoming the largest concentration camp, in history.

Chapter 8:

Gaza by Sea and by Land

⌘ ⌘ ⌘

Comedy Octopuses: Bella:
Friday, 29 August 2008

Gaza waters extend twelve miles off the coast; after 12 miles, one is in international waters at that point. However, Israeli gunboats regularly patrol the waters at the six-mile point, shooting at any boats that cross this line; they say they are imposing this limit. (Our Greek friends find this particularly upsetting because throughout thousands of years, the Mediterranean was always free for its entire people to sail until now. This restriction makes for poor fishing, something to do with the sea being too warm for many fish that close to shore. I guess also it's a small area for everyone to fish in. But more to the point, Israeli gunboats don't just shoot at boats that cross this arbitrary six-mile line, but also at boats three miles out, two miles out and even at people on the beach.

So the Free Gaza boat and a bunch of us dispersed on about five or six small wooden fishing boats headed out on August 25th . Our boats were flying a lot of our flags for the occasion, including both the American and the Australian ones flying upside down by accident rather than design, I think! We decided to go catch some fish beyond the six-mile point, steaming on to eight miles. However, not so far from the coast because the smudge skulking on the horizon suddenly began moving along what appeared to be an intercept line, shaped up to be a spiky grey Israeli ship, all angles and whirling technical things, plus deck-mounted guns.

The fishermen had been showing people multiple bullet holes in both the boats and themselves from earlier incidents. On the first little boat the speedy Israeli ship would reach, Eliza and I watched with adrenalin pumping a bit and climbed up to the stern in the usual tradition of being visible (which could be interpreted either as internationals in the area or here, we'll make it easier for you to shoot us).

Then another Israeli ship appeared from the other direction. A third joined them, and then they began to circle our little group of boats. But that turned out to be pretty much it for most of the rest of the day; six Palestinian boats fishing, three Israeli boats circling menacingly—except you can't pull off menacing for hours and hours without following it up. After it became apparent they were not going to attack, they just simply weren't that interesting anymore.

Not as interesting as fishing! Man, fishing is bizarre. And damn hard work. The sun blazed the whole day and the only shade was inside the wheelhouse or a few feet beside it. About five men, plus two young boys, were on the boat working, hauling nets, and winding heavy ropes and cables. It was only a small boat, with blistered paint and rusted metal, but its owner was very proud of its engine, which roared deafeningly and which he told us would go faster than the Free Gaza easily. It ran on bottle after bottle of cooking oil; one more thing like powered milk and in fact almost everything edible here comes through despite the Israeli siege. How? Via the hundreds of tunnels between Gaza and Egypt.

When it came time to bring up the nets, Eliza and I perched on the roaring, steaming engine's roof, combining a patch of shade with avoiding twisting ropes while going slowly deaf, and watched everyone work to raise the nets and empty them onto the boat's floor. What a spectacle of mass death! Thousands of fish of all descriptions, all flapping about desperately, incredibly strange colored and shaped, all gasping their last. Disoriented crabs and small bemused octopuses (octopi?) clambered over one another in slow drunken bewilderment, at which I wanted to laugh, but couldn't, since most were living their last moments. The two boys slipped about among the fish, examining the odder ones and throwing the occasional one back. Something flounder-like had this lucky escape, after a long study, the boy smiling at Eliza's and my obvious relief that at least one sea creature got to live to swim another day. A blackened cooking pot and gas cylinder contraption (lit blithely by the youngest boy) provided tea and coffee, and later in the day a big fat fried fish each for me and Eliza and lots of little fish for the fishermen (no doubt the nonsaleable ones) for lunch. It was the best fish I had ever tasted.

During the day we had been alternating with the captain on the VHF radio, liaising with the other English speakers, and eventually the Free Gaza had to call a halt to things because of limited fuel. Our fishermen were loathe to leave, and lagged behind, fishing as they went, eventually stopping altogether when some problem happened with the nets.

Our captain radioed for the others to leave without us, and we hung about while they began fixing the problem. To our great joy, Eliza and I understood we could swim. Completely out of sight of land in any direction, we leapt into the gleaming Gaza Sea. Our boat maneuvered itself a short distance from us in a slightly worrying manner (swimming in long sleeves and long trousers isn't easy) but stopped after a bit, so we caught up, and they hauled us back in. As I sat on the rug on the bow drip-drying, drinking my first lusciously sweet and minty Palestinian tea in three years, I couldn't have been happier.

While all this had been happening, two Israeli ships packed up and went home, and one lurked on the horizon in a slightly bored manner. As soon as we set off, however, it took off after us, catching up at an alarming rate. Our captain asked us to radio the Free Gaza to ask them to come back for us. As soon as this was agreed, the Israeli ship stopped. We radioed them back, "Don't worry. Ship stopped. Don't come." At which it began again to advance speedily. We radioed again, and again it stopped. We began to catch onto the game when this was repeated a third time. Finally it decided to do what initially looked like an attack but turned out to be just making some sort of point—it came full speed toward us, circled us once as close as it could so that our boat would be rocked by its heavy wake, and resumed following us from a distance.

So Eliza and I, full of fish and covered in salt, settled back on the deck with my iPod. The shuffler provided a soundtrack of Blondie's "Maria," Ani di Franco's "Not a Pretty Girl," Billy Bragg's "Internationale," Nancy Kerr and James Fagan's "Tiller Song," and Crowded's House's "Don't Dream, It's Over." Occasionally one of us would open an eye, squint toward the Israeli ship, announce, "Nope—guns still not pointing at us. That's nice."

"Best catch in four years," our captain said wistfully, as we headed toward the shore. Finally we caught up with the other boats, which were waiting to arrive in port with us. As we pulled in, we watched all the seasick sunburnt journalists being helped off the Free Gaza. Vik waved at us from the deck, shouting "Free Gaza… two and Israel… zero!"

Gaza from North to South
Dr. Bill:

Some would say the limited cargo we could bring on two small Greek fishing boats that sailed to Gaza was largely symbolic, a drop in the bucket in terms of Gaza's greater needs. This is certainly true in terms of the overwhelming humanitarian needs being deliberately denied to 1.5 million human beings. Some of the more cynical of Israel's apologists have gone as far as to claim our mission is nothing more than a big publicity stunt. But for over a hundred young children at the *Atfaluna Society for the Deaf* in Gaza City, our mission will make a world of difference: the gift of hearing. That's about how many hearing aids we brought on the boats as gifts donated by the California-based Palestine Children's Welfare Fund. Such high-tech devices have been deemed a security threat to the state of Israel. So many Gaza children have been denied the ability to hear.

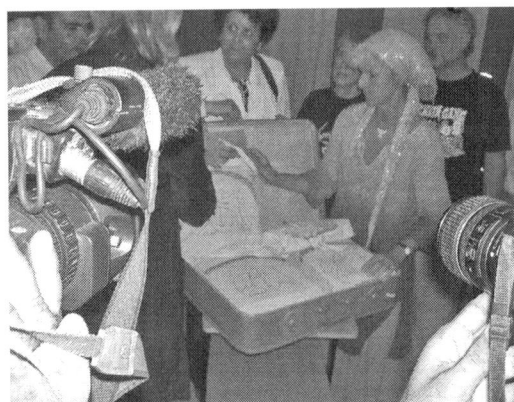

Edith Lutz opens suitcase full of hearing aids for Atfaluna Society for children with hearing impairments

There are hundreds of Gaza's children who are deaf because of the usual congenital causes and to infections. But there are also many who suffer hearing loss becaue of acute severe noise exposure. There are bombs and artillery shells. And then there are loud explosions due to low altitude sonic booms from Israeli fighter jets that have flown immediately overhead in efforts to collectively scare the population. It is always much easier to devastate than to heal. There are children in Gaza who will spend years suffering the consequences of some reckless Israeli F-16 fighter pilot's joyride.

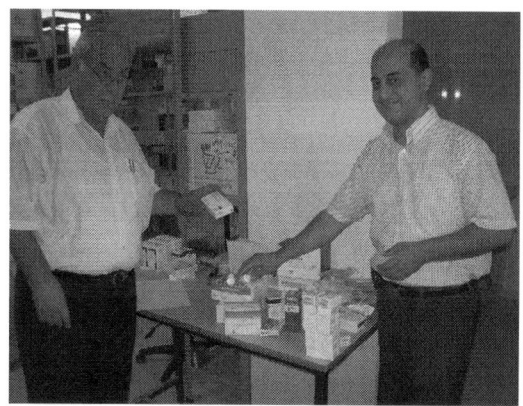

Dr. Yussef Mousa, Chairman of the Union of Health Work Committees, and Dr. Akram Nasser, accept the aid cargo of medicines the Free Gaza boats brought them for Al-Awda Hospital

For the surgical crew at Al Awda Hospital in Jabalya, our mission will mean that several necessary operations can now proceed thanks to new stocks of anesthetic supplies that have been in short supply. For patients who use a clinic in Beit Hanoun, they will now be able to get an electrocardiogram in their own clinic instead of having to travel to the hospital. This is courtesy of some benevolent physicians in Greece who financed two machines. A second ECG machine will be delivered to another small clinic in need.

Lauren Booth, Dr. Mona Farra' and local women at Beit Hanoun Clinic

These are only a few small gestures in the greater scheme of things, yes. But they produce tangible results for a few in need. But more importantly, we have opened up a route. In subsequent voyages, future Free Gaza movement boats will bring larger quantities of medical supplies and other cargo ashore. This is only the beginning.

More importantly, our gifts will hopefully raise more awareness in the world community about what is lacking here and about the adverse humanitarian and environmental consequences of this cruel blockade. I hope the world's powers will put a stop to this and soon. Then and only then can the bigger issues be addressed. After nearly a year since the Annapolis so-called peace conference, these fundamental consequences of the Israeli siege of Gaza have barely been mentioned.

Our delegation visits factories whose production has been curtailed and in some cases, shut down because essential supplies critical to ongoing factory operations have been blocked. Now the unemployment rate hovers at over 45 percent for the entire Gaza Strip. In some of the refugee camps, the unemployment rate is over 80 percent.

We participate in a peaceful demonstration in Gaza City on behalf of agricultural workers who are equally devastated. Peaceful, direct action like this has a long tradition here in Gaza and other parts of Palestine. If Israel and the West were really serious about wanting to stop what they call "terrorism," one would think that they would respond positively to peaceful demonstrations that call attention to abuses of fundamental human needs.

Most of Gaza's limited agricultural land lies along the border with Israel. In the agricultural community of Beit Hanoun, for example, over 60 percent of the olive and citrus groves in the area have been ripped out by Israeli militarized bulldozers and tanks. The Israeli's claim that this wanton destruction is necessary for their security, since Qassam missiles have sometimes been fired from these orchards. Israel's security always comes at the expense of Gaza's security. It is hard to see how this bizarre and lopsided "security arrangement" can lead to anyone's long-term well-being and safety.

In many areas along the border, the 'security zone' has been widened by 300 meters, always at the expense of the people of Gaza and never at the expense of the Israeli's. Valuable farmland becomes a no-man's-land. Palestinian farmers are often shot at from Israeli positions on the other side of the borders while they are trying to tend to their crops. Then when it becomes time to export the crops, attempts to earn a living are further undermined. Time-sensitive perishable products of farmers like carnations or fresh strawberries whither away while sitting for too long at the border. Israel deliberately delays their transport and exports are denied to these farmers.

Weekly protest for agricultural workers

We march with hundreds during their weekly demonstration up to the gates of the UNSCO office. The gates are locked shut and no one answers the door. The local UN agencies can do nothing to help the locals other than to voice the plight of these farmers to the UN general assembly. The UN Security Council and its five permanent members dominate the general assembly. Efforts to respond to Israel's cruel policies are vetoed continuously by its chief enabler, the United States.

We also participate in the weekly demonstration with families of prisoners who are held by Israel. They hold pictures of their loved ones. Some have been imprisoned for more than ten years without due process. There are over 11,000 Palestinian prisoners languishing in Israeli jails. These family members protest nonviolently here in Gaza City every week demanding to be heard. When will the outside world ever listen?

These people have relatives in Israeli Prisons; over 11 thousand political prisoners are currently held by Israel

Next, our bus, filled with Free Gaza movement passengers and local Palestinians from our host groups, heads south toward the city of Rafah, which borders Egypt. We want to get an assessment of the current situation there.

There is no way of telling by casual observation, but this main north-south road, *Salah Al-Din,* is a part of one of the oldest thoroughfares in human history. It has been called different names over the millennia, but it been a part of the main highway that follows the coast between Morocco and Turkey for over 5,000 years. Unfortunately right now, it is virtually impossible for Gaza's local citizens to travel any further than the forty kilometers between Beit Hanoun in the north and Rafah in the south. The Israelis, and 'applied political pressure through the Americans over the Egyptians', have the local people living alongside this main arterial of the millennia clogged, and sealed off from the rest of the world.

En route we make a stop at Nuseirat Refugee Camp about halfway down the Gaza Strip. Nuseirat is one of four middle camps. The others are Bureij, Maghazi, and finally Deir al Balah, right next to the town of Deir Al Balah, which carries the same name. Before these four camps' creation in 1948, the area was farmland, and there still exists a wee bit of farmland in the limited spaces between the four camps. These four middle camps now collectively comprise a population of over 132,000. And these are the smaller four of the eight refugee camps in Gaza. Jabalya Camp north of Gaza City has 107 thousand people. Beach Camp has around 81 thousand. Rafah Camp has over 97 thousand, and Khan Younis Camp nearly 62 thousand inhabitants. The populations of these camps do not include the larger cities and smaller towns that surround them.

What distinguishes refugee camps in Gaza from the towns that often carry the same name is that the camps are essentially devoid of open land. People are packed into these camps like sardines. Families are crowded together in cinder-block apartments with the roof left incomplete. This has become a classic feature of modern Gaza architecture. The top floor is left undone with rebar pilings for future construction of higher floors to house more people when there are future generations. There is no room to build outward—only upward. The population of the camps keeps growing.

At the Nuseirat Children's Center, teenage students perform traditional Palestinian *Dabke* dancing for us. This is an art form that developed before 1948 in more spacious Palestinian villages north of Gaza before the Catastrophe or *Nakba,* put them in this overcrowded situation. The great-grandparents of today's dancers come from these villages; before they were forced into these camps by the creation of Israel. Many of these former Palestinian villages are now destroyed. Now the memories of theses villages are preserved through dances like the *Dabke* in refugee camps like Nuseirat.

We head further south, past the rubble of the former *Abu Holi* checkpoint, which was finally destroyed in September 2005, along with two adjacent former Israeli illegal settlements. Before August 2005, there were about 8,000 Israeli squatters in Gaza. These settlements, along with the various Israeli-only bypass roads and military bases that supported them, controlled about 40 percent of the Gaza Strip and made it off-limits to local Palestinians. These restructions included about a third of the Gaza beachfront, the former *Gush Kativ* block of settlements. Once again, the security and safety of 8,000 Israeli settlers came at the expense of over 1.5 million Palestinians confined in Gaza.

When the settlements were here, the IOF had the entire Gaza Strip bottlenecked between north and south at *Abu Holi* checkpoint. This was the only way for Palestinians, since all other north-south roads were off-limits to them. On a whim, the IOF could completely shut off north-south traffic in the Gaza Strip, and they often did. When Israeli settler traffic needed to use the overpass between settlements on either side of the highway, the Palestinian traffic would be stopped, at times for hours just to let a few Israeli settler cars pass. When there were incidents of Palestinian armed resistance, it was much worse. The checkpoint was completely shut off, and family members would be separated for days. Many travelers were stuck here. There used to be large tents and portable restrooms in *Abu Holi's* fields along the road that served as temporary housing for motorists and passengers who were stuck.

I passed through *Abu Holi* checkpoint a couple times in 2003. The traffic was shunted through a chute, with concrete barriers on either side, spy cameras, and multiple spooky concrete guard towers with slits in them so that Israeli guards could see out, yet vehicle passengers could not see in. All of that is gone. The concrete slabs and settlements on opposite sides of the highway are just ugly piles of rubble now. The Israelis blew up everything before they pulled out in 2005.

The next major city to the south is Khan Younis, which means *Jonah's Inn* in Arabic. It was founded in the fourteenth century as a way station to protect caravans, pilgrims and other travelers who plied this main route. Today it has nearly 200,000 inhabitants, including its adjacent refugee camp. And finally we get to Rafah, which has been in existence since at least 1300 BC. It has a current population of 130 thousand people, of which 84 thousand live in refugee camps. Before 1979 when the Sinai Peninsula was given back to Egypt as part of the Camp David Peace Accords negotiated between Carter, Sadat, and Begin, there had been no distinct border here.

Before 1967, Egypt controlled the area and between '67 and '82, the Israelis controlled both sides of Rafah. As a result, Rafah experienced natural growth to the south. Then in 1982 after Israelis withdrew from the Sinai, a line was drawn in the sand, a gate was built, and the people of Rafah were separated into an Egyptian side and a Gaza side. But many families continued to have relatives on both sides. There was a natural commerce and connection between the two Rafahs.

The border between Egyptian and Gazan Rafah in 1985

During the late 1990s, the Israeli military authorities tried even harder to disconnect Rafah from the outside world. They built an iron wall to separate Egyptian from Gaza Rafah. The local residents responded by building tunnels. The ruthlessness of the Israeli occupation authorities then became even more apparent. Between 2002 and 2005, they destroyed over 2500 homes and made 20,000 Palestinians homeless in the occupied Palestinian territories. Two thirds of these home demolitions occurred in Rafah, and about 10 percent of Gaza Rafah's entire population was made homeless. The Israeli occupation authorities claim that they uncovered about ninety tunnels in this way. The no man's land was widened to 300 meters, and the area was given the Orwellian misnomer **Philadelphi Corridor**—brotherly love! It has been anything but. When I visited this corridor in 2003, there were Israeli tanks and C-9 militarized Caterpillar bulldozers combing through the rubble of what were once apartment buildings. There were several Israeli sniper towers; if you stepped out into the open, you risked being shot immediately. Still, I was taken by local boys on a cat-and-mouse expedition inside the damaged apartments along the perimeter, so I could experience the danger for myself.

Rafah border in November, 2003, 2 weeks after 2000 people were made homeless by Ariel Sharon in 1 night due widespread demolition of apartments adjacent to the iron barrier.

The Rafah border in 2006. The Israelis call this the Philadelphi Corridor. 'Brotherly Love'

In 2006 when I visited the Rafah border again, it was much better, after the Israeli "redeployment" from Gaza. The Israelis and the sniper towers were gone from the immediate area. The iron and concrete wall still existed, and probably spycams that you couldn't easily see. Near the former site of the pharmacist Nasrallah's home, where Rachel Corrie was killed, there stood a community garden.

By then you could safely walk right up to the iron wall and cross right where you would have been killed by an Israeli sniper a year and two months before. You could then look through a slit in the iron wall along one of its seams, and see Egypt a few centimeters away on the other side. By 2006, more new tunnels had been built, with more underway. Another man-made humanitarian catastrophe and all the indifference—all this death and wanton destruction was for nothing. Now we have a lot of bitter people whose lives have been collectively devastated, with the world paying virtually no attention. But the people of Rafah remain determined to survive any way they can.

Breach of the Israeli built iron wall. January, 2008

In January 2008, there was a brief period of hope. Local Palestinians took matters into their own hands. They used explosives to blow up the iron wall. No one was killed or injured. For a brief time there was euphoria. Hundreds of thousands of Palestinians and Egyptians crossed back and forth to briefly rekindle ancient relationships; the people of Gaza were able to re-stock essential supplies for a week. In Gaza City today there are now frequent sightings of shiny red motorcycles that were all bought in the nearby Egyptian town of El Arish, during that week of limited freedom. Then, Egypt, under pressure from Israel and the USA, closed the border again. They built a yellow stone wall that we can now see and that I am told was financed by American taxpayers—another thing I am supposed to be *proud* of?

The Israeli-Palestinian conflict here is a game of inches, just like WWI. Palestinians have gained a few inches in this ground game along the border in Rafah. So many innocent people have been sacrificed in this back-and-forth inching along.

It is now August 2008. Our FG delegation bus drives right up and over the line where the iron wall used to stand to the new stone wall with Egypt, where we file out. There are still a few piles and fragments of iron wall strewn about that the Hamas authorities have not yet removed. Now the locals can stroll right up to the stone wall on the Egyptian line and shout, *"Ahlan-Wa-Sahlan!"(WELCOME)* to the Egyptian guards sitting in their towers on the other side of the stone wall. Compared to the Israelis, the Egyptian soldiers are much less likely to shoot.

The area remains a widened undeveloped corridor, except where new military bases now stand, and where hundreds of Hamas militiamen train. Hundreds of tunnels connecting Gazan to Egyptian Rafah run below us. Ironically, this is right where IOF bases and sniper towers once stood a few years ago. A lot of bad money has been poured on top of bad money to reinforce this border here in Rafah. Still, people gotta live, and they will continue to find ways around whatever barrier the West puts up here. The world's powers have done nothing to solve the underlying neglected humanitarian needs here in Palestine, which lead to armed conflict. Some so-called peace process this is! What a farce!

We head back up to Khan Younis to the city offices and meet the mayor. We journey to the West up against where refugees from Khan Younis camp used to try to exist alongside the Gush Kativ block of settlements. These settlements denied locals access to the sea for so many years.

Now they can travel to the sea without being sniped at. But now the new land acquired from the former settlement is on the brink of a catastrophic, occupation-caused environmental disaster that could be easily prevented. Because of extreme rationing by the Israeli occupation authorities of fuel to the area, the local sewage treatment plant is limited in how much sewage it can process. Consequently, a huge cesspool is building up west of Khan Younis. This cesspool lies up the hill from perhaps the most beautiful beach in Gaza, which was formerly a part of the Gush Kativ settlement block.

The water tables here have been among the best in Gaza; hence the location of this former settlement. Palestinians now have access to this area again. We visit this beach, and some of us swim in its crystal-clear, aquamarine waters. It is still beautiful. Only problem is that if the cesspool uphill keeps building up without proper processing of sewage, it could rupture and contaminate the delicate high-quality water table below it and spoil the adjacent beach and coastline.

Our bus heads back toward Gaza City via the coastal road, formerly reserved for Israeli settlers only, and off-limits to Palestinians for many years. There is abundant vegetation; this is probably the most scenic area in the Gaza Strip. Musheir Faraa' is from these parts. He was born and raised in Khan Younis but now lives in Sheffield, England, where he is a civil engineer and Palestinian rights activist. His family has property around here and his two sisters, who are both physicians, have been among our hosts here in Gaza. He mentions that he wonders how Jeff Halper is doing.

Jeff Halper arrived with us on the boats. He is the only Jewish Israeli citizen among us who is currently living in Israel. In fact, Jeff's home in Jerusalem is only about an hour's drive away from the Gaza border with Israel at Erez Crossing. So instead of taking a 33 hour boat trip back to Cyprus, and then an airplane trip back to Tel Aviv, Jeff thought he would just cross directly back into Israel from Gaza. Since there are Israeli laws prohibiting Israelis from traveling to Gaza, we are all curious to find out what will happen. Jeff left our hotel in Gaza City for the Erez crossing with Israel this morning. Jeff left me his two mobile phone numbers yesterday, so I try to contact him. I call the first number and there is no answer. I call the second number, and Musheir talks to Jeff's wife in Jerusalem. Jeff has been arrested and taken into custody at Erez crossing.

Chapter 9:

End of an Odyssey

⌘ ⌘ ⌘

Jeff Halper:

Jeff Halper in Gaza

September 1, 2008

Now, a few days after my release from jail in the wake of my trip to Gaza, I'm posting a few notes to sum things up.

First, the mission of the Free Gaza movement to break the Israeli siege proved a success beyond all expectations. Our reaching Gaza and leaving has created a free and regular channel between Gaza and the outside world. It has done so because it has forced the Israeli government to make a clear policy declaration: that it is not occupying Gaza and therefore will not prevent the free movement of Palestinians in and out (at least by sea).

Israel's security concerns can easily be accommodated by instituting a technical system of checks similar to those of other ports. Any attempt on the part of Israel to backtrack on this by preventing ships in the future from entering or leaving Gaza with goods and passengers, including Palestinians, may be immediately interpreted as an assertion of control, and therefore of occupation, opening Israel to accountability for war crimes under international law, something Israel tries to avoid at all costs.

Gone is the obfuscation that has allowed Israel to maintain its control of the occupied territories without assuming any responsibility: from now on, Israel is either an occupying power accountable for its actions and policies, or Palestinians have every right to enjoy their human right of traveling freely in and out of their country. Israel can no longer have it both ways. Not only did our two little boats force the Israel military and government to give way, but they also changed fundamentally the status of Israel's control of Gaza.

When we finally arrived in Gaza after a day and a half sail, the welcome we received from 40,000 joyous Gazans was overwhelming and moving. People sought me out in particular; eager it seemed to speak Hebrew with an Israeli after years of isolation from Israel. The message I received by people of all factions during my three days there was the same: How do we (we in the sense of all of us living in their country not just Palestinians or Israelis) get out of this mess? Where are we going? The discourse was not even political: what is the solution: one state or two? It was just common sense and straightforward, based on the assumption that we will all continue living in the same country and this stupid conflict, with its walls and siege and violence, is bad for everybody. "Don't Israelis see that?" people would ask me.

The answer, unfortunately, is "no." To be honest, we Israeli Jews are the problem. The Palestinians years ago accepted our existence in the country as a people and are willing to accept ANY solution. It is us who want exclusivity over the land of Israel; it is us who cannot conceive of a single country, who cannot accept the national presence of Palestinians (we talk about "Arabs" in our country), and who have eliminated by our settlements even the possibility of the two-state solution in which we take 80 percent of the land.

So it's sad, truly sad, that our "enemies" want peace and coexistence (and tell me that in HEBREW), and we don't. Yeah, we Israeli Jews want "peace," but in the meantime what we have—almost no attacks, a feeling of security, a "disappeared" Palestinian people, a booming economy, tourism, and ever-improving international status—seems just fine. If "peace" means giving up settlements, land and control, why do it? What's wrong with the status quo?

When in Gaza I also managed to see old friends, especially Eyad El-Sarraj of the Gaza Community Mental Health Program and Raja Sourani, director of the Palestinian Center for Human Rights, whom I visited in his office. I also received honorary Palestinian citizenship, including a passport, which was very meaningful to me as an Israeli Jew. When I was in Gaza everyone in Israel, including the media who interviewed me, warned me to be careful, to watch out for my life. They asked me if I was scared. Well, the only time I felt genuine and palpable fear during the entire journey was when I got back to Israel. I went from Gaza through the Erez checkpoint because I wanted to make the point that the siege is not only by sea. On the Israeli side I was immediately arrested, charged with violating a military order prohibiting Israelis from being in Gaza, and jailed at the Shikma prison in Ashkelon.

In my cell that night, someone recognized me from the news. All night, right-wing Israelis physically threatened me, and I was sure I wouldn't make it till the morning. Ironically, there were three Palestinians in my cell who kind of protected me, so the danger was from Israelis, not Palestinians, in Gaza as well as in Israel. (One Palestinian from Hebron was in jail for being illegally in Israel; I was in jail for being illegally in Palestine.) As it stands, I'm out on bail. The state will probably press charges in the next few weeks, and I could be jailed for two or so months.

I now am a Palestinian in every sense of the word: On Monday I received my Palestinian citizenship, and on Tuesday I was already in an Israeli jail.

Though the operation was a complete success, the siege will only be genuinely broken if we keep up the movement in and out of Gaza. The boats are scheduled to return in two to four weeks, and I am now working on getting a boatload of Israelis. My only frustration with what was undoubtedly a successful operation was with the fact that Israelis just don't get it and don't want to get it. The implications of our being the strong party and the fact that the Palestinians are the ones truly seeking peace are too threatening to their hegemony and self-perceived innocence.

What I encountered in perhaps a dozen interviews, and what I read about myself and our trip written by "journalists" who never even attempted to speak to me or the others, was a collective image of Gaza, the Palestinians and our interminable conflict that could only be described as fantasy. Rather than inquire about my experiences, motives, or views, my interviewers, especially on the mainstream radio, spent their time forcing their slogans and uniformed prejudices on me. It was as if giving me a space to explain myself might deal a death-blow to their tightly-held conceptions.

Ben Dror Yemini of the popular *Ma'ariv* newspaper called us a "satanic cult." Another suggested that a prominent contributor to the Free Gaza movement was a Palestinian-American who had been questioned by the FBI, as if that had to do with anything (the innuendo being we were supported, perhaps even manipulated or worse, by "terrorists").

Others were more explicit: Wasn't it true that we were giving Hamas a PR victory? Why was I siding with Palestinian fishermen-gun smugglers against my own country, which sought only to protect its citizens? Some simply yelled at me, like an interviewer on Arutz 99. And when all else failed, my interlocutors could always fall back on good old cynicism: "Peace is impossible. Jews and Arabs are different species. You can't trust them." Or bald assertions: They just want to destroy us. Then there's the paternalism: Well, I guess it's good to have a few idealists like you around…

Nowhere in the many interviews was there a genuine curiosity about what I was doing or what life was like in Gaza. No one was interested in a different perspective, especially if it challenged his cherished slogans. No one was going beyond the old, tired slogans. Plenty of reference, though, to terrorism, Qassam missiles, and Palestinian snubbing our valiant efforts to make peace and none whatsoever to occupation, house demolitions, siege, land expropriation, or settlement expansion, not to mention the killing, imprisonment, and impoverishment of their civilian population. As if we had nothing to do with the conflict, as if we were just living our normal, innocent lives and bad people decided to throw Qassam rockets at us. Above all, there is no sense of our responsibility or any willingness to accept responsibility for the ongoing violence and conflict. Instead just a thoughtless, automatic appeal to an image of Gaza and "Arabs" (we don't generally use the term "Palestinians") that is diametrically opposed to what I've seen and experienced, a slavish repeating of mindless (and wrong) slogans that serve only to eliminate any possibility of truly grasping the situation. In short, a fantasy Gaza as perceived from within a bubble carefully constructed so as to deflect any uncomfortable reality.

The greatest insight this trip has given me is understanding why Israelis don't get it: a media composed of people who should know better but who possess little critical ability and feel more comfortable inside a box created by self-serving politicians than in trying to do something far more creative: understanding what in the hell is going on here. Still, I formulated clearly my messages to my fellow Israelis and that constitutes the main content of my interviews and talks:

(1) Despite what our political leaders say, there is a political solution to the conflict and there are partners for peace. If anything, we of the peace movement must not allow the powers that be to mystify the conflict, to present it as a "clash of civilizations." The Israeli-Palestinian conflict is political and as such it has a political solution.

(2) The Palestinians are not our enemies. In fact, I urge my fellow Israeli Jews to disassociate from the dead-end politics of our failed political leaders by declaring, in concert with Israeli and Palestinian peacemakers: We refuse to be enemies.

(3) As the infinitely stronger party in the conflict and the only occupying power, we Israelis must accept responsibility for our failed and oppressive policies. Only we can end the conflict.

Let me end by expressing my appreciation to the organizers of this initiative: Paul Larudee and Greta Berlin from the US, Hilary Smith and Bella from the UK, Vangelis Pissias, a Greek member of the team who provided crucial material and political input, Dr. Mona El Farra and Dr Eyad Sarraj of the International Campaign to End the Siege of Gaza, Jamal al-Khoudary, an independent member of the PLC from Gaza and head of the Popular Committee Against the Siege, and others, including the wonderful group of participants on the boats and the great communication team that stayed ashore.

Special appreciation goes to ICAHD's own Angela Godfrey-Goldstein who played a crucial role in Cyprus and Jerusalem in getting the word out. Not to forget our hosts in Gaza (whose names are on the Free Gaza Web site) and the tens of thousands of Gazans who welcomed us and shared their lives with us. May our peoples finally find the peace and justice they deserve in our common land.

Jeff Halper is the Director of the Israeli Committee Against House Demolitions (ICAHD).

Chapter 10:

Gone but not Forever

⌘   ⌘   ⌘

Dr. Bill:
August 27-28 2008

This morning, I along with Takis Politis, a university professor of information tech-nology at the University of Tsessalia in Volos, Greece, and Tasos Kourakis, a Greek MP and also a podiatrist and professor of genetics at University of Aristoteles in Salonica, head out separately from the others on our FG delegation. Dr. Khamis El-Essi takes us to the Islamic University in Gaza City. Its campus is right next to the more secular University of Al Azhar. Al Azhar has more affiliations with Fateh, while the Islamic University tends to favor Hamas. I have visited Al Azhar University before. It has a pharmacy and medical school. So does the Islamic University.

The campus at Islamic University. Some of these buildings were subsequently destroyed by the Israeli Air Force in January 2009

Based on their respective affiliations, there was armed conflict between students of these universities in the summer of 2007. There is still some evidence of damage and graffiti on the buildings here at the Islamic University, stemming from the June 2007 internecine warfare, but most of it has now been repaired. The campus is otherwise quite attractive, with modern buildings alongside mosques with tall minarets.

We are taken to the office of Professor Kamel Sha'ek, the president of Islamic University. Professor Sha'ek did his undergraduate work at Cairo University in Egypt. He then received postgraduate degrees in construction management at Colorado State University and also in the UK and Spain.

Meeting with Kamel Sha-ek, the President of Islamic University.

Before 1967, there were no universities in the West Bank and Gaza Strip. At that time, students had easy access to universities in Jordan, Egypt, and the outside world. After the Israeli occupation in 1967, coming and going from Gaza became more difficult. Universities in the West Bank were successfully established in Hebron, Bethlehem, Birzeit, and later in Abu Dis, east of Jerusalem.

In Gaza, the Islamic University was the first university to be established in 1978, nine years after the occupation began. Al Azhar University was then established in 1992. According to Professor Sha'ek, Islamic University's enrollment is currently 60 percent female and 40 percent male. They have hosted exchange students from other countries in the past, but this has become more difficult with the siege.

Information Technology lecture hall at Islamic U which has state-of-the-art computer terminals at each desk.

We are taken to an information technology lecture hall, which has state-of-the-art computer terminals at each desk. Later, we visit the molecular genetics lab and then the anatomy lab, with modern three dimensional anatomy models, which can be viewed in cross sections. Computerized virtual anatomy lesions are viewed on computer terminals instead of cadaver dissections. We meet briefly with about twenty-one female second-year medical students who are all dressed conservatively and wearing the hijab.

We depart the Islamic University and Dr. Khamis drives us in his small economy car, which has been converted to burn propane instead of petroleum. Propane is currently in greater supply and therefore less expensive because of the siege. There are also "falafel mobiles" driving around Gaza, which burn vegetable oil and other biodiesel products. The siege has made the local population very creative and innovative.

We arrive at *Al Wafa'* Rehabilitation Hospital on the northeastern margins of the Gaza Strip, about a half kilometer from the barrier with Israel. We head upstairs to the main nurses station. On the wall there are pictures of two male nurses who are now martyrs. But these martyrs were not involved in any sort of armed conflict. They were simply trying to do their job as nurses.

On February 7, 2003, the area where Wafa' Hospital is located was under an incursion by IOF. These two nurses were moving patients upstairs on the men's coma ward. They both were shot and killed by a single bullet fired through the window by an Israeli sniper, who was perched on the top of the adjacent building immediately to the east of Al Wafa' Hospital. You can still see where the lone bullet penetrated through the glass here on the coma ward. The IOF claimed that they did not know this was a hospital, yet there is clearly a white flag with a red crescent posted on the northeast corner of the hospital, and "Al Wafa' Rehabilitation Hospital" clearly written on the eastern side of the building in Arabic and English (but not Hebrew). These are easily seen from the sniper's position. This episode was reported widely throughout Gaza, but it never really made the news in the USA. It should have. Maybe it's because it is very hard to explain how shooting nurses doing their job on a coma ward represents "self defense."

Maybe it is better not to report the story at all than to confuse the American public with a true story that goes against prevailing dogma that our main stream media is trying to instill. Many who control the mainstream media in the USA feel it is better that their countrymen not to know about such ugly situations. They want to portray the more powerful Israeli bullies as the main victims in this conflict.

While the American public continues to be treated like mushrooms about the realities in Gaza, we tour wards full of people with shattered lives who have been forgotten by the outside world, but not by Al Wafa' Hospital: A school teacher who was shot in the head and survived in a persistent vegetative state; a man shot through the spinal cord and now permanently paralyzed. We also see genetic cases that produce orthopedic disabilities, like three girls from the same family who need specialized attention in order to walk. Because of the isolation in Gaza combined with traditional clanship, there are frequent marriages between distant cousins, and thus relatively high genetic diseases here.

The sun sets on the final night before the FG boats are ready to set sail again back to Cyprus. Our hosts in the Popular Committee to End the Siege have a big gathering in the Legislative Council building to send us off. The sun rises. My, how the five days here in Gaza have gone by so quickly!

I am not ready to leave yet. I can't! This whole boat project took much longer than expected to get here and consequently has left us all with much less time in Gaza than we had initially anticipated. I have friends here from previous visits that I haven't been able to see yet. We are told that the border with Rafah, which has only been open for six days so far during 2008, will now be open for two more days this last weekend in August. Internationals will be allowed to exit, along with limited numbers of the tens of thousands of desperate Palestinians who will crowd both sides of the border with Egypt, trying to get out, and trying to get back in.

Besides medical patients trying to seek specialty care abroad, there are many more local Gazans with time-sensitive reasons for wanting to travel outside like college students, who have already been studying abroad, have made it home, and become stuck here. Now they want to resume their studies at universities abroad before their credentials run out. Unfortunately, endless crisis and endless uncertainty about virtually everything is now a way of life in Gaza.

Ten of the original international passengers who arrived five days ago on the boats have decided to stay. Four of us plan to leave through Rafah this weekend, and six others plan to stay on for longer periods of time and do solidarity work here.

Before departure, we have a final gathering on the veranda at Al Deira Hotel. Ismail Haniyeh and other dignitaries from the local government are with us here for a big send-off. Speeches are made in English and Arabic, and the cameras roll with footage to be seen all over the world, except in America. We each are awarded Palestinian citizenship, including a brand new Palestinian Authority VIP passport! I get to meet Dr. Mahmoud Az-Zahar, who was trained as a general surgeon, but is also a cofounder of Hamas. Two of his sons have been assassinated by Israel in targeted raids. His first son was killed during an attempt on Az-Zahar's own life in September, 2003. An Israeli F-16 dropped a large bomb on his house in the Rimal neighborhood of Gaza City, and while he was only slightly wounded, his son Khaled and a personal bodyguard were killed. Twenty others were wounded, including his daughter Rima. His house was destroyed, and ten other houses nearby were damaged, as well as the nearby Al-Rahman mosque. Over two thousand mourners attended the funeral for those killed. His second son was killed in a targeted assassination in January of this year.

I give Dr. Az-Zahar a baseball hat with a Native American design and a logo that says, Native Pride. Chief Sitting Bull was also a freedom fighter because he would not stay on the reservation. He was considered a "savage" by the calvary. When

Custer tried to rein him in at Little Bighorn, he had the gall to fight back. Many Americans consider Sitting Bull a hero.

Commemorative poster for Free Gaza Movement at El Deira Hotel

Leaving with the Free Gaza Boats are local Palestinians from Gaza who have been unable to get out by other means. These include several college students, a family, a woman separated from her husband, and a boy with a high-level amputation suffered from an Israeli mortar shell, seeking specialty care abroad.

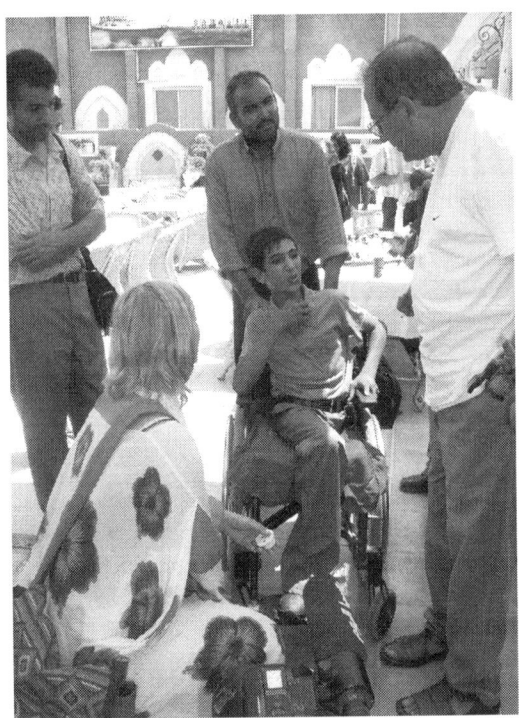

Sa'ed Mosleh, his father Khaled, with Dr. Eyad Sarraj and Lauren Booth

It is getting time for the boats to leave. So we head down to the marina by bus. It takes time to prepare the boats for casting off. There is both happiness and melancholy as Palestinian passengers say good-bye to their families on shore, not knowing if or when they will be able to return to Gaza.

Palestinian Family aboard Dimitris K (Free Gaza) leaving Gaza Port

Maria Del Mar aboard Dimitris K (Free Gaza) pulling out of Gaza Port

It is getting later in the day. The boats' departure is behind schedule, and there is growing anxiety that there is limited daylight. It would be best if the boats were able to make it out into international waters before the sun sets, in case they have any run-ins with the Israeli Navy. Finally, the boats pull out from the marina at 3:30 P.M. With top speeds at just over six nautical miles, this leaves just enough time to get out beyond the twenty-mile limit before the nightfall.

Those of us from the Free Gaza movement who have decided to stay head back to the veranda at the Al Deira Hotel where we can see the two boats being escorted out to sea by Gaza fishing vessels. A half hour later, the fishing vessels turn around toward shore, and we can see four Israeli warships closing in from the north and south around the FG boats. At sunset, we are relieved to receive word that our vessels have made it out into international waters without any direct interference from the Israeli Navy, only intimidation, which we can live with.

**Liberty and Free Gaza escorted out by Gaza Fishermen;
Israeli warship approaching on right horizon**

**Sa'ed entertained by Nikos Bollos and freshly
caught tuna, on the way to Cyprus**

From Bella: Newsflash! Boats Almost Back!

Friday, 29 Aug 2008

The *Free Gaza* and the *Liberty* are arriving back at Cyprus any minute now, safe from their return journey that began yesterday. They are carrying seven Palestinian passengers who (according to the requirements of the Cyprus authorities) have valid visas or second passports, yet physically could not leave Gaza because of the siege. Our Israeli passenger Jeff however was the first to head home, through the

Erez checkpoint before the boats left, and he has since been charged with illegally entering Gaza, and is under house arrest for a few months I think (much better outcome than the twenty-year treason charge originally threatened).

I'm still here with nine others (may have to leave tomorrow or may be able to stay another week). We had an action today at Erez border accompanying a female patient named Majdeya to the crossing in face of threatened fire if we proceeded. She's been trying for seven months to get to her scheduled operation in an East Jerusalem hospital to have a spinal tumour removed. Didn't get her in, but did get a "promise" of "by Sunday when her current operation is due" and didn't get shot either which was nice. (I do wish people wouldn't sing things like "We shall overcome" during what might be our final moments though, especially out of tune...)

Here's an article from the Israeli press, interesting particularly because of the official comments...there really is potential to sail again in a few weeks, if ONLY we can get some big donors to cover our debts so we don't have to sell the boats to do it that way.

Israel allowed two boats carrying international activists and seven Palestinians to leave Gaza on Thursday and sail without interruption back to Cyprus.

The boats had been allowed to dock in Gaza harbor last Saturday after the government decided not to clash with the 45 human rights activists aboard and play into what officials said was a clear provocation intended to damage Israel's public image.

The Free Gaza movement said that among the Palestinians who left Gaza were five children, including 10-year-old Saed Mosleh from Beit Hanoun, who the group said had lost one of his legs to an Israeli tank shell. He left Gaza with his father to seek medical treatment abroad. Also on board was the Darwish family, who will be reunited with its relatives in Cyprus.

"I can't believe we're finally able to leave for medical treatment," said Khaled Mosleh, Saed's father. "This is a miracle of God."

Out of the 45 activists who arrived on Saturday, nine will remain in Gaza to do long-term monitoring, the movement said.

The Free Gaza movement plans to return to Gaza with another delegation in the near future and to ask the United Nations, the Arab League and other international organizations to organize similar sea-based operations.

Israeli defense officials said Thursday that there was no set policy on how

Israel would react in the event that another ship coming from international waters tries to enter Gaza. Officials said that as of now, Israel knows of no plans for other boats to set sail for Gaza, and that if other boats did try to enter, Israel would decide how to handle the situation on a case-by-case basis.

"Each case will be examined individually," one official said.

In Thursday's case, the official said Israel had been aware of who was on board the ships - including the identity of the Palestinians - and had not interfered since none of the passengers posed a security risk.

"None of the passengers was dangerous to Israel, and they were not coming into

Israel, so there was no reason to stop them," the official said. "If a boat, however, tried to take wanted Hamas terrorists out of Gaza, that would be a different story."

Greta Berlin Arriving in Cyprus:

We arrived safely last night. The trip home was much less eventful than the trip to Gaza and much less emotional. On board my boat, the *Free Gaza*, was a family of Palestinians who had not been let out of the concentration camp called Gaza for five years. The mother had given birth to her youngest son four years ago, and the family, living in Cyprus, had not seen him. The joy on the faces of Hana's family was worth waiting the extra time to leave. We had to make sure that the Cypriot authorities would allow them in.

On board the *Liberty* was a ten-year-old boy whose leg had been shot off by the Israeli military. He was from Khan Younis. The story (and I haven't been able to verify it yet) is that he was standing with his friend as an Israeli tank invaded his town. A sniper shot him through one leg, and when he stood to run, the sniper shot him through the other one, causing huge damage to the leg. It was amputated at the hip. Again, we had to wait for Cypriot authorities to give permission for him to transit to another country.

On the first page of the *Cyprus Mail* is a photo of the boy with Osama, one of our organizers. Even though we came in at 9:00 P.M., the media was all over the quay waiting for us. Although we didn't get seasick this time, many of us, because we are so exhausted, are feeling the land effects today, swaying as we try to walk down the streets.

It has been a week of overriding joy, sadness at the condition of so many sick and wounded Palestinians, hope for the future, and disbelief that we not only arrived safely but left safely. As we pulled out of Gaza yesterday, seven Israeli naval vessels surrounded the Palestinian fishermen who joyfully escorted us six miles out. The last view we had of Gaza was of the seven gunboats surrounding the fishermen. We've heard from our Israeli sources that they arrested four of them.

As usual, the Palestinians will face the wrath of the Israeli military because they had egg on their faces and will take it out on the weakest.

Chapter 11:

Showdown at Erez Crossing

⌘ ⌘ ⌘

From Donna Wallach

August 29-31, 2008

I along with others from the Free Gaza movement decided not to return with the SS Free Gaza and SS Liberty to Cyprus. Instead we chose to remain in the Gaza Strip for a while to continue the work of breaking the siege.

Throughout the time I am staying here I will participate with the others in various actions in Rafah, Gaza City, and other areas throughout the Gaza Strip, including going out in fishing boats to challenge the Israeli Navy who prevent the Palestinian fishermen from fishing more than six miles out. In addition, we are reorganizing ISM Rafah, to do Palestinian-led solidarity work here.

This past Friday, Majdeya Abu Shawesh, a sixty-four-year-old Palestinian woman from Al Nuseirat Refugee Camp, Gaza Strip, arrived to the Erez crossing accompanied by all of the remaining members of the Free Gaza movement, as well as other sick patients needing specialty health care abroad like a girl with severe burns and a boy with a deviated nasal septum needing plastic and reconstructive surgery. Majdeya has been suffering for seven months with a tumor on her spine. Without the necessary surgery granted her by St. Joseph Hospital in Jerusalem, she will continue to become progressively more paralyzed and will live in constant pain.

We FG members walked in front of her as a protection for her to not be shot by the Israeli soldiers guarding their border. She was in a wheelchair that was pushed by Vittorio, the Italian member of our group. Slowly, we approached the Israeli side, holding our arms in the air and many of us clutching our passports. A Palestinian man was the liaison between Dr. Mona El-Farra, the main organizer of this action to take this sixty-four-year-old woman to cross the Erez checkpoint and the Israeli "authorities."

The Palestinian man kept on telling us that we needed to stop because the Israelis told him that they were going to shoot us. We decided it was more important to challenge this crime against humanity: Israel not permitting this woman to receive the urgent medical treatment she needed. So we continued to walk toward the Israeli gate with our arms up in the air.

Erez from Gaza side, crossing no-man's-land to the border

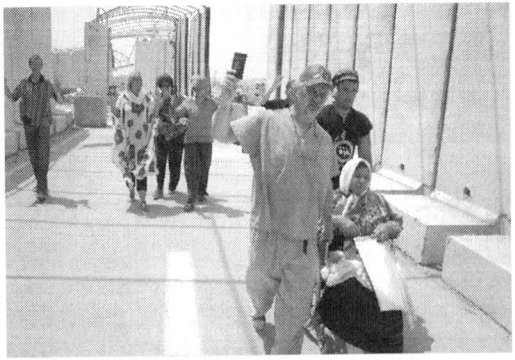

Entering the tunnel toward the Iron Gate

We finally reached the Israeli gate without a shot being fired, not a bullet nor a tear gas canister nor a sound bomb. In the end, the Israelis heartlessly told the woman she had to go back home, but could return an eighth time.

On Sunday the thirty-first of August, we from FG arrived at about 9:00 A.M. from Rafah, the southernmost area in Gaza Strip, to Erez crossing, which is the northern most area in Gaza Strip. We came to continue standing in solidarity with this woman from Al Nuseirat refugee camp in central Gaza. We arrived late, and she and Dr. Mona El-Farra had already left for the border.

We gathered inside the crude fenced-in area where all Palestinians and others wait for permission to cross the dirt pathway across the widened no man's land to arrive at the Israeli gate. We waited hours. Then we heard that the woman was turned back again, with the ridiculous and contradictory excuse that a member of her family must accompany her into Israel and on to the hospital in Jerusalem.

This woman came back but was not defeated in her determination to cross the border. She had become accustomed to this kind of treatment by the Israeli Authorities. Almost all the members of her family have been wrongfully blacklisted, meaning that they cannot enter the apartheid state of Israel. Finally, the woman's seventy-five year-old husband was granted permission to enter Israel with her.

After he arrived at Erez, and the paper work for him was filled out, they went off to the Israeli side. We continued to wait in the heat to hear that she had crossed and was inside the Israeli ambulance that would take her to the Jerusalem hospital and to her surgery, which was supposed to have started on this Sunday, and now would be delayed a bit longer.

Dr. Mona El-Farra told us that she continued to tell the Israeli authorities that members of the Free Gaza movement were waiting at Erez to ensure that she would enter this time. She told them that we were willing to die. We would walk again to the border even if the soldiers would shoot and kill us. We would do whatever it takes so that the Israelis would allow her to enter, which they finally did. The eighth time was the charm for this very brave and courageous woman, sitting in a wheelchair, who defied the Israelis with all of their gunpowder.

From Dr. Mona El Farra':

Hello all:

I am alive and active, and I will never give up.

I am fine, but the whole situation in Gaza is so frustrating and not easy to handle day after day. It is not easy living under such circumstances, while the borders are closed, and one and a half million of us live under collective punishment.

The success of the Free Gaza movement gave us some hope for the future; it was a small act but great and courageous, too. A few determined, strong activists did the miracle: in an unprecedented voyage, the first boats to arrive from international waters to Gaza shores in forty-one years. A lot of work can be done to make change, to ring the bell, to wake up the deaf, silent, and blind international community and their governments. What is happening in Gaza under the siege and the occupation is more than a human-rights violation—it is a war crime.

I was with the Free Gaza movement and their reconstituted Gaza International Solidarity Movement at Erez crossing last Sunday (the northern border between Gaza and Israel). We were there to create pressure for Israel to let one of the many patients who are stranded in Gaza, out for treatment. We succeeded in the end, as this patient was permitted transfer to St. Joseph's Hospital two days after our action, after seven hard months of bureaucratic delay. She needed subspecialty treatment of her spinal cord tumor, which was slowly making her more paralyzed. The hard question is: Why should it take all these extravagant efforts to let one patient in great need for critical surgery and specialty care out of Gaza?

It is a fundamental, basic need; it is the right of each individual to get health care! Access to health care is a fundamental, basic need. BUT IN OCCUPIED PALESTINE THE STORY IS DIFFERENT.

Two hundred thirty-eight patients died last year while waiting to be issued permits to leave Gaza for treatment via the borders. Hundreds are waiting, including many children. We are not talking about politics: about Hamas or Fateh, or who is or is not controlling Gaza. We are talking about a basic humanitarian and human rights issue.

From Gaza with love

Dr. Mona El Farra'

Chapter 12:

Exiting Gaza: Takes One and Two

⌘ ⌘ ⌘

Dr. Bill:
Friday, August 29, 2008

We go to the Erez crossing again, where we walked in solidarity with our Palestinian brothers and sisters singing "We Shall Overcome," and "Give Peace a Chance." Using my best Reagan imitation, I shouted, "MR. OLMERT, TEAR DOWN THIS WALL! We could hear frantic shouting in Hebrew from behind the concrete guard towers but could see no one. We made it right up to the Iron Gate. This gate was sealed shut, of course.

But this time, the cameras were rolling—**Al Jazeira, Ramattan,** and **Press TV** were present. And for a moment, the whole world was witnessing Israel denying medical care to a poor, defenseless woman and others. If there were only Palestinians among us, and whether or not cameras were rolling, I am sure that the Israeli soldiers would have shot and that the world would have barely noticed. That is sad commentary but true, unfortunately.

A few Palestinians on the other side of the gate shook hands with us through the iron pickets. Now we were blocking their return to Gaza. There is no way we could physically move this woman any farther, and then the Israeli guards threatened to close the border and deny our new friends on the other side of the gate their way back home. So we finally retreated with their pledge that she might get across in a couple of days.

Dr. Mona takes us a couple kilometers southeast to the border town of Beit Hanoun. I have some unfinished business I want to tend to. I want to visit the Al Athamna family, nineteen who were massacred by Israeli shelling while they slept in their large family apartment on the early morning of November 8, 2006. Several neighbors also died that morning, and more than forty-five were wounded. Archbishop Desmond Tutu was sent by the UN to investigate this massacre, but he was held up by Israel. He was unable to enter Gaza until seventeen months afterward.

**29 August 2008 Free Gaza Movement visits
the Al Athamna family, 21 months after
they were massacred.**

At that time during November 2006, I was volunteering with the Palestine Medical Relief Society. I entered Gaza and visited Beit Hanoun a week after the Israeli siege surrounded and isolated this town. The morning after the tanks and military bulldozers pulled out, the artillery massacre of the El Athamna family immediately followed. When I visited with members of this extended family a week later, they were still in the early stages of their collective grief.

The Israeli missile attack hit the stairwell first, impeding evacuation.

I have thought about this family often in the ensuing months. How could I forget them? I just couldn't leave their collective tragedy behind me because it is the worst I had ever seen. I have sent them money, which seemed like an awkward, empty gesture at the time, given the enormity of their loss. But it was all I could do. I couldn't change the indifference of our stand-in US ambassador to the United Nations, John Bolton, when he vetoed a UN resolution condemning this act. But as a US citizen, I feel somehow responsible.

Today, their large cinderblock apartment looks much the same as it did during that horrific November day back in 2006, except the stairwell, which had been blown wide open by the first artillery shells that struck the apartment that day. It has again been sealed. Family members feel Israel attacked the stairwell first to impede exit from the building. Survivors, who still needed to use that stairwell, no longer risk accidentally tripping and falling to their death. This was certainly possible the last time when I climbed through the ruins of this apartment. The gaping holes made by artillery rounds in the wall in front of their building have been repaired, as have the huge holes in the walls and ceilings of the apartment units themselves.

Majdi with the memorial poster of his family.
The roses represent the women who were killed

Surviving Al Athamna family members a week after the attack

I ask for Majdi El Athamna, who was my previous contact. He had told me back then that he was, "Only alive by the will of God." He lost his son and three brothers that day, and his wife and other son were in critical condition at the hospital. Majdi is not available right now; maybe he is not here, or maybe he just can't deal with it. We do not ask further. So Majdi's mother greets us all and invites us into the ground-floor foyer adorned with all the memorial posters honoring the lost family members.

16 of 19 members of Al-Athamna family massacred in their own apartment, November 8, 2006 buried here in the sand

No, their grief has not really eased with time. This blow has been much too devastating. Our visit today seems like we are pulling off a scab. Majdi's mother is again moved to tears, as she recounts losing three sons and five grandchildren in one ten-minute attack. She tells us the story in great detail, as well as the story of those permanently wounded. There are still, the seriously injured survivors, some of who are around us today. One child, who looks about fifteen years of age, suffered a serious head injury. The entire right side of his skull is caved inward. He moves with a coarse jerky gait, and his eye wiggles back and forth constantly. His intellect is damaged, for sure, and his speech is impaired. Two years ago, he was a normal child. Family members plead with us to get him out of Gaza, so he can see a neurosurgeon who can fix all this.

I know damn well that his severe disabilities will not respond to neurosurgery or much else at this point. He will be damaged for the rest of his life as a result of the Israeli artillery attack on his family. Another child is hopping around the room on one leg because the other one was amputated below the knee—a direct result of the carnage that day. His family claims that he still does not have an artificial leg.

Perhaps something meaningful could be done for this child. The level of sorrow in this family, nearly two years after the fact, is overwhelming.

I offer the grandmother a Native American hat decorated with a rose—another meaningless gesture given the enormous cruelty of it all, but it is all I have at the moment. It is clear that the survivors of this extended family are living in grinding poverty; their collective sorrow has been largely forgotten by the world. We say good-bye to the Al Athamna family and head back to Gaza City for a rest. Tomorrow, four of the ten of us Free Gaza movement passengers that remain will try exiting through Rafah to Egypt.

Bella: Subject: No. Twenty: Casablanca on the Gaza Sea[3]

The outdoor restaurant overlooking the sea that belongs to the Al Deira Hotel has been nicknamed Casablanca-without-the-alcohol by Dr Bill. Here, we internationals and Palestinians alike sit, looking out over the moonlit water, sharing a naguilla pipe and discussing rumors about the Rafah border. Will it open? If so, when? . . . and, for whom?

People tell each other about what documents they have obtained, what connections they have made, which consulate may be arranging a visa for them. They show pictures of the husbands, wives, children, and lovers who are waiting in other lands. They talk about their "coordination" toward getting out.

Until now, this border with Egypt, the only way Palestinians with no other passport may come or go from Gaza, has opened six days this year. But we hear it will open again for two days before Ramadan begins this Saturday and Sunday. No, Tuesday until Thursday. Definitely Saturday but Sunday is unsure. Saturday, but only for the sick traveling for treatment. No, Saturday for foreign passport holders, and Sunday for the sick. Maybe also Monday, the first day of Ramadan. No, not Monday… only if your name is on the published list. No, you can try even if your name is not published.

We internationals catch the underlying anxiety, move as the locals do from table to table, to sit briefly. What did you hear? Who can give permissions? Write your name on this list. Dr. Eyad will make for us the contact. Our new Palestinian passports will make things better for us. No, they will make things worse for us.

---

3   Sharyn Lock, **Gaza Beneath the Bombs** (London, :Pluto Press, 2010), p, 205

Over the last days, I call the Australian consulate who offers no help or information other than to note that Israel says those who arrive by the boat must leave by the boat. What does Israel's opinion have to do with the Egyptian border, I wonder? The British consulate however comes to meet us and says our best chance is to leave on the Saturday—after this it may be impossible, even for us. I forlornly let go of my wished-for extra week. We will leave at 7:00 A.M., with a police escort. This will get us past many gates.

This last is obviously not my favorite idea, but I have a plan to bring four Palestinians with me, and so I'm taking any special treatment I can on behalf of them.

N and K are two lovely sisters, who have tried four times over nine months to leave to take up their study visas in Spain and have not even been let out through the Palestinian side. Now the visas are running out, and Spain has told them to go to Cairo to renew them. (Spot the obvious problem with that?) "Do you have arrangements waiting from the Egypt side?" I ask them, wondering if they have a place to stay if the border crossing occurs late. "If we cross, we have a whole LIFE waiting for us!" replies N. J has no arrangements but wants to go to study. W came from Paris for a visit back home to Gaza one and a half years ago has been unable to get back out. He has an activist French wife (married against all her principles as the only possible route to a shared country) with whom he has been trying to reunite. She has been waiting for him in Paris these past few years.

We bid them good-bye on Friday night, but Vik and I sit up late in Casablanca with Dr Dolf, who serenades us on oud with traditional songs until early morning. I smoke naguilla in the hope of easing some of my sadness at leaving. My favourite song contains lyrics along the lines of "don't ask me what is my address, I have no home in this world. I am everyone, in every place, and no place is mine."

We meet our Palestinian friends again, virtually at the same table, again in the early morning, so we can sit together and wait for the call to go. They arrive at 7:00 A.M., and we are not told to come until 2:00 P.M. Most Palestinians have been queuing at the border since 7:00 A.M., so we are lucky to be able to sit here by the sea, telling stories of romance and visas. W describes meeting his fiancée during a Paris demonstration. J calls; he's gone directly to Rafah and thinks he will try independently of us.

Dr. Bill's Account:

Saturday, August 30, 2008

Following the departure of the FG boats, three of us are staying at Dr. Eyad Sarraj's apartment in Gaza City. Bella is staying with Dr. Mona Farra', and the other six activists are in the process of moving to Rafah and being absorbed into the community; there, they will breathe new air into a reconstituted International Solidarity Movement in Gaza.

Since 2003, after the killing of Westerners like Rachel Corrie, James Miller, and Tom Hurndall, the Israeli occupation authorities made it virtually impossible for ISM activists to cross from Israel into the Gaza Strip. ISM has continued to be active in the West Bank, where it is more difficult for the Israeli occupation authorities to control their entrance and exit. In Gaza, there has been only one entrance for internationals: the Erez checkpoint. Consequently, it has been easier for ISM to be blocked from Gaza. But the sea route now opens new possibilities.

Bella, Lauren Booth, and I plan to exit Gaza today through Rafah. Bella (Sharyn Lock) needs to get back to the UK, where she is scheduled to begin midwifery school in a couple of weeks. Lauren Booth plans to get reunited with her husband and two daughters, who have been waiting for her in France. I need to get back to work as a family and ER physician in a small town on the lee side of the Cascade Mountains back in central Washington State. My first office day is supposed to be in about a week.

We are all at the home of Dr. Eyad Sarraj, waiting for word that the border is open for us. We play American and British music, and copy a few CDs for Dr. Mona. Finally we hear that a police convoy will take us to Rafah.

Our convoy leaves Gaza City on some sort of James Bond, white-knuckle, high-speed chase down the Salah Al-Din highway past pedestrians and donkey carts. We are not all flattered by the VIP treatment—some of us are upset by it. I am glad for all of us that our drivers are skilled, and no one gets hit or injured. It seems to be more dangerous than necessary though.

We clear the Palestinian gate, and I hand my remaining shekels through the fence to a Palestinian boy on the Gaza side of Rafah. If things go as planned, I will be spending Egyptian lira from now on. We pass through the departure terminal on the Palestinian side that was built by the Israelis and receive departure stamps in our passports.

We have completed the hurry up part of today's journey. Now it is time for the wait part. We load our luggage on a bus full of Palestinians who are also trying to get out. There is a queue of buses all jam-packed with Palestinians and maybe a few Egyptians. Now nothing moves for hours, as we sit and stand in the heat on these overcrowded buses. We are told that we are waiting for the Egyptian authorities to clear buses full of Palestinians who are trying to enter Gaza.

Since this is only the seventh day that the Rafah border has been open all year, there are too many people trying to cross all at once. The Egyptian clerks who process the people trying to cross are overwhelmed. It seems that decisions about who gets through and who gets sent back are quite arbitrary. After two and a half hours in the intense heat, we all get off of the bus in the middle of no man's land, with walls and barriers all around us. We sit in the grass and wait an hour more. Finally we get back on the bus, which creeps along at a snail's pace. An hour later, we finally clear the Egyptian gate at the yellow stone wall. We see Egyptian police in full riot gear, poised to close the border for the night behind us. They are there to quell any un-rest that might break out when the Palestinians who have been waiting all day are turned back.

We enter the arrival terminal, which is filled with thousands of Palestinians trying to get through this final hurdle and be accepted into Egypt, now only a few meters away. ("Give us your tired, your poor, your huddled masses, yearning to be free.") The four of us Westerners are escorted to a VIP waiting room where we wait an ad-ditional hour. Finally, we are told, "We are ready for you." We follow an Egyptian of-ficial who is holding our passports toward the Palestinian side. We ask why we are being sent back to Gaza and are told that, "You cannot pass because you entered Gaza illegally by the sea." Illegally? I see my friend Marwan from Gaza City who is trying to exit. He says he will make some phone calls on our behalf, but it is better if we are not seen together right now as it might hinder his chances to get out.

We sit on our suitcases to discuss our options. We could refuse to leave and get arrested by Egypt. Maybe then we might get deported, which might be okay since we are just trying to get home anyway. The only problem with this plan is that we might be denied entry if we ever wanted to enter Egypt again in the future.

Next we are told that we are holding up Palestinians who want to pass, and that the whole border will be closed until we leave. This is funny and certainly not nec-essary. We are not threatening anyone or anything. It is the same line the Israeli border guards gave us yesterday at Erez. Finally, Tawfiq Jabber, the Palestinian chief of police from Gaza is sent over to cajole us back over to the Gaza side. He explains how he has been separated for years from his wife, who lives in Lebanon, for similar reasons. This all seems absurd. We are all unarmed international human rights activists, and clearly pose no danger to Egypt. One might be able to understand that Israel would block us but Egypt? This is understandable only if you consider who wields the real power here: Israel and the USA. Israel is the biggest recipient of US foreign aid in the world, receiving an average of over $3 billion a year in military aid alone. Israel has received about 20 percent of US foreign aid to the whole world these last forty years, and that aid has been unconditional, given the "special relationship" between the USA and Israel.

Guess who the second biggest recipient of US foreign aid is? Egypt. Why? … For making peace with Israel, as part of the Camp David Peace Accord in 1978. But this aid is conditional. It gives Israel and the USA the strings to control the puppets within Hosni Mubarak's regime. The US has provided around $2 billion a year to the Mubarak regime in Egypt for the past thirty years. About $1.3 billion in military aid that keeps the regime in power. That way, it can force Mubarak to do the bidding for the US and Israel. Egypt is a poor country. I am sure that $3 billion a year from the US government is a lot more important to them than we are. So if Israel and its USA proxies want to punish us for entering Gaza by boat without Israel's permission, so be it! We are now political footballs, to be kicked back and forth as part of a greater geo-political strategy that is beyond us; each country carefully guarding its goalposts at Erez and at Rafah. It is annoying, but it is also a manifestation of a much deeper problem.

Lauren Booth is highly organized. She has speed dial and is on the phone immediately with contacts at the British Consulate, who are very polite and sound helpful and hopeful. "The British are more polite that way than the Americans," she explains. "The Americans are blunt and tell it to you rudely to your face." Because she is a resident there, and they are already helping Lauren, Bella is also in touch with the British Consulate. I am stuck. I have no phone numbers for the US embassies in Tel Aviv or Cairo. Besides, it is the Labor Day weekend in the US, so their offices are all probably closed until Tuesday. Here, Ramadan will be starting on Monday, which complicates matters even further. Besides, I don't have much confidence right now that my American embassy will help me out much anyway.

Yesterday at Erez, Donna Wallach had the number for the US embassy in Tel Aviv. I dialed the number to request assistance to cross into Israel with our Palestinian patients. I was referred to three phone numbers at the US consulate in East Jerusalem. Two of the numbers at the consulate had tape-recorded messages, and the third was answered by a hostile-sounding woman who gave me the endless runaround, saying in essence, "There is nothing we can do." Maybe the embassy in Cairo will be more helpful. But I don't see myself starting that project until Tuesday, after the American Labor Day weekend is over.

The British consulate gets back to Lauren and advises us to return to Gaza City for the night and try again tomorrow morning. Now it is dark, and we are still here in Limbo between the fences. Now we are hanging out at the Palestinian border office. We request a ride back to the Palestinian gate, so we can get a taxi back to Gaza City. We must wait for evening prayer to be finished. After prayer, we must wait further for some unexplained reason. We grow hungry and one of the guards goes out to the Palestinian Rafah side and brings us back some Falafel sandwiches, which we appreciate, but we just want to get back to Gaza City and get some rest. As we wait, some of us, including me, grow more tired and more irritable.

This situation is a sad result of years of no diplomatic process because if there is no real diplomacy, a standoff ensues. With a heavy-handed and brutal military response from Israel, the counterresponse of oppressed Palestinians is to elect a hard line government with a more centralized governing style. The tragedy now is that foot soldiers, like those around us here, cannot even make the most rudimentary and mundane decisions, like driving us and our luggage a half kilometer back to the Palestinian gate. It has to go up the chain of command, and this is taking hours.

Finally, we decide to force the issue. We grab our bags, and start walking toward the Palestinian gate. The Palestinian border guards drive after us. There is shouting between us and tempers flare. Finally they drive us back to the gate and make arrangements to get us to Gaza City by taxi; as good hosts, they insist on covering the cost. We depart amid tensions, and get back to Gaza City at 9:30 P.M., totally exhausted and sweaty. We will try again tomorrow.

Sunday, August 31, 2008

We awake at 06:00, only to find out that Egypt and Gaza have fallen back to Standard Time, while Israel and the West Bank are still on Daylight Savings Time; so it's really only 05:00 here and 06:00 an hour's drive north in Jerusalem. This adds to the confusion in terms of "coordinating" our departure with outside intermediaries, as if we didn't have enough confusion already yesterday.

Ken O'Keefe joins us today in our attempt to exit Gaza. He needs to get back to his pregnant wife in London who is due in a month. We arrive at the border gate in Rafah at 09:00, Gaza Standard Time. We spend two hours on the Palestinian side of Rafah having coffee and playing with local Palestinian boys. Bella has brought tennis balls for them to play with. I try teaching them how to juggle and amuse them with my physical comedy shtick. There is laughter all around, and the stoic Hamas border guards look at us with puzzled faces. They do not seem to know what to make of it all.

After two hours, we clear the Palestinian Gate and the terminal. Our passports are stamped for exit a second time. Today, there will be no prolonged waiting on buses for us, even though that is the fate of Palestinians trying to cross. Instead, we are taken to the same waiting room as last night, where we will lounge around in more comfort until the Egyptian side decides whether or not to clear us. We see the same guards that we were in a shouting match with last night. There are apologies all around and forgiveness. From noon until the evening, Lauren is on the phone repeatedly with the British Consulate and her husband Craig in France. Both are working on our behalf. At 13:00, Dr. Mona El-Faraa' calls us to tell us that the elderly lady with the spinal cord tumor that we escorted to Erez crossing two days ago has finally made it across after seven months of efforts, and is now on her way to Jerusalem. We spend the day drafting a press release using Ken's computer, which we will release along with a press conference on Tuesday; here it is:

LIKE PALESTINIANS, HUMAN RIGHTS WORKERS DENIED EXIT THROUGH EREZ CHECKPOINT TO ISRAEL AND THROUGH RAFAH CROSSING TO EGYPT

FOR IMMEDIATE RELEASE

GAZA (2 Sept. 2008) - Four foreign nationals from the UK, USA, Ireland, and Australia, who helped peacefully challenge the siege of Gaza by traveling through international waters with the Free Gaza movement, have so far been refused exit to Israel via Erez crossing, or to Egypt via Rafah crossing.

For over two years Israel has severely restricted access to Gaza, blocking aid shipments and trade. As a consequence, Gaza's economy has collapsed, forcing most industries to close and dramatically increasing malnutrition rates among children. Eighty percent of families in Gaza are now completely dependent on United Nations food aid.

Travel outside of Gaza has been likewise blocked by Israel. Over 200 people have died as result of not being able to leave Gaza for medical treatment. Hundreds of Palestinian students, accepted to universities abroad, have also been denied exit visas by Israel.

Among the internationals currently stranded in Gaza are Irish activist and former Hawaiian legislator Kenneth O'Keefe, British journalist Lauren Booth, the sister-in-law of former British Prime Minister Tony Blair, and Dr. William Dienst, a family and emergency room physician from the USA.

This refusal of entry by Israel and Egypt effectively confines the internationals to the forty by ten kilometer enclave of Gaza, along with 1.5 million Palestinians, likewise sealed off from loved ones who live abroad and denied freedom of movement for purposes of education, medical care, leisure, or work.

The four internationals attempted to peacefully exit Gaza through Israeli-controlled Erez crossing on August 29th; Israel denied the exit, stating that the activists had entered Gaza illegally by sea, even though that voyage had been formally allowed by the Israeli Foreign Ministry and Internal Affairs Ministry, according to newspaper reports. An official statement by Israel's Defense Ministry (August 25th) declared the Free Gaza movement did not violate any laws, and that their action posed "no security threat" (Ha'aretz).

Diplomatic channels are trying to negotiate the exit of the human rights workers, who wish, like Palestinians, to exercise their human rights under Article 13 of the Universal Declaration of Human Rights: (1) Everyone has the right to freedom of movement and residence within the borders of each state and (2) Everyone has the right to leave any country, including his own, and to return to his country.

At 16:30, Islam Shathawan, the police spokesperson for the Palestinian government visits us. He tells us that Dr. Eyad El-Sarraj has been in touch with the British Embassy and the Arab League to work on our behalf. There is supposed to be a decision at 8:00 P.M., though not clear whether that is Gaza/Egyptian time or Israel time.

Afterward, we are visited by Dr. Ghazei Hamad, from Prime Minister Ismail Hanieyeh's office. Dr. Hamad is the former spokesman of the Palestinian government in Gaza. "Well you could always consider using the tunnels," he finally says to our pleas of frustration. He tells us there are currently over 100 tunnels between Gazan and Egyptian Rafah. "But the Israeli's say they destroyed ninety tunnels when they destroyed thousands of homes along the border," I answer. "Yes," he answers back. "Every time they discovered a tunnel, we built two more." The only problem is that if we use the tunnels, we could still be apprehended in Egypt or be in big trouble when we try to leave through the Cairo Airport.

We wait until 9:00 P.M. and are finally told that the Egyptians have refused our entry and that we must turn back; another thirteen-hour day of total futility. Our Palestinian brothers driving us back to Gaza City a second time say this is nothing. For them it is much worse. And now the Rafah border is closed again, and tomorrow, Ramadan begins.

Bella: Shot at and Refused Travel: We Are All Palestinian!
Tuesday, 2 September 2008

Hi, all,

I've asked Bradford University how long I can reasonably hang onto my midwifery place without there being too little time left for it to be taken up by someone else. They've said Thursday.

I started to think optimistically about a life here if losing the university place is beyond my control. But the Australian embassy rep ("Why are you in Gaza? Don't you know it's dangerous?") is implying that they will only continue to negotiate my exit if I promise to leave WHENEVER they get me a way out. EVEN if it's too late to go to university, which is the main thing I'm going home for this soon. Because "negotiations are happening at a very high level, and it would compromise their integrity and future safety of Australians if I 'change my mind' about wanting to leave." All of this in the patronizing tones normally used by one's arresting officer.

"Anyway," he added. "You can't stay there, you're illegal. You don't have a visa." (Guess who gives out visas for Palestine? You're right—it's not the Palestinians.)

"I've got a Gaza port entry stamp," I offer. "They made it specially!"

"That doesn't mean anything, you need a visa."

"Oh, would a Palestinian passport do?" I ask. A loud silence.

I ring the British consulate for advice. As usual, the chap there offers understanding and respect, but in the end unfortunately has to disclaim me for lack of citizenship. I ring my UK support person. He listens to me move from anger to frustration to tears to a decision to agree to their terms and still try to get home to study.

So there we have it. I'm waiting to see what happens next. I'll potentially end up out of Gaza, without a degree to begin, wanting to be back here but have no way in. Just like all the Palestinians waiting on the border, like my host Dr. Mona's sixteen-year-old daughter, who is missing school and rings from Jordan every day to say, "I want to come home."

Meanwhile, members of the newly reformed Rafah ISM were out with the fishing boats, crossing the six-mile limit line and thus being fired on. Without internationals, the Israelis aim to wound or kill the fishermen and damage the boats. With internationals however, they just fired around the boats and across the bow all day. Harrowing, but not actually deadly—and the fishermen brought home ten times the fish the boats normally bring back from inside the Israeli enforced six-mile limit.

Just like everyone else...
Thursday, 4 September 2008

These are difficult days. I'm staying with Dr. Mona, one of our hosts here, but without concrete plans to leave or to stay, I feel very much in Limbo. I think by the end of the weekend I have to arrange a home. That will help a lot. Right now I feel both lost and lonely. But I am ashamed to say so when my situation is so much better than all 1.5 million other people who live here, and thousands of young people who lose their study places and scholarships in other countries daily. I filled out my online enrollment form today, but it felt a bit of an empty gesture. The university didn't yet tell me to give up the place, but they will. On Saturday I will go to find out about starting midwifery study here; I'm a little late, but I'm hopeful it can be arranged.

Chapter 13:

Setting Nets with Gaza Fishermen While Facing Down the Israeli Navy

⌘ ⌘ ⌘

Gaza Fishermen repairing their nets

Vittorio Arrigoni's Account of an Israeli Shooting and Harassment:
September 9, 2008

When at a distance that our fishing boat's captain estimated to be seven nautical miles from the coast, we dropped our nets, and started fishing. The Israeli warships rushed to reach our position. One of the warships, which was located at a distance less than 200 meters alongside of our fishing boat, opened fire in our direction at least four times during the day. It was intimidating fire directed into the water, but some bursts almost touched the hull of our boat. A shot fired from a cannon almost reached us. Making attempts to obtain radio contact with the Israeli ship useless. Soldiers on the Israeli warship used megaphones to order us to evacuate the area. Afterward, they were shooting. Actually, they had been shooting even before they ordered our fishing boat to evacuate. Once, they shot at our fishing nets and then tried to damage them further by sailing directly over them.

Unfortunately our big mistake was not having either still cameras or video. We will bring these supplies, plus megaphones, which we will use exactly like the Israeli war vessel does. I consider these essential for future fishing missions.

Despite these intimidations, the fishing was rich and profitable; we brought ashore quantities of fish ten times greater than the Palestinian fishermen's usual catch.

**Vittorio Arrigoni, right, participating
in protest on behalf of fishermen**

ISRAELI NAVAL VESSELS FIRING ON UNARMED FISHING BOATS AND HUMAN RIGHTS WORKERS [1]

(OFF THE COAST OF GAZA) 1 September 2008 - Israeli Naval vessels are currently firing on unarmed Palestinian fishing boats and international human rights workers off the coast of the Gaza Strip. The fishing boats are several miles off the coast of Gaza City, in Palestinian territorial waters. As of 11am (4am EST) no one had been injured, but live ammunition is still being fired in the direction of the civilian boats.

The unarmed boats went to sea at dawn this morning, in an attempt to fish in their own waters. Six international human rights workers from five different countries

1. http://www.freegaza.org/en/home/56-news/422-israeli-naval-vessels-firing-on-unarmed-fishing-boats-and-human-
rights-workers

accompanied the fishermen in the hopes that their presence would deter the Israeli military from firing on the fishermen. In the past the Israeli military has shot and killed unarmed Palestinian fishermen for trying to fish in their own waters.

International Human Rights Observers accompanying the fishermen are:

Vittorio Arrigoni, Italy, Georgios Karatzas, Greece, Adam Qvist, Denmark Andrew Muncie, Scotland, Donna Wallach, USA, Darlene Wallach, USA

YouTube Video: Shooting on Palestinian Fishing Boats (1:36)
September 9, 2008

Video: http://www.youtube.com/watch?v=yTUYivihoTE

Tomorrow another fishing day in Gaza Territorial waters has been organized; on board with us we will have the first German television channel and some Arab journalists.

The world has to know, to open its eyes, react, and face up to what is happening just few miles away at sea from Gaza coasts.

In the attached video, which was shot by one of my partners on board, it's clearly visible how our fishing boat was bombarded from machine-gun fire coming from an Israeli warship. These kinds of attacks occur almost daily. Murders and wounding of Palestinian fishermen, who are only guilty of trying to sail more than three nautical miles from the shore, have occurred. This limit is an illegal and arbitrary one imposed by Israeli authorities. The Oslo Agreements established that the maximum limit is twenty miles from the coastline and the Bertini Agreement, stipulated in August 2002 between UN and Israel, set this distance at twelve miles.

Some days ago, our presence on board as internationals avoided death or wounding of Palestinians; we wish that tomorrow the presence of television cameras will work as a deterrent for any criminal Israeli action.

We, nonviolent people, will accompany nonviolent fishing boats at a distance not more than ten miles from the coast. Their fishing is one of the few sources of nourishment for a destroyed Gazan economy.

In the 1990s, when fishing boats could sail from the strip's coast and reach a distance equal to twelve miles, fishermen could bring ashore, sell, and also export almost 3.000 tons of fish every year. In 2007 just 500 tons of fish were harvested from more than 3,500 professional fishermen along the forty kilometers of the Gaza Strip coast; now from among these 3,500 fishermen just 700 are still working today in an economical field that was able to sustain at least 40,000 people as mechanics, fishmongers, and thousands of families of local fishermen.

It's always more difficult to find fish in the sea close to the Gaza Strip's coast; pollution and extreme exploitation has made this water contaminated and void of much commercial fish. This is one of the reasons why tomorrow we will accompany the fishing boats far from the seashore hoping for another miraculous day of fishing.

The ability to sail twenty miles out would allow Gaza fishermen the chance, during the springtime, to meet schools of sardines migrating from the Nile delta to the Turkish sea. Staying at less than six miles from the coast is almost impossible for them to find large groups of fish. According to the Palestinian Centre for Human Rights, Israel never allowed Palestinian fishermen to sail and reach the twenty miles established by the agreements.

Gaza fishermen state that they cannot go beyond more than two and one-half miles without being exposed to the risk of Israeli gunfire, and the risk of having boats and nets destroyed while Israeli patrols push them toward shore. This situation, which has been going on since 2003, has worsened during the last years with the presence of Israeli rockets and helicopters used against the fishermen.

According to the Rafah Fishermen's Union, Israeli war boats patrol the sea, in the southern part of the Strip, 24 hours a day, seven days a week, under the pretext of keeping security and fighting weapons traffic. During 2007 more than seventy fishermen were arrested, their boats destroyed together with nets and fishing equipment. For months, thousands of fishermen didn't have the permission to leave the port.

"In a report published by Israeli human rights group *Bet'selem*, some fishermen's stories were collected. Ismail Basleh was fishing on the first of January 2007 with his brother Samir and his friend Aymen al-Jabur. In the distance they saw an Israeli warship approaching; after stopping at less than thirty meters from them, it starting shooting into the air. The Israeli captain then, ordered Ismail to follow them for six kilometers, to turn off engines, and swim in cold water toward them. The warship was slowly moving away, and Ismail was about to drown. The rest of story reported by Bet'selem is about bound arms and legs, threats and intimidations, sleep deprivation, and demeaning and inhuman treatments. Adnan al-Badwil described also his misadventure when he was fishing with his brother at 5:00 A.M.; they had just pulled up the nets with the fish when they heard some shooting in the dark. The boat was hit, it started oscillating, and then both men fell into the water. Three members of the crew were wounded and treated for three days in the hospital. But, despite all the risks for their own lives, Gazan fishermen still go out with their boats and try to go over the three-mile limit. They feel they have to in order to survive.

Nowadays they often can only use rowing boats since there is no more fuel in Gaza. This is not due to the high price of oil, but because Israel doesn't allow fuel to enter the strip. Israel keeps pushing forward an embargo that appears as a general collective punishment for an entire population.

Tomorrow we will dedicate our fishing day to three fishermen who, some days ago were arrested and, against the religious laws of Ramadan, forced by the soldiers to eat and drink, breaking their fast and their religious commitments. We will mainly dedicate it to two fishermen recently wounded, Mohammad Ani As-Sultan, nineteen years old, and Hussam As-Sultan di Ani, thirty-two years old, who was hit in his head and still in critical condition. These crimes can no longer remain in silence.

Please, spread the video
And stay, on shore as offshore, human.
Stay human.
Vittorio Arrigoni.

Update From Gaza on Fishermen Accompaniment this past Saturday

Andrew Muncie, Scottish National and Human Rights Worker
September 9, 2008

On Saturday the sixth of September, human rights workers from the Free Gaza Movement and the International Solidarity Movement again accompanied Palestinian fishermen on their fishing boats in Gaza territorial waters.

It was just 09:30 in the morning, and we were only four miles out to sea, having barely left Gaza's coastline behind, when the Israeli gunboat's heavy machine gun opened up, spraying the wake around our hull with bullets.

There was no surprise. We'd just spent the previous ten minutes watching as this same gunboat harried another vessel from our fishing fleet. It would accelerate into an attack run, only to veer off at the last moment before collision, battering the fishing boat with its wake. It would pull alongside screeching threats and commands to stop over the megaphone. Throughout, its machine gun barked menacingly, peppering the air and water around the boat with bullets.

When our turn came, our skipper just stuck steadfast to his course, neither slowing down nor speeding up. The crew continued preparing the nets, only pausing briefly to consider the crack of the machine gun and the trajectory of the bullets that were coming their way. This morning they were determined that they were going to fish.

They had to fish. How could they stop and turn back now? Why would they stop when they hadn't even reached the so-called "six-mile limit"? This is not some agreed perimeter, not some internationally recognized boundary, indeed not even a border that had ever been officially declared or communicated to them, but just an arbitrary and elastic space delineated with the threat of gunfire.

And of course this gunboat was probably just toying dangerously with the fishing boats as others like it had done so often before. These shots were most likely simple warning shots. Not like those that hospitalized two fishermen three days ago. Not like those that killed fourteen of their colleagues in the last few years. If you are a Gaza fisherman, you can never be sure when it will be your time to get injured or shot.

As expected, the gunboat got bored, perhaps even embarrassed with its failure to force some sort of response. It withdrew and began patrolling slowly back and forth, as if nothing had happened.

This respite was welcome but brief. In the early afternoon, another gunboat appeared on the horizon, heading in our direction at full speed. It tore in and out of our fleet again and again, weaving between our boats as if we were flags in a slalom ski course. A few bursts from its machine gun, and it left just as promptly as it had appeared.

Before long the light began to fade. All in our fleet were heading back to Gaza City while dragging their nets for the last time that day. We waited eagerly in anticipation of *Iftar* and the time when we could break our fast. Two of the men had already begun preparing the Ramadan supper, frying fish and prawns from that day's catch. We gazed out across the sea, calculating how long it would be before the low sun finally met the horizon.

Suddenly, another gunboat appeared with a definite menace apparent in its speed and course. Its cannon roared twice, the shells narrowly missing one of the leading boats, exploding in the water. Tracer bullets then pierced the dim light streaking across the sky just as the gunboat swerved again and went in for another target. Its cannon roared a third time, and we tried to film, but the light was now so dim, and the boat far away. But it mattered not. The fishermen insisted we stop because the Ramadan supper was ready and their course was already set.

From Bella: Israeli Gunboat Rams Palestinian Fishing Boat
Thursday, 11 September 2008

The last day I went out fishing, the Israeli gunboats shot at us for a while in the morning. They threatened in Arabic over the megaphone to arrest the fisherman and take them to Israel. This happens constantly and sometimes the boats are damaged or sunk after the arrests. They threatened to start shooting directly at the boat, but they didn't. It's common for boats or fishermen to be hit. They actually went and sat on the horizon for most of the day, after announcing more politely in English "This is a closed area. You must leave." O.J. responded over channel 16 that these were Palestinian waters, over which they had no jurisdiction, and they were firing upon unarmed people.

As the sun set, the sea turned silver, and the fisherman served up the day's catch to break the Ramadan fast, the gunboat came back for a special Ramadan drive-by shooting before heading home - the flash of automatic fire drawing a line toward the bow where I was filming, wondering if they were going to stop when they reached me and the boat. They did, to begin again at the other end of the boat, and follow it up with a few explosion type things. Then they went home for their dinner too, we presume, and we ate our fried fish. Our first catches were small, but the last one very big, so the fishermen were happy.

Then yesterday:

Israeli Military Gunboat Rams Unarmed Palestinian Fishing Vessel

(GAZA COASTAL WATERS) 10th September 2008 – An Israeli military gunboat rammed an unarmed Palestinian fishing vessel today at high speeds. The gunboat smashed through the upper hull of the fishing boat, careened over the top, and landed on the other side.

Extensive damage was caused by the impact to the fishing boat. The hull was badly damaged, and virtually the entire deck area, all the equipment on it, and the canopy above the deck were severely damaged. Unusually, all of the crew happened to be in the cabin or at the fore at the time. Had they been on deck they would have had little chance of survival.

A Gazan fishing boat, after being rammed by an Israeli Warship.
Darlene Wallach, ISM observer, inspecting the damage.

Via a megaphone, the Israeli military aboard the gunboat then made the threat that:
"When the internationals leave Gaza, you will all be made to pay."

Human rights observers from the International Solidarity Movement and from the Free Gaza movement have recently been accompanying Gazan Fishermen during their work. The fishermen are constantly harassed, threatened, and attacked by the State of Israel, in flagrant violation of international law and maritime law. Israel has been attempting to impose an illegal "no-go" area six miles off Gaza's coast through employment of lethal force against unarmed fishing boats. However, and this is not unusual, today's attack happened within the so-called "permitted" six-mile area.

The ISM regards the project of accompanying unarmed Palestinian fishermen as a long term commitment. Some of the human rights observers currently undertaking this work are long-term volunteers who will be in Gaza for the indefinite future. More long-term volunteers are expected to bolster their number within the next few weeks.

For more photos of the damage, see:
http://www.flickr.com/photos/29205195@N02/sets/72157607231701711/

Vittorio Arrigoni: What is Terrorism?
September 17, 2008

What is terrorism?

For a Russian citizen, terrorism is a kamikaze from Chechnya who blows himself up in a Moscow theater.

For a Grozny citizen, terrorism is Russian military that razed to the ground his town.

For an American soldier based in Afghanistan, terrorism is the mujahaddin exploding a car bomb in front of an American army base.

For Afghan people living at the border with Pakistan, terrorism is the NATO bomb dropping from 10,000 meters distance on a marriage party, tearing to shreds dozens of civilians.

For a European tourist spending his holidays in the Sharm El-Sheikh American army base, terrorism is an act of violence and bombing against a holiday village.

For an Egyptian living in a dusty village in the desert just a few kilometers from that artificial paradise, terrorism is a government funding this dctatorial power with thousands of euros coming from his tourist business, while his sons are dying of starvation.

As we can easily understand, it's quite complicated to find a clear and unequivocal definition of terrorism; given that the question itself is so controversial, the answer strictly depends from what side we are observing the bloodshed and in which side we are counting victims among friends and relatives.

A few days ago

Nine/eleven victims were sadly commemorated with a day of rememberance and mourning for the whole of humanity, not only for New York citizens or for Chileans looking back on thousands of people dead and disappeared after the Pinochet coup.

But I'm wondering how many 9/11s are taking place every day around the world and every day here in Gaza where 1.5 million innocent people are dying slowly, cut off into the biggest open prison ever built in the world.

In the video, which I'm kindly asking you to spread, we can see a tangible example of terrorism showing every day off the Gazan coasts. It is a clear and definitive terrorism that doesn't admit to objections or uncertainties about its definition.

It's a "made-in-Israel" terrorism. These are fishermen that often go farther offshore, where the sea is more generous for fishing. A few days ago, they paid a high price.

On Monday the tenth of September, at about 5:00 P.M., at a distance of six miles from the Gazan coasts, in Palestinian waters, an Israeli military gunboat deliberately rammed at high speed one of the fishing boats that day without internationals on board. The impact was devastating for the fragile Palestinian fishing boat, the Israeli military gunboat ran into one side of the fishing boat, literally passing over it and then going on over and sailing on the opposite side. Marks from the Israeli engine turbines are perfectly visible on the fishing boat's bow.

Luckily the boat was fishing at that time, and it was, therefore, steady, and buoyant in water, otherwise it would have tipped over with all the crew, which would have certainly died. Even more luckily, all members of the crew were astern cooking the meal that would have interrupted the Ramadan fast, at about 6:00 P.M. Unluckily, damages for the owner of the boat amount to 50,000 dollars, maybe more. Fixing them in a short time will be impossible, since in Gaza under siege, it is not possible to find all the necessary materials.

The only wounded person for this crazy terrorist attack, according to some military sources in Tel Aviv, was an Israeli soldier, since that suicidal action seriously compromised also the Israeli crew's lives.

Palestinian fishermen try every day to go offshore and do their job to survive, but they are always victims of Israeli attacks, which, against every international agreement and all human rights, as a general punishment, force them in a fishing area limited at six miles from the coast, even though attacks often happen at just three miles offshore.

Our presence as internationals, equipped with video cameras, work as a deterrent toward these daily crimes and Israeli terrorism. A boat captain told me that he was contacted by radio from an Israeli warship and threatened in Hebrew: "When the internationals will leave Gaza, our revenge will be dreadful." It's therefore a vital need for these innocent people that a group of internationals are always present here in Gaza.

I invite all European and American citizens to come here and actively participate in the defense of human rights, joining all of us ISM activists, against every crime, and Israeli terrorism, to be human.

Stay human. Vik from Gaza, Vittorio Arrigoni

See Vittorio's video of a Palestinian boat damaged by Israeli naval forces at: http://uk.youtube.com/watch?v=9E7nqVEOmsE

Chapter 14:

Marooned in Gaza: Life in the "World's Largest Prison"

⌘ ⌘ ⌘

By Lauren Booth

Never has so much bile been written about Lauren Booth since she broke through, with others in the Free Gaza movement, the Israeli naval blockade of Gaza and found herself unable to escape. Here, in a passionate reply to her critics, she describes everyday life in the "world's largest prison" from a unique Gazan perspective: cut off from her home and children after six weeks...and with no idea of what each day will bring.

This morning I have two wake-up calls. The first is the dawn call to prayer from the surrounding mosques. It is a deep-throated Islamic yodel that lulls me in and out of sleep. The second is a distant rumble like thunder; it is the Israeli Navy firing at Gazan fishing boats.

This morning the distant booming has been more prolonged than usual. I walk down to the dock to see what is happening. It is early, but the sun is already blazing. Horns scream and the broken roads are a mish-mash of rusting cars, ageing motorcycles and a multitude trying to avoid the potholes and rocks that litter the way.

I wander past breeze-block apartments peppered with bullet holes. There is no cement here, so most new buildings are half-built shells. I pass a group of primary school girls dressed in dark green uniform blouses worn over jeans for modesty. They are skipping through the chaos, chatting carelessly. For a moment I imagine I am taking my own children to school. It could be a long time before I am granted that privilege again.

At the port, a large crowd has formed. People are shouting and gesticulating wildly. In among the decrepit vessels with paint peeling off them stands a boat whose front has been ripped apart. A couple of dejected young men sit amid the wreckage, threading worry beads around and around their fingers. An old man in a traditional white Arabic shirt shouts out at anybody who will listen, "This is what Israel has done to me. It has destroyed me."

During the night, Israeli patrol vessels had attacked the small Gazan fishing fleet, as they have done many times before. The Israelis have imposed a "no-go" zone six miles from Gaza's coast. This time a gunboat had smashed through the upper hull of this fishing vessel, leaving it a useless wreck. It was the third boat to be destroyed in a matter of weeks. I shield my eyes from the sun as the man repeats over and over that such a repair would cost "fifty thousand dollars!" And who has that kind of money in this broken land?

Then I shudder as I realize this is an act of revenge by an Israeli force furious with the fishermen who greeted me and forty-five other foreigners when we arrived on peace boats on the Gazan coastline last month, breaking the Israeli blockade for the first time. The Israeli military aboard the gunboat had shouted at the fishermen through a megaphone: "When the foreigners leave Gaza, you will all be made to pay." The people around the boat shrug. As they say in the Gaza Strip: *"Hak al dyniah."* [This is the life.]

**Mohammed El Hesy, captain of fishing boat rammed
by Israeli warship, and his crew**

And now this is my life, too. Because I find myself stuck in the same boat—trapped in Gaza, hundreds of miles away from my home and children. Much has been written about my visit to Gaza at the end of August on board one of two peace boats from Free Gaza. Many of the comments about my part in the mission to highlight the plight of this tiny strip of land have been highly critical. I have been accused of naivety and stupidity. Jan Moir, in a particularly acerbic piece, went so far as to say I am gloating over my predicament. "Still, no matter how much Booth bleats behind the barbed wire, she is still managing to look quite pleased with herself," she wrote in the *Daily Mail*. I can assure her that it's no fun not knowing when you will see your children again.

I will say that I was naïve to believe I could come to Gaza, a land where human rights are so routinely ignored and abused, and expect my own to somehow be respected. The plan had been to land in Gaza as part of the first international boats to arrive on its twenty-five-mile coastline for forty-one years, and then turn around and get out.

Following that event, I, and a handful of others decided to stay in Gaza for a couple of days and then leave through the land border. We were told it was being opened also for international passport holders like us. But when we got there, our exit was blocked after nine hours of Limbo inside the no man's land between the Egyptian and Palestinian checkpoints at Rafah. We were banned from leaving by the Israeli authorities who wield tacit control over the Egyptian authorities. So here I am stuck in this foreign land.

I am living among the people I am reporting on, seeing their world first-hand, their struggle with polluted water, broken sewage works, decaying schools and hospitals, and half-empty shops. Like so many mothers here, I am living out of a half-open suitcase, separated from my children, ready to leave at a moment's notice, yet emotionally preparing myself for the fact I may have to stay indefinitely.

Gaza is a twenty-five-mile by four-to-seven-mile strip of land between Israel and Egypt, home to 1.5 million Palestinians and occupied by Israel for forty years. In 2005, Israelis pulled their settlers out of Gaza but still control the area to this day. A year later, they designated it a no-go zone after the surprise election of Hamas.

It is where BBC correspondent Alan Johnston was kidnapped last year and held for 114 days. He was one of the last international journalists based full-time in Gaza after most Western news agencies had deemed the area too dangerous. Some aid agencies have since withdrawn staff. And yet I have felt very safe in Gaza. I walk freely through the city center and the camps at either end.

Hamas has been very careful about security since taking power. 'No more kidnappings on their watch' is their message. So I have been issued two bodyguards—Ali, a newly wed twenty-four-year-old, and a younger man, Mohammed. They have both been carrying handguns. Their protection seemed fairly pointless until three weeks into my stay, when I was woken with a jolt at 4:00 A.M. by machine-gun fire.

The people I was staying with tried to assure me it was unlikely to be anything more than Hamas police carrying out training sessions on the beach. I suspected fireworks, this being Ramadan. Every night for weeks, boys with cherry bombs that explode loudly have been amusing themselves in the alleyways of the camps by lighting them and flinging them against walls or into bins. But the booms got louder and closer. Then the sirens began.

There was a violent clash between the police and a heavily armed militia group, The Army of Islam, responsible for much of the violence in Gaza and the kidnapping of Johnston. For hours I lay sleepless. It seemed like the shooting would never stop. The periods of silence became excruciating as we all tensed, waiting for the ratta-tat-tat of the machine-gun fire to break the quiet.

After the eleven-hour battle, the British consul in Gaza called me. "Limit your movements today. Do not go to the south at all, which is not to say the north is safe. In fact, stay inside if you can." It later turns out that this was a decisive battle, with eleven militiamen and two policemen shot.

Many other members of the radical faction were rounded up and three truckloads of weapons confiscated, part of the Hamas pledge to clean up the streets. This was the first violence that I had encountered in three weeks. Two days previously it had been considered by the head of police safe enough for me to travel to Rafah, the most dangerous part of Gaza, without security.

My voyage to Gaza at the end of August was on board *Free Gaza*, part of a two-boat flotilla that sailed from Larnaca, Cyprus. It was a day-and-a-half of muesli bars, rolling stomachs, and cups of half-spilt tea. My shipmates were a variety of people from around the globe, keen to highlight and even break Israel's siege of the Gazan residents, a form of collective punishment that is illegal under international law.

I said good-bye to my husband and children at our home in France, fully expecting to be back in two weeks. I don't expect people to understand what drives someone to join a mission that is dangerous and even unlikely to succeed, but I felt I needed to stand up for something I believe in.

On the day we left Larnaca, Dr. Bill, Jeff Halper, and Tom Nelson each said the same thing every time they see me:

"Lauren! You're our human shield. I'm sticking to you like glue, buddy!" I don't let them know how certain I am that, if he had the choice, Tony Blair would probably applaud the Israelis getting rid of me. Dragging my inappropriately vast, pink, Barbie-style suitcase below deck on the *Free Gaza*, a cold shiver runs down my spine. I think "If these people are relying on MY name to keep us safe, we're in serious trouble!"

During the night before we had sight of land, our entire satellite system was maliciously scrambled, leaving all but one of our six phones useless. Then just before dawn, aboard the *SS Free Gaza*, the radio system crackled into life. For a minute,

Hebrew music floated into the dark cabin. This weird infiltration of another culture was suddenly interrupted by a heavily accented voice. "*Free Gaza*, this is the Israeli Navy. Turn back." After thirty-two hours, and two years of planning, no one had any intention of turning round.

As we approached the Gaza City skyline, in the distance we spotted a group of boats and heard people shouting. We quickly realized that we were being serenaded in Arabic. In complete contrast to the response from the Israeli Navy, the Gazans were delighted by our arrival. Happily, the Israelis could hardly have risked bombing us out of the water; we had rather counted on this.

In the harbor it was chaos. I was amazed to see tens of thousands of men, hijabed women, and children all jostling for the best position. After we moored, we began our first days in Gaza under heavy police protection at the Al Deira hotel. It is an unlikely paradise in this desolate land. The bedrooms have Wi-Fi, and the hotel's restaurant is a terrace that overlooks the sea.

But it was a brief stint. After the boats returned to Cyprus, I moved, preferring to stay with local families. I quickly came face to face with the hardships of living in a country that has been cut off by the Israelis for nearly two years. I met a young teacher who had been trapped in Gaza for two years. Wissam is married to a French woman and had been living in Paris until he returned to Gaza to see his family in 2006. During his visit the border was closed. He has been trying to leave ever since. As he talked I noticed his brown, yellow teeth. It is a common sight in Gaza, where the dreadful water strips off the enamel, but the people have no choice but to keep drinking it. Gaza's only power plant was targeted in a bombing raid by Israel and since then there has not been enough power to properly clean the water. According to the World Health Organization, 90 percent of the water is not fit for consumption.

When Hamas won control of the Palestinian Authority government in the 2006 elections, Israel effectively sealed all its borders with Gaza and restricted the entry of even basic food items such as fruit, milk and other dairy products, wheat flour, rice, sugar, salt, cooking oil, and frozen foods. The lack of adequate food supplies is obvious all over Gaza. I visit a health center with Dr. Mona El Farra, the author of the award-winning blog "From Gaza with Love." It is midmorning, so the center is packed with young mothers, most in *hijab* or the full-face *nikab*. There is noise, but only from the mothers. The forty-plus infants in their arms are mostly silent. A green liquid in bowls and cups is being prepared by medical staff. I am struck by the smell. It is the pungent stench of ill health.

Ruwaida Farra Jalla, thirty-two, hands me her baby, and I help to stuff the mix of puréed vegetables and added minerals into the poor child's mouth. She appears to be a newborn, with the wizened features of an old man. Her frilly green dress hangs off her meager, unmoving limbs. *Selsabile* is nine months old but weighs just eleven pounds. She is chronically malnourished. Another near-starved infant is handed to me, a baby with the blonde-red hair I have been surprised to see so prevalent in barefoot youngsters from Rafah to Beit Hanoun.

Sawsan Alsiwaisy, the baby's mother, shakes her head when I ask if she too is blonde beneath her burkha. Dr. *Al-Wahaidi* explains that this coloring, pallid skin and pale hair, is a direct attribute of malnourishment, more often than not a sign of lack of protein. In the past decade, this clinic has seen the cases of severe nutritional distress rise from 4,500 to 16,000. I ask another mother, *Ghada Jibreil*, what she feeds her children at home. She replies, "All that I have. Dry bread dipped in tea." None of the women's husbands have jobs, nor do their older sons and only a handful of their fathers or uncles have work.

British journalist Lauren Booth carries a Palestinain baby who suffering malnutrition during her visiting to the Ard Al-Insan Society clinic in Gaza City

The unemployment rate in the Gaza Strip now stands at 45 percent, higher than almost anywhere else in the world. In the camps themselves the figure is much higher. Since Israel's blockade began, nearly 95 percent of all factories operating in Gaza have been closed down. Repeated shutdowns of electricity and fuel sources are contributing to the humanitarian crisis.

In 2006, Israeli prime ministerial adviser Dov Weisglass was quoted as saying that the idea behind the closure policy was "to put the Palestinians on a diet but not make them die of hunger." Some of these children will die as a direct result of poor nutrition due to the closures. Many more will be condemned to a marginal existence with physical and intellectual stunting of their growth and development.

There isn't much to do here. The beach is the main place where families go to enjoy themselves. I am keen to swim, but I am told that as a woman I must go early in the morning when I will not be seen. I am advised to swim far from the shore. The sewage system is near collapse and each day 77,000 cubic meters of raw and partially treated sewage is discharged into the sea

So I am taken out by a fisherman. We go about half a mile out before it is deemed safe enough to swim. It's the first time I've ever swum in the sea in my clothes. There is an item of clothing here called a *burkhini*: lightweight trousers and a loose-fitting shirt that Muslim women can swim in. I wear the nearest equivalent I can muster from my suitcase. After my swim I emerge onto the beach, my salty clothes clinging to me. It is still early and a group of fishermen watch as I walk ashore. I traipse down the beach squishing around in my wet clothes, but I suspect my blonde hair draws more attention than my wet attire.

Dried and changed, I wander around the city. I stop at the PLO flag shop. Like all the nonessential stores here, there is no one inside but the rather dejected owner. He leaps to his feet and hands me box after box of incredible trinkets. Yasser Arafat key rings, Hamas bookmarks, pins of dead martyrs, etc. I settle for a T-shirt that says Free Gaza and a mug with iron bars printed on it and the rather cheery legend, Smile. You're in Gaza, The Biggest Prison in the World.

Before the Free Gaza boat had left to return to Cyprus, leaving myself and ten others who wanted to stay and carry out humanitarian work, I had been assured that I would be allowed to leave via Rafah, the only connection to the outside world for ordinary Palestinians. This border crosses into Egypt and has been open for just eight days this year. It is an essential doorway to the world—a way for people and goods to get into and out of this stricken land.

I join the crush of humanity in a bus heading across Rafah's no man's land. The bus, like virtually all the public transportation in Gaza, has no air-conditioning. It broke down ages ago, and there are no parts to fix it. This is no joke as it's over 35°C inside. The bus stops with a jolt. Inside the Rafah terminal, it is utter chaos. It amuses me later to read a report in an Egyptian newspaper pronouncing the opening "a well-organized success." To British eyes, it's a scene straight from Terminal 5 Heathrow during the height of summer, and more—families sprawled, dejected on the floor, men yelling at the authorities, and snappy police in uniforms with riot truncheons and guns strapped to their waist.

My passport is taken away and still not returned after an hour-and-a-half. I am starting to panic when I spot a familiar face. It is the teacher, Wissam. Despite still not having the right papers he is hoping he will be allowed to cross the border. He has not seen his wife, who lives in France, for two years. I leave Wissam talking to his wife on his mobile. He is sure this time he will get through. I have wandered outside to escape the chaos and panic in the terminal for a moment.

I hand a tennis ball to Mohammed, my security guard. I brought several tennis balls to Gaza to give to children at checkpoints, who get bored. We take turns rolling the ball at a can, a point awarded every time it is knocked down. Another young man in a black suit who Mohammed describes as "Mr. Qassam, Mr. Rocket" joins us. We enjoy the game, shouting and cheering at every loss and gain until we attract the attention of a middle-aged man in a T-shirt and black trousers. A gun strapped to his belt and his full beard denotes his authority. He shouts furiously at my companions and then strides away. A masked gunman belonging to the military wing of the Palestinian group Fateh controls a tiny enclave within the Rafah border of the Gaza Strip.

I quickly pick up the ball, assuming our games are over. But then my colleague Ken O'Keefe and I are led to a secluded patch near to some stables where the police horses are looked after. A serious young man marks a line in the dirt track. We are to play handball with Hamas. It is one of the most bizarre experiences of my stay in Gaza. The break lifts my spirits, but I am soon brought back down to earth when I return to the terminal.

The Egyptians maintain the border has only been opened to humanitarian traffic, and we are again not allowed to leave. The Egyptian authorities add that if we hang around the terminal, they'll close the checkpoint, and no one else will cross today. The official who tells me this news pleads with me to go.

Complaining about mistreatment at checkpoints leads to collective punishment. It is an uncannily precise echo of the threat made to me by the IOF when I tried to exit via Erez into Israel just the day before.

I learn later that Wissam, along with 200 other Gazans, was turned back, too.

The city of Rafah is also home to a vast refugee camp in the south, known during the pre-Hamas days for running gun battles and bloody familial feuds.

Driving into the area a few days later, a local photographer named Abed and I pass through four checkpoints where cars are routinely stopped by police, and their contents checked for weapons. At the far side of the camp are tunnels. There are over 150, it is said, through which all kinds of goods travel illicitly from Egypt to the shops and homes of the Gaza Strip.

A large group of men is gathered at sundown, chatting amiably, surrounded by new shiny red motorbikes. In January, Hamas destroyed the Iron Walls built by the Israelis south of Rafah. 200,000 Palestinians passed through into Egypt in a few days. They came back loaded with essentials like batteries, electrical goods, building materials, and all kinds of medicine. The young men all bought Chinese motorbikes from the nearby Egyptian city of El Arish. With petrol so scarce and parts for cars in ever shortening supplies, the solution to travel problems here is to go by two wheels.

I stand with a group of middle-aged businessmen who want to pose for photos. The tunnels, once secret passageways regularly bombed by the Israelis, are now spoken of quite openly. Egyptians on the other side take bribes to turn a blind eye to the boxes of goods that go through. The tunnels are nicknamed the "Gazan subway."

I mime pulling a rope to the men inviting me to test a flashy motorbike for size. They are surprised. Not many from the outside world know how the system inside the tunnels actually works. People and goods are lowered into the dug-out holes and put into boxes attached to one another by ropes. It takes just fifteen minutes for the Rafah teams to heave materials and human cargo back up and out into the Rafah sunshine; or more likely the darkness. As I peer over at the tunnels, I contemplate my very unique journalistic perspective. I now know what it is like to live under siege, unable to escape, and to work in a place where all the normal rules of civilized society do not apply.

Chapter 15:

What Did You Do on Your Summer Vacation?

⌘ ⌘ ⌘

From Dr. Bill:
September 2-7, 2008

After our press release, Ken, Lauren, and I hold a press conference at the head-quarters of the Palestinian news agency Ramattan; we have started trying to play hardball. We have been stuck here for over four days. We feel we have given the consulates, politicians, and the diplomats long enough to "coordinate." We thank Israel for giving us the opportunity to personally experience what it feels like to be deprived of the ability to travel, just like one and a half million Palestinians from Gaza, who have it much worse than we do. At the press conference, Dr. Eyad Sarraj and Dr. Mona Faraa' make appeals in Arabic on our behalf.

This press conference doesn't seem to have much effect. The Ramadan pace works against us, as several reporters fail to file their reports to their news agencies in a timely manner. Ramadan is fasting and family time, which takes priority over us. A few things we said in English have also come back to bite us in the butt. Online article headlines the next day state: Boat Activists Blame Egypt for Blocking Gaza Exit. This is not exactly the spin that we wanted, and it could compound bad feelings among the Egyptians and make our situation more complicated.

That evening we hold a candlelight vigil with women who are separated from their families outside of Gaza. The following morning, I go to work trying to extricate myself from Gaza and get back home. I e-mail my friends and family back home to try to help me out. I write the following e-mail to the US Embassies in Egypt and Israel and also send it by fax:

2 September 2008
To Whom It May Concern
Re: Exit from Gaza

My name is Dr. William L. Dienst Jr. I am a family and emergency room physician from Omak, Washington, USA.

For the past month, I have been the chief medical officer for the Free Gaza movement boats. As you may know, we successfully sailed from Cyprus and entered Gaza port directly from international waters in accordance with international maritime law. We are the first such boats to enter Gaza directly from the sea since June 1967, a time span of forty years.

Our two boats, the *Liberty* and the *Free Gaza*, returned to Cyprus on 28 August 2008. I stayed on in Gaza to coordinate the delivery of medical supplies to local Gaza hospitals and clinics, and to try to assist patients who require transfer out of Gaza for medical reasons.

I have since attempted to leave Gaza on 29 August through Erez crossing into Israel but was denied; in fact, our group of unarmed Palestinians and human rights workers was threatened with being fired on by the Israeli border guards. We proceeded anyway to the Iron Gate and fortunately we were not shot at. The Israeli's would not open their iron gate, however; so we were forced to retreat.

On 30 August and 31 August 2008, I along with three other internationals from the UK, Ireland, and Australia, attempted to leave Gaza through the Rafah Crossing into Egypt. We spent nine hours on Saturday and another thirteen hours on Sunday there trying to get across, so we can travel home. We were kept in Limbo until the very end on each day before being denied exit. At the end, the stated reason given to us for their refusal was that we entered Gaza by sea. I can only speculate about the real motivations behind Egypt's refusal at this point, so I won't. All I can say is it comes as a complete surprise.

If you could assist in helping me exit from Gaza, I would appreciate it. I have a plane ticket to Europe, and I am scheduled to leave Frankfurt, Germany, and then on to Spokane on Saturday, 6 September 2008. I am scheduled to start back at work seeing my patients at Family Health Centers in Tonasket, Washington, on Monday, 8 September 2008.

Respectfully,
Dr. William L. Dienst Jr.

The next day, I get the following responses from US Consulates in Israel and Egypt:

Request Transfer out of Gaza through Erez
From: Zahner, Luke V (ZahnerLV@state.gov)

Sent: Wed 9/03/08 7:29 AM

Dear Dr. Dienst,

On Sunday, the Consulate General passed on your request for exit through Rafah to the Egyptian authorities. Today we contacted the Israelis about possibly facilitating your exit through Erez. The response from the Israeli authorities was that their standing policy is anyone entering Gaza "illegally" – i.e., by sea – cannot exit through Israel. The other issue, however, is that even if they were to permit exit through Erez, you could be subject to arrest by the Israeli authorities.

We will continue to be in contact with the Israeli authorities to see how you might exit Gaza, but for the moment at least, the Erez crossing does not appear to be a viable option.

Please keep us informed of any developments, and we will definitely do likewise.

Luke Zahner
U.S Consulate General – Jerusalem

And:

RE: Request transfer through Rafah out of Gaza
From: Consular, Cairo NIV (ConsularCairoNIV@state.gov)

Sent: Wed 9/03/08 7:58 AM
To: William Dienst

Dear Sir,
Thank you for your e-mail message.

Unfortunately, we are not able to accommodate your request as we are not able to overrule any Egyptian authorities.

Regards,
Consular Staff

Since we are all stuck, we decide to keep doing productive things here while we wait for the diplomatic ice to break.

We meet with Mr. John Ging, an Irishman and the current director of UNRWA in Gaza. He feels Israel's policies, since its Supreme Court declared Gaza a "hostile entity" in September 2007 is lunacy in terms of humanity, legality, and logic.

Mr. John Ging, 3rd from left, Director of UNWRA in Gaza

Creating a man-made catastrophe does not resolve any problems; it compounds them. Israel's Gaza policies are clear violations of International Law, and the Geneva Conventions. And it defies logic, creating a self-fulfilling prophesies of hopelessness, which produces violence. The borders have been open for only a few select UN officials and politicians who must tow a more ridiculous line in order to be let in and out of Gaza.

There has been a ceasefire in effect for over two months, and still Israel has not lightened up on the siege. The so-called Quartet keeps issuing empty platitudes and does nothing. There is presently a more positive security situation and there is no reward.

As Archbishop Desmond Tutu has said, this is an abominable situation, with an appalling lack of an international reaction. There is no agricultural support. Buffer zones are widened as farmland is destroyed, and people in Rafah are displaced and living with relatives now in more overcrowded conditions. Gaza now receives less social support from the outside than a prison. This is absurd on the sixth anniversary of the Universal Declaration of Human Rights, and the sixth anniversary of the Palestinian Nakba.

Mr. Ging believes that the international community needs to restore the belief that nonviolent action such as the present ceasefire will lead to positive results. Local Gazans will need escape from total despair. The international community needs to demand from Israel, "Why is the border still closed, and when are you going to open it?" The international community needs to insist that action be taken, especially for Gazans with time-sensitive situations like medical conditions that need specialty treatment outside, and college students whose future careers are jeopardized by this blockade.

My wife and support network back home are now pushing all the buttons to get me back home. Marianne Torres in Spokane creates an ad hoc committee to Free Dr. Bill Dienst from Gaza. Washington State Congresswoman Kathy McMorris-Roger's office phone starts ringing off the hook. My support network back home also starts calling my Washington State Senators Maria Cantwell and Patty Murray's office to intervene. And my friend, Jim Ennes, a survivor of the Israeli attack on the USS Liberty in 1967, and author of the book, *Attack on the* Liberty, is in touch with his friend, former Senator from South Dakota James Abourezk, who is in touch with Egyptian authorities:

Dear Dr. Ramadan:

As you can see from the e-mail from Dr. Dienst, he has been blocked from exiting Gaza both by Israel and by Egypt.

It's a bit embarrassing to have an American doctor, who is trying to help people, held up by political considerations.

I hope you can have your government allow him to exit Gaza so he can come home.

Many thanks.

Jim Abourezk
Former U.S. Senator, South Dakota

We do get action from Washington State Congresswoman McMorris-Rogers and Senator Cantwell also.

The next day I go out with the Palestine Medical Relief Society's mobile health van down to the town of Deir Al Balah, in the central Gaza Strip along the coast. I volunteered a lot with these mobile health vans in the West Bank and Gaza when I was here in 2006.

Outside mobile clinic, Deir Al Balah, Gaza

Since then, their main office in Gaza was bombed by Israel, and they have had to move. Their medical infrastructure is starting to fall apart now compared to when I visited before. Basic medical supplies that were previously well stocked are now lacking. We spend a very frustrating morning seeing desperately poor patients needing medications and specialty care that we do not have: e.g., a man with chronic pain from compression fractures in his spine and a woman with kidney failure who needs to see a kidney specialist but lacks the resources to do so.

It is Ramadan, and the mobile clinic is not as busy as usual. So we leave early and head back to Dr. Eyad's house for an afternoon Ramadan rest. In the evening,

Dr. Khamis, the rehab specialist from Al Wafa' hospital drops by and asks if I would be willing to work a few Emergency Room shifts at the main hospital, Al Shifa. There are plenty of Palestinian doctors in Gaza who speak perfect Arabic. I do not. "Why do you need me?" I ask.

"Because there is a crisis at the hospital. Two girls died last night of meningitis and pneumonia."

"Why the crisis?" I ask further.

"The Fateh doctors are on strike," he answers."

"Why are they on strike?"

"Because their bosses in the West Bank have told them that if they work, they will not get paid, and if they don't work, they will," he answers.

I don't like the sound of this. "Tell you what," I finally say. "Let's set me up for a four-hour shift and see how it goes."

"I will let you know," Dr. Khamis says. He never does. The next day, I am summoned to another physician's apartment for coffee. I am warned not to get involved. "Hamas is trying to use you." I am told that several of the Fateh physicians who went on strike have now been thrown in jail by Hamas. This is extremely sad. Under extreme isolation and pressure, the whole medical system is imploding.

I am getting frustrated, and I start thinking of other, perhaps unconventional means of getting out. I am also extremely enraged about the minimal coverage that the Free Gaza movement and the Gaza Siege are receiving in the American media. I start plotting a master prank to get me out, and perhaps bring Jerusalem-based reporters from the *New York Times*, CNN and Fox to the Al Deira Hotel to cover all the action. I explain my twisted plan to Dr. Eyad El Sarraj. "The Western media wants to report on terrorism and kidnapping in Gaza, right? If it bleeds, it leads," I explain.

"What they need is a good kidnapping of a Westerner to get them to leave their cushy-little assignments in Jerusalem and come to Gaza. So let's arrange for me to slip out through the tunnels in the middle of a Ramadan night. Then I can be smuggled down to the Red Sea resort of Sharm El Sheikh, were I can blend in as a Western tourist. I will even shave and get a haircut. Meanwhile you can claim that I have disappeared. We can make up a name of a fictitious previously unknown "terrorist group" that calls in and claims responsibility for my abduction."

"I will bet that those American reporters will be racing across Israel to Erez crossing to cover the scoop. The Israelis will let them right through to report the bad news about those Palestinians. Pundits back home will then make total asses of themselves condemning the "terrorists" and perhaps condemning us for being "so naïve." I can then sneak across the Red Sea to Jordan on a fishing boat. It's not very far from Sharm Al Sheikh. Then after the pundits make total asses out of themselves, I can show up at a press conference in Amman and explain how it was all a joke."

"That is an interesting idea," Dr. El Sarraj responds; he smiles, but says no more. I want him to hook me up with the folks who know the tunnels. "So you want me to introduce you to the true underworld of Gazan society?" he chuckles. A few days later, I start pressing him again to line me up with the tunnelers. "I believe you have a tunnel fetish," remarks Eyad El Sarraj, the psychiatrist.

On Sunday morning, September 7th, Lauren Booth wants to attend church. We go to Sunday Mass at Gaza's only Catholic parish, with Monsignor Manuel Musallam, nicknamed the pope of Gaza, presiding. Having grown up with the Catholic Church, it is interesting to try and follow the familiar mass in Arabic.

Later we visit the Jabalya Rehabilitation Society in Jabalya refugee camp. This school also cares mainly for students who are hearing impaired. We meet with Ahmed Abdullah, the chairman and a former UNRWA school headmaster. Mr. Abdullah was a child in a village now in Israel, just southeast of Ashkelon. In 1948, his entire family was killed by Jewish militias. He somehow escaped to Gaza. He says that he still has love in his heart in spite of all this. So "Why do they hate us?" he asks rhetorically. "We don't hate the US. We just hate Israeli apartheid. You want peace and security? Then give me justice and a stable future as a fellow human being. End the Jewish apartheid state and begin the secular democratic state," he explains further.

We head north and visit a poor family who is also devastated because their three children all suffer from a genetic disease that leaves them with severe cognitive disabilities. Then we head north to *Um Nasser* Village. The children of Um Nasser Village are the descendants of **Bedouweean** [wanderers in Arabic]. They peer into our van with a mixture of curiosity and fear. For the only white people they have seen before have been dressed in Israeli military fatigues and had come to kill them.

Um Nasser village lies beneath a giant cesspool—one that was breached. In March 2007, Um Al Nasser village in northern Gaza was completely flooded with sewage when a six and one-half acre septic cesspool containing 20,000 cubic meters of sewage water collapsed, killing five people and rendering hundreds homeless.

The children of Um Nasser village have the features of all the wanderers that have traveled the Negev desert and wider Middle East: African, Arab, and European; but they are no longer wanderers, because they are trapped. They look distinctly different from other Palestinian brethren. When we get out of the van, the children run away. It is clear that they have been abused by white people. They call me and Lauren **"Yahud"** [Jew]. I have to explain to them that we are **Maseehee** [Christians]. I am not sure these children know the difference.

Um-NASSIR VILLAGE, GAZA - Lauren Booth, talks with a handicaped son of an unemployed Palestinian man Hassan Abu Hashesh

Um Nasser village lies wedged beneath the cesspools to the south, and the Berlin Wall and ominous watchtowers separating it from Ashkelon, Israel to the north.

There used to be Israeli settlements to the east, but now there are sand dunes again.

While I am being interviewed in Um Nasser village by Russian television, I get the call from Dr. El Sarraj:

"I have bad news for you; you will not be able to use the tunnels because the Egyptians will now allow you to exit Rafah on the surface. Sorry to disappoint you," he jokes. This has been an ongoing amusing banter between us ever since I explained my crazy idea to use the tunnels and try to create an international media incident. I was serious about the idea. I don't think Dr. Eyad ever was.

I tell my dear friend, Dr. Eyad, "That it's okay. I am sure I can manage it."

Dr. Jamal Khoudary, the chairman of the Popular Committee Against the Siege calls me a few minutes later and asks me how quickly I can return to Gaza City and be ready to leave through Rafah.

I say an abrupt good-bye to Lauren Booth who is still stuck here. I will be out of Gaza and in Egypt in just two hours. I hop a ride from the Russian news crew and leave all the sadness of Um Nasser village behind.

I get back to Dr. Sarraj's house for some lighting-speed packing and some quick good-byes to Dr. Eyad's family: Nisreen, and two-year old Ali which are tearful and hard. We are not sure why I am being released now, while my colleagues are being left behind. Dr. El Sarraj thinks it has to do with counterpressure from my American Senators and Congresswoman.

Mr. Khoudary is outside to bid me good-bye as I jump into a van. Before I know it, I am heading at normal speeds to Rafah for the last time. We drive right though the Palestinian Gate without stopping. This is real express service. The no man's land is empty because the border is closed to Palestinians. I am taken through the Egyptian gate while I am talking on the phone to a Mr. Stanley Heller, who is an American reporter who calls me from Connecticut serendipitously. As I give him a live description of my departure from Gaza, I enter the Egyptian terminal for the last time. A few minutes later, I am outside on the curb having cleared the entire Rafah border in less than twenty minutes. To get through Rafah, you have to pull the right strings, politically speaking. I am just not sure at this point which strings were pulled by my friends back home on my behalf. A few months later, I read an e-mail response to former Senator Jim Abourezk, which also may have made the difference:

On Mon, Sep 8, 2008 at 4:30 AM, Amr Ramadan wrote:

Dear Senator Abourezk,

Since your call on Thursday and I have been working with Cairo to see how best to help with Dr. Dienst's situation.

As you are aware, he hasn't entered Gaza through a port controlled by Egypt.

Moreover, the Rafah crossing was opened only for "Palestinians" in an attempt to ease the economic situation in Gaza. However, due to the humanitarian purpose of his presence in Gaza, the Egyptian Authorities were able to accommodate his case and allowed him to leave Gaza through the Rafah crossing late yesterday. He should be coordinating his return to the US with the American Embassy in Cairo now. I hope this brings good news to his family and all those concerned with his case.

I wish to thank you for bringing his case to our attention.

Best.
Sincerely,
Amr Ramadan
Charge d'Affaires
Embassy of Egypt to the U.S.
3521 International Court NW,
Washington, DC 20008.

Lauren Booth's Departure from Gaza
September 21, 2008

It was six thirty in the morning and the center of Rafah, in Gaza was heaving. Mohammed my personal security guard and friend, blasted through the traffic of donkey carts and school children. His driving was even more crazed than usual. He was almost as tense as I was. It was the third time we had driven to the Egyptian border each time hoping I would be allowed out of Gaza.

Each of the two previous times, I had been turned back after all-day ordeals, my passage refused at the end of those two days by the Egyptian authorities. My original intention on coming to Gaza by sea had been to stay just under a week and then head home to France. I hadn't considered the vagaries of the Egyptian border authorities. Having a passport plus an oral agreement that you can pass through the crossing had counted for nothing twice before.

This time I was really desperate to get across. I had been stuck in Gaza for more than four weeks. Students who I had been with had managed to escape from Gaza by paying the all-important baksheesh [bribe] to someone on the Egyptian side. Today I had only three hundred dollars in various pockets; would that be enough?

It all started well enough. Within half an hour of entering the airport-style terminal building on the Palestinian side, I had an exit visa stamp on my passport. But then to my horror I was led by Gaza police officers to the same building I had spent thirteen hours in previously.

"Not the room of doom!" I said trying to make light of the situation, even as my heart sank toward my dirt-covered sandals. It had been seven weeks since I had seen my daughters Alexandra and Holly or my husband Craig. Just under a month of that time I had been an increasingly stressed resident of the Gaza strip, unable to leave as Israeli diplomats leaned on Egypt to punish those of us on the siege breaking boats for visiting the region without their permission to do so.

I missed my family so badly I didn't allow myself to think of them for more than a moment. It was an exquisite kind of torture not knowing when I might see them again. I had met several women who hadn't seen their children in the West Bank for more than a year, one poor lady who hadn't seen her parents for fifteen years.

In the room of doom I laid out several chair cushions on the floor and forced myself to sleep. I lay there for nearly three hours before raised Arabic voices turned my blood to ice. "What do you mean they must ALL go back to Gaza NOW?" I looked at my friends and colleagues, a highly respected Sheikh and a young man with bullet injuries both Palestinian and both needing medical treatment in Cairo. Suddenly I was surrounded by armed guards. "You can go. Only you. Leave now now now now!" I turn to my friends to say, "What? Sorry it's like this, why me? No I can't leave them..."

This is how it is at Rafah: divide and conquer, with no time for warmth, handshakes, and kind words. Linger when your "coordination" comes through, and you can miss your chance to go home, see your children, and leave this concentration camp. I am in the terminal building on the Egyptian side of the Rafah crossing. Mothers in burkhas sit on broken suitcases held together with rope. A young girl of about five has arms covered in bandages; I stroke her hair as I am hustled into another office. She doesn't react at all, just stares at her feet. The atmosphere of powerlessness and despair is dizzying. Today I am a VIP it seems. A large man in a sweaty shirt smiles and takes my passport. "Okay?" he asks and I try to force a smile back at him; a grimace is all I can manage. Outside in the main building names are shouted out by officials: Hussan...Ahmad...Dijani. Husbands and fathers who have accidentally pleased distant officials will leave; many will not pass and will never know why.

I ask the fat man behind the desk looking through piles of green Palestinian passports if he speaks English. He does not. "This system is a disgrace," I say to him, in a friendly tone. He looks at me curiously. "You should be ashamed of your part in this. Are you proud to be destroying lives today?" I wave my hands around randomly and chuckle just for good measure. The official shakes his head he doesn't understand. I go to a window in the midst of the human misery and pay for my exit visa. An armed guard in the red beret of the army, waves me toward a corridor that says arrivals.

I step outside into the sunshine. It has taken me three attempts and twenty-nine hours, including more than seven hours on this third try to get through this border, but I am in now in Egypt. I am free to resume my life. My first thought is, "Will I ever see Gaza again?"

Chapter 16:

Farming and Fishing in the Gaza Strip

⌘ ⌘ ⌘

Donna and Darlene Wallach

1. (GAZA) On Monday, 15 September 2008, international human rights volunteers with the International Solidarity Movement and Free Gaza movement joined the Palestinian Union of Agricultural Work Committees (UAWC) in symbolically planting trees in the buffer zone in *Fukharee,* east of Khan Younis and north of Rafah.

The buffer zone was established by the IOF on one of Gaza's prime agricultural areas. The zone is a no-go area roughly 300-500 meters wide along the entire eastern border of the Gaza Strip. In this buffer zone, farmers are violently prohibited from farming their land, and these areas have become very dangerous for the Palestinians to live and farm in.

The Israeli buffer zone is another form of siege that denies the Palestinians the right to livelihood, feeding their families, freedom of movement, and to live in peace. This is all happening during the so-called ceasefire.

ISM volunteers met at UAWC office in Khan Younis before joining with a few hundred activists. Two buses and four cars transported all the volunteers, the trees, and the shovels to *Fukharee,* close to the border with Israel. Upon arriving some people noticed the tell-tale dust of an Israeli tank as it appeared from behind some trees off in the distance.

All the volunteers got off the buses and started walking toward the fields holding three banners and chanting "Free, Free Palestine" in Arabic. Various news agencies and independent video cameras recorded the event.

We dug holes and managed to plant about 100 olive, guava, and citrus trees. Although the ISM volunteers were there to both join Palestinians as they reclaimed their land and demand that Israel stop destroying the crops in the area, the action was primarily symbolic. The UAWC plans to continue doing various similar actions throughout the Gaza Strip in and near the buffer zones.

--Donna Wallach, international human rights monitor, writing from Occupied Gaza

Fishing boat in Gaza City marina

2. (GAZA) On Wednesday 17 September 2008, I (along with two other international volunteers) went out with three different fishing boats from the Gaza City port to trawl for fish. We left the port at about 8:30 A.M.

For more details and videos about farming in Gaza, see: http://farmingunderfire.blogspot.com/

I was on a boat with fishermen I already knew. We went out about seven and a half miles, put out the net, and began to trawl. It wasn't long before an Israeli Navy gunboat approached, and circled around. The fishermen requested from me to speak with the Israeli Navy. I did make contact with them, telling them, "We are Palestinian fishermen fishing in the waters off Gaza. Palestinians have the right to fish in Gazan waters. They have the right to a livelihood and to feed their families."

Someone on the Israeli Navy gunboat said in Hebrew that it was forbidden for the Palestinian fishermen to be out past six miles. I replied that according to International Law, the Palestinian fishermen had the right to fish beyond twelve miles in their territorial waters. His response was to call me "bitch." Soon after that the gunboat opened fire on the fishing boat, aiming, what appeared toward the center of the boat. The fishermen quickly pulled in their nets, not wanting their boat or any of the equipment to be damaged by the gunfire.

We headed back toward the Gaza coast until we reached about six miles out and began trawling again. The gunboat came by again and circled around menacingly. Off in the distance we saw the large Israeli Navy gunboat that has the water cannon stationed at the fore of the boat. We were expecting to get drenched but were pleasantly surprised when it continued past us without stopping or even aiming the water cannon at us.

The Israeli Navy contacted the boat via VHF, again reiterating that it was forbidden for them to fish out beyond six miles. This is an abomination! The large quantities of fish are out beyond the six-mile limit, as are the larger fish. The fishermen need to be able to fish in their territorial waters, when and where they want.

It is an outrage that Israeli Navy gunboats patrol the territorial Gazan waters at will. They harass, threaten, shoot, damage, and terrorize the Palestinian fishermen, their boats, and fishing equipment. The Israeli Navy often limits the Palestinian fishermen from fishing beyond three or four miles, and sometimes they aren't permitted to fish at all.

This would not be tolerated any place else in the world.

Fishing is one of the few sources of Palestinian food left in Gaza. The IOF has destroyed much of the farmland and established an illegal buffer zone on much of the agricultural farmland within Gaza, denying Palestinian farmers their livelihood and the right to feed their families. This has made 80 percent of the Palestinians living in Gaza Strip totally dependent on food aid from the UN.

It is time that these collective punishments upon the entire population of Gaza Strip end. The Palestinian people have the human right to live in freedom. Parents have the human right to provide for their children. Children have the human right to go to school and students have the human right to attend university. Farmers have the right to farm their land and fishermen have the right to fish in their own territorial waters. This siege must end.

Please, be creative; put pressure on the apartheid state of Israel to end the siege now. Tell your families, your friends, and your coworkers that this situation can no longer be tolerated. Ban the Israeli Navy from the territorial waters of Gaza!

Donna Wallach, international human rights monitor, writing from Occupied Gaza

3. Gaza City, Palestine. On Thursday 18th September 2008, at least seven Palestinian fishing boats left Gaza City port to fish in Gazan territorial waters. Today the Israeli navy boat with the water cannon was not seen, so there was no damage to any fishing boats and nobody was injured from high-powered water spray. However, the Israeli soldiers on two Israeli Navy gunboats that were patrolling were exceptionally aggressive and arrogant. One of the gunboats sailed by all of the fishing boats and fired at them, going from boat to boat.

Israeli soldiers on a second gunboat were harassing the fishermen, yelling out to them in Hebrew and in Arabic that it was prohibited for them to fish past six miles. The soldiers on the gunboat were informed that according to International Law, the Palestinian fishermen have the right to fish at least twelve miles out. Their response was laughter. Later on in the afternoon, this same gunboat was positioned in a very threatening way in the water close to one of the Palestinian fishing boats. One of the soldiers was yelling at the captain of the boat in a derogatory tone of voice and using condescending language telling him to stop fishing and to go back to Gaza. Almost the entire day the Israeli Navy gunboats harassed the fishermen, either shooting at them or threatening to.

Every day and night Palestinian fisherman try to fish, and every day the Israeli Navy does what it can to prevent them from feeding their families and making a living. The eyes of the world need to watch what is happening. The people of the world need to put an end to this constant harassment and attack on Palestinians trying to earn a living and to feed their families. Palestinian fishermen have the right to fish in their own waters.

4. Gaza City, Gaza Strip, Palestine, 19 September 2008. On the morning of the 19th day of Ramadan, about five Palestinian fishing boats left Gaza City port for another day of trawling off the coast of Gaza Strip. It was a very clear day, and I could easily see the coast the entire day.

When the boat I was on reached seven miles out, an Israeli Navy gunboat speedily approached and fired at the fishing boat. One of the soldiers called for the captain of the boat and yelled at him to stop. Continuing in a derogatory tone of voice, the

Israeli soldier told the captain to only sail up and down the coast and not to go farther out into the sea. The captain told the soldier that he needed to go out ten miles to trawl for fish. I also spoke to the gunboat and reiterated that the fishermen needed to go out ten miles. This time the gunboat did not continue to fire upon this boat. I think in the end we only went out to eight miles. For the remainder of the day we were able to trawl for fish in relative peace.

However, just after the sun went down, after the meal for breaking the fast for the day, an Israeli Navy gunboat fired upon another Palestinian fishing boat, and we heard over the VHF radio an international tell the Israeli Navy "We are Palestinian fishermen fishing in Palestinian waters. Stop shooting!"

In the evening, the captain of the boat told me that it costs him $1,000 a day of diesel fuel to power his fishing boat. Considering that the catch for the day was small, as it often is for the Palestinian fishermen up and down the coast, it is hard to understand how they succeed to make a living. In addition to the exceptionally high cost of fuel, there are either no spare parts for broken, damaged, or lost equipment, or the cost of the spare parts are ten times the normal cost. The Israeli siege continues to impact every aspect of Palestinian life. The siege must end, now!

5. Gaza, 20 September 2008. Members of ISM in the Gaza Strip accompanied Palestinian fishermen from the port of Gaza. When they were approximately four nautical miles offshore, an Israeli gunboat approached the fishing vessel was approached and proceeded to circle it continuously for a while. Shortly after the gunboat withdrew, a larger naval vessel approached from the northeast. It began to spray the fishing boat with high-pressure water from a cannon mounted on its bow. Fortunately no one was injured during the attack, and no damage was done to the boat, largely because the fishermen had taken measures to protect it such as boarding up the windows. The same boat suffered a similar assault again later in the day. A second fishing vessel in the vicinity was observed also being attacked by water cannon. In the afternoon, an Israeli gunboat closed in on the fishing boat carrying ISM members and fired live ammunition in very close proximity to the boat.

Report by Darlene Wallach, ISM and FG volunteer

6. Gaza City, Gaza Strip, Palestine, 21 September 2008. About five fishing boats trawled the coast from the Gaza City port. I was on a boat that had been hit by water cannon the previous day, and many of the nets had been damaged as a result.

The crew spent most of the morning repairing the nets and at 11:40 A.M., we finally left the port for a full day of trawling.

At 12:30 P.M. in the distance we saw two Israeli Navy gunboats; one was very large and was equipped with the water cannon. The regular sized gunboat started patrolling between three fishing boats that were in the same area. At 12:55 P.M. that gunboat started harassing and shooting at one of the fishing boats. I don't know how far it was offshore, but it definitely wasn't beyond six miles. At 1:10 P.M. that same gunboat shot at the boat I was on and a soldier yelled, "Go south."

After some time passed and the gunboat was no longer in the area, the captain of our boat steered toward the north. There are larger fish in the northern Gazan waters, and apparently very tasty, and the fishermen REALLY wanted to catch as many of those fish as they could this day.

As we continued sailing northeast, we saw the gunboat with the water cannon pass in the distance. At 1:40 P.M. we saw another regular sized Israeli Navy gunboat approaching. It moved alongside in a threatening move as if to say: don't go out any further into the sea! Ten minutes later the water cannon gunboat arrived and dowsed our boat and most of the crew with high-powered blasts of water. One crewmember, Ahmed, fell on the slippery deck and hurt his knee.

For some unknown reason the gunboat only water cannoned us once for a brief time, causing no damage to the boat or the nets. I do not know what impact the water cannon has on the fish; much of the highpowered blasts of water hit the sea and often times the net, too. In any case, as in previous occasions, the smaller gunboat positioned itself on the opposite side of our boat from the water cannon gunboat, ready to shoot and posing a threat, besides blocking us in from escape from the deluge of high-powered water. In addition, there were strong waves from the movement of the larger gunboat making our boat rock from side to side and increasing the danger from the blasting water and wet, slippery deck.

Later, around 3:10, another Israeli Navy gunboat approached very quickly and forced us away from our position in the north of the Gazan territorial fishing waters. Soldiers were shouting to go south, among other things. The gunboat continued to circle our boat in very close proximity and was threatening to shoot. As we changed course and headed south, the gunboat proceeded to circle the boat for a while, and then left.

After the gunboat had been gone for a while, the captain of our boat changed course again and returned to the north, heading closer to shore, the goal of catching that specific fish had not been abandoned. At 4:00 *P.M.* an Israeli Navy gunboat quickly approached, as it drew nearer I spoke on the VHF informing the navy, "We are Palestinian fishermen, we are pulling in our net of fish. We have the right to be here. These are internationally recognized Gazan fishing waters. Over." I repeated this a number of times.

Finally a soldier on the gunboat arrogantly replied: "You don't have the right to be here. Take your fish and go south." We continued to pull in the net and headed south and out to sea. Only two nets full of fish and neither of them were big catches; however, they did succeed to catch a number of boxes worth of the type of fish they wanted, and for that, they were happy.

The fishing boat headed into port after the sunset, and after eating the evening meal breaking the Ramadan fast for the day, they dropped me off, thanked me for my support, and headed back out to sea for an entire night of fishing. They had been fishing for two days and nights already.

Vittorio Arrigoni: We Will Keep On Going Offshore Fishing
October 5, 2008

I went to Al-Awda hospital to have my stitches taken out. A fairly good scar now marks my skin for life (courtesy of Israel), the pattern like the teeth of a voracious mechanical shark that infests this sea, hunting his besieged victims, Palestinian fishermen.

How much innocent blood will spill in the Gazan Sea? In these days of rough weather, I'm waiting for the sea to calm its anger and to allow us to go offshore again, to claim the violated right to live—or at least survive with these people who are rightfully off shore harvesting their country's sea.

There are many reasons why we go out fishing with Palestinian fishermen; some of them are concrete, some others are more symbolic but no less essential.

One fishing day with us on board, according to the fishermen, is equivalent to one week of ordinary work offshore. Without internationals, they don't dare sail more than few miles from the port, where usually fishing is very poor. If they try to go further they risk death or if they're lucky, "just" injury. It's worth remembering that before the siege was imposed by Israel, there were more than 3,500 fishermen working along the forty kilometers of the Gazan coasts; today just 700 of them are still trying to survive in a field which was used to be able to provide jobs for at least 40,000 people, if you consider mechanics, fishmongers, etc., as well as thousands of local fishermen that now are surviving with enormous difficulty.

The day after one of our fishing actions, the fish are sold at the market at a knockdown price. When the volume of fish is bigger, prices go down, and more mouths will eat. The owners of some of the fishing boats, before we arrived, had the serious intention of selling them because of the very high price of the fuel and the absence of a reliable future income. Since we arrived they've told us many times how our support, in addition to helping increase their incomes, has also acted as an injection of hope at a hopeless time.

In addition to the clearly visible achievements obtained with our fishing actions, there are some others more symbolic but equally edifying. With Free Gaza and Liberty we opened the Gaza port. With the rudimentary Palestinian fishing boats, we try every day to open the sea, aware of the fact that this is not important only for the fishermen, but for all the Palestinians. This is the reason why we work with them as they attempt to claim their right to live a life free from confinement, from the siege and from the Israeli crimes against humanity.

If the Israeli army believes they put me out of action by wounding me I just want to make a statement for them: you're deluding yourselves.

I, Vittorio Arrigoni, with Darlene, Donna, and others fellow travelers committed in this mission for the protection of human rights. We will never retreat from facing these abuses of justice, legality, and freedom. You will have to kill all of us and accept this responsibility in front of the world and before God, who both in the Torah and in the Koran doesn't justify in any way the cold-blooded murder of innocent people.

I would like to talk with the Israeli soldiers who attack us every day (the day I was wounded I could see them well enough to see the whites of their eyes). I would like to ask them if they really believe that they are defending Israel when they shoot at unarmed civilians, internationals or Palestinians, while we are simply fishing on Palestinian vessels.

As a pacifist I don't wish it in any way, but I would really not be surprised if one day, one of these young Palestinian fishermen, from whom Israel steals the hope of a worthwhile life, who has accumulated grief upon grief for fathers, friends, and brothers killed, wounded or buried for years in an inhuman Israeli prison - chooses to leave the fishing nets and shoulder a Kalashnikov.

Because this is what Israel is teaching the young Palestinians, with its warships, raids, the military occupation of borders, imposing the siege as a collective punishment and denying all human rights. In this way, by teaching hate to its innocent victims, Israel becomes responsible for the risk all Israeli people face, from Ashkelon to Tel Aviv.

We will keep on going offshore fishing, not scared by the threats made against us by the Israeli navy, until politics, high-class activism and the politically committed civil society cease to turn their back on the "moral issue of our times" as Nelson Mandela defines the Palestinian issue.

We want to show to the Palestinians who adopted us, that in this world a minority group of men and women are still awake, ready to challenge the conspiracy of silence and those who face this tragedy with indifference.

I believe that, everywhere on the planet, there are still many human beings immune to the virus of indifference and selfishness, and this is the reason why I'm making a plea: don't leave us to do this alone, don't turn your back on your brothers and sisters burdened by terrible injustice.

Come here to help us or support us in other ways.
Even from a distance be near us.
Stay human.

Vittorio Arrigoni

Chapter 17

Kidnapped in Gaza Waters

⌘ ⌘ ⌘

Vittorio Arrigoni
December 6, 2008

Last Tuesday the sea was a placid, liquid blanket, unruffled and as smooth as oil when Darlene, Andrew, and I, human rights activists with the ISM sailed from the port of Gaza on three Palestinian fishing boats. The warm sun, clear blue sky, and complete absence of wind had led us to expect a plentiful day's catch for our fishermen friends.

(http://www.palsolidarity.org/)

Around 11:00 A.M. we were intercepted and circled by eight Israeli military boats opening fire against the fishing boats, obstructing our way, after which they proceeded to kidnap us three internationals and fifteen Palestinian fishermen. They abducted us and stole the boats.

We were about six miles from the coast of Gaza, which according to international law, is unequivocally in Palestinian waters, since the Oslo Treaty gives the Palestinians sovereignty up to twenty miles from the coast of the strip; that means ours wasn't an arrest but a full-blown abduction, with the fishing boats stolen rather than confiscated. It was a veritable terrorist blitz: Israeli Navy Special Forces, commandos, balaklava-wearing, armed to the teeth, all to stop just three small wooden boats that could barely stay afloat.

I tried to ask the highest-ranking Israeli officer whether they were planning to kill me. I could see more than ten pistols, guns and cannon barrels pointing at me, following my every move. Before the Israeli soldiers boarded the fishing boat, I asked him and the other soldiers what kind of obsessive fear Israel nurtured that a bunch of simple Palestinian fishermen within their own sea zone, trying to catch just enough fish to feed their families could incite such a reaction? The Israeli officer, so iron-willed and authoritarian when barking orders in Hebrew at his soldiers and in English (with a distinctly Australian accent) at me, had nothing to say in reply to my simple query. These soldiers, all muscles and stony coldness, are trained to kill a man in less than a second (or less when he's Palestinian), without even batting an eyelid. But it's obvious they're unable to willingly grasp the meaning of simple terms such as "right to exist" and "right of sustenance."

Since we were far from Israeli borders, I told the Israeli officer I didn't recognize his authority or his right to kidnap me, and my friends, the fishermen. I, therefore, decided I would present passive resistence. I climbed onto the cabin roof, and then onto the iron structure used as a jib to lift the fishing nets, at the boat's stern. Three soldiers followed me, pointing guns in my face. Their eyes behind the black balaklavas seemed to me like the best representation of hatred that I had ever seen; a hatred taught in years of lessons learnt by heart, on how to best defeat an enemy, even when that enemy doesn't exist.

Not in the least bit intimidated, I asked them whether they intended to kill me, and if so to go ahead and finish off their job then and there. Go ahead and kill a civilian, a disarmed Italian on a Palestinian fishing boat, fishing with his Palestinian friends in Palestinian waters. A fourth soldier came forward, and I recognized the weapon he was holding—a taser gun. I told him the truth, that I have a heart condition. His weapon could have given me a cardiac arrest. The soldier got closer, the officer gave him the order, and I turned my back on both of them, so as not too feel too much compassion for them. The soldier shot me in the back, an electric shock that knocked me right out. Then all four soldiers tried to push me down the three-meter leap, down onto the stern's steel floor that could have caused several broken bones. I lunged forward and leapt into the sea, swimming slowly with what strength I had left. I swam toward the shore on the horizon, toward Gaza, toward my home. Indifferent to the intimidating bullets hitting the water a few centimeters from my head, I swam for a good half hour, followed at a short distance by the eight warships. But when my teeth started to chatter uncontrollably, and the palms of my hands turned blue, I had to give in and let the soldiers pull me out of the water, beating me up as they did so. I narrowly missed getting hypothermia.

When we got to the port of Ashkelon, Darlene, Andrew, and I were marched out of the Israeli warship and were met by a scenario reminiscent of the Holocaust. It was something that reminded me of *Schindler's List*, or the horror-imbued prose of Primo Levi. All the fishermen were made to kneel, stark naked, chained at the ankles and handcuffed with their arms behind their backs, and blindfolded. These were the conditions they had been made to travel in, on an open deck for fifty nautical kilometers. Why? For what reason on earth does Israel, through its army and government, soil its reputation with such crimes against the civilians of Gaza on a daily basis? Why does it impose these collective punishments? Preventing harmless fishermen from catching fish a few miles from the coast, in their own water zone, and more generally starving Gaza's population held captive in its siege, certainly doesn't favor the peace process nor will it give Israel more security. The exact opposite is true.

We three internationals were lead into a prison at Ben Gurion, followed by another one in Ramle, where we immediately went on a hunger strike to ask for the immediate release of the Palestinian fishermen, which eventually took place. I was held for six days in that Israeli jail in terrible conditions, in filthy and claustrophobic cells, crawling with insects and parasites that feasted on my skin. But coming from Gaza, I was used to being held under chains. Through Israel's will, Gaza is the biggest open-air prison in the world. All the industries have had to close down, over 80 percent of the population survives under the poverty line, and the highest rates of unemployment in the world are recorded in Gaza, where there's no electricity or fuel. Hospitals need medicine, and the vast majority of the population needs food and the bare essentials. The Israelis only hauled me from one open-air prison to an enclosed prison, where at least, unlike in Gaza, they regularly serve rations; and both electricity and drinking water are available almost daily.

But I was denied the most basic of human rights, such as the right to contact my attorney or consulate. Furthermore, I am keen to speak out against the prison of Ramle, twenty kilometers from Tel Aviv, where hundreds of African refugees, mostly Ethiopian, Eritrean, and Sudanese, are virtually buried alive. They have perfectly valid UN visa passes; in any civilized country they would have been assigned accommodation and the bare essentials to survive. They're fleeing from war—they're no terrorists. But once again, when it comes to human rights and more generally to international law; Israel has demonstrated that they speak just a bunch of hollow words outside their borders, as well as within them. I'll do everything in my power to let the inhuman conditions of my inmates be known. I promised them I would.

In the end, Andrew, Darlene, and I were deported. We didn't appeal to an Israeli court so as not to legitimize our arrest, which is considered a kidnapping under international law.

Our lawyers will battle it out to have the fishing boats returned. Besides the financial loss suffered by the boats' owners, what's really aggravating us is the thought of fifty unemployed fishermen, and about thirty Palestinian families without a means of sustenance for the last week.

Those boats stolen by Israel are a symbol of the siege under which Gaza is forcibly held, the illegality bordering on terrorism with which the Israeli Army operates outside its territory.

Personally, I, Vittorio Arrigoni, declare that I'm a lion. The more I get flogged, the more they jail me, the steelier my will to fight for human rights becomes. It was no laughing matter for Gandhi and his companions to shake off the British occupation, nor for Mandela to defeat the apartheid that reigned supreme in South Africa. Neither the wounds inflicted on me in these months in Gaza nor has my last confinement sufficed to make me take a single step back on the path toward the nonviolent civic struggle I undertook. It's a moral matter that spells freedom for the Palestinians, and simultaneously peace and security for the Israelis.

Stay human.

Vittorio Arrigoni, ISM and Free Gaza activist.

Chapter 18:

Stealing Gaza's Gas

⌘ ⌘ ⌘

David Shermerhorn

by David K. Schermerhorn
April 19, 2009

There is an historical connection between the Gazan community and offshore fishery. In recent times, some 3,000 fishermen in over 700 boats made their livelihood in the waters off the shores of Gaza. Before 1978 when the fishing area included the sea off the Sinai coastline the area covered some 75,000 square kilometers. The larger boats are about twenty meters in length and usually carry a crew of seven. They are typically trawlers using downriggers to lower their nets to the ocean bed. Currently their main catch is bream or sardines that average between eight and fourteen inches. Smaller craft, *hassakas,* normally deploy their nets a few hundred meters off shore. The nets are then hauled in by hand. These catches are very modest.

On September 13, 1993 the Oslo Agreement was signed marking the basis for a peaceful accord between Israel and the Palestinians. The 1994 GAZA-JERICHO AGREEMENT outlined specific steps needed to realize the general provisions of the Oslo Agreement.

Under its terms the Gazan fishermen were free to use a marine corridor extending twenty nautical miles from the Gaza shore bounded by restricted, or border, zones to the north and south abutting Israeli and Egyptian waters.

However, beginning in late 2000, the Israeli military initiated a continuing campaign of intimidation and harassment against fishing boats that ventured near or beyond a six nautical mile limit. (1) Their patrol boats attacked and harassed the fishermen on a daily basis. To date the Israelis have killed fifteen and wounded over 200 fishermen.

Among the warships used were ones in the Dabur and Dvora classes. Their armaments include twenty mm to thirty mm cannon, machine guns, automatic grenade launchers, plus high-pressure water cannons. Some have 700-mile ranges and top speeds of fifty-two knots. Originally they were built in the US but, in recent years, they are constructed by Israel Aircraft at a plant in the Negev.

No formal notice or explanation of restrictions was ever given to the Palestinians. Instead any regulations have been written and enforced by Israeli machine guns and water cannons. Since the Operation Cast Lead "ceasefire" their attacks have become more aggressive, often occurring within a few hundred yards of the shore. Even the people of Gaza, walking on their beaches have been wounded by gunfire intended for the fishing boats. The fishermen continue to be killed, wounded, or arrested. Their boats continue to be targeted or impounded. The noose of the siege grows tighter.

Israeli Attack on Gazan Fishing Boats…WHY? A TIMELINE

For the first fifty years after Israel's founding, the country explored extensively for natural gas or oil deposits with little success. Approximately 400 onshore and twenty-five offshore mainly exploratory wells were dug during that period. Israel was obliged to import 85 percent of its energy needs by buying coal and petroleum products from Egypt, Russia, Mexico and elsewhere.

- September 13, 1993 – The Oslo Agreement was signed laying the basis for peaceful relations between Israel and the Palestinians.

-May 4, 1994: PLO Chairman Yasser Arafat and Israeli Prime Minister Yitzhak Rabin signed the Gaza-Jericho Agreement as part of the subsequent procedures called for in the Oslo Agreement.

Article XI established three maritime activity zones that extended twenty nautical miles out to sea from the coast of Gaza. (2) Two narrow zones running parallel to the boundaries of Egyptian and Israeli waters were designated no fishing areas. Under the terms of the agreement the larger remaining zone "will be open for fishing, recreation, and economic activities." For the next six years the Gazan fishermen operated freely within the zone with no major confrontations by the Israelis.

In addition the UN Convention on the Law of the Sea, part V, describes an Exclusive Economic Zone (EEZ) that would grant Gaza control of all seabed assets up to 200 nautical miles from its shore. (3) There is speculation that vast deposits of natural gas are located beyond the twenty-mile maritime activity zone. Such a resource would give Gaza the potential of becoming another Dubai in a relatively short period if they were allowed to develop their own deposits. (4)

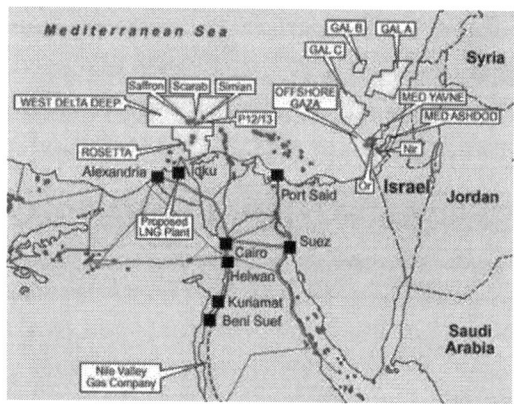

Eastern Mediterranean Gas Fields off the coasts of Egypt, Gaza and Israel (From Israeli Invasion and Gaza's Offshore Gas Fields by Michel Chossudovsky: 9 January2009, Pacific Free Press

An interview regarding Maritime Activity Zone and EEZ:

-1999 -The British Gas Group (BG Group) discovered a vast deposit of natural gas within Gaza's Maritime Activity Zone: Over 1.3 trillion cubic feet equal to 150 million barrels of oil were estimated to be there. Located about fifteen miles off the coast, the deposits were named Gaza Marine one and two. It was estimated that there were sufficient reserves to generate electric power for all Palestinian needs for a decade and still have a surplus to export. (5)

- On November 8, 1999, Chairman Yasser Arafat signed an agreement giving BG Group 90 percent interest and 10 percent to Consolidated Contractors Company, an Athens-based Palestinian entity connected to the PLO. They and the Palestinian Investment Fund (PIF) had the option to later assume up to 40 percent interest. A final allocation of the rights continues to be contested between BG Group, Israel, Egypt, and the Palestinians in obscured ongoing negotiations.

- July 25, 2000: Yasser Arafat walked out on the Camp David meeting. (6)

-September 27, 2000: Yasser Arafat traveled nineteen miles off the Gaza coast to light the first flare stack flowing up from the natural gas deposit. An Israeli oil consortium had contested the Palestinian rights to the gas but this suit was overturned in an Israeli court. Original estimates for development and production expenses were in the area of two billion dollars. Profits were estimated at another two billion dollars.

In the initial stages BG considered running an underwater pipeline twenty nautical miles from Gaza Marine directly to Gaza where it would be used in retrofitted generators to provide power. Excess gas would be piped to the West Bank or converted to liquid natural gas (LNG) for export to foreign buyers. (7)

This plan was abandoned when Ariel Sharon announced that the Israelis would never buy the gas directly from the Palestinians. At that point the BG Group negotiated with Egypt to run an undersea pipeline to a plant at El-Arish, Egypt. The gas would then be piped to Israel so that they would not have to deal directly with the Palestinians.

Under pressure from Tony Blair, BG Group was forced to negotiate with the Israelis instead who wanted the pipe to run directly to Ashqelon. Those discussions were so long and contentious that ultimately the BG Group closed their Israel office and again began dealing with Egypt. (8)

- September 28, 2000: Ariel Sharon visited the Temple Mount despite warnings by Arafat and other leading Palestinians. The predictable riots and deaths following this provocation marked the beginning of the second Intifada. As a result, Sharon was elected prime minister in February 2001. (9) He reaffirmed that Israel would never buy gas from the Palestinians. After the outbreak of the second Intifada, the Israelis began an ever-tightening blockade of Gaza with fewer and fewer trucks and no foreign boats allowed to enter.

- Late 2000: Attacks by Israeli patrol boats against Gazan fishing boats began and have continued to this day. These attacks started only after the discovery of the natural gas deposits and five years before Hamas freely won the legislative elections on January 25, 2006. (10) It is apparent that these assaults on the fishermen had nothing to do with security or with Hamas. Instead it had everything to do with Israel controlling a four billion dollar resource belonging to the Palestinians.

-In the late 1990s Noble Energy, based in Houston, TX, began explorations for natural gas off the Israeli coast in conjunction with Israeli partners Avner Oil and Delek Drilling.

March, 2000: Nobel Energy announced the discovery of the Mari-B natural gas deposit located approximately fifteen miles off shore and close to the Gaza marine zones. Initial estimates projected reserves exceeding 1 trillion cubic feet of natural gas. In 2003 a platform was completed and gas began flowing through a pipeline to Ashqelon. Until 2009 the Mari-B reserve remained the only sizable reserve found in Israeli territory. Although it was a significant deposit it did not approach meeting Israel's energy needs and was a finite resource.

While there is no hard evidence supporting speculation at this time it appears quite possible for the Israelis to access the gas deposits located in Gaza marine from the Mari-B platform. Slant drilling techniques now allow bits to reach up to 25,000 feet horizontally from a standing platform. Iraq accused Kuwait of stealing its oil using such a technique before the first Gulf War. (11)

October, 2001 – Following the 9/11 attacks the US State Department included both Hamas and Hezbollah on their terrorist list.

August, 2002: In response to a request from Prime Minister Sharon, the secretary-general of the United Nations appointed Ms. Catherine Bertini as his personal humanitarian envoy to assess the humanitarian needs of the Palestinians. At the end of her visit to the area, she made numerous recommendations including one that dealt with the fishing boats. In her report, she included a list of "Previous Commitments Made by Israel."

Item two states: "The fishing zone for Palestinian fishing boats off the Gaza coast is twelve nautical miles. This policy needs to be fully implemented." (12) But it never was.

Despite Bertini's recommendations, Israeli attacks became more frequent on fishing boats that passed a six-mile limit. Most boats carried a GPS, so they can determine their exact positions. Some captains were intimidated by the Israeli threats and turned back before crossing the no-go line. Others continued to go farther out despite the increased danger of attack. The fishery closer to shore has collapsed after so many boats were forced to operate in such a limited area. In addition the waters near shore are polluted due to sewage pouring in from broken pipes. This is one more example of an infrastructure crippled by the Israelis. (13) Before the siege, Gaza's fishermen caught 3,000 tons of fish each year. Now it is less than 500 tons.

The most productive fishing months for the Gazans are in the winter and spring. At that time an annual migration of fish traveling from the Nile Delta to Turkish waters pass through the zone ten miles and further from shore. The incentive to go beyond the six-mile limit is very strong.

In addition to firing cannons and machine guns at or near the fishing boats the Israelis periodically introduce noxious chemical substances into the water fired from their boats that leaves a foul odor on any fish or crewmen on deck. It is probable that the chemicals are the same used by the Israelis in crowd control on land. Under the Chemical Weapons Convention of 1997 it is specified "Each state party undertakes not to use riot control agents as a method of warfare." (14)

On occasion, the patrol boats have purposely rammed into fishing boats, damaging the vesselss and endangering the crew. Numerous times the Israelis have forced fishermen to jump into the water and remain there for up to three hours until they are exhausted and close to hypothermia.

Periodically, the Israelis impound fishing boats and take them and their crews to Ashdod, Israel or some other port. The crewmen are generally released after being photographed and interrogated. The boats are held for indefinite periods. Captured fishermen report that the Israelis pressure them to become informers in exchange for the freedom to fish. (15)

9/12/05 – Israel announced that it had ended the occupation of Gaza and withdrew its forces. But it continued to maintain control of air and sea lanes as well as all border crossings on land. The amount of vehicular traffic remained extremely limited and never approached a typical pre-occupation daily level. The ability for persons to enter or leave Gaza continued to be restricted. Permission or denial for passage was often arbitrary and unpredictable. The conditions of an occupation continue to prevail.

1/25/06 – Hamas won seventy-six of one hundred and thirty-two seats in the Palestinian Legislative Council in an open honest election. After a bloody battle with Fatah elements that were supported by both Israeli and US interests, Hamas took control of Gaza. Israel and the United States immediately reiterated that Hamas was a terrorist organization and that they would continue to have no public contact with it. The restrictions at the border crossings were tightened further with even more severe limitations on the admission of produce, materials, medicines, and people. Anemia and malnutrition are widespread as a result.

Early June 2008 – Israeli Defense Minister Ehud Barak instructed the Israel defense forces to secretly prepare for an invasion of Gaza, later known as Operation Cast Lead. (16)

June, 2008 –Israel contacted BG Group to propose renewing negotiations over the natural gas deposits. Actual negotiations overseen by Ehud Olmert were taking place in October 2008. It appears that Israel wished to reach an agreement with BG Group before the secretly planned invasion began. (17)

6/19/08 – Hamas and Israel signed a six-month truce agreement calling for cessation of rocket firings by Hamas and military incursions by Israel. In May 2008, over 300 rockets had been fired. Hamas was lead to believe that significant increase in shipments would be allowed to enter Gaza. Before the truce, roughly seventy trucks were allowed to bring provisions into Gaza each day compared with some 900 permitted before the Israeli clamp down in 2000. Hamas was led to believe that a similar flow of traffic would be restored. Instead Israel allowed only an increase from the seventy to ninety trucks. (18)

8/23/08 – Two boats, the *Liberty and Free Gaza* sailed into Gaza Harbor from Cyprus carrying forty-four international supporters of the Palestinians. They were the first vessels to break the Israeli siege in forty-one years. The venture had been organized by the Free Gaza movement (freegaza.org).

I was aboard the ship Free Gaza and again on two other trips to Gaza aboard the *Dignity* that was later rammed and badly damaged by an Israeli warship.

10/31 & 11/9/08 – I joined other international observers traveling aboard three separate Gazan fishing boats. We went to document events and locations and to hopefully serve as deterrents against attacks by Israeli gunboats. On both days we were harassed by machine gun and cannon fire and explosive charges landing within a few feet of our boat. Several times each day the largest of the three Israeli patrol boats came within fifty feet of our vessel as they bombarded the deck and cabin with a high pressure water cannon. Any fish, loose equipment, or crewmen caught in the torrent were at risk of being washed over the side. All the cabin windows had been previously smashed by such assaults and were now quickly boarded up when the patrol boats approached. An Italian observer with us had been wounded previously by flying glass, requiring a number of stitches in his back

According to the crew, attacks of this sort occurred every day when a fishing boat approached or passed the six-mile limit imposed by the Israelis. This pattern of attack began in 2000 after the natural gas discovery was made.

11/18/08 – Israeli naval vessels attacked three Palestinian fishing boats located seven miles off the coast of Deir Al Balah, clearly within the limits permitted in the 1994 Gaza-Jericho Agreement. Fifteen Palestinian fishermen and three international observers were kidnapped and taken with the boats to Israel. The fishermen were held for a day and then released. The boats were eventually returned but damaged. The internationals were jailed in Israel for many days and then deported.

11/5/08 – IOF forces killed six Palestinians while supposedly searching for a tunnel passing under the border. By continuing to enforce the siege the Israelis had never honored the conditions of the truce. But this incursion by the IOF was such a blatant violation that it effectively terminated even the semblance of a truce.

According to the Israeli Intelligence Heritage Center one rocket had been fired from Gaza in September and two were fired in October before the IOF incursion. Israeli spokesman Mark Regev conceded that Hamas had not fired these few rockets.

During the next five weeks 237 rockets were fired into Israel. (19) The provoked increase in rocket fire was Israel's public justification for launching the long planned Operation Cast Lead despite offers by Hamas to renew the ceasefire. (20)

11/18/08 – An Egyptian court ordered the government to stop shipping natural gas to Israel. Under a 2005 agreement, Egypt agreed to deliver 1.7 billion cubic meters of gas to Israel over a fifteen-year period. The gas had begun to flow in May 2008. A lawsuit followed seeking to bar delivery since the Parliament had not given its approval. The court supported the lawsuit and its findings are being appealed. (21) The potential cutoff of the gas from Egypt gave Israel even more incentive to take control of the Gaza marine deposits and to deny any benefits to Palestinians, whether Hamas or Fatah.

12/27/08 – Israel began bombing Gaza as phase one of Operation Cast Lead. The Gaza harbor was bombed during the hostilities, damaging a number of the fishing boats.

1/18/2009 – Israel declared a ceasefire, ending Operation Cast Lead.

1/24/2009 – A father and his daughter walking on a Gaza beach were wounded by gunfire from Israeli ships shooting at Gazan fishing boats.

2/14/2009 Gazan Coast Becoming A No-Go Zone

On Saturday, 14 February 2009, twenty-three-year-old Rafiq abu Reala was shot by Israeli naval forces while fishing in Gazan territorial waters, approximately two nautical miles out from the port of Gaza city. He was in a simple fishing vessel, not much larger than a rowing boat, with a small outboard engine, known locally as a *hassaka*. Rafiq, his brother Rajab and another friend were following the course of a shoal of fish. A group of five more *hassakas* were out at the time, about a kilometer to the west of Rafiq's boat, further out to sea. An Israeli naval gunboat approached the area and began shooting at the other *hassakas*, which quickly changed course and headed east, back toward shore.

Suddenly Rafiq realized the gunboat was bearing down on their *hassaka*. As he recounted the events of that day, Rafiq likened the predatory nature of the naval vessel to that of a wolf. It circled their fishing boat and began shooting heavy ammunition in their direction. The three terrified fishermen threw themselves down flat in the bottom of their boat. The Israeli captain ordered them via megaphone to raise their nets and leave the area. At this point the gunboat was less than twenty meters from Rafiq's *hassaka*. The second time the gunboat came around no attempt was made to communicate with the fishermen. Rafiq was desperately pulling in the nets with his back facing the gunboat. An M-16 assault rifle was fired, hitting him twice with explosive dum-dum bullets, which peppered his back with shrapnel from the bullets themselves.

The force of the shots threw him in the water, plunging him down about six or seven meters below the surface. Rajab asked their friend to control the boat while he rescued Rafiq. Being a strong swimmer, he dove in after Rafiq and pulled him out of the water into the *hassaka*. However, Rafiq was unconscious by this time. The outboard was being slowed down by the weight of the nets so they headed toward another *hassaka* 300 meters away where they dumped the nets. The fishermen in this vessel had a mobile phone and made an emergency call. The stricken *hassaka* reached port at the same time as the ambulance arrived and Rafiq was taken to al-Shifa Hospital in Gaza city in serious condition.

It could take Rafiq months to fully recover, but he has a family to support. He married just six months ago, and his wife is now expecting their first baby. After five years of working as a fisherman, he has experienced Israeli naval forces firing warning shots on many occasions, but this was the first time he has been directly targeted. However, Rajab survived being shot in the chest by the Israeli Navy two and a half years ago. Rafiq described the level shooting on Saturday like an open war. Fishermen were attacked from Wadi Gaza, south of Gaza city, all the way to the northern border of Gaza. A number of *hassakas* were targeted that day, some vessels sustaining serious damage from the shooting.

Palestinian fishermen have come under daily assaults from Israeli gunboats since Israel announced a unilateral ceasefire that supposedly came into force on 18 January. Reports of heavy gunfire and even missile fire are now becoming the norm. Rafiq is the third Gazan fisherman to be shot by the Israeli Navy during this non-existent ceasefire. On 26th January, Alaa al-Habil was shot in the lower leg while trawling less than one nautical mile off the coast of Gaza. On 6 February, Mahmoud al-Nadar was shot in both legs while one and one-half nautical miles off the coast of Rafah in the south of the Gaza Strip. Nowadays it is unthinkable for fishermen to venture beyond three nautical miles from the Gazan coast, with many vessels staying just meters from the beach. However, Gazan territorial waters reach twelve nautical miles offshore—indeed, the Oslo Accords grant a fishing zone extending as far as twenty nautical miles

Israel is attempting to create arbitrary no-go zones in the sea, enforced solely by the gun. They might succeed if it weren't for the resilience of the fishermen. All this is akin to what is happening on land. The IOF has declared an area of Palestinian land a kilometer in from the Green Line a closed military zone, affecting an audacious land grab that threatens to swallow a vast swathe of rich agricultural land all the way along the eastern length of the Gaza strip. (22)

-January 2009 – Noble Energy announced the discovery of a vast deposit of natural gas some fifty miles off the Haifa shoreline. Named Tamar One, it is estimated to hold five trillion cubic feet and be able to produce 50 percent more than the daily capacity of the old Mari-B site. The stocks of Noble Energy and its partners Delek Group and Avner Oil have soared since the announcement. (23)

-March 30, 2009 – Noble Energy announced the discovery of another major deposit at Dalit, located about thirty miles off shore from Israel. Production estimates have not been released but the two discoveries are considered sufficient to cover Israel's energy needs for many years. (24)

-Attacks by Israeli gunboats on the Gazan fishermen continued unabated. Between March 2009 and early April at least three Gazan fishermen have been injured, twenty-four abducted to Israel and eleven boats confiscated.

- April 12, 2009 – An unmanned fishing boat blew up about 300 yards off the Gaza coast. The IOF claims that it had been booby trapped in an attempt to attack an Israeli patrol boat. They cite this account as justification for their "monitoring" of Gazan boats and for the latest restrictions that limit fishing to a zone within two miles of the coast. Palestinian observers on shore claim the vessel was sunk by gunfire from an IOF ship. (25)

Although the violations of law and basic human rights to the Gazan fishermen pale in comparison to the recent horrors that unfolded throughout Gaza during Operation Cast Lead, they must not be overlooked. And they must be seen within the context of another attempted theft of a valuable Palestinian resource.

Former IOF chief of staff Moshe Yallon typified Israeli arrogance and indifference when he stated, "The Palestinians must be made to understand in the deepest recesses of their consciousness that they are a defeated people." (26) The resilience and the resourcefulness of the fishermen and of all the people of Gaza in the face of the horrors they have suffered clearly gives the lie to Moshe Yallon's arrogance. They are not victims. They will prevail.

David K. Schermerhorn traveled to Gaza three times in 2008 aboard boats organized by Free Gaza (freegaza.org). He was also on board the Challenger 1 when it was attacked by Israeli commando forces on May 31, 2010.

Chapter 19:

For *Dignity* and Beyond

⌘ ⌘ ⌘

Written by Free Gaza Media Team, Ramzi, Greta and Huwaida

The successful initial voyage of SS *Free Gaza/Dimitris K* and SS *Liberty/Agios Niko-laos* marked only the beginning of several fruitful voyages from Cyprus to Gaza and back.

The Second Breaking of the Siege: the Dignity's Maiden Voyage

On October 28, 2008, we made our second voyage to Gaza, this time aboard the *Dignity*, a new ship, better able to make the journey in the rough winter weather. Although Israeli warships trailed our small ship when we approached Gaza, they did not attempt to use force against us, and we were able to once again break through their blockade.

Aboard the *Dignity* were twenty-seven doctors, lawyers, journalists, and human rights workers, representing twelve different countries. The passengers included Palestinian legislator Mustapha Barghouti, Nobel Laureate Mairead Maguire, and Italian opera singer Joe Fallisi, who gave Gaza's first ever opera concert. The passengers also included Caoimhe Butterly, a renowned human rights worker who stayed on as the first Free Gaza coordinator, working alongside the Palestinian NGO Network and the Popular Committee Against the Siege, our partner organisations inside Gaza.

After watching the *Dignity*'s arrival, Fida Qishta, the local coordinator for the International Solidarity Movement (ISM) in the Gaza Strip, said, *"If Gaza is free, then it's our right to invite whomsoever we wish to visit us. It's our land, and it's our sea. Now more groups must come, not only by sea but also the crossings at Erez and Rafah must be opened as well. This second breaking of the siege means a lot, actually. It's the second time in two months that people have come to Gaza without Israel's permission, and that tells us that Gaza will be free."*

The Third Breaking of the Siege: Parliamentary Delegation

In November 2008, the *Dignity* made its second successful voyage to Gaza, carrying 24 Passengers. On this voyage, the Free Gaza movement joined with the European Campaign to end the Siege to bring over a ton of medical supplies to Gaza, accompanied by eleven past and current European parliamentarians from England, Ireland, Scotland, Wales, Italy, and Switzerland, including the Baroness Jenny Tonge, Lord Nazir Ahmad, and Clare Short, the former British secretary for international development.

They were part of a much larger group of fifty-three European parliamentarians who had been denied entry to the Gaza Strip earlier in November. Journalists from Al Jazeera, Ha'aretz and the Independent (UK newspaper) were also on board for a three-day fact-finding tour of the Gaza Strip. The passengers also included Eva Bartlett, a Canadian activist who remained in Gaza to increase the number of international human rights workers there.

The *Dignity*, with 11 members of various European Parliaments, looks towards shore as they arrive in the port of Gaza

In addition to delivering medicines, the parliamentarians toured hospitals, schools, agricultural centers, and Gaza's power plant, as well as meeting with their counterparts in the Palestinian Legislature.

The *Dignity* left Gaza on the 10th of November carrying an additional eight Palestinians for the return journey, including the secretary for the Independent Union for the Labour Leagues in Gaza. He came aboard the *Dignity* to speak to syndicates and university students in Spain, and encourage them to participate in breaking the siege on Gaza. Also on board was an elderly Palestinian couple. After suffering from a stroke in 2007, the husband was not allowed out for treatment through either Rafah or Erez. The couple had not seen their children since the siege began in 2006.

"We're thankful that we were able to deliver these badly needed medical supplies," said Dr. Arafat Shoukri, chair of the European Campaign to End the Siege. *"However, the unfortunate truth is that these supplies are only symbolic. Until the siege ends once and for all, innocent people will continue to unnecessarily suffer and even die."*

The Fourth Breaking of the Siege: The Student Delegation

On December 8, 2008, the Free Gaza movement sent in a "students" delegation, headed by professors Mike Cushman and Jonathon Rosenhead of the London School of Economics and the British Committee for Universities for Palestine (BRICUP). The delegation toured schools and universities in Gaza to assess the impact of the siege on education, and successfully brought out eleven Palestinian students who had been accepted to universities abroad but were unable to exit Gaza because of the Israeli siege. They are just a handful of the over 700 Palestinian students who have visas to study at universities in Europe but have been forbidden to leave by Israel and Egypt—another example of the collective punishment on the civilian population of Gaza.

According to Rosenhead and Cushman, *"As academics, we are particularly pleased to be traveling on the* Dignity *on this mission to enable at least some of the hundreds of students trapped in Gaza by the Israeli siege to get out and take up their places at universities round the world. This siege is an affront to any idea of academic freedom or human rights. How can anyone justify preventing young people from fulfilling their potential and learning how to serve their community more fully?"*

Also on board the *Dignity* on this voyage was a British surgeon, Dr. Sonia Robbins, traveling to Gaza to volunteer in local hospitals. Dr. Robbins had worked in Gaza previously but had been prevented from returning by the siege. The boat also carried a Palestinian who had been denied the right to see his family in Gaza for several years, international human rights workers, and journalists.

The *Dignity* carried a ton of medical supplies and high-protein baby formula. Two human rights workers remained in Gaza to join the teams working there, including Ewa Jasiewicz, who joined Caoimhe Butterly as our cocoordinator on the ground in Gaza.

The Fifth Breaking of the Siege: The Qatari Delegation

On December 19, the Free Gaza movement returned to Gaza once again, this time with two envoys from the Qatari Eid charity, in partnership with the people of Qatar. With this historic journey, Qatar became the first Arab nation to ever break the siege of Gaza. Envoys from Qatar assessed hospitals, schools, and civilian centers, and established the foundations for future, lasting partnerships between Qatar and Gaza.

The boat passengers included three human rights workers who remained in Gaza. They included Italian Vittorio Arrigoni, who had been on board the first Free Gaza mission, had remained in Gaza to do human rights work including the accompaniment of fishermen, and had been kidnapped at sea by the Israeli Navy and subsequently deported from Israel. Also on board was Natalie Abou Shakra, from Lebanon, who became the first Lebanese activist to work long-term in Palestine— breaking another aspect of the siege that denies anyone from Lebanon the right to enter Palestine. Among the other passengers were two Israelis, including Neta Golan, one of the founders of the International Solidarity movement.

Lubna Masarwa, a Palestinian human rights activist stated that: *"We are unarmed civilians carrying desperately needed supplies to other unarmed civilians...[but] Gaza doesn't need charity. What Gaza needs is sustained political action aimed at overcoming this vicious siege."*

Declared Alze Al-Qahtani, one of the Qatari envoys: *"This is just the beginning..."*

Gaza Today: This is only the Beginning[5]

By Ewa Jasiewicz – Gaza City

December 27, 2008

As I write this, Israeli jets are bombing the areas of Zeitoun and Rimal in central Gaza City. The family I am staying with has moved into the internal corridor of their

5   Reprinted from *Palestine Chronicle*, http://www.palestinechronicle.com/view_article_details. php?id=14538

home to shelter from the bombing. The windows nearly blew out just five minutes ago as a massive explosion rocked the house. Apache's are hovering above us, while F16s soar overhead.

UN radio reports say one blast was a target close to the main gate of Al Shifa hospital, Gaza and Palestine's largest medical facility. Another was a plastics factory. More bombs continue to pound the Strip.

Sirens are wailing on the streets outside. Regular power cuts that plunge the city into blackness every night and tonight is no exception. Only perhaps tonight, it is the darkest night people have seen here in their lifetimes.

Over 220 people have been killed and over 400 injured through attacks that shocked the strip in the space of fifteen minutes. Hospitals are overloaded and unable to cope. These attacks come on top of existing conditions of humanitarian crisis: a lack of medicine, bread, flour, gas, electricity, fuel, and freedom of movement. Doctors at Shifa had to scramble together ten makeshift operating theaters to deal with the wounded. The hospital's maternity ward had to transform their operating room into an emergency theatre. Shifa only had twelve beds in their intensive care unit; they had to make space for twenty-seven today. There is a shortage of medicine—over 105 key items are not in stock, and blood and spare generator parts are desperately needed. Shifa's main generator is the life support machine of the entire hospital. It's the apparatus keeping the ventilators and monitors and lights turned on that keep people inside alive. And it doesn't have the spare parts it needs, despite the International Committee for the Red Cross urging Israel to allow it to transport them through Erez checkpoint.

Shifaa's head of casualty, Dr. Maowiye Abu Hassanyeh explained, "We had over 300 injured in over thirty minutes. There were people on the floor of the operating theater, in the reception area and in the corridors. We were sending patients to other hospitals. Not even the most advanced hospital in the world could cope with this number of casualties in such a short space of time."

And as IOF chief of staff Lieutenant-General Gabi Ashkenazi said this morning, "This is only the beginning."

But this isn't the beginning; this is an ongoing policy of collective punishment and killing with impunity practiced by Israel for decades. It has seen its most intensified level today. But the weight of dread, revenge, and isolation hangs thick over Gaza today. People are all asking, "If this is only the beginning, what the end will look like?"

11:30 A.M.

Alberto Acre, a Spanish journalist, and I had been on the border village of Sirej near Khan Younis in the south of the strip. We had driven there at 8:00 A.M. with the mobile clinic of the Union of Palestinian Relief Committees. The clinic regularly visits exposed, frequently raided villages far from medical facilities. We had been interviewing residents about conditions on the border. Stories of olive groves and orange groves, family farmland bulldozed to make way for a clear line of sight for Israeli occupation force watchtowers and border guards. Israeli attacks were frequent. Indiscriminate fire and shelling sprayed homes and land on the front line of the southeastern border. One elderly farmer showed us the grave-sized ditch he had dug to climb into when Israeli soldiers would shoot into his fields.

Alberto was interviewing a family that had survived an Israeli missile attack on their home last month. It had been a response to rocket fire from resistance fighters nearby. Four fighters were killed in a field by the border. Israel had rained rockets and M16 fire back. The family, caught in the crossfire, never returned to their home. I was waiting for Alberto to return when ground-shaking thuds tilted us off our feet. This was the sound of surface-to-air missiles and F16 bombs slamming into the Hamas police stations, and army bases. They also bombed in Gaza City, in Deir Balah, Rafah, Khan Younis and Beit Hanoun.

We zoomed out of the village in our ambulance and onto the main road to Gaza City, before jumping out to film the smoldering remains of a police station in Deir Balah, near Khan Younis. Its name, which means 'place of dates', sounds like the easy semislang way of saying take care, Deir Baal - Deir Balak

Eyewitnesses said two Israeli missiles had destroyed the station. One had soared through a children's playground and a busy fruit and vegetable market before impacting its target.

Civilians Dead

There was blood on a broken plastic yellow slide, and a dead donkey with an upturned vegetable cart beside it. Aubergines and splattered blood covered the ground. A man began to explain in broken English what had happened. "It was full here. Three people dead and many, many injured." An elderly man with a white kefiyyeh around his head threw his hands down to his blood drenched trousers. "Look! Look at this! Shame on all governments! Shame on Israel! Look how they kill us. They are killing us and what does the world do? Where is the world when we are being killed here—hell upon them!' He was a market trader who was present during the attack. He began to pick up splattered tomatoes he had lost from his cart, picking them up jerkily and quickly putting them into plastic bags. Behind a small tile and brick building, a man with bloody legs was sitting against a wall. He couldn't get up and was sitting, visibly in pain and shock, trying to orient himself.

The police station itself was a wreck, a mess of crisscrossed piles of concrete, broken floors upon floors. Smashed cars and a split palm tree blocked the road. We walked on, hurriedly, with everyone else, eyes skyward at four apache helicopters, their trigger mechanisms supplied by the UK's Brighton-based EDM Technologies. They were dropping smoky bright flares, as a defence against any attempt at Palestinian missile retaliation. Turning down the road leading to the Deir Balah Civil Defence Force headquarters we suddenly saw a rush of people streaming across the road. "They've been bombing twice. They've been bombing twice," shouted people. We ran too but toward the crowds and away from what could possibly be target number two, a ministry building our friend shouted to us. The apaches rumbled above.

Arriving at the police station, we saw the remains of a life at work smashed short; a prayer mat clotted with dust, a policeman's hat, and the ubiquitous bright flower patterned mattresses, burst open. A crater around twenty feet in diameter was filled with pulverized walls and floors and a motorbike, tossed toylike on its side, in its depths.

Policemen were frantically trying to get a fellow worker out from under the rubble. Everyone was trying to call him on his Jawwal mobile phone. Fire licked the underside of what used to be a room but was now just three feet high. Hands threw back rocks, blocks, and debris to reach the man.

We made our way to the Al Aqsa Hospital. Trucks and cars loaded with the men of entire families were speeding to the hospital to check on loved ones, with horns blaring without interruption.

Hospitals on the Brink

Entering Al Aqsa was overwhelming—pure pandemonium, charged with grief, horror, distress, and shock. Limp blood-covered and burnt bodies streamed by us on rickety stretchers. Before the morgue was a scrum, tens of shouting relatives crammed up to its open double doors. "They could not even identify who was who because the bodies are so burned," explained our friend. Many were transferred, in ambulances and the back of trucks and cars to Al Shifa Hospital. The injured couldn't speak. Causality after casualty sat propped against the outside walls outside, being comforted by relatives, wounds temporarily dressed. The more seriously injured were inside. Relatives jostled with doctors to bring in their injured, wrapped in blankets. Drips, blood-streaming faces, scorched hair, and shrapnel cuts to hands, chests, legs, arms, and heads dominated the reception area, wards, and operating theaters.

We saw a bearded man, on a stretcher on the floor of an intensive care unit, shaking involuntarily, legs rigid and thrusting downward—a spasm coherent with a spinal cord injury. Would he ever walk again or talk again? In another unit, a baby girl, no older than six months, had shrapnel wounds to her face. A relative lifted a blanket to show us her fragile bandaged leg. Her eyes were saucer wide and she was making stilted, repetitive, squeaking sounds.

A first estimate at Al Aqsa hospital was forty dead and 120 injured. The hospital was dealing with casualties from the bombed market, playground, Civil Defence Force station, civil police station, and also the traffic police station. All leveled. A working day blasted flat with terrifying force. At least two shaheed (martyrs) were carried out on stretchers out of the hospital. Lifted up by crowds of grief-stricken men to the graveyard to cries of "La Illaha Illa Allah," [there is no god but Allah].

Who Cares?

And according to many people here, there is nothing and nobody looking out for them apart from God. Back in Shifa Hospital tonight, we meet the brother of a security guard who had had the doorway he had been sitting in and the building (Abu Mazen's old HQ) fall on his head. He said to us, "We don't have anyone but God. We feel alone. Where is the world? Where is the action to stop these attacks?"

Majid Salim stood beside his comatose mother, Fatima. Earlier today she had been sitting at her desk at work at the Hadije Arafat Charity, near Meshtal, the headquarters of the security forces in Gaza City. Israel's attack had left her with multiple internal and head injuries, a tube down her throat, and a ventilator keeping her alive. Majid gestured to her, "We didn't attack Israel. My mother didn't fire rockets at Israel. This is the biggest terrorism to have our mother bombarded at work."

The groups of men lining the corridors of the overtaxed Shifa hospital are by turns stunned, agitated, patient, and lost. We speak to one group. Their brother had both arms broken and has serious facial and head injuries. 'We couldn't recognize his face because it was so black from the weapons used," one explained. Another man turns to me and says, "I am a teacher. I teach human rights. How can I teach my children about the meaning of human rights under these conditions, under this siege?"

It's true; UNRWA and local government schools have developed a human rights syllabus, teaching children about international law, the Geneva Conventions, the International Declaration on Human Rights, and the Hague Regulations to try to develop a culture of human rights here to help generate more self-confidence and security and more of a sense of dignity for the children. But the contradiction between what should be adhered to as a common code of conduct signed by most states, and the reality is stark. International law is not being applied or enforced with respect to Israeli policies toward the Gaza Strip or on '48 Palestine, the West Bank or the millions of refugees living in camps in Lebanon, Jordan, and Syria.

How can a new consciousness and practice of human rights ever graduate from rhetoric to reality when everything points to the contrary both here and in Israel? The United Nations has been spurned and shut out by Israel, with Richard Falk, the UN's special rapporteur on human rights, held prisoner at Ben Gurion Airport before being unceremoniously deported this month. An international community that speaks empty phrases on Israeli attacks like "we urge restraint…minimise civilian casualties."

The Gaza Strip is one of the most densely populated regions on the planet. In Jabaliya camp alone, Gaza's largest, 125,000 people are crowded into a space two-kilometers square. Bombardment by F16s and Apaches at 11:30 in the morning, as children leave their schools for home reveals a contempt for civilian safety as does the eighteen months of a siege that bans all imports and exports and has resulted in the deaths of over 270 people as a result of a lack of access to essential medicines.

A Light

There is a saying here in Gaza that we spoke of jokingly last night: At the end of the tunnel…there is another tunnel. Not so funny when you consider that Gaza is being kept alive through the smuggling of food, fuel, and medicine through an exploitative industry of over 1,000 tunnels running from Egypt to Rafah in the South. On average one to two people die every week in the tunnels. Some embark on a humiliating crawl to get their education, see their families, or find work on their hands and knees. Others are reportedly big enough to drive through.

Last night I added a new ending to the saying: At the end of the tunnel, there is another tunnel and then a power cut. Today, there's nothing to make a joke about. As bombs continue to blast buildings around us, jarring the children in this house from their fitful sleep, the saying could take on another twist. After today's killing of over 200, is it that at the end of the tunnel, there is another tunnel, and then a grave or a wall of international governmental complicity and silence?

There is a light through, beyond the sparks of resistance and solidarity in the West Bank, '48 and the broader Middle East. This is a light of conscience turned into activism by people all over the world. We can turn a spotlight onto Israel's crimes against humanity and the enduring injustice here in Palestine, by pressuring our governments; demanding an end to Israeli apartheid and occupation; and broadening our call for boycott, divestment and sanctions, and for a genuine, just peace.

Through institutional, governmental, and popular means, this can be a light at the end of the Gazan tunnel

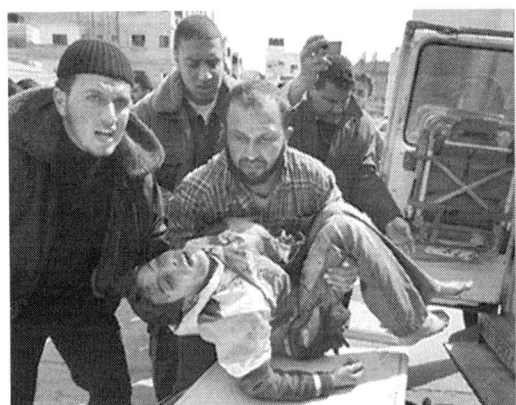

Child victim of Israeli sniper fire

The Sixth Attempt at Breaking the Siege: the Ramming of the *Dignity*

In response to the Israeli massacres in Gaza at the end of December 2008, the Free Gaza movement sent the *Dignity* on an emergency mission of mercy to besieged Gaza. Aboard the ship were over three tons of medical supplies, three surgeons to volunteer in hospitals and clinics in Gaza, Dr. Elena Theoharous, a member of the Cypriot Parliament, and Cynthia McKinney, former US congresswoman and Green Party presidential candidate.

On December 30, the *Dignity* was attacked by the Israeli Navy at approximately 6:00 *A.M.* (UST) in international waters, roughly ninety miles off the coast of Gaza. Several Israeli warships surrounded the small, human rights boat, intentionally ramming it three times. According to ship's captain Denis Healy, the Israeli attack came, *"without any warning, or any provocation."* Thanks to the heroic efforts of its captain and crew, the ship was able to stay afloat and made its way to safe harbor in Lebanon without the loss of life.

Also on board was Caoimhe Butterly, our Gaza cocoordinator, who stated that, *"The gunboats gave us no warning. They came up out of the darkness firing flares and flashing huge floodlights into our faces. We were so shocked that at first we didn't react. We knew we were well within international waters and supposedly safe from attack. They rammed us three times, hitting the side of the boat hard. We began taking on water and, for a few minutes, we all feared for our lives. After they rammed us, they started screaming at us as we were frantically getting the lifeboats ready and putting on our life jackets. They kept yelling that if we didn't turn back they would shoot us."*

The Dignity after being deliberately rammed by an Israeli Warship

The Seventh Attempt to Break the Siege: the Spirit of Humanity

Immediately following the ramming of the *Dignity*, the Free Gaza movement secured a new boat, the *Spirit of Humanity*, and attempted another emergency mission to besieged Gaza. Aboard the ship were thirty-six passengers and crew, representing seventeen different nations. They included doctors, journalists, human rights workers, and five European parliamentarians representing Belgium, Greece, Italy, and Spain. The mercy ship also carried tons of desperately needed medical supplies that were meant for hospitals in the Gaza Strip. The ship was forced to turn back by the Israeli Navy, which threatened to fire on the unarmed civilians on board if they continued toward Gaza.

Fouad Ahidar, a member of the Belgian Parliament who sailed aboard the *Spirit of Humanity*, stated that, "I have five children that [were] very worried about me, but I told them 'you can sit on your couch and watch these atrocities on the television, or you can choose to take action to make them stop.'"

During the massacre, the United Nations failed to protect the Palestinian civilian population from Israel's flagrant violations of international humanitarian law. Israel has closed off Gaza from the international community and demanded that all foreigners leave. But Huwaida Arraf, an organizer with the Free Gaza movement, stated, "We cannot just sit by and wait for Israel to decide to stop the killing and open the borders for relief workers to pick up the pieces. We are coming in. There is an urgent need for this mission as Palestinian civilians in Gaza are being terrorized and slaughtered by Israel, and access to humanitarian relief denied to them. When states and the international bodies responsible for taking action to stop such atrocities chose to be impotent, then we,-the citizens of the world, must act. Our common humanity demands nothing less."

Too Much to Mourn in Gaza[6]

By Eva Bartlet

09 January 2009

Gaza Strip: After finishing a shift with the Palestine Red Crescent Society yesterday morning, we went to the United Nations-administered al-Fakhoura school in Jabaliya, which was bombed by Israeli forces, killing at least forty displaced people who were taking shelter there. When we arrived, prayers were happening in the street in front of the school. I'd seen prayers in open, outdoor places in Palestine and Egypt. But these days, when I see a mass of people praying, in front of al-Shifa hospital, in the streets of Jabaliya, I think of the mosques that have been bombed, and of the loss of lives and sanctuaries. And yesterday I thought of the loss of another safe haven.

The grief was very evident, as was the indignation: "Where are we supposed to stay," one man demanded. "How many deaths is enough? How many?" It's the question that has resounded in my mind since the attacks on 27 December.

Across Fakhoura street from the school, about fifteen meters down a drive, a gaping hole in the Deeb family house revealed what had been happening when it was hit by a shell. Rounds of bread dough lay where they'd been rolled out to bake. Amal Deeb was in her thirties, a surviving family member told us. When the missile struck, it killed her and nine others in the extended family's house, including two boys and three girls. Another four were injured, one having both legs amputated.

6   http://www.countercurrents.org/bartlett090109.htm and http://electronicintifada.net/v2/article10146.shtml

Approaching the house, the stench of blood was still strong, and was visible in patches and pools amid the rubble of the room. Later, in Jabaliya's Kamal Adwan hospital, nine-year-old Ahlam lay conscious but unsmiling, unresponsive. The woman at her side explained her injuries: shrapnel lacerations all over her body, and deeper shrapnel injuries in her stomach. Ahlam didn't know nine of her family members were killed.

Returning to the street in front of the Fakoura School, mourners had gathered, ready to march, to carry the dead and their pieces to their overcrowded resting place. Flags of all colors mixed in this funeral march: no one party dominated, it was collective grief under collective punishment.

So many people had joined the procession through the narrow streets that the funeral split, taking different streets, to reach the cemetery. At the entrance to the cemetery, decorated cement slabs mark the older graves, laid at a time when cement and space were available. The most recently buried bodies, instead, show in sandy humps, buried just low enough to be covered but not properly so. Cement blocks mark some graves, leaves, and vines on others. And some were just barely visible, by the raise in earth. But it was too packed, too hard to estimate where a grave might be, no possibility of a respectfully spaced arrangement.

"Watch where you step," Mahmoud, a friend, told me, pointing to a barely-noticeable grave of a child.

The enormity of the deaths hit me. After twelve days of killing and psychological warfare, I'd become less shocked at the sight of pieces of bodies, a little numb, like a doctor might, or a person subjected to this time and again. I was and I remain horrified at the ongoing slaughter, at the images of children's bodies being pulled from the rubble astonished it could continue but adapted to the fact that there would be bodies, maimed, and lives ruined. I stood among sandy makeshift graves, watching men digging with their hands, others carrying corpses on any plank long enough—corrugated tin, scraps of wood, stretchers—to be hastily buried. As the drones still flew overhead and tank shelling could be heard 100s of meters beyond, it all become too much again. I wept for all the dead and the wounded psyches of a people who know their blood flows freely and will continue to do so.

Hatem, the other day, told me to be strong as Palestinians, for Palestinians. And I try, though each day brings assassinations no one could have imagined. Out of touch with all the other fragmented areas of Gaza, I read of the Samuni family and see photos of a baby girl pulled from the rubble of a house shelled by an Israeli warplane. Mohamed, a photojournalist, has photographed many of those killed in Israel's bombings of houses. And today Hatem crumbled, though he is strong. It's all too much.

Nidal, a Palestine Red Crescent Society medic, told how he was at the Fakhoura School when it was shelled. His aunt and uncle live nearby, and he'd been visiting friends at the school. "I was there, talking with friends, only a little away from where two of the missiles hit. The people standing between me and the missiles were like a shield. They were shredded. About twenty of them," he said.

Like many Palestinians I've met, Nidal has a prior history of loss, even before this latest phenomenal assault on civilians. Only twenty years old, Nidal has already had his father and brother killed, martyred it is said here, by sniper's bullets. His right hand testifies his part in the story: "Three years ago, the Israeli army had invaded our region [Jabaliya]. One soldier threw a sound bomb at us and I picked it up to throw away. It went off in my hand before I could throw it away." Sound bombs are used against nonviolent demonstrations against Israel's wall in the occupied West Bank villages of Bilin and Nilin, and many youths learn at a young age how to chuck them away. But Nidal's stubs of fingers show that he wasn't so lucky. However, he is luckier than his father and brother. And luckier than two of his cousins, his aunt's sons, who were in the area where missiles were dropped at the UN school. They, twelve and twenty-seven years old, were killed.

Osama gave his testimony as a medic at the scene after the multiple missile shelling. "When we arrived, I saw dead bodies everywhere. More than thirty. Dead children, grandparents . . . Pieces of flesh all over. And blood. It was very crowded, and difficult to carry out the injured and martyred. There were also dead animals among the humans. I helped carry fifteen dead. I had to change my clothes three times. These people thought they were safe in the UN school, but the Israeli army killed them, in cold blood," he said.

Mohammed K., a volunteer with the Palestine Red Crescent Society, was elsewhere when the UN safe haven was shelled. "We were in Jabaliya, at the UN 'G' school, to interview the displaced people taking shelter there. We wanted to find out how many people were staying there, where they'd left from and why exactly, and how safe they felt in the school. While we were there, we heard the explosions, saw the smoke, and wondered what had been hit. It was Fakhoura."

A Lebanese Attempt to Break the Siege: The Tali

Efforts by Free Gaza movement inspired others to sail to Gaza and try to break the siege. There were unsuccessful attempts by Libya and Iran to sail cargo to Gaza. A cargo ship sponsored by Lebanese promoters and carrying activists and supplies set sail in February, 2009 from Lebanon en route to the Gaza Strip in defiance of an Israeli blockade on the coastal Palestinian territory.

The Togo-flagged ship *Tali* (brotherhood in Arabic) carried about sixty tons of medicine, food, toys, books, and stationery, as well as eight activists and journalists. The ship set sail from Tripoli in northern Lebanon, and then stopped in Larnaca, Cyprus, for inspection before continuing to Gaza, where organizers said it was scheduled to arrive midweek. The trip had not been cleared by Israeli authorities who turned back similar aid boats trying to reach Gaza, said one of the journey's organizers, Hani Suleiman. Before departure from Tripoli, organizers had to change ships after port authorities declared the larger boat unsafe. But the second ship, the *Tali*, was not equipped to carry the eighty Lebanese and foreign activists and journalists who were planning to set sail. Only eight people ended up boarding the ship just after midnight. Maan Bashour, a pro-Palestinian Lebanese involved in the organization of the trip, said the remaining activists were trying to find another boat to take them to Gaza.

"There will be other boats," Bashour told the Associated Press. "We will keep sending them. The whole point is to tell the world that the Lebanese people reject the [Israeli] blockade on Gaza."

One of those on board was Theresa McDermott, a Free Gaza volunteer who was also a passenger on the first Free Gaza boat, which reached Gaza in August 2008:

Eight P.M. (CET) M. writes: "T. just phoned to say they have been approached by two Israeli gunboats, which are hovering around, and there are two Israeli helicopters overhead. The Israelis told the captain of *Tali* that he cannot go to Gaza and, according to T.; the Israelis told him they would sink the boat if it proceeds. He refused to turn around and told them he is responsible for his boat and he is going to Gaza. The Israelis said the boat cannot go to Gaza, and it appears they will try to force it to *El Arish*, but the captain intends to push forward. (And having been aboard the *Tali*, I think it will take more than a ramming to sink it.) T. will let us know if anything more happens. They are in international waters but some distance from Gaza water.

Greta Berlin writes:

Theresa, one of the original Free Gaza volunteers was on this boat, the *Tali*. Free Gaza organizers helped in Cyprus to get the boat inspected and then sent on to Gaza. Please make your outrage heard as, once again, Israel, the bully of the Eastern Mediterranean, gets away with piracy. On board was an elderly patriarch from Jerusalem as well as several Lebanese human rights watchers. According to eyewitnesses, the passengers were beaten and much of the boat destroyed. We are checking the status of the units of plasma loaded on board, because, if the stories are accurate that the Israeli Navy thugs turned off the generators, this badly needed plasma will be destroyed very quickly. You can follow the story in Al Jazeera English and Al Jazeera Arabic.

Theresa McDermott, who went to Gaza with the first and second Free Gaza movement voyages in August and October 2008, had responded to a call for support by internationals from a Lebanese humanitarian aid organization to take a voyage to Gaza aboard the Togo-flagged ship, *Tali*, and was one of only nine passengers aboard the cargo ship. On February 4, 2009 Israeli gunboats intercepted it, boarded, and forced the ship to Ashdod port in Israel. Theresa was found in Ramle prison four days later after being "disappeared" by the Israel government when she was forcibly removed from the Lebanese seaborne aid mission to Gaza.

All the passengers and crew aboard were released on Thursday, February 5 except Theresa and two Indian crewmembers. Nobody realized they had not been released. Between Thursday evening and Sunday morning there was no word about her whereabouts except several false stories saying that "Britons" had departed to London. Finally on Sunday, she was able to call her family in Scotland to say she was in Ramle prison in Israel. She was also able to let people know about the two Indian crewmembers who were also still in jail after being taken off the *Tali* along with her. Even the Indian Embassy hadn't been informed. They were deported to India on February 11th and Theresa was deported to the UK on the 16th.

According to Al Jazeera journalist Salam Khodr, when the ship was boarded, the passengers were beaten and kicked by Israeli soldiers before being removed from the ship, although Theresa was not harmed during the boarding or arrest. Israeli officials provided no information about why she had been detained, what the charges were, and why her detention was concealed. She was deported on the grounds that she had entered Israel illegally, but it has to be asked how this can be the case when she was actually brought into Israel at gunpoint by the Israeli armed forces.

Members of the Scottish Parliament including Pauline McNeil, Sandra White, and Hugh O'Donnell, who were part of a fall delegation to Gaza aboard the Free Gaza boat, *Dignity* worked with the British government to ensure that she received the protection she needed, and she appreciated the attention of the Embassy once they were able to locate her.

The Israelis found only medical and other humanitarian aid on the *Tali* but refused to return the ship. The status of its humanitarian cargo is unknown.

Also see: http://www.youtube.com/watch?v=MCb3apCJ4Ql&feature=channel_page

Chapter 20

The Spirit of Humanity versus Pirates of the Mediterranean

⌘ ⌘ ⌘

Absurdity Is the Norm in the Gaza Strip

Stephanie Westbrook
June 15, 2009

Upon returning home from Gaza, a friend commented, "It must have been horrifying seeing all the destruction." And it was. The twenty-two-day Israeli assault on the Gaza Strip laid waste to an already ravaged territory.

The landscape is dotted with piles of rubble of bombed out buildings, the twisted iron and aluminium of destroyed factories, once green fields, reduced to sand and dirt by Israeli tanks, apartments with two meter holes in the walls and toppled minarets of mosques turned to ruins.

But as devastating as bearing witness to the destruction was, it was the absurdities of the siege, the total blockade of Gaza imposed by Israel and Egypt that really affected me. Gaza itself remains frozen in time; for nearly five months after the ceasefire, aside from a few rare cases in which cinder blocks have been used to fill gaping holes in the sides of buildings, no reconstruction whatsoever has begun. The blockade keeps the necessary building materials out of Gaza.

While travelling throughout Gaza with a delegation of mostly US citizens organized by Code Pink, the absurdities of the siege presented themselves over and over.

At Al Shifa Hospital, the largest in Gaza, we saw state-of-the-art isotope scan and radio therapy machines in the oncology department that cannot operate because the radioactive material as well as a calibration tools have been refused entry by Israel. A row of dialysis machines sat unused, lacking the required fluids. As medical conditions in Gaza deteriorate because of the siege, many look for medical care abroad. However, the sealed borders prevent them from travelling. We met the director of an orphanage who had already lost the vision in one eye, was losing it in the other. He had been unable to obtain permission to travel to Egypt for eye care.

Power outages are regular occurrences. The Gaza power plant simply cannot keep up with the demand because of a lack of fuel, which is blocked by Israel, as is supplemental electricity produced in Israel. There are both scheduled blackouts of eight to ten hours, as well as spontaneous outages.

While touring the Al Shifa Hospital, the minister of health apologized for the heat in the room, saying their generator must be reserved for higher priority uses than air conditioning. Families are forced to carry their loved ones up the stairs, the elevators shut down during blackouts.

The centers working to create employment opportunities for Gaza's women inevitably fall prey to the siege. Power cuts bring the sewing machines making dresses and linens to a standstill. Even the embroidery thread used to make traditional handicrafts must be smuggled in through the tunnels.

The siege has also taken its toll on the father figure. According to Dr. Zeyada of the Gaza Community Mental Health Program, with well over 50 percent unemployment due to the siege, children see their fathers as unable to provide for them. And during the war, they saw that their fathers were also unable to protect them. Children have started looking to other role models, and make easy targets for those who, unfortunately, have no desire for peace.

Education suffers under the siege. At a UN vocational training center in Khan Younis, the library consists of roughly twelve bookcases, but only two had any books at all, with half being photocopied manuals. The textbooks destined for the center have been held up in a storage facility in Jerusalem; the Israelis simply refused to allow them in. The center is also unable to get the raw materials for their metal and woodworking courses.

Sharif, a university student studying business administration in his second year, is understandably proud of having top marks in his facility. His friends have nicknamed him the Genius. Sharif has been awarded a scholarship at Portland University in Oregon starting this fall. Unfortunately, the irrationality of the siege is likely to prevent him from being allowed to go. "If I can't get authorization by August, there goes my scholarship."

A professor at Al Aqsa University has been offered a position at the University of Manchester; however, he has been denied permission to travel. Professors are also unable to travel to attend international conferences. And students in the English department have a tough time finding native speakers with which to practice the language; getting into Gaza is almost as difficult as getting out!

Numerous projects for which funding has already been approved are currently suspended for the simple fact that the materials to complete them are not allowed in. Turkey has donated funds for a new university library and PalTel, the Palestinian telecommunications company, has allocated funds for an information technology center. Both projects remain in Limbo, victims of the siege.

An official with the UN Relief and Works Agency remarked that it is also a problem to get the actual banknotes in. UNRWA, which provides services to more than 1 million registered refugees in the Gaza Strip, is often only able to get money in to pay the salaries of their 10,000 employees, while money to fund projects is blocked.

Not only are Palestinians restricted in their movement in and out of Gaza, but also within. In late May, Israel began dropping thousands of leaflets near the border areas warning the people of Gaza not to come within 300 meters of the border or they would be fired on. Farmers are forced to risk their lives in order to work their fields that fate has placed too close to the border. The same restrictions are imposed on Palestinian fishermen. The sound of shots pierce the silence nightly, as Israeli gunboats fire on fishing boats that dare to venture far enough away from the shore in order to catch fish to sell and provide a living for their families.

These are the absurdities that have become the norm in Gaza. But perhaps most absurd of all is how anyone can believe that Israel's severity in the closures, the destruction of the economy and social fabric of the Gaza Strip, will serve to convince Palestinians to place their trust in International Law.

What we in the international community must do is to heed the call we heard repeatedly from the people of Gaza: work to break the siege so that they can take care of themselves.

Hedy Epstein Attacked Yesterday

Written by Greta Berlin|
18 June 2009

Hedy Epstein, our wonderful eighty-four-year-old Holocaust survivor, the woman who has been determined to come with us to Gaza this year, was attacked yesterday while walking home in her hometown in Missouri.

"Someone came up behind me and pushed me with both hands, throwing me to the ground. I cut an artery in my chin, and my knees are black and blue. I've got several stitches in my chin right now. When I looked up to see him, he was running as fast as he could away from me," said Hedy this morning.

When talking to her friend's husband, he said, "Listen, in St. Louis if someone is going to push you, they are after your purse. This was a targeted attack. And, if anyone else has either been attacked or been threatened, we want to know, because the police here need to know."

Last year when we were getting ready to go on our first trip to break Israel's blockade of Gaza, many of us were threatened by Israel firsters. Some even bragged that they would blow up our boat, sink it, or kill our children. Lauren Booth, the sister-in-law of Tony Blair, was threatened that her children would be killed. Those of us organizing the project were threatened as well. It didn't stop us then, and it won't stop us now.

In January when Hedy was interviewed on TV about Israel's war crimes in Gaza, she got several threatening phone calls, "We're going to come and find you, and we will take care of you."

This message needs to go out far and wide to everyone appalled that pro-Israel thugs would push an eighty-four-year-old woman to the ground in an attempt to hurt her and scare her from coming. When I hung up today, the last words Hedy said were, "Can I come later? Would you put me on the next trip?'

The answer is a resounding YES."

Press Releases: Brick by Brick

By Free Gaza Team

(Larnaca, 18 June 2009) In the final week in June, the Free Gaza movement will set sail on its eighth mission to break Israel's horrific siege and collective punishment of 1.5 million Palestinians in the Gaza strip.

"The Israelis violated international law by ramming the boat I was on which was carrying medical supplies to Gaza. Therefore, I never got to Gaza. Especially after Operation Cast Lead, I want to go to Gaza, and if I'm lucky, one day, I'll also get to visit a free Palestine," said former Representative Cynthia McKinney, one of the passengers coming back.

Mairead Maguire, the Nobel Peace Prize winner from Ireland is also going back, "I am going to Gaza to show my love and support for the people of Gaza who continue to suffer under Israeli siege and occupation, yet whose spirit of nonviolent resistance inspires all who believe in equality, freedom and justice," she stated.

"It is crucial that we continue sending boats to Gaza to challenge Israel's criminal closure on the Strip," said Huwaida Arraf, delegation leader of the June voyage. "Gaza does not need our charity but needs us to stand up against the forces that continue to deliberately deny an entire people their human rights.

International donors pledged over $4 billion to rebuild Gaza, and yet none of them are doing anything about the fact that Israel is not allowing any building supplies into Gaza, not to mention thousands of other items such as anesthetics, oxygen and cancer treatments, chlorine to treat the water supply as well as paper, books and toys for children; even tea and coffee have been banned."

This voyage will be the first attempt to challenge Israel's naval blockade on the Gaza Strip since an Israeli gunship brutally rammed the *Dignity* in December 2008, and nearly sank the *Spirit of Humanity* with all on board in January.

Boat by Boat

By Free Gaza Team

(Doha, 22 June 2009) The Free Gaza movement will sail 240 miles from Cyprus to Gaza, its eighth mission to break Israel's draconian siege on 1.5 million Palestinians there. In the holds of the *Spirit of Humanity* will be tons of cement and suitcases full of toys, crayons, and coloring books for the children, all items banned by Israel's government.

Two of the organizers, Huwaida Arraf and Greta Berlin, as well as the Honorable Cynthia McKinney, former US Congresswoman from Georgia, held a press conference yesterday in Doha, Qatar. All three called on the world to recognize Palestinian human and civil rights…rights that have been denied for sixty-one years.

"People in Gaza are being made to live in subhuman conditions. Children are dying, and governments are silent. It is important to continue sending boats to Gaza to challenge the criminal blockade enforced by the Israeli military," said Ms. Arraf.

The group emphasized that what they are taking is only a token of what the people of Gaza need. They are hoping to buy a cargo boat, to bring in larger amounts of building supplies via the sea route they aim to open. They ask for the financial support of people around the world to purchase this ship.

Speaking to Al Jazeera and eight other news organizations, Ms Arraf emphasized, "International donors pledged over $4 billion to rebuild Gaza, yet none of them are doing a thing about the fact that Israel allows no building supplies into the territory. So we are leaving for Gaza to tell the world to do something."

When asked what guarantees the group has received from the Israeli government, both Berlin and Arraf frowned. "We do not seek permission from or coordinate with the Israeli authorities. Israel has grossly abused its authority as an occupying power, daily violating the human rights of Palestinians, and imposing collective punishment on them. It is past time for the international community to stop abetting Israel's illegal closure policy," stated Ms. Arraf.

Mile by Mile

By Free Gaza Team

(Larnaca, 24 June 2009) As the Free Gaza movement gets ready to set sail on our eighth mission, many of our passengers are reflecting about why we are sailing to besieged Gaza.

Ahmed is returning to his home in Gaza. Israeli occupying forces will not allow him to see his mum. "I have tried to go home for six years, and for six years I have not been allowed to see my mother, and she is terribly ill. This is my chance to go home. I must go home."

Sixteen nations are represented on this voyage. Many of us have travelled thousands of miles to show the world that we will not stand by while the Palestinians of Gaza continue to be violated.

"I've flown in from Bahrain to tell my sisters in Gaza that we will never rest until the world knows what has happened to them," stated Juhaina, a young woman from Bahrain.

"When we left last August, I told the people of Gaza we would come back, and I've flown 5,000 miles to keep that promise," said Mary Hughes Thompson, one of the co-founders of the movement.

"I am returning to the friends that I made when I went in October," said Mairead Maguire, Nobel peace laureate. "They must know that we have not and will not forget them."

The tons of cement that our small boat carries are just a token of what is needed to rebuild the Gaza strip, but the hope in the hearts of the passengers cannot be measured by weight. Miles and miles they have travelled to get to Cyprus, miles more they will travel tomorrow to get to Gaza. The *Spirit of Humanity* will proudly fly the flags of sixteen nations, the flags of people who are determined not to forget the horror of an occupation that has lasted forty-one years.

Formal Notification of Intent to TravelJune 24, 2009

To: The Israeli Ministry of Defense, Fax: 972-3-697-6717

To: The Israeli Ministry of Foreign Affairs, Fax: 972-2-5303367

From: The Free Gaza movement

This letter serves as a formal notification to you, as the Occupying Power and belligerent force in the Gaza Strip, that on Thursday, June 25, 2009 we are navigating the motor vessel *Spirit of Humanity*, and the motor vessel *Free Gaza*[6] from the Port of Larnaca to the port of Gaza City. Our vessels will be flying the Greek flags, and, as such, fall under the jurisdiction Greece.

We will be sailing from Cypriot waters into international waters, then directly into the territorial waters of the Gaza Strip without entering or nearing Israeli territorial waters.

We will be carrying medical supplies in sealed boxes, as well as crayons, coloring books and toys for children, cleared by customs at the Larnaca International Airport and the Port of Larnaca. We will also be carrying 300 bags of cement delivered directly from the supplier to the Port of Larnaca. There will be passengers and crew on board from fourteen different countries. Our boats and cargo will have received security clearance from the Port Authorities in Cyprus before we depart.

As it will be confirmed that neither we, the cargo, any of the boats' contents, nor the boats themselves constitute any threat to the security of Israel or its armed forces, we do not expect any interference with our voyage by Israel's authorities.

On Tuesday, December 30, an Israeli Navy vessel violently, and without warning, attacked our motor vessel *Dignity*, disabling the vessel and endangering the lives of the sixteen civilians on board. This notice serves as clear notification to you of our approach. Any attack on the motor vessels, *Spirit of Humanity* and/or *Free Gaza** will be premeditated and any harm inflicted on the people on board will be considered the result of a deliberate attack on unarmed civilians.

A copy of this notification has been sent to the embassies of the civilians who will be on board.

Free Gaza Boat *Spirit of Humanity* Departs Cyprus

(LARNACA, 29 June 2009) - The Free Gaza boat the *Spirit of Humanity* departed Cyprus at 7:30 A.M. on Monday, 29 July. Twenty-one human rights and solidarity workers representing eleven different countries were aboard.

Over 2,400 homes were destroyed in Gaza during the Israeli massacre in December/January, 490 of them by F-16 airstrikes, as well as thirty mosques, twenty-nine educational institutions, twenty-nine medical centers, ten charitable organizations, and five cement factories.

Each kit carries a small amount of supplies for a single family, representing sectors of civil society currently being blockaded by Israel: agriculture, building and reconstruction, education, electricity, health, and water and sanitation. Although over four billion dollars in aid was promised to Gaza in the aftermath of the Israeli onslaught, little humanitarian aid and no reconstruction supplies have been allowed in.

---

*The *Free Gaza* was unable to make the voyage due to controversial restrictions from Cypriot Port Authorities having to do with seaworthiness of the vessel.

SPOT Signals from Spirit: Their Meaning
By Free Gaza Team
29 June 2009

The SPOT locator, onboard Spirit, along with GPS position, can send three signals: okay, help, and emergency.

The okay signal means everything going well, and is sent every half an hour/hour.

There may be some occasions when they miss out a signal due to being busy or asleep but they will definitely send when there is anything happening.

A help signal doesn't mean that we need help, just that the Israelis have made contact and are around but haven't stopped us yet, they will send a help signal as soon as they do contact us and will continue to send a help signal while they're around. This is only for your information not necessarily for action although a contact with them to say "we know you're in contact with the boat, please leave it alone, and don't harm it or the passengers" may be useful. If they leave *Spirit* alone again, they'll go back to okay

If they suddenly go from help to 'not sending', that will mean that they have boarded and have us from sending, don't worry we should be fine only a wee bit frustrated. There is a chance that they may miss the occasional signal, so wait until two or three are missing before deciding that we've been boarded.

If they do get into difficulty, they'll send an emergency signal out to alert the relevant search and rescue teams; we seriously don't expect to have to use that one but if used, it will bring us help very quickly.

URGENT ALERT - Israeli Navy Surrounding *Spirit* and Threatening to Open Fire

By Free Gaza Team
29 June 2009

At 1:40 A.M., the Israeli Navy surrounded the *Spirit* while in international waters off the coast of Israel as it is on its way to the Gaza Strip. We got a call from the boat saying that they were being threatened, told to turn back, or they would be fired on.

Huwaida Arraf, one of the delegation leaders, was on the phone with the Israeli gunboats, and we could hear her saying, "You cannot open fire on unarmed civilians" several times. At this writing, they are surrounded by several ships shining bright lights at the *Spirit*.

Call Off Your Attack Dogs - Cynthia McKinney

By Free Gaza Team | 30 June 2009

We just spoke to the passengers. Everyone is okay, but the situation is still very tense. They continue to be surrounded by Israeli warships that are threatening to open fire. The Israeli Navy is actively jamming all navigation systems in violation of international maritime law, endangering the people on board.

Former US Congresswoman, Cynthia McKinney, speaking from on board the SPIRIT, stated, "I am extremely angry. We demand that the Israeli government call off their attack dogs. We are unarmed civilians aboard an unarmed boat delivering medical and reconstruction aid to other human beings in Gaza. Why in God's name would Israel want to attack us and threaten our safety and welfare? I call on President Obama and the international community to intervene now to prevent this situation from escalating with potentially drastic results to the civilians on board."

Since the boat's navigation equipment is being jammed, it has turned westward in order to stay in international waters. The captain and crew are working from the most ancient of navigation equipment...the compass, to stay clear of Israeli waters.

Update on the Spirit
Written by Free Gaza movement
June 30, 2009

Dear Friends,

We just spoke again with our people aboard the *Spirit of Humanity*. The Israeli Navy is continuing to try and intimidate the ship, and is actively jamming its radar, GPS, and navigation systems in direct violation of international maritime law. This jamming is extremely dangerous and directly threatens the welfare and safety of everyone aboard our civilian ship.

Because their instrumentation is being jammed, they are using compass and paper to attempt to navigate. They are in international waters, and they believe their location is approximately 110 kilometers off of the town of Hadera. Everyone is tired but determined. They are not being deterred by the Israeli aggression and are continuing toward Gaza. Please help them.

We Do Not Seek a Confrontation

Written by Free Gaza movement
June 30, 2009

"All we want is to reach Gaza. We do not seek a confrontation."
Activists aboard Gaza justice boat demand they be allowed to visit their friends & family in besieged Gaza, and deliver their cargo of medical supplies, children's toys, and reconstruction kits. They invite the world to join them.

(At sea 60 km off the coast of the Gaza Strip) - Human Rights activists aboard the Free Gaza ship, the SPIRIT OF HUMANITY, today demanded that the Israeli Navy immediately stop threatening them.

"This aid is desperately needed by the people of Gaza," said Mairead Maguire, winner of the Noble Peace Prize and Pacem in Terris Award for her work in Northern Ireland. "President Obama has called upon the Palestinians to abandon violence but Israel is denying them the right to non-violently resist the siege of Gaza."

The unarmed justice ship departed Larnaca Port in Cyprus at 7:30 A.M. Monday with its crew of twenty-one human rights activists, humanitarian workers, and journalists from eleven different countries, including Nobel laureate Mairead Maguire and former U.S. Congresswoman Cynthia McKinney. The boat, a converted ferry, hopes to arrive in Gaza Tuesday afternoon, following a grueling thirty-hour sea voyage.

Huwaida Arraf, chairperson of the Free Gaza movement and delegation cocoordinator for this voyage, said, "All we want is to reach Gaza. We want to visit our friends and deliver our cargo of medical supplies, children's toys, and reconstruction materials. Our ship was searched and received security clearance from the Port Authorities in Cyprus before we departed."

Arraf continued, "We do not seek a confrontation. We have travelled from Cypriot waters to international waters and will enter Gazan waters. We've never gone anywhere near Israel. Israel's closure of Gaza is an act of collective punishment and a blatant violation of international law. We call upon our governments to take action to uphold their obligations under the Fourth Geneva Conventions. If they won't or until they do, we will act. We will come to Gaza again and again until this brutal siege is broken. We invite the good people of the world to join us."

Israel Attacks Justice Boat; Kidnaps Human Rights Workers; Confiscates Medicine, Toys and Olive Trees

By Free Gaza Team

30 June 2009 [23 miles off the coast of Gaza, 15:30pm] – Today, the IOF attacked and boarded the Free Gaza movement boat, the *Spirit of Humanity*, abducting

twenty-one human rights workers from eleven countries, including Noble laureate Mairead Maguire and former U.S. Congresswoman Cynthia McKinney. The passengers and crew are being forcibly dragged toward Israel.

"This is an outrageous violation of international law against us. Our boat was not in Israeli waters, and we were on a human rights mission to the Gaza Strip," said Cynthia McKinney, a former US Congresswoman and presidential candidate. "President Obama just told Israel to let in humanitarian and reconstruction supplies, and that's exactly what we tried to do. We're asking the international community to demand our release so we can resume our journey."

According to an International Committee of the Red Cross report released yesterday, the Palestinians living in Gaza are "trapped in despair." Thousands of Gazans whose homes were destroyed earlier during Israel's December/January massacre are still without shelter despite pledges of almost $4.5 billion in aid, because Israel refuses to allow cement and other building material into the Gaza Strip. The report also notes that hospitals are struggling to meet the needs of their patients due to Israel's disruption of medical supplies.

"The aid we were carrying is a symbol of hope for the people of Gaza, hope that the sea route would open for them, and they would be able to transport their own materials to begin to reconstruct the schools, hospitals and thousands of homes destroyed during the onslaught of Cast Lead. Our mission is a gesture to the people of Gaza that we stand by them and that they are not alone" said fellow passenger Mairead Maguire, winner of a Noble Peace Prize for her work in Northern Ireland.

Just before being kidnapped by Israel, Huwaida Arraf, Free Gaza movement chairperson and delegation co-coordinator on this voyage, stated that: "No one could possibly believe that our small boat constitutes any sort of threat to Israel. We carry medical and reconstruction supplies, and children's toys. Our boat was searched and received a security clearance by Cypriot Port Authorities before we departed, and at no time did we ever approach Israeli waters."

Arraf continued, "Israel's deliberate and premeditated attack on our unarmed boat is a clear violation of international law and we demand our immediate and unconditional release."

We are NOT the "Story": It's Not Just Our Twenty-One Kidnapped Passengers

Written by Ramzi Kysia and Greta Berlin
July 1, 2009

On June 30th 2009 IOF forcibly boarded the Free Gaza boat, *Spirit of Humanity*, and kidnapped 21 human rights workers and journalists who were on their way to deliver much needed humanitarian and reconstruction supplies to besieged Gaza. Those abducted by Israel include Nobel peace prize laureate Mairead Maguire and former U.S. Congresswoman Cynthia McKinney.

Since their kidnapping, tens of thousands of people around the world have mobilized to demand their immediate and unconditional release. The Free Gaza movement would like to thank everyone who has made a phone call, sent a fax or email, written a letter, or organized a demonstration on behalf of our twenty-one imprisoned friends.

With respect, it is not enough. We are not the story. Since it's founding in 1948 the State of Israel has regularly kidnapped and tortured Palestinians, throwing them into forgotten prisons where they can languish for years. Today, over 11,000 Palestinian political prisoners endure torture and isolation in Israeli jails, outdoor prison camps, and secret black sites without benefit of due process. The prisoners include men, women, and children. They come from all walks of life: doctors, journalists, parliamentarians, workers, resistance fighters, homemakers, students, and others.

They are our sisters and brothers.

The twenty-one passengers aboard the Spirit of Humanity have been illegally incarcerated for their solidarity work with Palestine. 11,000 other members of our common human family are already imprisoned simply for being Palestinian.

The Siege of Palestine is not simply the physical blockade against Gaza. The Siege includes the hundreds of checkpoints throughout the West Bank that separate families and communities and shatter any prospect for a viable Palestinian state. The Siege includes the millions of Palestinians in Diaspora, many of them dumped in squalid refugee camps in Jordan, Lebanon, and elsewhere. The siege is ever-present throughout all aspects of Palestinian life.

This siege is only strengthened when we pay more attention to the injustice done to twenty-one international solidarity workers than we do to the much greater injustices already being committed against millions of Palestinians.

We in the Free Gaza movement implore all the good people around the world who have working so hard to secure the release of our friends to "adopt" a Palestinian prisoner. We ask you to learn about the crisis and take on the cause of an individual prisoner as your own.

Break the Siege! Reach out to Palestine!

Ireland's Foreign Affairs Minister Calls for Release of Irish Activists Detained

By Free Gaza Team
July 2, 2009

"Ireland's Foreign Affairs Minister Micheál Martin today called for the swift release of two Irish nationals currently detained in Israel following the June 30 seizure of a boat en route to Gaza with humanitarian aid.

The two, Nobel Peace Prize winner Mairead Maguire and Derek Graham, are awaiting deportation following the seizure of vessel The *Spirit of Humanity*. In a statement, Minister Martin said his department has been closely following the situation and was in ongoing contact with Israeli authorities.

"My immediate priority is ensuring the safety and welfare of Ms. Maguire and Mr. Graham and securing their release as soon as possible," the minister said. "I have been assured by the Israeli authorities that they are both well and are being properly treated. An officer from the Irish Embassy in Tel Aviv visited yesterday with Ms. Maguire and Mr. Graham to provide assistance and will endeavor to make a further consular visit today.

"I would again renew my call for the release of Ms. Maguire and Mr. Graham as well as the other nineteen passengers detained on the *Spirit of Humanity*," he added. "I would also call upon the Israeli Government to ensure that the humanitarian supplies for the people of Gaza being transported on the *Spirit of Humanity* are made available as soon as possible to the Palestinian authorities for distribution."

The minister called the current Israeli blockade of Gaza "completely unacceptable" and called for all border crossings into the coastal salient to be opened to humanitarian and commercial traffic."

UN Expert Denounces Seizure of Aid Boat by Israeli Forces

Written by Free Gaza movement
July 2, 2009

GENEVA - The UN special rapporteur on the situation of human rights in the Palestinian territories occupied since 1967, Richard Falk, denounced the unlawful naval seizure by an Israeli gunboat on the high seas of a ship carrying medicine and reconstruction material to blockaded people of Gaza.

"This Israeli action implements its cruel blockade of the entire Palestinian population of Gaza, in violation of Article 33 of the Fourth Geneva Convention that prohibits any form of collective punishment directed at an occupied people," said the human rights expert.

Mr. Falk pointed to a recent report on the impact on health resulting from the two-year blockade, issued by the International Committee of the Red Cross. He stressed that Israeli actions not only restrict such vital supplies as food, medicine, and fuel to bare subsistence levels, but has in unprecedented fashion, disallowed the entry to Gaza of building materials and spare parts needed for repairing some of the widespread damage caused by its attacks on the Strip that took place for twenty-two days starting on December 27, 2008.

"Such a pattern of continuing blockade under these conditions amounts to such a serious violation of the Geneva Conventions as to constitute a continuing crime against humanity," added the independent human rights expert.

The boat in question had been inspected in response to Israeli demands before departure by the port authorities in Cyprus to determine whether there were weapons on board. None were found, and Israeli authorities were so informed.

Nonetheless, the twenty-one peace activists on the boat were arrested, held in captivity, and have been charged with 'illegal entry" to Israel even though they had no intention of going to Israel

Interview from a kidnapped passenger, Adie Mormech[7] - Prison Cell, Givon Jail, Ramle, Israel

July 4, 2009

Adie Mormech, one of twenty-one human rights workers and crew taken prisoner on Tuesday, 30 June when his boat was forcibly boarded by the Israeli Navy, has spoken by mobile phone from his prison cell at Givon jail, Ramle, near Tel Aviv.

In a brief interview with Andy Bowman of Manchester's Mule newspaper, Mr. Mormech gave the following account:

How are you being treated?

It's bad, but the conditions are okay for me, I've not been beaten up, they're a bit nasty sometimes and when they boarded the boat we had our faces slammed against the floor. It was bad for the older women like Mairead.

The four other UK nationals are in the cell with me. There are fourteen of us in the seven by seven meter cell that includes the toilet and shower; so very crowded.

It's very hot, and there's only a tiny window. We get awakened at six in the morning for an inspection and have to stand to attention, and then they repeat that at 9:00 A.M., and we are only allowed out of the cells for a few hours each day.

They keep giving us forms to sign, but they are in Hebrew, so we don't. Although I'm able to cope here, other people are less comfortable than me in the situation. If we're here for a long time like some of the other people in here have been, then it will be tough.

---

7   Interviewed by Andy Bowman, from Mule Newspaper, www.themule.info Based out of Manchester in the U.K., Mule Newspaper is a small indy media outlet. They punch above their weight, providing good progressive and investigative journalism as volunteers.

Have you had access to a lawyer yet?

We have, and at the moment we're discussing what to do about our deportation. They've taken our personal items like laptops, cameras, phones, and many other valuables, and we want to find out where these are. They obviously want to deport us as quickly as possible, but some of us are thinking about fighting the deportation. Firstly on the basis that if we get deported we won't be allowed into the occupied West Bank or Israel for another ten years, but also, because we didn't intend to come here to Israel, we intended to go to Gaza, and went directly from international waters into Palestinian waters. There is nothing legal about what Israel has done to us grabbing us like this. We're considering fighting the deportation on the grounds that we shouldn't accept and legitimize this barbaric military blockade of Gaza.

If you challenge the deportation could you remain in prison for a while longer?

Yes we could; there are some people that need to get home, but some will challenge. And for those it will be a few more weeks in prison at least, we expect.

And you?

I'm veering toward challenging it on the basis that it's a scar on my name to accept that I shouldn't have been here, but in fact I have every right to go to Gaza just as everyone else does. That's the whole point of these voyages and that's the principle we want to stick to.

Have they told you what has happened to the cargo of the boat?

No, we don't know what they're doing with it. We've been told a lot of lies so far about where we're going and what's happening to us, so we just don't know. They're already prepared to deprive the people of Gaza of a lot of aid anyway.

What is your message to people back in the UK?

This is not about us here in the cells, it's about the denial of human rights to the people of Palestine, and in particular the inhumane blockade of Gaza. People must not forget about what is happening to Gaza. At the moment they are even being denied food and medical supplies. After the carnage of the 1,500 people killed in January, we won't forget and we'll keep on going and keep fighting for the human rights of the people of Palestine.

Letter from an Israeli Jail,

By Cynthia McKinney
July 4, 2009

This is Cynthia McKinney and I'm speaking from an Israeli prison cellblock in Ramle. [I am one of] the Free Gaza twenty-one, human rights activists currently imprisoned for trying to take medical supplies to Gaza, building supplies, and even crayons for children, I had a suitcase full of crayons for children. While we were on our way to Gaza, the Israelis threatened to fire on our boat, but we did not turn around. The Israelis hijacked and arrested us because we wanted to give crayons to the children in Gaza. We have been detained, and we want the people of the world to see how we have been treated just because we wanted to deliver humanitarian assistance to the people of Gaza.

At the outbreak of Israel's Operation Cast Lead [in December 2008], I boarded a Free Gaza boat with one day's notice and tried, as the US representative in a multinational delegation, to deliver three tons of medical supplies to an already besieged and ravaged Gaza.

During Operation Cast Lead, US-supplied F-16s rained hellfire on a trapped people. Ethnic cleansing became full-scale, outright genocide. U.S.-supplied white phosphorus, depleted uranium, robotic technology, DIME weapons, and cluster bombs, new weapons creating injuries never treated before by Jordanian and Norwegian doctors. I was later told by doctors who were there in Gaza during Israel's onslaught that Gaza had become Israel's veritable weapons testing laboratory…people used to test and improve the kill ratio of their weapons.

The world saw Israel's despicable violence thanks to al-Jazeera Arabic and Press TV that broadcast in English. I saw those broadcasts live and around the clock, not from the USA but from Lebanon, where my first attempt to get into Gaza had ended because the Israeli military rammed the boat I was on in international waters. It's a miracle that I'm even here to write about my second encounter with the Israeli military, again a humanitarian mission aborted by the Israeli military.

The Israeli authorities have tried to get us to confess that we committed a crime. I am now Israeli prisoner number 88794, in prison for collecting crayons to kids.

Zionism has surely run out of its last legitimacy if this is what it does to people who believe so deeply in human rights for all that they put their own lives on the line for someone else's children. Israel is the fullest expression of Zionism, but if Israel fears for its security because Gaza's children have crayons then not only has Israel lost its last shred of legitimacy, but Israel must be declared a failed state.

I am facing deportation from the state that brought me here at gunpoint after commandeering our boat. I was brought to Israel against my will. I am being held in this prison because I had a dream that Gaza's children could color and paint that Gaza's wounded could be healed, and that Gaza's bombed-out houses could be rebuilt.

But I've learned an interesting thing by being inside this prison. First of all, it's incredibly black: populated mostly by Ethiopians who also had a dream like my cellmates, one is pregnant. They all are in their twenties. They thought they were coming to the Holy Land.

Original audio message available here: http://freegaza.org/it/home/56-news/984-a-message-from-cynthia-from-a-cell-block-in-israel

They had a dream that their lives would be better. The once proud, never colonized Ethiopia [has been thrown into] the back pocket of the United States, and become a place of torture, rendition, and occupation. Ethiopians must free their country because superpower politics [have] become more important than human rights and self-determination.

My cellmates came to the Holy Land so they could be free from the exigencies of superpower politics. They committed no crime except to have a dream. They came to Israel because they thought that Israel held promise for them. Their journey to Israel through Sudan and Egypt was arduous. I can only imagine what it must have been like for them.

And it wasn't cheap. Many of them represent their family's best collective efforts for self-fulfillment. They made their way to the United Nations High Commission for Refugees. They got their yellow paper of identification. They got their certificate for police protection. They are refugees from tragedy, and they made it to Israel. Only after they arrived, Israel told them, "There is no UN in Israel."

The police here have license to pick them up & suck them into the black hole of a farce for a justice system. These beautiful, industrious, and proud women represent the hopes of entire families. The *idea* of Israel tricked them and the rest of us. In a widely propagandized slick marketing campaign, Israel represented itself as a place of refuge and safety for the world's first Jews and Christians. I too believed that marketing and failed to look deeper.

The truth is that Israel lied to the world. Israel lied to the families of these young women. Israel lied to the women themselves who are now trapped in Ramle's detention facility. And what are we to do? One of my cellmates cried today. She has been here for 6 months. As an American, crying with them is not enough. The policy of the United States must be better, and while we watch President Obama give 12.8 trillion dollars to the financial elite of the United States it ought now be clear that hope, change, and 'yes we can' were powerfully presented images of dignity and self-fulfillment, individually and nationally, that besieged people everywhere truly believed in.

It was a slick marketing campaign as slickly put to the world and to the voters of America as was Israel's marketing to the world. It tricked all of us but, more tragically, these young women.

We must cast an informed vote about better candidates seeking to represent us. I have read and re-read Dr. Martin Luther King Junior's letter from a Birmingham jail. Never in my wildest dreams would I have ever imagined that I too would one day have to do so. It is clear that taxpayers in Europe and the US have a lot to atone for, for what they've done to others around the world.

What an irony! My son begins his law school program without me because I am in prison, in my own way trying to do my best, again, for other people's children. Forgive me, my son. I guess I'm experiencing the harsh reality, which is why people need dreams. [But] I'm lucky. I will leave this place. Has Israel become the place where dreams die?

Ask the people of Palestine. Ask the stream of black and Asian men whom I see being processed at Ramle. Ask the women on my cellblock. [Ask yourself:] what are you willing to do?

Let's change the world together and reclaim what we all need as human beings: Dignity. I appeal to the United Nations to get these women of Ramle, who have done nothing wrong other than to believe in Israel as the guardian of the Holy Land, resettled in safe homes. I appeal to the United State's Department of State to include the plight of detained UNHCR-certified refugees in the Israel country report in its annual human rights report. I appeal once again to President Obama to go to Gaza: send your special envoy, George Mitchell there, and to engage Hamas as the elected choice of the Palestinian people.

I dedicate this message to those who struggle to achieve a free Palestine, and to the women I've met at Ramle. This is Cynthia McKinney, July 2nd 2009, also known as Ramle prisoner number 88794.

Report from the Kidnapped Passengers in Ramle Prison

By Free Gaza Team
July 4, 2009

On Monday, June 30, Twenty-one passengers going to challenge the blockade of Gaza on board the Spirit of Humanity were seized by the Israeli Navy and taken to Israel against their will. All their equipment was taken and some of were roughed up. All were thrown into prison to await Israel's decision on how and when they would be deported.

The majority of the group ended up in Ramle Prison. Those of us who are Free Gaza organizers had been hearing some news from them, statements, interviews, and letters since they arrived. From the first night, the Free Gaza Twenty-one have been busy trying to get news out of the prison about the illegality of Israel's actions in relation to themselves and the other inmates inside Ramle Prison who have no voice.

Report from E: I received a 2:00 A.M. phone call during one of the first sleepless nights from Ramle Prison to let me know that in one of the cells, four of the FG group had been busy writing a press release on an old phone one of their cellmates had loaned them. It had taken them hours to write the press release. They were just ready to send it out. 'Could I check my e-mail to see if I had received it?'

Since that first night I have been hearing more increasingly about the plight of the other inmates of the prison; men and women who have not nearly as good an opportunity as our folk for media coverage of their stories and not nearly as good an opportunity as our folk of ever getting out of Ramle Prison.

To Fathi Jaouadi, Adie Mormesh, Ishmael Blagrove, and Captain Denis Healy, the situation of their fellow inmates is something they want to talk about and act upon. Fathi wanted to pass on news of what they have been doing inside Ramle prison; he wanted to let everyone who supports the Free Gaza movement know that 'Free Gaza members are never lost for things to do when it comes to trying to expose Israel's appalling treatment of not just Palestinians, but all people who come to Palestine and get caught up in Israel's abuse of justice and the law.'

Fathi Jaouadi has been actively involved in Palestinian rights since he was fifteen years old. Now in Ramle prison, he has already managed to organize a meeting with a UN representative and to raise the issue of the other inmates with him. He said that the UN official has agreed to follow up on some of the cases; Fathi has also been in contact with local NGOs to raise the issue of many of the inmate's situations. He told me he wants to focus on the fact that none of the inmates have any access to legal advice or help, most of the inmates have not been able to contact family to let them know of their situation and none of the inmates have committed anything that warrants them to be held indefinitely inside Ramle prison.

Fathi is in the process of collecting statements from all the inmates, and he is translating them from Arabic. He says the majority of the inmates in their cell are from Arab countries, and they have not had access to their embassy officials. He will follow up with the UN and other organizations once he is released and contact all the families and give statements and details to the relevant embassies.

Ishmael Blagrove is a well-known documentary filmmaker and has been speaking extensively about the Palestinian struggle for more than twenty years. In Ramle prison, he has been working tirelessly to get contact with refugee councils and organizations in Britain to present to them the case of the refugees inside. He says that many of the men from neighboring Arab countries just want to go home, they don't want to stay in Israel and yet they are not being given the opportunity to speak. Ishmael says that many of the inmates are entitled to legal representation, but they do not know this, nor do they have any idea how to contact any refugee organization to advise them. Ishmael is in the process of establishing links between the refugee councils in Britain and the inmates of his cell in Ramle Prison.

Fathi and Ishmael have already established channels to publish these issues in Britain on their release.

When we called Ramle Prison today Fathi said that Adie had just finished his daily English lesson with the inmates. Adie is reportedly very happy with the progress of his students and said this morning they had successfully completed an intense session on Past Participles. Adie Mormesh has also been very active for the rights of Palestinians for many years. He spent two weeks in the West Bank with the Olive Coop (Zeitoun) and Action Palestine in 2007. He worked with and documented the boycott, divestments, and sanctions campaign and participated in the World Social Forums for Palestine in Porto Alegre and Mumbai in 2003 and 2004. He has now become a teacher of English in Ramle prison.

Captain Denis Healey, who has been the Free Gaza movement's captain since October 2008 and bravely steered the *Dignity* to safety in December (when she was attacked by the Israeli Navy), has also been quite busy; he has been giving in-depth lectures to his fellow inmates about life at sea. Apparently there are many interested parties amongst the inmates; some hope that they may pursue a life on the sea when (and sadly if) they ever get out. They are full of questions as to the procedure of getting qualified to work on and sail boats in the Mediterranean, and Captain Denis is giving them a good run down on what they should do to follow such a dream.

This is how four of our passengers have been keeping busy during the past week, they wanted to let you all know; they also said they realize the news they are sending out is not new to any of us. We have all been working with these issues of injustice for years. But that doesn't mean that every new story about the violation of human rights, about the cruelty, brutality, and flagrant misuse of justice by Israel should not be published.

Our friends are stuck in Ramle prison, because they tried to visit the war-stricken people of Gaza, and they are furious at what they are seeing. They know they have generated media interest around the world, and that sooner or later, they will leave Ramle Prison, but they also know that the other inmates of the prison have no such privilege, and without our interest in them, they could well be stuck inside Ramle prison for the rest of their lives, or exiled to some foreign country that is not their home, facing a life without family or loved ones to share it with. And so it is for the 11,000 Palestinian prisoners at present inside Israeli jails. Every one of them has a story that ought to be heard.

Statement #1 taken by Fathi Jaouadi
From Ramle Prison

3rd July 2009
My name is M.
I am 26 years old.
I am a Palestinian born in Al Quds (Jerusalem) and I hold a birth certificate showing this. My family comes from a village called Sour Bahr.

We have two houses there owned by my grandfather who fled in '48 to Jordan and left the houses with my Aunt.

When I was five years old, I went with my family to Jordan to bring back the papers that proved our ownership of these two houses. We stayed in Jordan for two years and then, when we had all the papers we came back to Sour Bahr.

I lived all my life in one of the houses and some of my family lived in the other. We always used to make our way between our two houses, which were only minutes apart from each other.

However when the Wall was built, it split our two houses apart. It used to take minutes and then it took four and one-half hours to go from house to house.

The house I lived in was in the West Bank, the other on the side of the Wall that is Al Quds.

When I was 16 I began the process to try and obtain an Israeli ID, so that I could continue to enter Al Quds and go to our house that was on the other side of the Wall.

Every day my mother would go to the Interior Ministry to try and obtain my ID. She contacted many lawyers about the case but although she worked on this for eight years, there was no result. During this time I tried often to visit our house on the

Al Quds side of the wall and every time I was caught by the Israeli forces and sent back to the West Bank.

When I was 24 years old I had a fight with a friend, I was caught by Israel during the fight and imprisoned for one and a half years.

I am a normal Palestinian trying to live a normal life. I am not involved in any political movement, and I have no security issues with Israel. I am just trying to live my life, but when I had served my time in prison for fighting with a friend, Israel could not decide where to release me.

My birth certificate said Al Quds but I had no Israeli ID. When Israel started investigating, they discovered that when I was five years old I had gone with my family to Jordan for two years.

It was then that I was told by an Israeli judge that the Law states, "Any Palestinian who spends two years outside Israel has no right to return."

I have since seen the Judge twice in the past two months. And he has told me that I will be returned to Jordan. But Jordan has refused to accept me. So now I have been told I will just have to wait in prison.

I am very depressed now and hate my life. I am afraid of how long they will make me wait. It could be years. I am afraid I will be sent to Jordan. I have no one in Jordan. I was there when I was five years old! All my family is in Palestine. I know if they send me to Jordan I will never be allowed back into Palestine. I will never be allowed to see my family again. And I have done nothing.

I just want to be allowed to live a simple life with my family and the people I know and love in my own land.

Statement by Tun Dr. Mahathir Mohamad
July 5, 2009

Former Malaysian PM Tun Dr. Mahathir bin Mohamad Condemns the Abduction and Detention of Cynthia McKinney, Mairead Maguire and members of the Free Gaza movement by Israel

It was indeed shocking to hear about the detention of vessels carrying humanitarian aid and the abduction and arrest of the volunteers on board the Gaza-bound ships. The fact that the Israeli Government committed these acts while the ships and volunteers were in international waters reflects the arrogance of the Zionist administration. That it was committed with such impunity, with total disregard of the international community further emphasizes how dangerous Israel is to the global peace equation.

To add insult, President Barack Obama had very recently said that Israel must allow humanitarian aid be channeled to the Palestinians in Gaza who are dying due to the stranglehold imposed by Tel Aviv.

We demand that the Israeli Government to immediately release the volunteers and the vessels including the aid on board unconditionally.

Failing which we expect President Obama to walk the talk and take Israel to task and to ensure the immediate release of the volunteers and boats.

We hope President Obama is aware that the volunteers include an upright American former Congresswoman Cynthia McKinney as well as Nobel Laureate Mairead Maguire.

DR MAHATHIR BIN MOHAMAD
Chairman
Perdana Global Peace Organization

Update on UK Detainees

Written by Free Gaza movement
July 5, 2009

We have just heard that at least three of the six British Free Gaza detainees are being put on a flight to London in the morning, due to arrive at Heathrow at 13:30

We are currently unable to make contact with the group, which has been moved to cells at Ben Gurion airport detention center. Once we have confirmation that they are on the morning flight, we will post to our Web site: www.freegaza.org

If you live in the London area, please try and make it down to Heathrow to meet them. We expect to have journalists at the airport to report on their deportation, and we are trying to arrange for a press conference in London for later in the afternoon.

Poem from Prison by Mairead Maguire

July 10, 2009
"Spirit of humanity"

As long as
The people of Palestine
Have no liberty, no freedom
Those of us with a voice to speak
Must speak

As long as
The children of Gaza
Live in fear of Israeli
Bombs and occupation
Those of us with a voice to speak
Must speak

As long as
Six million Palestinian refugees
Are deportees around the world
Those of us with a voice to speak
Must speak

As long as
Millions of god's children
Are hungry, imprisoned, and without hope
Those of us with a voice to speak
Must speak

Because it is in speaking
We find our liberty, our freedom
And no prison bars can take away
Our peace, our love
Which is the true spirit of humanity
(for Gaza and the Palestinian people)

Mairead Maguire - Nobel peace laureate (in Ramle - Israeli prison)
I July 2009, http://www.propheticimagery.com/Spirit percent20of percent20Humanity.htm

The Ship that Wanted to Break the Blockade of Gaza but Was Captured by Israel

Written by Eva Boss
July 17, 2009

On the thirtieth of June the Israeli Navy boarded the Free Gaza boat *Spirit of Humanity* when it was approaching Palestinian waters off the Gaza Strip. The boat was towed to the Israeli port Ashdod where the twenty-one persons on board were arrested. Only after almost a week had passed, they were released and deported to their respective countries of origin.

It was the eighth attempt that the Free Gaza organization made to break the blockade on the Palestinian Gaza Strip, where a majority of the people are dependent on aid organizations for their survival. The borders are closed. The inhabitants cannot leave, and Israel only allows in the most necessary items for the inhabitants not to starve to death.

Spirit of Humanity in the port of Larnaca before leaving. The boat was boarded on the 30 June by the Israeli Navy, who towed the ship to the Israeli port of Ashdod.

The *Spirit of Humanity*, a tourist ferry from Greece, had left port of Larnaca on the twenty-ninth of June, loaded with three tons of medicine, toys, and building materials including a symbolic sack of cement. Israel does not allow any import of material for rebuilding houses that had been destroyed during the war around the turn of the year, the rationale being that the material could be used for attacks on Israel by Hamas.

Also onboard were twenty-one solidarity workers and journalists. Among them was the Irish Mairead Maguire who in 1976 won the Nobel Peace Prize, and American Cynthia McKinney, former Congresswoman. It was the second trip for both.

"The Palestinians in the Gaza Strip asked me to come back, and I promised to do so. Things have become worse since I was there last time. Israel has violated both international law and the Geneva Conventions. The world must not forget the Gaza Strip. They have to force Israel into lifting the siege," said Mairead Maguire before setting off.

The youngest on board was Adam Qvist, twenty-three, from Denmark, who also went on his second trip. "For me this is a chance to come back. Last time I stayed five weeks and worked with the fishermen. The Israelis shot at us when we sailed out, but warning shots only. When we are not on board, it's more serious. All the fishermen here have scars from shots at their legs," he tells us.

Adam Qvist in port Larnaca just before his first voyage to the Gaza Strip in August 2008, when the organization Free Gaza succeeded in breaking the blockade

At night after their departure, they were contacted by the Israeli Navy, which threatened to open fire if they didn't turn around. The boat continued in spite of this and in spite of its radar and navigation system being blocked.

"They tried to force us into Israeli waters," reports Denis Healey, who navigated by the compass. But when the boat approached Palestinian waters they were stopped. The boat was surrounded and boarded. "They said we had been in Israeli-controlled waters, since there is an embargo on the Gaza strip," he adds. When the boat was towed in to the port of Ashdod, the people on board were arrested on the grounds of having entered into Israel illegally. The Israeli authorities explained that humanitarian goods should legally be passed overland through Israel. But no building material is allowed. The Free Gaza organizers were indignant and held a press conference in Nicosia, Cyprus.

"They took the boat and the passengers against their will and brought them to Israel. This is illegal. They came from Cyprus through international waters. We want everyone to know that we did not violate any law. Where is the world, the UN, the EU? We only demand from Israel to follow the law," said Ramzi Kysia.

"The boat was in the area that the Oslo agreement grants to the Palestinians for fishing and economic development. The agreement was signed by the Palestinian leader at that time, Yassir Arafat, and Israel's Prime Minister, Yitzhak Rabin, in 1993. The area has even been acknowledged internationally," states Ramzi Kysia.

Greta Berlin, one of the five founders of the organization Free Gaza, aboard of the Spirit of Humanity

It was the third time that Israel prevented a Free Gaza boat to approach the Gaza Strip. Two times in last winter the boats were stopped with the explanation that there was a war going on. One of them, the Dignity, was rammed and damaged so severely that she later sank in the port of Larnaca, in Cyprus, before repairs had been finished.

However, in the year before the Free Gaza boats made their way through to the Gaza Strip five times where they were enthusiastically received. The first two boats broke the blockade in August 2008 and the organization views that event as a victory.

When the boats went back, they had Palestinians on board who were prohibited from leaving the country by the Israeli authorities. Students with scholarships abroad were a part of the group, as well as a boy who had lost a leg in a shell attack and hoped to get prostheses abroad.

It was the first time boats reached the Gaza Strip for more than forty years. A Palestinian attempt in 1988 failed, since somebody blew up the boat in the harbor of Limassol.

Further boats were able to sail into the harbor of Gaza in October, November, and December, thus breaking the siege. On one of these boats the Palestinian parliamentarian Mustafa Barghouti from the West Bank was on board. This was his only way to visit the Gaza Strip.

A group of European parliamentarians also went on the journey and came back with promises that they would do their best within the EU to lift the blockade.

Hugh O'Donnell, member of the liberal democrats in the Scottish Parliament, was very upset about the distress he saw in Gaza. He told about broken dialysis machines that had to be dismantled in order to save spare parts for the only functioning one, and about a two-months-old baby with a heart defect in an incubator and that would soon die because the Gaza Strip lacks medical resources.

"This is a shame. I only once saw a place that was similarly ghastly. This was Kosovo during the war," said O'Donnell.

The Palestinian parliamentarian Mustafa Barghouti participated in one of the trips to the Gaza Strip last year in October. This was his only way to get there. Israel only exceptionally allows trips between the Gaza Strip and the West Bank.

The last unsuccessful trips have not moved the Free Gaza group to surrender. They are now looking for new boats that can replace the captured *Spirit of Humanity* and the sunken *Dignity*. They hope to make a new attempt in some months.

"We have learnt not to go with one boat only, therefore we are looking for at least two boats," says Greta Berlin. "We are looking for a passenger boat and a cargo boat.
The money for the boats is coming from donors from all over the world. The smallest sum someone donated was one and a half dollar; the largest amount was $100,000. People give what they can in order to help the isolated Palestinians."

The organization Free Gaza is politically independent and the boats are unarmed. Each time the boats are checked by the Cypriot authorities to make sure they do not import any weapons to the Gaza Strip.

Free Gaza and Palestine
Huwaida Arraf

August 3, 2009 edition of: *The Nation.*

Last month I led a group of twenty-one human rights workers on a boat from Cyprus to challenge Israel's naval blockade of the Gaza Strip. We carried toys, medicine, olive tree saplings, toolkits, a fifty-kilo bag of cement, and school supplies on our small converted ferryboat.

At 2:00 A.M. on June 30, almost eighteen hours into the 230-mile journey, a colleague awakened me. The Israeli Navy was calling our boat on the VHF radio. "You are navigating toward a blockaded area. You are hereby ordered to change your course. If you do not, we will be forced to use <u>all necessary force to stop you.</u>"

Nervous after a previous boat of ours was dangerously rammed at sea in December by the Israeli military, I replied, "Israeli Navy, this is Arion (the registered name of our ship *Spirit of Humanity*). We are twenty-one unarmed civilians carrying aid for the Palestinian people of Gaza. Any blockade on Gaza is unlawful as you are the occupying force in the territory and are therefore responsible for the wellbeing of the civilian population there. As our boat, its cargo, and the twenty-one civilians on board do not constitute any kind of threat to Israel or its armed forces, you are obliged to allow us entry. We are proceeding to Gaza. Do not use force against us."

Shortly thereafter our navigational systems were disabled for nearly four hours as the warnings continued. In their "final" warning to us, the Israeli Navy threatened to open fire. "Israeli Navy, we are unarmed civilians; do not use force against us. Do not shoot." We did not stop.

We were boarded by force. Before we were separated, I saw Navy forces grabbing my husband, Adam, around the neck. He is a filmmaker who has made documentaries from Palestine to Darfur. Later, I learned that outside of my view, these government-sanctioned pirates pummeled Adam in order to wrest his video camera from his grasp.

Though I know it could not have been easy for him, Adam did not fight back. He was a multisport athlete in high school, threw out Manny Ramirez stealing second and is one of those rare individuals who bring a football player's intensity to peace work. But like the rest of us, Adam insists on using nonviolent means to resist Israel's military occupation.

And though in his widely hailed Cairo speech President Obama made an implicit call for nonviolence as the means to challenge the Israeli occupation, the Obama administration made no public statement on our behalf nor did it do so three months ago, when my dear friend Bassem Abu Rahme was killed while nonviolently protesting Israeli expansionism in the West Bank that threatens to destroy his village of Bil'in.

My colleagues and I invested time and energy in this difficult journey and put our lives at risk because for too long the international community has been complicit in Israel's crimes against the Palestinian people. For too long, diplomats and world leaders have paid lip service to Palestinian human rights. For too long, the Palestinian people have been told to wait: in the checkpoint line, on the peace process, to have your rights recognized, and for freedom.

Students I met on a recent successful voyage to Gaza certainly did not want to wait to be slowly suffocated and drained of their dreams. So desperate were they to escape their confinement in Gaza to obtain higher education abroad that they asked us to drop them in international waters and they would swim the rest of the way to Cyprus. This was youthful madness, but indicative of how trapped people in Gaza are today.

I was born in the blanket of freedom of the United States. My parents immigrated here, knowing that I could not be free in my homeland. But today I use my freedom to struggle as a Palestinian for my friends and relatives who endure the yokes of occupation, oppression, discrimination, exile, internment, and apartheid.

Most Palestinians in the occupied territories have not lived a day free of Israel's occupation, and Palestinian citizens of Israel continue to live as a discriminated-against minority. Just the other day, Israel's housing minister, Ariel Atias, declared,

"We can all be bleeding hearts, but I think it is unsuitable [for Jews and Palestinians] to live together [in Israel]."

This is the Israel the United States funds with billions each year. Under the leadership of President Obama (or any American president) support for this sort of raw bigotry makes no sense and is antithetical to our most cherished principles. Yet when Israeli leaders utter such contemptible language it is ignored. When Israeli soldiers fire lethal weapons at unarmed, peaceful protesters it is too often ignored. When Israeli naval boats become pirate ships, boarding a vessel that poses them no threat, arresting and beating American citizens, it is ignored.

It is ignored and Israel continues to enjoy the patronage of the United States and to present itself as a moral beacon for the world. But my generation finds racist language like that of Atias—and the actions that result from such outdated thinking—abhorrent.

We find it unacceptable that Palestinians continue to be asked to wait, to improve our self-government and to be patient as we build ourselves toward the same rights that people elsewhere take for granted. With the fourth Palestinian generation born into refugee camps, with a new generation in Gaza being raised poorer and more desperate than the last, with my land being carved and sliced and walled for the exclusive benefit of one ethno-religious group, I say we cannot wait.

The question facing the world now must no longer be about where to squeeze a Palestinian state. The only relevant question is how to advance the immediate freedom of ten million Palestinians. There can be no more waiting, no more prevaricating, no more negotiations on that simple, beautiful human concept—freedom.

We will be free. President Obama can expedite the process by putting pressure on Israel, or he can sideline himself and the process for the next eight years. Sooner or later, however, Israel's subjugation of us will be overturned. The current situation is untenable. Whether we live in two states or one state with equal rights for all like South Africa and, indeed, the United States, we will achieve our freedom. What South Africa was to students in the 1980s, Palestine is fast becoming to younger generations increasingly repulsed by the entrenchment of Israel's dual system of law, domination of another people and ongoing confinement of 1.5 million Palestinians to a tiny parcel of land in Gaza.

So, yes, this was only one tiny humanitarian boat to Gaza. But Israel's heavy-handed action shows how much is at stake and how shaky Israel's grip over another people becomes when the world's citizens speak out and take action, even as governments fall short.

Threatened and Beaten On the Way to Gaza

By Adam Shapiro
Huffington Post Contributor Updated: 07-17-09 05:35 PM

I departed Cyprus with twenty others on June 29 in a converted ferry carrying humanitarian provisions intended for Palestinians in Gaza cut off from the world by the Israeli military siege. Our intent was to bring Palestinians toys, medicines, toolkits, olive tree saplings, and one fifty-kilo bag of cement while breaking the sea barrier Israel maintains to imprison Palestinians in their coastal territory.

An independent filmmaker, and human rights advocate, I planned to document the trip and life in Gaza.

Approximately half of Gaza's population is under age 18. These children suffer the consequences of an Israeli imposed economic collapse ostensibly intended to undermine Hamas rule. As with Iraq, the sanctions serve only to devastate a population and decimate civil society.

At 2:00 A.M. on June 30, somewhere off our starboard side, an Israeli warship shone its searchlights at our boat. A voice called on the radio, "You are navigating toward a blockaded area. You are hereby ordered to change your course. If you do not, we will be forced to use all necessary force to stop you."

These waters are patrolled unchallenged by the Israeli Navy. Our call for help to a UN ship we knew to be in radio range when our boat was intentionally rammed by the Israeli Navy in December 2008 went unanswered.

We counted eight Israeli warships and four zodiac boats with boarding parties and divers in hot pursuit. About an hour earlier, an F-16 executed flyovers. This was US-supplied and American taxpayer-subsidized force all to stop one bag of cement from reaching a ghetto and human-made disaster area.

In a flurry of activity, we were boarded. Those of us with video cameras bore the brunt of the over-zealous navy forces. We were beaten to break our grasp on the video cameras. I have documented events from Afghanistan to Darfur to various locations around the Middle East, but until then, I had never been physically attacked on account of my work. Israel's military censor continues to hold the evidence and I expect never to retrieve it. With the evidence gone, much of the media have treated the event as though it never occurred.

Instead of sailing into Gaza's bombed and broken port, we were kidnapped at gunpoint, taken to a foreign country, and imprisoned. Instead of delivering toys to children in Azbet Abed Rabbo, where in February I met families living in tents (again) because their homes were left in rubble by Israel's December-January invasion, we stood at attention for a prison guard to check our cell. As other governments spoke up publicly for their citizens, the US government was notably silent.

As for Gaza, Palestinians there are worlds away from hoping for equal rights. Day to day survival is the priority. The International Committee of the Red Cross recently issued a report, "Gaza: 1.5 million people trapped in despair," in which it details that nothing has been rebuilt that was destroyed during Israel's Operation Cast Lead, over 70 percent of Gazans live in poverty, and malnutrition is on the rise among the most vulnerable - the children of Gaza. Trauma is a foregone conclusion.

The World Health Organization has reported that one-third of children under five and women of childbearing age are anemic.

It is in this context of despair and a complete lack of governmental will to challenge Israel in which a generation of Palestinians is growing up in Gaza worse off than their great grandparents who fled there in 1948. Our small boat tried to break the apathy that permits blockade and siege. We were ordinary civilians, taking a risk on the high seas, confronting the region's most powerful navy, because despite all the words describing the situation in Gaza, nothing is improving. In fact, after the immediate outcry following Israel's winter invasion, Israel again started reducing the number of trucks allowed to enter Gaza.

The Berlin Wall did not fall in a day.

Adam Shapiro is a human rights advocate and documentary filmmaker. His latest film is "Chronicles of a Refugee."

On the Right of Resistance
By Ramzi Kysia

July 27, 2009

"If you are neutral in situations of injustice, you have chosen the side of the oppressor."
- Desmond Tutu

We live in an era defined by its brutality. Our challenge is whether to accept this or to take the risks necessary to transform our world commons in beloved community.

A year ago this August, forty-four ordinary people from seventeen different countries sailed to Gaza in two, small wooden boats. We did what the world would not do - we broke through the siege of Gaza. Over the last year the Free Gaza movement has organized seven more voyages, successfully arriving to Gaza on five separate occasions. Ours remain the only international ships to reach the Gaza Strip in over forty-two years.

In the Middle East, the struggle for justice is an uncertain endeavor in the best of times. On all sides human rights workers are beset with difficulties and distress. The Arab states are tyrannies, their peoples subject to secret police, arbitrary arrest, torture, and oppression. Within their societies, the Arab world is equally fractured by ethnic and class tensions, poverty, and political stagnation. From the outside, from the West, the Middle East faces both open and covert acts of intimidation, intervention, economic destabilization, and even war, invasion, and mass killings.

Standing astride all these troubles, blocking near every attempt at progress in the region are the twin colossi of big oil and Israel. Seldom have a people been cursed with burdens more bitter, more devastating, and seemingly more intransigent than have the Arabs with oil and Israel.

Nowhere is this truer today than in Gaza. In 1999, British Gas discovered huge natural gas fields, worth billions of dollars, in Palestinian territorial waters off the coast of Gaza. Israel has already built a horizontal pipeline to siphon off gas from at least one of these fields. If there is an unspoken reason for the siege of Gaza - this is it.

Israel maintains effective control of all points of entry and exit to Gaza, as well as de facto control of Gaza's revenues and economy. As such, and despite the closure of settlements in Gaza in 2005, Israel remains an occupying power in Gaza as in the rest of Palestine. As an occupying power, Israel is responsible for the wellbeing of the people it occupies and cannot legally impose a blockade, particularly one the collectively punishes the entire population of Gaza. These are clear crimes and the Israeli government and military should be prosecuted for them.

For the last three and a half years the Israeli siege has become increasingly ruthless. Less than twenty percent of normal trade is allowed into Gaza today. The siege has caused the local economy to collapse, leading to steep increases in unemployment, poverty, and childhood malnutrition rates.

Because of Israel's siege there is little fuel to run Gaza's power plant so electricity is scarce and intermittent. Without electricity, water and sanitation systems do not function. On March 27, 2008 two elderly women in their seventies, a teenage girl, and two babies were killed by a flood of sewage in Um Naser. Last year alone, well over sixteen billion litres of raw sewage had to be dumped in the sea, turning the Mediterranean into a toilet and creating a public health disaster.

Gaza is a tiny coastal plain, barely twenty-five miles long by four to seven miles wide. It does not have the ability to independently support the one and a half million human beings who live in one of the most densely populated places on the planet. Two-thirds of Gaza's people are refugees, driven out of historical Palestine during Israel's founding war in 1948. Over half the population are children.

Israel has a long history of violence against Palestinian children. A few examples: In December 2004, the IOF shot and killed seven-year old Rana Siyam. Earlier that year, nine-year old Raghda Alassar was shot and killed in her school while she was taking an English test. Thirteen-year old Iman al-Hams was shot seventeen times by the IOF as she was walking home after class in Gaza. An Israeli captain went up to her corpse and shot her again in the head, dead checking the schoolgirl. The IOF prosecuted him, but not for murder. He was charged with "illegal use of his weapon," and despite admitting that he emptied his entire magazine into a little girl, he was found "not guilty."

Over the summer of 2006, the IOF killed three-year-old Bara Habib, three-year-old Rajaa Abu Shaban, six-year-old Rawan Hajjah, nine-year-old Aya Salmeya, and over thirty-five other children just in Gaza alone. On January 16, 2007, the IOF killed ten-year-old Abir Aramin, the daughter of a Palestinian peace activist, as she was walking home from school. These are only a handful of cases. The Israeli human rights organization B'tselem estimates that over 900 Palestinian children were killed by the Israeli military between 2000 and 2008.

Israel has already recreated the worst aspects of the Warsaw ghetto in Gaza, transforming this small strip of land into the world's largest open-air prison, and the humanitarian condition of the one and a half million men, women, and children illegally incarcerated in Gaza is now at its worst point in the last forty-two years of Israeli occupation.

But there are darker histories waiting to be reborn. The simple and terrifying truth is that Israel is pushing the world on a path toward genocide. We are all en route to the slow-drip destruction of the Palestinian people. This reality must be forcefully confronted and fully overcome before it's too late.

It's now been more than six months since the end of Israel's latest assault on the Gaza Strip, which led to the killing of over 1,400 Palestinians, and the people of Gaza are still living in rubble. Israel's hermetic closure has created a man-made and deliberately sustained humanitarian catastrophe. The continuing failure of the international community to enforce its own laws and protect the people of Gaza demands that we as private citizens directly intervene to take action commensurate with the crisis. We must act because our governments refuse to do so.

Regardless of Israeli threats or intimidation, Free Gaza volunteers intend to continue sailing unarmed boats to Gaza. Now more than ever we need the people of the world to join with us.

The siege of Gaza only serves to strengthen authoritarian structures on all sides of this conflict, entrenching centralized control, rallying people against a common enemy. The isolation of Gaza reinforces a belief that the world has forgotten Palestine, and little cares how Palestinians are forced to live or even whether they live or die.

In contrast, civil resistance and citizens' action movements are not only aimed against the injustices that we face but also strategies for social change. Nonviolent resistance empowers everyone with the knowledge that any among us can reach out, organize, and act to change the entire world. Time and again, history demonstrates that even the greatest of tyrannies can crumble to the ground when confronted with an organized and determined resistance.

Join us, whether in whole or in part. Join the Free Gaza movement, the International Solidarity Movement, and the BDS Movement. Join us and other campaigns in the struggle for justice for Palestine. We need volunteers to do research and writing, web updates, translation, graphic design, local organizing in their communities, and much more.

Become part of the resistance.

We are often told that resistance is either unwarranted or impossible. Liberal apologists for Israel, such as Thomas Friedman, are constantly demanding that Palestinians lay down their arms, all the while exhorting Israelis to pick them up in ever-increasing acts of violence and degradation.

When faced with violence in our world, our elites tell us that we have two - and only two - choices: capitulate to the violence, or go to war. Of course, which of these two choices is the right and proper course of action depends on who you are. Faced with Palestinian violence, Israelis must, rightly and properly, go to war. Faced with Israeli violence, Palestinians must, rightly and properly, capitulate. In Tel Aviv and Washington D.C. this is called "moral clarity:" the supposed necessity of pursuing Israeli security through deliberately creating massive insecurity among Palestinians. This is lunacy.

But even mainstream "peace" movements in the West try to delegitimize resistance by calling on both Palestinians and Israelis to renounce overt acts of violence, equating Palestinians who commit suicide bombings with Israelis who send F-16s, D9 military bulldozers, and Apache attack helicopters to level entire neighborhoods.

The problem is that the usually random and individual acts of violence by Palestinians against Israelis are not equal to the myriad structural oppressions and cruelties imposed on Palestinians through Israeli government policies. No Palestinian fighter jets bomb Israeli cities - because Palestine has no fighter jets. No Palestinian bulldozers demolish Israeli homes - because Palestine has no military bulldozers. No Palestinian soldiers invade Israeli neighborhoods, terrorizing the populace because there is no Palestinian army. The conflict in Palestine is a war of Israeli state terror against a largely unarmed and defenseless civilian population.

Even immoral and self-defeating acts of violence against Israeli civilians (such as some suicide bombings are) cannot be equated with the daily humiliations, terror, and death that Israel inflicts on Palestinians by deliberate policy. Contrary to its presentation in the mainstream media, this conflict is neither a righteous war against evil Arab terrorists, nor a religious or ethnic dispute between two opposing and equally self-justified groups of people. The Israeli/Palestinian conflict is the struggle of two irreconcilable and unequal causes: the struggle of an oppressed people for freedom, justice, and self-determination against their oppressors' struggle to maintain (and even expand) their domination. Under these circumstances resistance is not only a right it's a moral imperative.

With respect, just because some people have chosen to remain ignorant of the long and deep history of Palestinian nonviolent resistance - from the 1936 Boycott to Bil'in today - does not mean that it does not exist. The Free Gaza movement struggles in solidarity with an already vibrant Palestinian civil resistance.

Similarly, the other criticism of resistance that it is futile is equally mistaken. There is a widespread delusion among many that Israel and the Israeli lobby are simply too powerful to be challenged, let alone defeated. This is not the case.

On June 30th 2009, IOF forcibly boarded one of our boats, the *Spirit of Humanity*, and kidnapped 21 human rights workers and journalists who were on their way to deliver much needed humanitarian and reconstruction supplies to besieged Gaza, including Nobel peace prize laureate Mairead Maguire and former US Congresswoman Cynthia McKinney. They were held in jail for a week before being deported.

Though we were stopped on this particular voyage, it was not a "failure." In the month after our boat was hijacked, over 100,000 news stories, essays, blog entries, action alerts, and radio and television segments were made on Israel's violent response to our mission. It's true that the ordeal of our twenty-one volunteers pales in comparison to the 11,000 Palestinian political prisoners held in Israeli prisons. The seizure of our small cargo of three tons of medical aid and reconstruction kits is insignificant in light of the $4 billion (USD) of aid promised to Gaza, aid that has not and will not be delivered because of the Israeli blockade.

But that too misses the point. By choosing to violently confront and kidnap unarmed human rights workers on a mission of mercy, Israel publicly demonstrated both the illegality and the absurdity of the Gaza siege. The siege is abjectly not about "security." No one could possibly have believed that our small boat was a physical threat to Israel,

This public demonstration of the siege's illegality resulted in record action at the governmental level as well. Both the Irish and Greek governments formally intervened to protect their citizens and property. Despite having no diplomatic relationship and refusing to recognize the legitimacy of Israel's government, the King of Bahrain personally and successfully intervened to force Israel to immediately release the five Bahraini human rights workers kidnapped from the *Spirit*. The British parliament held a formal debate on the issue, and even the US State Department was forced to hold a national conference call on for family and friends of the kidnap victims, as well as for Arab-American civil rights groups.

This was unprecedented, but it's not enough.

The Free Gaza movement started our small part in this struggle in 2006. We began on hope alone. Many thought it couldn't be done, but we did it. We broke through the Israeli blockade. We will sail again, and we are absolutely determined to reach the Gaza Strip on our next voyage. We intend to nonviolently escalate our response. By sending a cargo ship, we will escalate the challenge to the blockade by bringing in significant amounts of banned reconstruction materials. By sending more boats on our next mission, we will significantly escalate the logistical difficulties Israel faces should they decide to violently attack us again. By sending even more parliamentarians, dignitaries, journalists, and human rights workers to accompany the boats, we will significantly escalate the political difficulties Israel faces should they decide to violently attack us again.

The journey to Gaza is dangerous. The Israeli Navy rammed our flagship, the *Dignity,* when we attempted to deliver medical supplies to Gaza during their vicious assault in December/January. In June, they hijacked our small boat and kidnapped everyone on board. Israel has even threatened to open fire on our unarmed ships, rather than allow us to deliver humanitarian and reconstruction supplies to the people of Gaza.

But the risks we take on our voyages are insignificant compared to the risks imposed every day upon the people of Gaza.

The purpose of nonviolent direct action and civil resistance is to take risks - to put ourselves "in the way" of injustice. We take these risks well aware of what the possible consequences may be. We do so because the consequences of doing nothing are so much worse. Any time we allow ourselves to be bullied, every time we pass by an evil and ignore it - we lower our standards and allow our world to be made that much harsher and unjust for us all.

Israel can threaten our boats and passengers. We will keep going. Israel can illegally disrupt our communications and navigation systems, and we will keep going. Israel can open fire around our boats, or attempt to ram and sink them. Israel can choose to forcibly board and highjack our boats, and abduct our volunteers.

It doesn't matter. We will keep going. Armed only with the love of justice, and in the rite of resistance we will go to Gaza again and again and again, until this siege is forever shattered and the people of Gaza have free access to the rest of the world.

Chapter 21:

The Freedom Flotilla

⌘ ⌘ ⌘

Escalating Our Efforts: Turning Concepts into Reality

By Huwaida Arraf

After Israel violently intercepted our last three attempts to reach Gaza by sea, we decided we needed a change of strategy. Some of our supporters began questioning the utility of continuing to send boats to Gaza; but for us, giving up was not an option. For one, the violence perpetrated against Palestinians on a daily basis in Gaza, and indeed throughout the Occupied Palestinian Territory, is greater than what we endured on the boats.

Furthermore, we refused to give in to the notion that military might and violence is stronger than the principles and rights we are fighting for. But to overcome Israel's apparent determination to put an end to our efforts, we had to make the cost of stopping our boats much bigger for Israel. Therefore, instead of sending one small boat with a few-dozen people and a symbolic amount of supplies to Gaza, we would need to send a flotilla.

From July 2009 to May 2010, we set to work on organizing this flotilla. We reissued our call for governments and international organizations to join us. We wrote letters to heads of state, particularly those states that pledged money to rebuild Gaza after Operation Cast Lead. In March 2009, donor countries pledged over $4.2 billion to rebuild Gaza, yet, according to a press release issued by UNRWA, by mid-August 2009, not one penny of this money had reached Gaza due to Israel's closure. Many of the governments responded, but only to reiterate their standard statements of concern for the welfare of Palestinians in Gaza. They did not commit to do anything about the Israeli policy that was decimating that welfare. We also set out to build grassroots support and involvement around the world. From Chile to South Africa, India to the United States, we met with groups, unions, parliamentarians, journalists, and other individuals to support our non-violent, direct action efforts to end Israel's strangulation of Gaza.

Because we were still a small group of activists, without a country, or even a big organization behind us, we aimed for a modest flotilla of three vessels—one cargo ship and two accompanying passenger boats, with many members of parliament, other high profile people, and media on board. We estimated that we would need at least Ð700,000 to make this happen. At the invitation of Former Malaysian prime minister Tun Mahathir Mohamad, we went to Malaysia. The First Lady of Malaysia, Datan Sri Rosmah, pledged the money for a cargo ship, but this was only half of what we needed. We spent months trying to raise the rest.

My husband Adam and I went to the Gulf. Many expressed verbal support for our efforts, but the financial support was not as forthcoming as we hoped, and needed. People had doubts about the utility of what we were doing, and preferred to channel their money toward humanitarian efforts. Although it is certainly understandable that one might prefer to help build a hospital, support an orphan, or send needed food and medicine to Palestine, "If that's where you invest 100 percent of your efforts without addressing the policies that leave Palestinians in need of this aid, you will be supporting them for the rest of their lives, their children's lives too!" I argued. We had originally hoped to sail by the end of the summer 2009, but we couldn't do it. We kept pushing the date back, September, October, November, January, but we still could not get the funds we needed to pull off the mission.

In January, our colleague Fathi Jaouadi informed us that Insani Yardim Vakfi (IHH), a large Turkish human rights and humanitarian relief foundation that operates in dozens of countries around the world, pledged five boats to the flotilla! Fathi had worked on this initiative for months, holding meetings with the officers of IHH before he was finally able to bring them on board. This represented a significant development, not only because of the number of boats added to the flotilla, but because a well-established humanitarian relief organization undertook to join us in a direct-action challenge to Israel's illegal closure policy. Other relief organizations and NGOs expressed verbal support for our efforts, but cited numerous restrictions that prevented them from joining us.

Over the next couple of months a few more groups joined the effort. In Sweden, an initiative called "Ship to Gaza" had been underway for approximately a year. There, activists were raising money to sail to Gaza, stopping at various European ports to load donated cargo and garner support along the way. They were modeling this effort after "Ship to Bosnia," a similar effort undertaken by Swedish human rights activists in 1995. Although the Swedish group had not reached their financial goal, and our effort was different than what they were planning, they decided to commit their resources to the flotilla.

Our Greek comrades from the maiden voyage had formed a group called "Ship to Gaza, Greece" and sought to join. The fact that Greeks and Turks, people with their own history of animosity toward each other, were going to work together for the sake of Palestine had strong political significance for both groups and underscored the power of our mission. The Swedish and Greek teams pooled their resources to buy a cargo ship. Then, the European Campaign to End the Siege of Gaza, a group that we had worked with before on our second and third voyages to Gaza, pledged a ship, and joined. On 3 April 2010, at a meeting in Istanbul, we announced the "Coalition to Break the Blockade on Gaza" and our plans to launch a flotilla to Gaza later in the spring.

As we were building this coalition, we were also busy readying our own vessels. On 30 March 2010, the Free Gaza movement purchased a 1,200-ton cargo ship at an auction in Dundalk, Ireland. The vessel had been impounded a year earlier following an inspection by the International Transport Federation (ITF), which found that its owners had exploited its Lithuanian crew members, failed to pay their wages, and subjected them to humiliating treatment. And so a vessel, which had been used to subject workers to modern day slavery, would now be used to promote human rights for the people of Palestine. We renamed the vessel, the *Rachel Corrie*, after the American peace activist killed by an Israeli bulldozer in 2003. In addition we purchased two small yachts, the *Challenger 1 – Al Sumoud* (Arabic for "Steadfastness") and the *Challenger 2 – Al Amal* (Arabic for hope) and were preparing the *Free Gaza* boat from our first mission to also sail so we could donate her to fishermen in Gaza.

The Mavi Marmara underway toward Gaza

Instead of acquiring five ships, IHH invested in one large vessel, a 1,060-person passenger ferry called the *Mavi Marmara*.[8] The European Campaign to End the Siege of Gaza purchased a military vessel converted into a passenger ferry called the *Sfendoni* (renamed *8000*, for the over 8000 Palestinian political prisoners in Israeli jails). Donations from people in Kuwait and Algeria allowed IHH to purchase two cargo ships, *Gazze I* and *Dafne Y* (renamed *Gazze II*). And the Greek/Swedish cargo ship, *Eleftheri Mesogios* (renamed *Free Mediterranean)* brought the number of vessels in our planned flotilla to nine.

Stress and tensions were high as we scrambled to overcome last minute obstacles to the launch of the flotilla. But, our spirits were even higher. Israeli leaders, including Foreign Minister Avigdor Lieberman, Defense Minister Ehud Barak, and their deputies threatened Israel would use all necessary force to stop us from reaching Gaza. While we did not underestimate the violence they could use against us, we believed we were protected by the public and high profile nature of our action, by all of the journalists we had on board the ships, and by the fact that Israeli leaders knew the Freedom Flotilla was a purely civilian effort. Furthermore, our cargo would be inspected by officials at each of the ports we departed from, confirming that we did not constitute any kind of threat to Israel's "security."

We did, however, threaten the legitimacy of Israel's closure on Gaza, as well as its ongoing abuses of the Palestinian people under the pretext of "security." Undoubtedly, the massive nature of our global, grassroots, direct action also constituted a threat to Israel's entire colonial apartheid project.

---

8   Even though the ship had a capacity of 1060 persons, for the sake of comfort, we decided to only put half that number of people on it.

Our ships departed from Ireland, Greece, and Turkey to meet at a pre-determined point in the Mediterranean Sea. On 30 May 2010, the Freedom Flotilla began the final leg of its journey to the besieged Gaza Strip with over 700 people from 36 countries on board seven vessels,[9] 10,000 tons of aid, and millions of volunteers and supporters around the world watching.

Israel's Intimidation Tactics Won't Stop Us: First Ship Sets Sail for Gaza!

By Free Gaza Team

London – 14 May 2010 – At 22:45 local time tonight, the *Rachel Corrie*, a 1,200-ton cargo ship, part of the eight-vessel *Freedom Flotilla*, set sail from Ireland on its way to the Mediterranean Sea. There, ships from Turkey and Greece will join her, then sail to Gaza.

This past week reports from Israel have indicated that the Israeli authorities will not allow the *Freedom Flotilla* to reach Gaza with its cargo of much-needed reconstruction material, medical equipment, and school supplies. According to Israeli news sources, clear orders have been issued to prevent the ships from reaching Gaza, even if this necessitates military violence.

The Free Gaza movement, which has launched eight other sea missions to Gaza, confirms that Israel has tried these kinds of threats and intimidation tactics before in order to try to stop the missions before they start. "They have not deterred us before and will not deter us now," said one of the organizers.

Ship to Gaza, Sweden, a *Freedom Flotilla* coalition partner, together with parliamentarian Mehmet Kaplan (Green Party) yesterday asked for an audience with the Minister of Foreign Affairs of Sweden, Carl Bildt, to discuss what measures the Swedish government and the European Union will take to protect the *Freedom Flotilla's* peaceful, humanitarian voyage. Earlier this week during a meeting with the European Campaign to End the Siege on Gaza, another coalition partner, Turkish Prime Minister Tayyib Erdogan expressed his support for "breaking the oppressive siege on the Gaza Strip, which is at the top of Turkey's list of priorities."

---

9   Due to mechanical troubles, which we suspect was a result of sabotage, the *Challenger 2*, was unable to continue as part of the flotilla. Also, Cyprus succumbed to Israel's diplomatic pressure, and did not allow us to take the *Free Gaza* out of port. The *Rachel Corrie*, although part of the flotilla, experienced delays (which we believe was a result of attempted sabotage) that put it a few days behind the other six vessels.

Coalition partners, Ship to Gaza, Greece and the Turkish relief organization IHH, stressed that the ships, passengers, and cargo will be checked at each port of departure, making it clear that we constitute no security threat to Israel.

Israel's threats to attack unarmed civilians aboard vessels carrying reconstruction aid are outrageous and indicative of the cruel and violent nature of Israel's policies toward Gaza. The *Freedom Flotilla* is acting in line with universal principals of human rights and justice in defying a blockade identified as illegal by the UN and other humanitarian organizations. Palestinians in Gaza have a right to the thousands of basic supplies that Israel bans from entering, including cement and schoolbooks, as well as a right to access the outside world. The *Freedom Flotilla* coalition calls on all signatories to the Fourth Geneva Conventions to pressure Israel to adhere to its obligations under international humanitarian law, to end the lethal blockade on Gaza, and to refrain from attacking this peaceful convoy.

"Treat Our Passengers and Cargo with Respect" says Senator Mark Dearey

(Dublin, May 21, 2010) The Free Gaza movement welcomes statements by the Irish Government to ensure the safety of the passengers and cargo currently making their way to the besieged Gaza Strip.

His Excellency Mr. Breifne O'Reilly, Irish ambassador in Tel Aviv, travelled to the Israeli Foreign Ministry in Jerusalem this week "to ensure a peaceful outcome which will enable the safe delivery of these humanitarian supplies".

The Free Gaza movement commends the Irish government for showing true international leadership regarding the illegal siege of Gaza and is calling for other governments to follow suit. The nine ship-strong flotilla, carrying more than 10,000 tons of medical, reconstruction and educational goods, has only been made possible by the actions and donations of citizens from more than sixty countries. A major donation was received from Malaysia, part of which was used to purchase and outfit the humanitarian cargo ship, *Rachel Corrie*.

For further information, visit http://www.counterpunch.org/berlin05182010.html

On Wednesday, Green Party spokesperson for foreign affairs and defence, Senator Mark Dearey, who has personally inspected the cargo onboard the *M.V. Rachel Corrie*, echoed the Ambassador's call stating: "Irish passport holders (must) be treated respectfully and be allowed complete their mission. It is the least we should be insisting on, given the gross abuse of Irish passports by Israeli agents in recent times." Senator Dearey, who has recently replaced Minister Ciarán Cuffe as spokesperson, was referring to Mossad's use of five bogus Irish passports when a Hamas official was assassinated in Dubai earlier this year.

Israel has yet to face sanctions from the Irish Government for this crime. Incredibly, demonstrating exactly what *chutzpah* means, Israel's director of European affairs, Naor Gilon recently asked the Department of Foreign Affairs not to "let" valid passport holders participate in this legal and necessary humanitarian mission to Gaza.

The governments of the United States and Israel both have the opportunity to show new maturity in their relationship with the Palestinian citizens of Gaza by ensuring that all threats to attack the "freedom flotilla" are withdrawn and its safe passage is guaranteed.

Senator Dearey has asked Oireachtas Members to keep a watching brief on the voyage, stressing: "It is beholden on Irish parliamentarians to offer what support we can to this legitimate humanitarian exercise, an exercise that [fellow Irishman] John Ging of the UN Relief and Works Agency has called for."

Second Ship Joins the Freedom Flotilla on Way to Gaza

By Greta Berlin

22 May 2010

[Istanbul, Turkey] Amid cheers and waving of Turkish and Palestinian flags, the *Mavi Marvara*, the second ship to join the Freedom Flotilla, left Istanbul this afternoon. Sponsored by the Turkish humanitarian organization, Insani Yardim Vakfi (IHH or Foundation for Human Rights, Freedoms & Humanitarian Relief), the ship will carry 700 passengers to Gaza as part of the 'blockade busting' flotilla. It joins eight other boats coming from three other countries carrying 10,000 tons of supplies to the Palestinian people, supplies that have been denied to them by Israel.

Boats will meet in the Mediterranean, and then turn toward Gaza to arrive at its besieged slice of beachfront by the end of May. Free Gaza movement's *Rachel Corrie* is already on her way from Ireland and is presently off the coast of Portugal loaded with cement, paper, and supplies for school children and medical equipment.

John Ging, head of United Nation's Relief and Works Agency (**UNRWA)** in the Gaza Strip since 2006 said, "We recommend the world send ships to the shores of Gaza, and we believe that Israel would not stop these vessels because the sea is open, and many human rights organizations have been successful in previous similar steps, and proved that breaking the siege on Gaza is possible."

We will Resist Israel's Attempts to Stop Us

By Free Gaza Team

(Heraklion, Crete, Tuesday, May 25, 2010)

As Israel continues to insist it will stop the seven-ship international Freedom Flotilla, two more ships departed from Greece to Gaza today.

A 2,000 ton cargo ship and fifty-person passenger ship owned by the European Campaign to End the Siege of Gaza, and Swedish/Greek Ship to Gaza campaigns left Athens to meet the *Freedom Flotilla* in international waters.

They follow hot on the trail of the cargo ships of Insani Yardim Vakafi (IHH's) and Free Gaza's *MV Rachel Corrie.* IHH's remaining 1,100 capacity passenger ship and cargo ship are to sail shortly from Turkey.

In Crete, the Free Gaza movement is readying its two passenger boats for their imminent departure. *Al Samoud* (the Steadfast) and *Al Amal* (the Hope Ship) were named by children from schools in occupied Gaza and Jerusalem.

Reports coming from the Israeli Navy say they will jam the flotilla's signals and communications, isolating those on board the ships, and barring the world from witnessing what could become a confrontation or prolonged naval stand-off. The strategy of the *Freedom Flotilla,* however, is to resist any attempts by the Israeli Navy to hijack its ships or to divide cargo ships from passenger vessels. "The message from Israel is clear: 'We will stop you. And no one can prevent us from stopping you.'" said Free Gaza chair, Huwaida Arraf. "However, we will nonviolently resist Israeli attempts to seize our boats. Thousands of people have contributed to making this flotilla a reality, and the people of Gaza are expecting us.

"We will not allow our flotilla to be divided. We will stay with our cargo ships. They are the core of the flotilla carrying essential construction materials denied entry into Gaza like cement, steel, and houses. This action is not a symbolic gesture but a concrete intervention to allow the people of Gaza to rebuild their lives with dignity," emphasized passenger, Aengus O'Snodaigh, TD Sinn Féin party, Ireland

Ewa Jasiewicz added, "We are not breaking the law. We are upholding it. We are acting out of necessity to prevent a greater crime from taking place—the collective punishment of 1.5 million people imprisoned in Gaza. The international community is complicit in this collective punishment and must break its silence. Respect for international law is not optional, it is obligatory."

E-mail from Marianne Torres in Spokane WA

May 28, 2010

According to a report from the webcam, one, possibly two of the boats, after having been certified, checked, examined, and given the okay, now inexplicably developed serious problems. At least one is having difficulty steering and is taking on water. Cyprus received their marching orders this time & will not allow them to land for repairs, even though they know they need help (I believe that refusal is in violation of maritime and international law.), and that there are European Parliament members aboard. A Turkish boat is going to retrieve passengers to take them to the meeting point.

Not a peep in American media except occasional one from Israeli perspective. www.witnessgaza.com

Israel's Disinformation Campaign against the Gaza Freedom Flotilla

By Free Gaza Team

28 May 2010

For over four years, Israel has subjected the civilian population of Gaza to an increasingly severe blockade, resulting in a man-made humanitarian catastrophe of epic proportions. Earlier this month, John Ging, the Director of Operations of the UN Relief and Works Agency for Palestine Refugees (UNRWA) in Gaza, called upon the international community to break the siege on the Gaza Strip by sending ships loaded with humanitarian aid. This weekend, 9 civilian boats carrying 700 human rights workers from 36 countries and 10,000 tons of humanitarian aid will attempt to do just that: break through the Israel's illegal military blockade on the Gaza Strip in non-violent direct action. In response, the Israeli government has threatened to send out 'half' of its Naval forces to violently stop our flotilla, and they have engaged in a deceitful campaign of misinformation regarding our mission.

Israel claims that there is no ongoing humanitarian crisis in Gaza. Every international aid organization working in Gaza has documented this crisis in stark detail. Just released earlier this week, Amnesty International's Annual Human Rights Report stated that Israeli's siege on Gaza has "deepened the ongoing humanitarian crisis. Mass unemployment, extreme poverty, food insecurity and food price rises caused by shortages left four out of five Gazans dependent on humanitarian aid. The scope of the blockade and statements made by Israeli officials about its purpose showed that it was being imposed as a form of collective punishment of Gazans, a flagrant violation of international law." [1]

Israel claims that its blockade is directed simply at the Hamas government in Gaza, and is limited to so-called 'security' items. When US Senator John Kerry visited Gaza last year, he was shocked to discover that the Israeli blockade included staple food items such as lentils, macaroni, and tomato paste. [2] Furthermore, Gisha, the Israeli Legal Center for Freedom of Movement, has documented numerous official Israeli government statements that the blockade is intended to put "pressure" on Gaza's population, and collective punishment of civilians is an illegal act under international law. [3]

Israel claims that if we wish to send aid to Gaza, all we need do is go through "official channels" and give the aid to them, and they will deliver it. This statement is both ridiculous and offensive. Their blockade, their "official channels," is what is directly causing the humanitarian crisis in the first place.

According to former US president Jimmy Carter: "Palestinians in Gaza are being actually 'starved to death,' receiving fewer calories per day than people in the poorest parts of Africa. This is an atrocity that is being perpetrated as punishment on the people in Gaza. It is a crime... an abomination that this is allowed to go on. Tragically, the international community at large ignores the cries for help, while the citizens of Gaza are treated more like animals than human beings." [4]

Israel claims that we refused to deliver a letter and package from POW Gilad Shalit's father. This is a blatant lie. We were first contacted by lawyers representing Shalit's family Wednesday evening, just hours before we were set to depart from

Greece. Irish Senator Mark Daly (Kerry), one of 35 parliamentarians joining our flotilla, agreed to carry any letter and deliver it to UN officials inside Gaza. As of this writing, the lawyers have not responded to Sen. Daly, electing instead to attempt to smear us in the Israeli press. [5] We have always called for the release of all political prisoners in this conflict, including the 11,000 Palestinian political prisoners languishing in Israeli jails, among them hundreds of child prisoners. [6]

Most despicably of all, Israel claims that we are violating international law by sailing unarmed ships carrying humanitarian aid to a people desperately in need. These claims only demonstrate how degenerate the political discourse in Israel has become.

Despite its high profile pullout of illegal settlements and military presence from Gaza in August—September 2005, Israel maintains "effective control" over the Gaza Strip and therefore remains an occupying force with certain obligations. [7] Among Israel's most fundamental obligations as an occupying power is to provide for the welfare of the Palestinian civilian population. An occupying force has a duty to ensure the food and medical supplies of the population, as well as maintain hospitals and other medical services, "to the fullest extent of the means available to it" (G IV, arts. 55, 56). This includes protecting civilian hospitals, medical personnel, and the wounded and sick. In addition, a fundamental principle of International Humanitarian Law, as well as of the domestic laws of civilized nations, is that collective punishment against a civilian population is forbidden (G IV, art. 33).

Israel has grossly abused its authority as an occupying power, not only neglecting to provide for the welfare of the Palestinian civilian population, but instituting policies designed to collectively punish the Palestinians of Gaza. From fuel and electricity cuts that hinder the proper functioning of hospitals, to the deliberate obstruction of humanitarian aid delivery through Israeli-controlled borders, Israel's policies toward the Gaza Strip have turned Gaza into a man-made humanitarian disaster. The dire situation that currently exists in Gaza is therefore a result of deliberate policies by Israel designed to punish the people of Gaza. In order to address the calamitous conditions imposed upon the people, one must work to change the policies causing the crisis. The United Nations has referred to Israel's near hermetic closure of Gaza as "collective punishment," [8] strictly prohibited under Article 33 of the Fourth Geneva Convention. All nations signatory to the Convention have an obligation to ensure respect for its provisions. [9]

Given the continuing and sustained failure of the international community to enforce its own laws and protect the people of Gaza, we strongly believe that we all, as citizens of the world, have a moral obligation to directly intervene in acts of non-violent civil resistance to uphold international principles. Israeli threats and intimidation will not deter us. We will sail to Gaza again and again and again, until this siege is forever ended and the Palestinian people have free access to the world.

Israel Threatening to Stop "Freedom Flotilla" to Gaza

By Free Gaza Team,

May 29, 2010

The ships from different locations are meeting in international waters in the Mediterranean and heading toward Gaza this weekend.

Those aboard the ships reportedly include over 30 parliamentarians from various countries as well as other notables. Among the Americans on board:

AMBASSADOR EDWARD L. PECK, JOE MEADORS, and COL. ANN WRIGHT

Ambassador Peck was chief of mission in Iraq and Mauritania and deputy director of the White House Task Force on Terrorism in the Reagan administration. Meadors is a survivor of the 1967 attack by Israel on the U.S. military ship the *USS Liberty* in which thirty-four Americans were killed. Wright is a twenty-nine-year US Army/ Army Reserves veteran who retired as a colonel and a former US diplomat who resigned in March 2003 in opposition to the invasion of Iraq. She just wrote the piece "The Audacity of the Free Gaza Flotilla: Breaking the Israeli Siege of Gaza May Lead to an Attack at Sea, Detention Camps and Deportation."

EU's New Foreign Affairs Minister Made a Statement!

EUROPEAN UNION Brussels, 28 May 2010

Statement by the spokesperson of High Representative Catherine Ashton on the flotilla sailing to Gaza

The spokesperson of High Representative of the Union for Foreign Affairs and Security Policy/Vice President of the Commission Catherine Ashton issued a following statement today:

"We strongly urge that all involved act with a sense of restraint and responsibility and work for a constructive resolution. The EU remains gravely concerned by the humanitarian situation in Gaza. The continued policy of closure is unacceptable and politically counterproductive.

We would like to reiterate the EU's call for an immediate, sustained and unconditional opening of crossings for the flow of humanitarian aid, commercial goods and persons to and from Gaza."

We're on our Way!

By Free Gaza Team

May 29, 2010

After tremendous pressure from the Greek Cypriots, reneging on their agreement with us:

http://www.cyprus-mail.com/cyprus/cyprus-stops-mps-joining-gaza-flotilla/20100529, we were forced to take our MPs and activists to Famagusta yesterday, on the Turkish/Cypriot side of Cyprus. We spent all day going from one port to the next, surrounded by helicopters and police. Clearly our deal with Cyprus officials had fallen through, and we ended up being pawns in a political soap opera. The Greek-Cypriot members of Parliament, the ones who had worked so hard to get us permission to leave, were outraged. These Parliament members finally told us to go to the North. If they could, they would. The Cypriot government said they made their decision because, "The Republic of Cyprus is fighting for its survival," but it didn't bow to pressure from Israel. As they said this, they bowed their heads.

We made a deal with the Cypriot government that we would board our high-profile passengers and members of Parliament from Cyprus. We would board with no media coverage. We would not bring our boats into Cyprus. We would take small boats out to our own ships and board past the twelve-mile territorial limit.

Authorities mandated that we couldn't even do that, essentially telling us that, even if we board small boats anywhere in Greek Cyprus from any port, we could not travel outside their territorial limits to go to Gaza. Twenty-seven people were supposed to board, including nine Cypriots and two Greeks. None of them could come with us.

Then our two American passenger boats mysteriously had mechanical problems at the same time. *Challenger II* was able to get fourteen delivered to the *Mari Marvara*, then limped into the harbor in Limassol after being harassed by Cypriot helicopters, essentially forbidding us to bring our wounded boat into port.

http://www.youtube.com/watch?v=BjGoe3Gi-ns&feature=player_embedded,

Our other boat, *Challenger I* headed toward Famagusta with sixteen passengers. It, too, was wounded, something wrong with the steering.

By the time we were jerked around yesterday, we had started at 7:00 A.M. By 10:00 P.M., we had nowhere to board, and our boats were out of commission. But we all have Gaza fever, and no one was giving up.

It has taken us all day to find someone on the Turkish side to ferry some of our passengers out to the flotilla, which has been patiently waiting five hours away from Cyprus. At 6:00 P.M., twenty of our passengers left for the flotilla, and the Swedish MP and the three German MPs are on board. Hedy is not, and we are heartsick that, once again, she will not be able to go to Gaza. The flotilla leaves for Gaza early in the morning and should arrive tomorrow afternoon. We have persevered... Al Samoud.

Fatima Mohammadi
May 29, 2010

If allowed in, this will be my third humanitarian aid convoy to Gaza. Each convoy has had its difficulties and its joys. The difficulty of this current convoy is that nearly 700 volunteers aboard 6 ships are attempting to enter the besieged strip through International waters – a completely legal activity – despite constant threats by the Israeli government to block, arrest and deport the entire convoy.

These threats have two effects in my opinion:

1) They highlight the severity and depth of the siege that Israel has imposed on Gaza for nearly four years, showing Israel to be the vicious occupier and instigator of hostility in the region that we know them to be, and

2) They strengthen the resolve of volunteers around the world, on this convoy and beyond, who are aware of the plight of the Palestinians and who actively seek a resolution to the unjust occupation and continued colonization of Palestine.

Of course, the joy of this convoy is the real potential it has to finally end the siege on Gaza… if it gains enough international support and attention in the crucial upcoming hours.

Currently, we are anchored in the Mediterranean Sea about a six-hour sail from Cyprus, where we have been awaiting two final ships. An American ship carrying members of Parliament from half a dozen European countries is supposed to arrive shortly, and the Irish boat, the *MV Rachel Corrie* follows shortly.

We will soon set sail toward Gaza, straight toward the threats of Israel to stop us at all costs, including by use of force. Rest assured, however, regardless of their tactics to stop us – force or delay – we will not turn back nor will we allow the Israeli military to board our ships. **(The ships are now on their way.)**

It is imperative to reiterate that this is an unarmed humanitarian aid convoy carrying the better part of one thousand volunteers from one and one-half years of age to eighty-eight years of age, from more than thirty countries.

What is surprising, however, is that although I *was* the only American on board as an IHH volunteer, traveling on my US passport, I have been joined by a few US citizens from various US organizations, including the Free Gaza movement, and discovered that we are eleven in all - including ex-military and government personnel, dual citizens, activists and medical volunteers. Most have been to Gaza at least once and are "used to" dealing with the threats of oppressive regimes and direct conflict with their police and military forces. And most of us still hope and expect the United States to take an openly supportive role of this convoy and to pressure Israel to allow our convoy into Gaza to deliver aid. Only time will tell…

In sum, we, the Americans on board the ships in this flotilla, and the collective *we*, volunteers and people of conscious from around the world, are relying upon the support of our fellow citizens and our respective governments to pressure Israel to 1) allow this humanitarian aid convoy into Gaza and 2) once and for all end this crippling and unjust siege of Gaza.

AS AMERICAN AS APPLE PIE

By Greta Berlin

(Cyprus, May 30, 2010) The Free Gaza movement now has two boats included in the *Freedom Flotilla* that is on its way to deliver 10,000 tons of supplies to the imprisoned people of Gaza. The third boat is being repaired.

Our two passenger boats, *Challenger I* and *Challenger II*, had mechanical problems on Friday, May 28, and were pulled into ports in Cyprus. After Cypriot port authorities on the Greek side denied our request to pull in for repairs, *Challenger I* limped into the port of Famagusta, on the Turkish side of Cyprus.

Both boats are flagged and registered in the United States, which means they are US territory.

Therefore we expect the US government to intervene if US property is wrongly confiscated by Israeli authorities as they have threatened. Israel has yet to return the *Sprit of Humanity*, which is registered under a Greek flag.

From Greta Berlin 23:00 Cyprus Time, May 30, 2010

Lubna: Greta, urgent! We have a threat from Israel
Me: Lubna. What is happening?
Lubna: Two Israeli ships coming toward us. So glad to see you here.
Me: Please try to stay on this so I can tweet it.
Lubna: They contacted the ship, asked who we are and disappeared. Now they are getting close to the ship. We can see them. Stay here. Three boats are coming, not two. Three Israeli boats; we are seventy-eight miles from Israel.
Me: I'll keep writing.
Lubna: People here are putting on their lifejackets; everybody preparing here.
Me: Okay. You are the lifeline to our Twitter account.
Lubna: We may lose the wireless; we didn't expect them now, and we thought they would arrive at the morning. Please stay in touch with the other boats.
Sent at 10:50 P.M.on Sunday
Me: We can't reach anyone
Sent at 10:52 P.M. on Sunday
Me: Where are you? Are you there?

Lubna has just reported that some kind of plane came over the ships, perhaps trying to block the satellite and it looks suspiciously like a drone, which would make sense.

Flotilla Greeted by Israeli Warships

Cyprus, May 31, 2010

At 11:00 P.M. Cyprus time and in international waters off the coast of Israel, the boats were contacted by the Israeli Navy. "Who are you and where are you going?" Our reply was that we were part of a flotilla and we were going to Gaza to deliver humanitarian supplies.

On the radar, the boats could see three Israeli warships shadowing us, and fifteen minutes later, a silent aircraft hovered over the flotilla.

One of our Hebrew speakers had found Israel's strategy and posted it to us (we have many inside Israel who help us, because they are outraged over what Israel does in their name.) It stated, "You will be boarded by highly trained, very efficient, and very SILENT commandos. They will use silent inflatable boats to get to your boats and both try to board your boats directly from the inflatables and by dropping divers into the water to climb onto the boats," so people were preparing for them to come up and over the sides of the ships.

Lubna Marsawa, Free Gaza's organizer on the Turkish passenger boat said in outrage, "Very few times in history has a flotilla delivering humanitarian goods been welcomed by military warships."

This is a call to the world from the people on the boats. "We are a civilian people doing what our governments have refused to do, challenge Israel's right to collectively punish 1.5 million Palestinians in Gaza by blockading their right to their own sea. This flotilla is bringing construction and educational supplies the people of Gaza and we are being met by Israeli warships."

Civilians Are under Attack by Israel

By Free Gaza Team

(Cyprus, May 31, 2010, 6:30 A.M.)

Under darkness of night, Israeli commandoes dropped from a helicopter onto the Turkish passenger ship, *Mavi Marmara*, and began to shoot the moment their feet hit the deck. They fired directly into the crowd of civilians asleep and at prayer. According to the live video from the ship, two have been killed, and thirty-one injured. Al Jazeera has just confirmed the numbers.

Streaming video shows the Israeli soldiers shooting at civilians, and our last SPOT beacon said, "HELP, we are being contacted by the Israelis."

We know nothing about the other five boats. Israel says they are taking over the boats.

The coalition of Free Gaza movement (FG), European Campaign to End the Siege of Gaza (ECESG), Insani Yardim Vakfi (IHH), the Perdana Global Peace Organization, Ship to Gaza Greece, Ship to Gaza Sweden, and the International Committee to Lift the Siege on Gaza appeal to the international community to demand that Israel stop their brutal attack on civilians delivering vitally needed aid to the imprisoned Palestinians of Gaza and permit the ships to continue on their way.

The attack has happened in international waters, seventy-five miles off the coast of Israel, in direct violation of international law.

Nobel-winning Elders Deplore Gaza flotilla attack

Johannesburg, May 31, 2010

The Elders group of past and present world leaders, including former South African president Nelson Mandela and Archbishop Desmond Tutu, on Monday condemned as "completely inexcusable" the deadly Israeli attack on a flotilla carrying aid for Gaza.

At least ten people are reported to have been killed when Israeli commandos raided the boats on Monday in an operation that has drawn international condemnation.

"The Elders have condemned the reported killing by Israeli forces of more than a dozen people who were attempting to deliver relief supplies to the Gaza Strip by sea," the twelve-member group said in a statement issued in Johannesburg, where it met over the weekend.

The group, which was launched by Mr. Mandela on his birthday in 2007 to try to solve some of the world's most intractable conflicts, called for a "full investigation" of the incident and urged the UN Security Council "to debate the situation with a view to mandating action to end the closure of the Gaza Strip." "This tragic incident should draw the world's attention to the terrible suffering of Gaza's 1.5 million people, half of whom are children under the age of eighteen," the group said.

Israel's three-year blockade of Gaza was not only "one of the world's greatest human rights violations" and "illegal" under international law, it was also "counterproductive" because it empowered extremists in the Palestinian territory, they said.

The Elders include six Nobel peace prize winners, former UN secretary general Kofi Annan, former Finnish president Martti Ahtisaari, former US president Jimmy Carter, detained Burmese leader Aung San Suu Kyi, and Mr. Mandela and Tutu.

Norway's first female Prime Minister Gro Brundtland, former Brazilian president Fernando Henrique Cardoso, former Irish president and ex-UN high commissioner for human rights Mary Robinson, Mozambican social activist Graca Machel, Indian women's rights activist Ela Bhatt, and Algerian veteran UN envoy Lakhdar Brahimi are the other members.

Cynthia McKinney Mourns the Dead of the Freedom Flotilla to Gaza: People of the US and the World must End Israeli Impunity Now!

31 May 2010

I am outraged at Israel's latest criminal act. I mourn with my fellow Free Gaza travelers, the lives that have been lost by Israel's needless, senseless act against unarmed humanitarian activists. But I'm even more outraged that once again, Israel's actions have been aided and abetted by a US political class that has become corrupted beyond belief due to its reliance on Zionist campaign finance and penetration by Zionist zealots for whom no US weapons system is too much for the Israeli war machine, and the silence of the world's onlookers whose hearts have grown cold with indifference.

I recently visited the offices of IHH, the Turkish humanitarian organization that sponsored one of the Freedom Flotilla boats, and that was targeted by the Israelis for its murderous rampage. Reports are still coming in as to the full extent of the senseless Israeli violence. Of course, I expect Israel's apologists in the press and in the United States government to shift into high gear to support Israel's lying machine. Take note of their names. The 12,000 Internet squatters/written word grenade throwers, hired by the Israeli Foreign Ministry to defend Israel and attack peace activists online, are already busy spreading their orchestrated disinformation in cyberspace. Be very careful what you read and believe from special interest press and the Internet. You could be reading one of Israel's hired hacks. As a news diversion from what Israel has just done, I suspect that we can also expect to see a lot of historical footage of war's atrocities on television: today is Memorial Day in the United States, a day long ago set aside to remember the sacrifices of US war dead.

I encouraged and supported U.S.S. *Liberty* veteran Joe Meadors's participation in the *Freedom Flotilla*. Unfortunately, the fate of the U.S.S. *Liberty* innocents on the high seas, while in international waters, has now been visited on the participants in the *Freedom Flotilla*, in large measure because of the congressional-and-presidential-level coverup of the 1967 Israeli attack on that US surveillance ship. Combine this with the failure of just about every other effort to hold Israel accountable for its crimes against humanity, war crimes, genocide, and crimes against the peace. Belgium and Spain changed their domestic laws of universal jurisdiction after Israeli appeals to do so. The entire musical-chairs-gang-of-rotating-Israeli-leadership are war criminals. During my imprisonment in Israel for attempting to take crayons to the children of Gaza, I called Israel a failed state. If Israel is threatened by unarmed, humanitarian activists (to the point of massacring them), then it is a failed state. Israel is a failed nuclear state.

Obama's most recent granting of an additional $205 million for Israeli "missile defense" is unconscionable, when in the same week, reports revealed for the first time, Israel's offer of nuclear weapons to apartheid South Africa. Just last week, a paper bearing the signature of former Israeli Prime Minister, Shimon Peres, was released by South Africa, revealing that in 1975, Israel could offer South Africa nuclear weapons "in three sizes." South Africa's then-minister of defense, P.W. Botha, was South Africa's signatory to the letter. This information would make the entire Obama Administration look sadly farcical as it points an accusing finger at Iran, except that U.S. obeisance to the Israeli blood-thirst is deadly serious…and with deadly outcomes.

Earlier this month, Israel was granted admission to the Organization of Economic Cooperation and Development (OECD), a direct affront to ongoing Boycott, Divestment, and Sanctions (BDS) efforts across the world. Once again, Israel has thumbed its nose at the global community—with bloody results—because it can.

I am proud to serve on the Bertrand Russell Tribunal on Palestine. Its next sitting will be in London, where we will examine corporate complicity in Israel's crimes against Palestine. The Tribunal will sit from November 5 - 7. Please put this on your calendar. We all must do what we can, where we are to end wars against the people at home and wars against human rights abroad.

Finally, a friend just sent a message to me saying that the Israelis had lost their minds. Sadly, based on the past, the Israelis could very well conclude that they can do anything--imprison me for trying to take love to the children of Gaza and kill humanitarian activists trying to do the same because they know, in the end, they'll get away with it. Instead, I would suggest that we are the ones who have lost our minds, our souls, our spirits, and our human dignity if we allow the Israelis to get away with murder—again—and we do nothing.

I am calling on the people of the United States to change course now.

On this Memorial Day 2010, I am stunned and outraged beyond belief while mourning the dead of the Freedom Flotilla to Gaza.

Update on Israeli Attack on Humanitarian Boats

By Free Gaza Team

[Cyprus – 1 June 2010]

The UN Security Council Calls for Impartial, Credible Investigation of Israeli Boat Raid. The raid in international waters, on the aid convoy headed to Gaza left at least sixteen civilians dead[10]. After an emergency session wrapped up in the early hours this morning, the council agreed to language condemning the acts that resulted in the deaths and injuries aboard the Turkish vessel *Mavi Marmara* and the European Campaign's vessel *Sfendoni*. The Council requested the immediate release of the ships as well as the civilians held by Israel.

The council called for a prompt, impartial, credible, and transparent investigation conforming to international standards. The council statement also reemphasized the importance of implementing U.N. resolution 1860, which calls for the unimpeded provision and distribution of humanitarian assistance to Gaza's 1.5 million residents. The flow of aid has been severely hampered by Israel's three-year blockade on the Gaza Strip.

Yesterday, Israeli-licensed attorneys filed two habeas briefs: one is asking for to release the passengers and the boats, so we can continue on our way to Gaza, since it was illegal to stop us in international waters. The other one is asking for information

---

10   The actual figure was later found to be nine civilians dead, one more brain dead but on life support

on all of the passengers, because there has been a total blackout on where the passengers are, who was wounded, and who was murdered.

Lawyers are only being allowed access for three hours every day from 13:00-16:30. They have the names of three Palestinians still in detention: Sheik Salah, Mohammad Zeidan and Lubna Marsawa.

Knesset Member Hanin Zoabi (Balad) who participated in the international flotilla to the Gaza Strip said, "It was clear from the size of the force that boarded the ship that the purpose was not only to stop this sail, but to cause the largest possible number of fatalities in order to stop such initiatives in the future.

Ships and their Flags

By Free Gaza Team - 01 June 2010

1. *Mavi Marmara* - Comoros Islands, Turkey; 577 passengers and crew, 300 Turks and 277 internationals including Palestinian/Israelis

2. *Gazze I* – Turkey; eighteen international passengers and crew

3. *Defne Y* (Gazze II) – Kiribati, Turkey; twenty international passengers and crew

4. *Sfendoni* (8000) – Togo; forty-five international passengers and crew

5. *Eleftheri Mesogios* (Sofia, Bulgaria) – Greece; eleven Greek and Swedish passengers and crew

6. *Challenger I* (Al-Sumoud) - U.S.; seventeen American and European passengers and crew

7. *Rachel Corrie* – Cambodia; twenty Irish and Malaysian passengers and crew

Total number of passengers on board all ships: 713 passengers

Israel is a Victim of its own Pathology!

By Eyad Sarraj, founder, Gaza Community Mental Health Programme

June 1, 2010

(Gaza City) Resorting to brute force is an expression of fear. Its deployment yesterday by the Israeli soldiers who raided and opened fire on the freedom flotilla on route to Gaza, killing more than ten civilians and injuring dozens more, will not serve Israel or treat its existential anxiety.

As a psychiatrist and a resident of Gaza, I understand Israel's reflexive use of force against civilians as a symptom of a structural pathology. Israel resorts to the use of maximum force as a form of intimidation. But this is the choice of the weak. It is quite possible that through Israel's actions, it is tightening its own noose.

More than a decade ago, the Israeli Prime Minister Benjamin Netanyahu published a book defending Israel's right to "a place under the sun". But it is the racist desire to create "a nation above nations" that is the desire of Zionist extremists. In this context, peace is an anathema; the siege and war on Gaza are legitimate and justified; Israel will use every possible means to avoid reaching a peace agreement with the Palestinians.

Indeed, Israel is marching rapidly toward becoming an apartheid state.

Due to the Israeli blockade of Gaza, the unemployment rate is near 50 percent. The World Bank has stated that 90 percent of water in Gaza is not suitable for human consumption, 80 percent of the population lives on less than a dollar a day, and 70 percent depend on charity for food supplies. Chronic malnutrition affects 15 percent of Gaza's children and its serious consequences for their cognition and growth will be felt for years to come.

The boats that the Israeli soldiers attacked were carrying food, medicines, and materials to build prefabricated homes for the people of Gaza. The freedom flotilla was a new attempt to break this Israeli blockade, condemned by the human rights community the world over.

The former US president Jimmy Carter has called the blockade an assault on civilization. Justice Richard Goldstone has rightly called Israeli actions crimes against humanity. So many voices, including those of many Jews, have called upon Israel to end this draconian siege.

One and a half million Palestinians remain prisoners of the largest open-air jail on earth since Israel's attack on Gaza began in December of 2008. Then, Israel's army demolished 15,000 homes, destroyed factories and ministries, and chopped off the minarets from mosques. Even the American School in Gaza, a sprawling establishment, was completely destroyed and Israel bombed schools run by the United Nations. Israel used illegal weapons against the people of Gaza during this war, killing hundreds and wounding thousands of civilians including children.

The attack on the freedom flotilla is just the latest act of Israel's violence. Now there is defiance in the streets of Gaza from people who demand that the world force Israel to respect them as human beings.

For the Palestinians, this is the time for us to be reunited. It is doubtful however if Palestinian factions will rise to the occasion and end their internal strife as their political alliances dictate otherwise. It is also doubtful that many Arab regimes will heed the calls from their people to break the siege on Gaza, as they are not independent from external political and economic pressure.

The mass killing of those on board the freedom boats has drawn condemnation around the globe with critical statements from the United Nations and from European capitals, but they fall short of forcing an end to the siege. As usual these capitals and the UN await a green light from the US. At any rate the Israeli killing of peace activists could be a turning point in the struggle to end the siege and the Israeli occupation.

Dr. Eyad Sarraj is the president of the Gaza Community Mental Health Programme and founder of the International Campaign to End the Siege of Gaza

Published in **The National**

Magistrates' Court Orders One Week Remand of Arab Political Leaders who Took Part in the Gaza Freedom Flotilla

ADALAH PRESS RELEASE, 2 June 2010

Legal defence team: "The court's decision to detain the Arab political leaders who took part in the Gaza Freedom Flotilla is discriminatory and constitutes selective prosecution. They are not being detained because of their Israeli citizenship but because they are Palestinian Arab citizens of Israel. Instead, the Israeli military, which attacked the ship and its passengers, should be investigated for violations of international law."

(Haifa, Israel) Last night, 1 June 2010, Judge Dina Cohen of the Magistrates' Court in Ashkelon, after a nine-hour hearing before a packed courtroom, decided to extend the detention of Arab political leaders—Mr. Muhammed Zeidan, the chairman of the High Follow-up Committee for Arab Citizens of Israel; Sheikh Raed Salah, the head of the Islamic Movement in Israel (northern branch); and Sheikh Hamad Abu Daabes, the head of the Islamic Movement in Israel (southern branch) —and Ms. Lubna Masarwa of the Free Gaza movement and Al Quds University for one week, until 8 June 2010.

The four Palestinian Arab citizens of Israel were arrested from the ship Mavi Marmara, part of the Gaza Freedom Flotilla, which was attacked by the Israeli Navy on 31 May 2010. Adalah Attorneys Hassan Jabareen and Orna Kohn, as well as Attorney Hussein Abu Hussein, and Attorney Khaled Zabargha of the Al Mezan Legal Center in Nazareth represented the four before the court.

While no indictment has been issued, the state argues that a range of criminal offenses could apply, including conspiracy to commit an offense, and possession and use of weapons. The state prosecution clearly emphasized in court that their request to remand the leaders was made in accordance with the state's policy of investigating and detaining citizens of Israel who participated in the Gaza Freedom Flotilla.

In the view of the legal defence team, the state's request and the court's decision contradict the basic principles of criminal law, which require that individuals should be criminalized solely on the basis of their individual deeds. The prosecution argued that the Israeli naval soldiers were attacked by the passengers on the ship; however, they did not furnish any evidence to demonstrate that one of these four individuals had participated in or were responsible for the attack.

Further, the legal defence team asserts that the decision discriminates against the detainees and amounts to selective prosecution due solely to their national belonging. They are not being detained because of their Israeli citizenship but because they are Palestinian Arab citizens of Israel.

The attorneys raised numerous preliminary arguments before the court in arguing for the release of the four leaders. They argued that the Israeli courts had no jurisdiction over the case, as the ship had been in international waters at the time of the Israeli Navy's attack. The state prosecution was unable to respond to the question of what the legal authority of the Israeli military was to attack the boat in international waters.

The attorneys also argued that the detention was illegal, prima facie, as the law requires those arrested to be brought before a court within twenty-four hours. In this case, however, the four individuals were kept in detention for almost forty hours before being brought to court. The state prosecution and the police argued that the hours of detention should be calculated only from time that the ship reached the Ashdod Port. The defence attorneys countered that since their liberty was taken from them when they were arrested on the ship, the detention began with their arrest. They were not allowed to meet a lawyer and were not brought before a judge within the limits of the law.

Adalah will submit an appeal against the decision to remand them in custody to the District Court of Beer el-Sabe tomorrow, 3 June 2010.

Notice of Blockade of Israeli Ships and Israeli Goods by Swedish Port Workers Union

By Bjorn Borg

Wednesday, June 2, 2010

Swedish Port Workers Union has today given notice of the blockade of all Israeli ships and cargo to and from Israel, which is managed by the union members. The blockade will be effective at 01:00 Tuesday, June 15 and lasts until at. 24:00 Thursday, June 24.

The reason for the blockade is the unprecedented criminal attack on the peaceful ship convoy In Gaza. Several peace activists were killed by Israeli commandos and other participants were detained without any reason.

Israel and Free Gaza Flotilla

By Free Gaza Team

June 3, 2010

CINDY and CRAIG CORRIE

Cindy and Craig Corrie are the parents of Rachel Corrie, who was killed by an Israeli army bulldozer in the Gaza Strip on March 16, 2003, while trying to prevent the demolition of the home of a Palestinian pharmacist, his wife and three young children.

A Free Gaza boat that is being readied to sail to Gaza is named for her. Among those on board are Irish Nobel Peace Laureate Mairead Corrigan-Maguire and former UN Assistant Secretary General Denis Halliday, who is also Irish.

The Corries, who have themselves been to Gaza twice and recently to Israel for a trial related to their daughter's killing, said today in a statement:

"We call on the U.S. government and governments of the world to act now. First, the well-being of all the flotilla passengers still in Israel must be secured, and the identities of those killed and injured must be released immediately. Second, governments around the world must demand an independent investigation into the attack upon the flotilla and the killings that occurred. An Israeli-led investigation into an international incident of this magnitude is unacceptable. Our family's own experience has made it all too painfully clear that the Israeli military is unable or unwilling to adequately investigate itself. Third, the U.S. and other governments can and must insist that other boats from the flotilla, including the *MV Rachel Corrie*, named for our daughter, be permitted to sail through international waters to Gaza unobstructed. Finally, we demand that the governments of the world act as courageously as did the activists on the Free Gaza flotilla and, themselves, break the illegal and immoral siege of Gaza."

Fifty-four Flotilla Passengers Admitted to Israeli Hospitals

Physicians for Human Rights (Israel) Press Release

04 June 2010

Waking up to Monday's events was disheartening and shocking, to say the least.

Throughout the ordeal, Physicians for Human Rights-Israel has remained in constant contact with senior physicians to try and find out the status of injured and deceased victims evacuated to Israeli medical centers. Despite our efforts to help individuals from all over the world who turned to us to help locate their loved ones, it was extremely difficult on Monday and Tuesday to receive official information from Israeli hospitals. Neither PHR-Israel staff, nor affiliated physicians were allowed into hospitals to gather testimony.

As a result of the lingering uncertainty, by Monday afternoon we issued an ***urgent letter*** to the director of medicine of the Israeli Ministry of Health and the director general of the Foreign Ministry asking them to set up an emergency hotline for the families of the injured and deceased. We also asked authorities to set up an emergency mechanism accessible to all the families of injured persons, especially those from countries that do not have diplomatic relations with Israel.

In Monday's waning afternoon hours, we submitted together with Adalah: The Legal Center for Arab Minority Rights in Israel and the Public Committee against Torture (PCATI) a **Habeas Corpus petition to the High Court of Justice**, demanding information about the health and whereabouts of hospitalized passengers.

Our petition received considerable local media attention. Articles can be found here:

http://www.haaretz.co.il/hasite/spages/1171580.html (Hebrew)

http://www.ynet.co.il/articles/0,7340,L-3897026,00.html (Hebrew)

http://news.walla.co.il/?w=//1681218 (Hebrew)

As a result of our petition, a list has been provided to Adalah with the names of hospitalized Flotilla passengers. Even with this list, it's still not possible to identify all of the passengers; authorities provided names in Hebrew and did not include ID numbers or countries of origin.

Yesterday morning, the Ministry of Health informed us that fifty-four Flotilla passengers had been admitted to Israeli hospitals Sheba, Hadassah Ein Kerem, Rambam, Beilinson, and Barzilai, and that surgeries had been/were being conducted at Sheba and at Rambam Hospitals. Last night, we received word that several patients were transferred from Beilinson Hospital to the medical facilities of the Israeli Prisons Service. In addition, according to information we've received, passengers have been made to sign off on deportation orders written in Hebrew, without understanding what they are being asked to sign.

As things stands today, we have yet to receive word from health officials regarding the establishment of an emergency hotline. We know that at least 31 flotilla passengers are still hospitalized, as well as three Israeli soldiers. We know that representatives from certain diplomatic missions visited hospitals both on Monday and Tuesday and that information on foreign nationals from countries without diplomatic ties with Israel is being coordinated by the ICRC. Since several individuals have undergone intensive care procedures, we feel it is crucial that families be able to reach their loved ones. For this reason, weve sent another urgent request to government officials demanding that families be notified of the medical status of their loved ones. In addition, yesterday we coordinated visits between lawyers and hospitalized Flotilla passengers at the Orthopaedics Unit at Beilinson Hospital.

From Gila Norich, Director of Development, Physicians for Human Rights Israel:

We believe that the violence and its tragic consequences necessitate an independent, international investigation. The Israeli government should publicize all documentation of the events, including materials that have been seized from passengers. Furthermore, as Israeli citizens, we call for the establishment of a National Commission of Inquiry to look into the decisions leading up to the events and for State actors take responsibility for their decisions.

Israel's decision to stop the Free Gaza Flotilla is further evidence of its ongoing control over the Gaza Strip. For the past three years, Israel has imposed a harsh and illegal blockade against the civilian population in Gaza amounting to collective punishment for political gain. This blockade includes limitations on the right to health, education, human and economic development, as well as a chronic dependence on foreign aid. These combined factors force the Gaza population to live their lives on the brink of perpetual humanitarian crisis. Through these actions, Israel violates the right of Palestinians to live in dignity, security, and freedom, and steers us further away from the possibility of a just and peaceful solution.

We look forward to providing additional updates in the coming days and appreciate your support.

Sabotage on the High Sea

By Greta Berlin

(Cyprus, June 4, 2010)

Colonel Itzik Tourgeman told the Knesset Defence and Foreign Affairs Committee on Tuesday that two more ships are on their way to try and break the naval blockade of Gaza. The head of research in the operations division said, "The ships have not reached their target as of today because covert action was taken against them." http://www.israelnationalnews.com/News/Flash.aspx/187299

We had suspicions about our two US registered boats, *Challenger I* and *Challenger II* and their mechanical problems as they sailed toward the flotilla, but we were not going to say anything unless we could prove it. Turns out we didn't have to prove it. Israeli mouthpieces did.

The Guardian ran a piece the same day, saying,

Israel gave strong indications today that its forces had secretly sabotaged some of the ships bound for Gaza as part of the freedom flotilla.

Matan Vilnai, the deputy defence minister, was asked on Israel Radio whether there had not been a smarter alternative to direct assault. He answered, "all possibilities had been considered…The fact is that there were less than the ten ships that were due to participate in the flotilla."

An unnamed Israeli defence force source who briefed the Knesset's foreign affairs and defence committee on the widely criticised armed interception of the flotilla at sea, also spoke of "gray operations" being mounted against the flotilla."

We were lucky that our two captains were superbly trained and able to offload the passengers safely.

So we are going to make sure the *Rachel Corrie* is well protected and that Israel is put on notice that anything that happens to her, the passengers and the crew will rest with Israel. As a result of these threats, we're going to pull *Rachel Corrie* into a port, add more high-profile people on board, and insist that journalists from around the world also come with us.

And sabotage happens with more than deeds. It also happens with words. In today's Haaretz, Barak Ravid reported,

"A diplomatic solution seems imminent to allow the humanitarian aid vessel the *Rachel Corrie* to dock without incident at the Ashdod Port. According to European diplomats and senior Foreign Ministry officials in Jerusalem, quiet messages have been exchanged over the past few days between Israel and the group operating the ship, to allow it to dock."

This, too, is sabotage in writing. We called Haaretz and the reporter. He did not return our call.

We have no intention nor would we ever have any intention of ever docking in Ashdod.

Lying About the Gaza Flotilla Disaster[11]

By MJ Rosenberg

It's been one lie after another in the US media about the Israeli attack on the Gaza-bound relief flotilla. No matter that the Israeli media views the whole incident as a debacle for Israel; in this country the Israel-can-do-no-wrong crowd is on overdrive defending the operation. As usual, facts don't matter to them. Except they do.

The first thing you need to know about the Gaza flotilla disaster is that the intention of the activists on board the ships was to break the illegal Israeli blockade. Delivering the embargoed goods was incidental.

---

11   Huffington Post, June 2, 2010,

In other words, the activists were like the civil rights demonstrators who sat down at segregated lunch counters throughout the South and refused to leave until they were served. Their goal was not really to get breakfast. It was to end segregation. That fact is so obvious that it is hard to believe that the "pro-Israel" lobby is using it as an indictment.

Of course the goal of the flotilla was to break the blockade. *Of course* Martin Luther King provoked the civil authorities of the South to break segregation. *Of course* the Solidarity movement in Poland used workers' rights as a pretext to break Soviet-imposed Communism.

The bottom line is that the men and women of the flotilla had every right to attempt to destroy an illegal blockade that Israel had no legal standing to impose and which was designed to inflict collective punishment on the people of Gaza. (There is no truth to the story that Israel would have delivered the goods on the ships to Gaza if asked; the Israelis never made that offer and, judging by years of precedent, would have blocked any delivery).

As for the Israeli argument that its soldiers were attacked, that is ridiculous. Israeli commandos were ordered to board a civilian ship in international waters and the government that sent them claims that the resisting passengers attacked them without provocation. This is like a carjacker complaining to the police that the driver bashed him with a crowbar that was under the seat. Neither carjackers nor hijackers should expect their victims to acquiesce peacefully.

Here are the facts about life in Gaza today: facts that only can be changed by breaking the blockade. These data come from the American Near East Relief Association (ANERA), which provides relief to Gazans to the extent permitted by the Israeli (and American) authorities. ANERA is neither "pro-Israel" nor "pro-Palestinian." It has no political agenda at all. It merely determines what human needs are and tries to respond to them.

Eight out of ten Gazans depend on foreign aid to survive.

The World Food Program says Gaza requires a minimum of 400 trucks a day to meet basic nutritional needs - yet an average of just 171 trucks worth of supplies enters Gaza every *week*,

Clothes that were held in the port of Ashdod for over a year were released into Gaza but arrived covered with mold and mildew, unusable.

Ninety-five percent of Gaza's water fails World Health Organization standards leaving thousands of newborns at risk of poisoning.

Anemia for children under the age of five is estimated at 48 percent.

Seventy-five million liters of untreated sewage are pumped into the Mediterranean Sea every day because piping and spare parts are not permitted.

During the 2009 bombing:

More than 120,000 jobs were lost as Gaza's industrial zone was destroyed, 15,000 homes and apartments were damaged or destroyed, and one-third of all schools were destroyed. None of these can be rebuilt because construction supplies are kept out by the Israeli authorities.

So what is the blockade about?

 It is not about stopping terrorism. Hamas has _repeatedly offered Israel_ an indefinite cease-fire in exchange for lifting the blockade. And, on a half dozen occasions, Israel accepted the deal but did not live up to its side of it. In fact, the 2009 war began after Israel ignored its commitments under the Gaza cease-fire agreement, continued the blockade, and then provoked the resumption of attacks on Sderot through a series of targeted assassinations of Palestinians (Israel claims that no cease-fire agreement curtails its right to kill any Palestinian it deems to be a terrorist).

Israel asserts that it will not accept any long-term cease-fire agreement with Hamas because Hamas does not recognize its right to exist. But Israel does not need the permission of anyone to exist—certainly not Hamas. All it needs from Hamas is an end to violence and that is precisely what Hamas is offering, in exchange for lifting the blockade.

This is not to say that Hamas need never recognize Israel. It should. But it is ridiculous to insist on recognition as a precondition for anything. Recognition would be the end result of negotiations, not a precondition for it.

But that is not what Israel wants. It wants to destroy Hamas because it is a "terrorist organization." And that makes sense until one realizes that the African National

Congress, Sinn Fein, the Israeli Irgun, the Algerian FLN, and a host of other resistance movements were called terrorist organizations before negotiations brought them to power. Former Israeli Prime Ministers Menachem Begin and Yitzhak Shamir were both unabashed terrorists prior to their entrance into respectable politics. And so what? If dealing with terrorists, as Israel has repeatedly done with <u>Hezbollah</u>, will help achieve a worthy goal, why not do it? After all, if negotiations fail, one can always walk away.

But Israel will not change its self-defeating policies until we change ours. And there is no evidence that is happening (at least, not until after the November elections, for obvious reasons).

For now, our policies are joined at the hip with Israel's. We support the blockade of Gaza. We oppose any efforts at reconciliation between Fatah and Hamas. We even back Israel's opposition to the Arab Peace Initiative, which offers Israel full peace and normalization of relations with every Arab country in exchange for the creation of a Palestinian state in the West Bank, Gaza, and East Jerusalem.

Enough is enough. The Obama Administration needs to join the rest of the world in demanding an end to the Gaza blockade as a first big step toward the resumption of negotiations.

The attack on the flotilla was one of the most disastrous blunders in Israel's history. At last, the whole world sees Israel's policy of collective punishment for what it is—a means to perpetuate the occupation forever. Only the United States government has chosen to close its eyes.

The occupation is killing Israel. And we are on the sidelines letting it happen. Some ally!

Rachel Corrie on Her Way

By Free Gaza Team

[Cyprus, June 4, 2010]

The *Rachel Corrie* is 150 miles away from Gaza in international waters and on her way. They will arrive on Saturday morning. The 1,200-ton cargo ship is the last ship from the Freedom Flotilla and is loaded with construction materials, twenty-two tons of paper and many other supplies that Israel refuses to allow into the imprisoned people of Gaza.

Some of the high-profile people on board:

Mairead Maguire is from Belfast, Ireland, a Nobel Peace Laureate (1976) and co-founder of Peace People, Northern Ireland. She was awarded the Nobel for her work for peace and a nonviolent solution to the ethnic/political conflict in Northern Ireland. Mairead went on the maiden voyage of *Dignity* in October 2008, the second successful voyage for the Free Gaza movement. She was also on board *Spirit* when Israel hijacked the boat in international waters, taking all twenty-one humanitarian passengers to Israel, where they were arrested, detained for a week in an Israeli prison and then deported.

Denis Halliday, from Ireland, a UN assistant secretary general from 1994-98. Appointed by SG Boutros Ghali, he served as ASG UN human resources management in New York and in mid 1997 to end 1998 as Head, Humanitarian Programme in Iraq to support the Iraqi people struggling under the genocidal impact of UN Sanctions. Since resigning from the UN in 1998, Halliday has delivered numerous parliamentary briefings, provided extensive media inputs and has given public/university lectures on Iraq, human rights, and the UN, in particular its reform.

Matthias Chang Wen Chieh is a Malaysian of Chinese decent. He is a barrister of thirty-two years standing and once served as the political secretary to the fourth prime minister of Malaysia, Tun Dr. Mahathir Mohamad. He is the author of three bestsellers, *Future Fast Forward*, *Brainwashed for War: Programmed to Kill*, and *The Shadow Moneylenders and the Global Financial Tsunami,* published in the US and in Malaysia.

Mohd Nizar bin Zakaria, Perak, Malaysia is a member of the Malaysian Parliament.

In addition, there is a three-member camera crew on board from Malaysia TV3 and journalist Shamsul Akmar bin Musa Kamal.

The passengers on board the ship have stated, "Communication is difficult and sometimes impossible, and there are many rumours out there started by Israeli authorities, but there is no way we are going to Ashdod. We are, for sure, on our way to Gaza."

MARTIN WANTS Rachel Corrie ALLOWED INTO GAZA

By Greta Berlin

Friday, June 4, 2010 22:27

The Irish government believes the MV *Rachel Corrie* should be allowed to reach Gaza, according to Minister for Foreign Affairs Micheál Martin. He said the ship should be allowed to proceed to Gaza and unload its humanitarian cargo: "If, as is their stated intention, the Israeli government intercepts the *Rachel Corrie*, the government demands that it demonstrate every restraint. Those on board the *Rachel Corrie* have made clear their peaceful intentions and have stated that they will offer no resistance to Israeli forces. Based on these assurances, there can be no justification for the use of force against any person on board the *Rachel Corrie*."

The minister has been involved in efforts to strike an agreement between both sides, but that was declined by the activists on the vessel. Mr. Martin said he had reached agreement with the Israeli government to allow the vessel dock in the Israeli port of Ashdod. The ship's cargo would have been unloaded and inspected under supervision from the UN and officials from his department. It would then have been transported to Gaza along with two activists.

In a statement Minister Martin said, "In my view, such an arrangement would have offered a useful precedent for future humanitarian shipments, pending the complete lifting of the blockade. **This proposal was put to those on board the *Rachel Corrie* who, on Friday afternoon, after careful consideration and having thanked the Government for its efforts, declined to accept it. I fully respect their right to do so and to continue their protest action by seeking to sail to Gaza.**"

The Irish Palestinian Solidarity Campaign said the offer "was unacceptable to those on the *Rachel Corrie*."

Israel Delivers Message to *Rachel Corrie*

Israel earlier proposed that the ship sail to the port of Ashdod, where it would "ensure that no weapons and or war material were on board."

Israel's Foreign Ministry Director General Yossi Gal said this "clear message" had been delivered to the *MV Rachel Corrie*.

'If the ship decides to sail to the port of Ashdod in Israel, then we will ensure its safe arrival and will not board it,' he said.

Speaking on RTE's **News At One,** activist and Nobel Laureate Mairead Corrigan Maguire said the vessel was progressing to Gaza and was expected to arrive in the twenty-five-mile exclusion zone at 6:00 A.M. Irish time tomorrow.

The IPSC said the vessel is now 100 miles from Gaza and will slow down through the night to avoid any confrontation in darkness.

Turkey has sent two medical planes to Israel to bring back five of its nationals wounded during Israel's attack on the flotilla.

The five, all men, are the last Turkish pro-Palestinian activists still being held in Israel.

The bodies of the nine people killed - eight Turks and a US citizen of Turkish origin - were returned to Turkey yesterday, along with nineteen wounded and 450 activists rounded up during the commando raid.

Rachel Corrie Equipment Jammed

By Free Gaza Team

5 June, 3:30 A.M.

The Ireland Palestine Solidarity Campaign (IPSC) has been contacted by the *MV Rachel Corrie* in the past few minutes. Jenny Graham reported that they had been followed by Israeli ships for about two hours, and that in the last few minutes, two ships were approaching from the port side. Ms Graham said that equipment on board had been jammed by the Israeli Navy, and that they expected their satellite phone to be jammed soon as well. The line was bad, and we were unable to determine the exact location of the *Rachel Corrie* relative to their destination.

On hearing of the news, Freda Hughes of the IPSC said, "We all hope that those on board the *Rachel Corrie* will remain safe and that there will be no repeat of Monday's terrible attack on the Freedom Flotilla. Our hearts are with you."

The *Rachel Corrie* is flying their Irish, Malaysian and Filipino flags at half mark as a mark of respect for their murdered comrades from the *Mavi Marmara* which was hijacked on Monday by Israeli commandos in an attack that left at least 9 people dead.

Speaking about Minister Micheal Martin's statement earlier, in which he said that those on board the *Rachel Corrie* had rejected a so-called deal that would involve them docking in the Israeli port of Ashdod, Jenny Graham said:

"We will have no part in a deal that involves us legitimizing the siege of Gaza. We intend to continue on our mission to deliver our cargo of aid and supplies to the people of Gaza. This has always been our intention."

Israeli Military Forcibly Stops Aid Boat To Gaza—Again

By Free Gaza Team

(Off the Gaza coast, 5 JUNE)

Just before 9:00 A.M. GMT this morning, the Israeli military forcibly seized the Irish-owned humanitarian relief ship, the MV *Rachel Corrie*, preventing it from delivering over 1,000 tons of medical and construction supplies to besieged Gaza. For the second time in less than a week, Israeli naval commandos stormed an unarmed aid ship, brutally taking its passengers hostage and towing the ship toward Ashdod port in southern Israel. It is not yet known whether any of the *Rachel Corrie*'s passengers were killed or injured during the attack, but they are believed to be unharmed.

The ship carried eleven passengers and nine crewmembers from five different countries, mostly Ireland and Malaysia. Before being taken hostage by Israeli forces, Derek Graham, an Irish coordinator with the Free Gaza movement, stated, "Despite what happened on the *Mavi Marmara* earlier this week, we are not afraid."

The 1,200-ton cargo ship was purchased through a special fund set up by former Malaysian prime minister and Perdana Global Peace Organisation (PGPO) chairman Tun Dr. Mahathir Mohamad. The ship was named after an American human rights worker, killed in 2003 when she was crushed by an Israeli military bulldozer in the Gaza Strip. Its cargo included hundreds of tons of medical equipment and cement, as well as paper from the people of Norway, donated to UN-run schools in Gaza.

According to Denis Halliday, "We are the only Gaza-bound aid ship left out here. We're determined to deliver our cargo." The *Rachel Corrie* had been part of the Freedom Flotilla, a forty-nation effort to break through Israel's illegal blockade, before being forced to drop off late last week because of suspicious mechanical problems.

The attack on the *Rachel Corrie* may spell trouble for Israel's relationship with Ireland. The Irish government had formally requested Israel allow the ship to reach Gaza. On 1 June, the Irish parliament also passed an all-party motion condemning Israel's use of military force against civilian aid ships, and demanding "an end to the illegal Israeli blockade of Gaza."

Nobel Laureate Mairead Maguire summed up the hopes of this joint Irish-Malaysian effort to overcome Israel's cruel blockade by saying: "We are inspired by the people of Gaza whose courage, love and joy in welcoming us, even in the midst of such suffering gives us all hope. They represent the very best of humanity, and we are all privileged to be given the opportunity to support them in their nonviolent struggle for human dignity and freedom. This trip will again highlight Israel's criminal blockade and illegal occupation. In a demonstration of the power of global citizen action, we hope to awaken the conscience of all."

IOF Admits It Doctored the Audio Tapes

By Free Gaza Team

(Cyprus, June 6, 2010)

The IOF *admitted today in a press release* that it doctored audio footage from its exchanges with the Gaza flotilla in order to paint the flotilla passengers as anti-Semites.

However, their comments made no more sense with this explanation:

"This transmission had originally cited the Mavi Marmara ship as being the source of these remarks, however, due to an open channel, the specific ship or ships in the "Freedom Flotilla" responding to the Israeli Navy could not be identified.

During radio transmissions between Israeli Navy and the ships of the "Free Gaza" Flotilla on 31 May 2010, the Israeli Navy ship attempts to make contact with the

'Defne Y' on channel 16. Other ships from the flotilla respond on the channel, without identifying themselves. At some point during the radio exchange the Israeli Navy is told by one of the ships to "shut up, go back to Auschwitz" (2:05) and "don't forget 9-11. (5:42)."

According to our Captain of *Challenger I*, Denis Healey, a man with twenty-five years of experience on the sea, there would be no way that anyone could communicate with each other without the entire fleet hearing the exchange. "There was no exchange like this by anyone on any boat during the entire time I was piloting the boat," said Denis.

Huwaida Arraf, the woman you hear on the radio, concurred. "The open channel is always the open channel, and everyone knows who is on the radio."

All radio transmissions on the sea are heard by all captains. Once again, Israel is caught in a lie trying to defend itself for the murder and mayhem it committed the morning of May 31, 2010.

We Will Be Back

By Free Gaza Team

(Cyprus, June 5, 2010)

Today, Israeli Prime Minister Benjamin Netanyahu hailed the peaceful outcome to the operation when they seized our ship in international waters in direct violation of maritime law. Through his speechwriter, he said, "We saw today the difference between a ship of peace activists, with whom we don't agree but respect their right to a different opinion from ours, and between a ship of hate organized by violent Turkish terror extremists,"

So we'd like to remind Mr. Netanyahu that the only hate evidenced on board all six boats on Monday morning came from the Israeli attackers. Israeli soldiers violently boarded the entire flotilla, beating, shooting, and hooding passengers as though they were in Abu Ghraib

"People had been shot in the arms, legs, in the head—everywhere. We had so many injured. It was a bloodbath," said Laura Stuart on board the *Marmara*, a British housewife and rescue worker.

She described frantic attempts to treat the injured in a makeshift sick room on the ship, and failed attempts to resuscitate some of the dead. For further information, visit http://www.stuff.co.nz/s/L1BG

Therefore, we are putting Mr. Netanyahu on notice that we are returning in the next few months with another flotilla, that his actions and the actions of his soldiers have energized thousands of people who have stepped forward with offers to help and participate on the next voyage. We'd also like to remind Mr. Netanyahu that seizing our ship, the *Rachel Corrie*, is yet another violent act from a long series of violent acts against civilians that Israel has committed this week.

Call from Gaza to the Citizens of the World to Break the Siege

Besieged Gaza, Palestine, June 2010

One-and-a-half years after the Israeli army perpetrated a massacre upon the population of Gaza, apartheid Israel commits another crime against partisans of Palestine in international waters. The world is moved at the plight of Palestinians and their supporters. All of the seven crossings between Gaza and Israel, including the Rafah Crossing—the only access Gaza has to the external world—remain hermetically sealed.

We request that the citizens of the world oppose this deadly, medieval blockade. We no longer rely on governments. The failure of the United Nations and its numerous organizations to condemn such crimes proves their complicity. Only civil society is able to mobilize to demand the application of international law and put an end to Israel's impunity. The intervention of civil society was effective in the late 1980s against the apartheid regime of South Africa. Nelson Mandela and Archbishop Desmond Tutu have not only described Israel's oppressive and violent control of Palestinians as apartheid, they have also joined this call for the world's civil society to intervene again.

We, therefore, ask people of conscience and civil society organizations to put pressure on their governments until Israel is forced to abide by international law and international humanitarian law. Without the intervention of the international community, which was effective against apartheid in South Africa, Israel will continue its war crimes and crimes against humanity, as articulated by the Goldstone report.

We call on civil society organizations worldwide to intensify the anti-Israel sanctions campaign to compel Israel to end to its aggression.

Signatory Organizations at http:

//www.freegaza.org/en/home/56-news/1215-call-from-gaza-to-the-citizens-of-the-world-to-break-the-siege

Our Deepest Sympathies

By Bianca Shaana and Niamh Moloughney

June 7, 2010

We in the Free Gaza movement would like to offer our deepest sympathy to the people of Turkey and particularly to the nine families who have lost loved ones. Twenty-eight children have lost their fathers because of the Israeli attack on the *Mavi Marmara*.

Britain's *Guardian* newspaper quoted Yalcin Buyuk, the vice chairman of the Turkish council of forensic medicine, as saying that the nine victims were shot a total of thirty times. Based on preliminary autopsy reports, two men were shot four times each and five others were shot either in the back of the head or in the back.

Ibrahim Bilgen, a sixty-year-old activist, was shot four times in the temple, chest, hip, and back. Nineteen-year-old Furkan Dogan, a US citizen of Turkish descent, was shot five times from less than forty-five centimeters away, in the face, the back of the head, twice in the leg and once in the back. Two IHH aid workers, Cevdet Kiliclar and Necdet Yildrim, were among the victims.

We in Free Gaza are proud and honored to work and be associated with the IHH and its honourable track record of humanitarian missions worldwide. As a human rights organization, it is hard for us to comprehend this kind of violence by Israel, especially when used against civilians embarked upon a humanitarian mission, such as that of the highly respected IHH. Furthermore it is appalling that the inflammatory remarks of Netanyahu, referring to them as "a ship of hate organised by violent Turkish terror extremists" should subsequently be repeated or even referred to by the media as anything but a pathetically transparent attempt to justify the inadmissible.

The facts are simple: The blockade of the port of Gaza is illegal, as deemed by international law and the UN. This point cannot be argued, the siege must end, the rights and dignity of the Palestinians in Gaza must be honoured. The port must be opened. Alongside of our partners in the Freedom Flotilla, we demand that Israel returns our boats including the *Spirit of Humanity*, detained by Israel since early 2009. The Free Gaza movement and our international partners intend to launch another flotilla at the first available opportunity. After that there will be yet another... and another... until this diabolical blockade collapses and steps toward peace are finally taken.

On June 6, another boat was announced by the *Jüdische Stimme*. Along with her partners, the EJJP and JJP (UK), they are sending a boat and call to world leaders to help Israel find her way back to reason, a sense of humanity and a life without fear. "Jewish Voices" expects the political leaders of Israel and the world to guarantee safe passage for their small vessel to Gaza, thus helping to form a bridge toward peace.

The FG and our partners would like to acknowledge and thank the many governments, in particular that of Ireland and Turkey, for their support for our mission. However, most importantly of all, we would like to thank the ordinary people from everywhere who contributed to the cargo and raised their voices together to spread the message worldwide: This siege of the Gaza strip and the imprisonment of its people must end.

In their Own Words: Survivor Testimonies from Flotilla, 31 May 2010

June 2010

For three days as they were held in captivity and unable to speak on their own behalf, Israel presented the massacre against civilian passengers on the Mavi Marmara and attacks on other flotilla ships as self-defense against a "lynching." Now that the passengers are returning to their home nations, the global community is hearing a much different story, not just regarding the incident but also their treatment afterwards once in custody. Please check the testimonials out at http://www.freegaza.org/boat-trips/survivor-testimonies. Brief excerpts from a few of these testimonials are included here:

From Onboard the Mavi Marmara:

Iara Lee:

"[The attack] was a surprise because it happened in the middle of the night, in the darkness, in international waters because we knew there would be a confrontation but not in international waters. Their first tactic was to cut all of our satellite communications and then they attacked. All I witnessed firsthand was the shooting. They came on board and started shooting at people…"

"We expected them to shoot people in the legs, to shoot in the air, just to scare people, but they were direct. Some of them shot in the passengers' heads. Many people were murdered—it was unimaginable…"

Lubna Masarwa[12]:

"When the Israeli military attacked the *Mavi Marmara*, we were deep in international water. That night, at 11:00 P.M., we saw two Israeli warships coming toward us. At about midnight we told the passengers to go to sleep. We thought the Israelis were only trying to scare us. We didn't believe they would dare do anything in international waters.

Later we saw a drone plane take off from one of the warships. At 4:00 A.M., we lost our Internet connection, and I understood that the Israelis were trying to cut us off from the outside world. I went immediately to call some journalists from the ship. This happened during morning prayers. As the passengers finished their prayers, the soldiers began to attack us.

Small Israeli vessels with tens of soldiers came close to the ship, a helicopter appeared above us, and gas bombs were thrown on the ship from all directions. Within minutes, people began carrying injured people off the deck and bringing them to where I was, on the second level of the ship. Later, people started bringing in bodies, first two bodies, and then another two. We put them on the floor and covered them with flags or whatever we could find.

Blood was pouring out of the bodies, from their heads…"

---

12 ***Midnight on the Mavi Marmara*** (London, O/R books, 2010, 44-42

Kevin Neish[13]:

"I saw them carrying this one IOF guy down. He looked terrified, like he thought he was going to be killed. But when a big Turkish guy, who had seen seriously injured passengers who had been shot by the IOF, charged over and tried to hit the commando, the Turkish aid workers pushed him off and pinned him to the wall. They protected this Israeli soldier…"

That was when Kevin found the backpack that the soldier had dropped. "I figured I'd look inside and see what he was carrying. And inside was this kind of flip book. It was full of photos and names in English and Hebrew of passengers on the ships. The booklet also had a detailed diagram of the decks of the *Mavi Marmara*…"

"I took detailed photos of the dead and wounded with my camera. There were two guys who had neat bullet holes side by side on the side of their head—clearly they were executed…."

Neish smuggled his photos out of Israel and into Turkey despite his arrest on the ship and imprisonment in Israel for several days. "I pulled out the memory card, tossed my camera and anything I had on me that had anything to do with electronics, and then kept moving the chip around so it wouldn't be found. The Israelis took all the cameras and computers. They were smashing some and keeping others. I put the chip in my mouth under my tongue, in my underwear, in my sock, everywhere to keep them from finding it." He finally handed it to a Turk who was leaving for a flight home on a Turkish airline. "After arriving in Istanbul, he gave the memory card to the Turkish aid group IHH, who's dead and wounded aid workers were in the photos. Many of the photos were published around the world."

"At one point when I was in the stairwell, a commando opened a hatch above, stuck in a machine gun, and started firing. Bullets were bouncing all over the place. If the guy had gotten to look in and see where he was shooting, I'd have been dead, but two Turkish guys in the stairwell, who had short lengths of chain with them that they had taken from the access points to the lifeboats, stood to the side of the hatch and whipped them up at the barrel. I don't know if they were trying to hit the commando or to use them to snatch away the gun, but the Israeli backed off, and they slammed and locked the hatch …"

---

13   As quoted by Dave Lindorff, http://www.counterpunch.com/lindorff06162010.html, June 16, 2010 and verified by Kevin Neish.

"They told us to be quiet. But at one point this Turkish imam stood up and started singing a call to prayer. Everybody was dead quiet, even the Israelis. But after about ten seconds, this Israeli officer stomped over through the squatting people, pulled out his pistol and pointed at the guy's head, yelling 'Shut up!' in English. The imam looked at him directly and just kept singing! I thought, Oh my God! He's gonna kill him! Then I thought, well, this is what I'm here for, I guess, so I stood up. The officer wheeled around and pointed his gun at my head. The imam finished his call to prayers and sat down, and then I sat down."

Aboard the *Challenger I*:

Huwaida Arraf:

"They started beating people. My head was smashed against the ground, and they stepped on my head. They later cuffed me and put a bag over my head. They did that to everybody."

On custody: "I asked them to at least give [my personal belongings] back to me, and they refused and forced me into a police van by pulling me up by my hair, my hands, and feet, and beating me in order to get me into the van. They drove me out of the port, stopped the car at some point—I'm not sure where because I was a little bit disoriented after being punched in the face and the jaw, and then they just opened the door and threw me out of the van. I think I must have passed out for a little bit because the next thing I knew there was a medic taking me into an ambulance. I was taken to a hospital and checked and released just a few hours later."

Dr. Fintan Lane:

"They stormed *Challenger 1* as if they were confronting terrorists. A stun grenade was thrown toward me before they boarded as I went to shut the door to the back deck; nonetheless, I got the door closed, and we piled up some furniture, including a heavy table, to slow them down. The only violence used was that deployed by the commandos. They tasered an Australian photojournalist and shot a young woman in the face with a plastic bullet. Extreme violence was used. I was stomped on and had a gun pointed into my face by an agitated commando, shouting that he was going to shoot me. His behavior was so intense that for a moment I genuinely feared for my life."

On treatment during custody: "I would not cooperate with my illegal detention in the processing area in Ashdod. I refused to hand over my passport, so my arm was painfully twisted behind my back for a prolonged period. Ken O'Keefe, the Irish-American passenger, suffered a severe beating at the hands of security officials at Tel Aviv airport before boarding, and his injuries were so bad that he had to be hospitalized; likewise, Fiachra O Luain from Ireland was beaten by a group of ten to twenty Israeli soldiers."

Aboard the *Sfendoni*:

Gene St. Onge

Commenting in reference to Israeli media's characterization of the takeover of the other boats, including the *Sfendoni*, which he was on, as rather routine and peaceful:

"This was not peaceful. I was kicked in the head.... As the commandos jumped on the ship, we attempted to protect the wheelhouse and the captain. We were able to crowd the inside of the captain's quarters. I was unable to because I was trying to protect another part of the boat.

By the time I got there I noticed that the captain was being pulled and hit. He sustained rather serious injuries. In the mean time, as I tried to get in I was thrown on the deck a couple times. One of my new friends whom I made on this trip, *Almahdi*, a Libyan Arab living in Europe, was hit with the butt end of a rifle, in his right eye. He fell to the deck. He was writhing in pain, trying to get away, but he was continually being kicked. When I saw that, I tried to help him. I was screaming 'Leaving him alone!' I kept getting pushed back.

Finally as I tried to get over to try to cover him, I was hit with something sharp, which I thought was a rifle. I was bleeding. And I was restrained with handcuffs."

Aboard the Sophia:

Henning Mankell[14]:

"We saw these black rubber boats coming with masked commando soldiers... they climbed aboard. They were very aggressive...there was an older man in the

---

14   More extended testimony by Henning Mankell in ***Midnight on the Mavi Marmara***, Bayoumi ed. (London, 2010,
21-27.

crew, he was perhaps a little slow, and they shot him in the arm with an electric gun which is very, very painful. They shot another man with rubber bullets."

The soldiers checked the boat and one soon returned saying they had found weapons. I have twenty-four witnesses to this. He showed me my razor, a one-use razor, and a box cutter he'd found in the kitchen. All my possessions were taken. They stole my camera, my telephone…even my socks."

"I think the Israeli military went out to commit murder." "If they had wanted to stop us they could have attacked our rudder and propeller, instead they preferred to send masked commando soldiers to attack us. This was Israel's choice to do this."

Aboard the *Rachel Corrie:*

Mairead Maguire with other members of Free Gaza aboard the Rachel Corrie prior to departure from Ireland

Mairead Maguire:

I accepted Free Gaza's invitation to go on what would be my third sailing on one of the Free Gaza boats. On my first journey in October 2008, on board the *Dignity*, we got into Gaza. During my second journey in June 2010, our boat the *Spirit of Humanity* was boarded illegally in international waters by Israeli Navy and all twenty-one human rights activists were kidnapped and taken illegally to Ashdod, arrested, held in prison for a week, and finally deported from Israel. This was an act of piracy in International waters by Israeli government commandoes.

May 31 (Monday) In the early hours of the morning (five to six hours out of Port of Malta) we received a call from media, to ask for our comments regarding the massacre on board the *Mavi Marmara*. This was the first sparse information we had about the massacre. The Malaysian passengers on board our boat managed to get in touch with their on-land support team who gave them as much information as they had obtained.

Derek Graham called a meeting of all passengers to inform us of the massacre, though at this stage full details were, as yet, unknown. We sat together in silence and prayer, in respect for all those who were killed and injured on board the *Mavi Marmara*, for their families, and for all those on board the Freedom Flotilla boats; all of whom we learned had been illegally boarded and taken to Ashdod, Israel. We lowered the flags to half-mast. We also stated our clear intention to continue sailing to Gaza.

There was tremendous media interest in the fact that this little boat was continuing, in spite of everything, to sail for Gaza. Many were following our journey. We heard that people were calling for our safe passage to Gaza, and in Malaysia, a special interfaith service had been held. We were not concerned for our own safety, rather we were concerned that the Turkish peace activists had been killed and injured; also that the people of Gaza were trapped in their open-air prison anxiously awaiting our arrival. We phoned some people in Gaza when we were off the shore and they said the people of Gaza were preparing for us, and hoping we would get through). We had been on the boat for six full days and after the tragedy of the Freedom Flotilla.

Outside in the big world, the propaganda machine was putting out lies and distortions about the *Rachel Corrie*. We received phone calls asking us if we were turning around or being diverted to Israel, or to Egypt, or talking to the Israeli government. We replied we were heading for Gaza, and we had had no contact to date with the Israeli Government.

June 5, Saturday, early in the morning: Whilst in international waters approximately sixty-five to seventy nautical miles from the Gaza coast, we began to be shadowed by two Israeli warships. We informed the Free Gaza movement and Perdana Global Peace organization and press releases were issued as these warships came closer and were joined by other vessels.

By 6.30 A.M., there were four Israeli vessels in sight. Both our satellite navigation equipment and our two satellite phones had their signals electronically blocked by the Israeli Navy, endangering the safety of our boat. All radio communication with the outside world was cut by the Israeli Navy, which was jamming the satellite equipment. This endangered all on board and we were left with no contact beyond localized radio communication with the Israeli Navy, who were jamming the satellite equipment.

The Israeli Navy radioed the *Rachel Corrie* and spoke to Derek Graham. This was the first time the Israeli Navy had made contact with the *Rachel Corrie*. The Israeli Navy gave warning to Derek (on channel 16) and told him we had no permission to enter the port of Gaza, as it was a closed Israeli military zone and to turn back. They told Derek the boat should go to Ashdod and they offered to deliver (with Derek Graham accompanying it) our aid into Gaza.

Derek replied their offer was not acceptable to us; as our mission was to deliver the aid to Gaza ourselves and break the siege. The Israeli Navy used the ship's former name, *MV Linda*, and not the *Rachel Corrie*, and this is a practice that breaches international maritime law. Derek informed them we were in international waters and had stopped our engines and were staging a peaceful protest. The Israeli Navy said they were going to board the boat…

Derek offered (four times) that the ship and cargo could be inspected by the United Nations or similar body, but this offer was not accepted. Many times we had made this offer of inspection by UN inspectors. At this point we were still in international waters, and outside Gaza's twenty-five-mile zone.

June 5, 11 A.M.: We saw two Israeli warships (about ten miles away), two Navy seal carriers, and six Zodiacs. We were warned that they were sending commandoes to board our boat. All passengers and crewmembers assembled in mid-ship awaiting their arrival. There was no panic. Everyone was perfectly calm.

There were thirty-five Israeli Navy seals (four of whom were women who searched the three women activists) and I dog. They came on board from their Zodiacs. All their faces were covered, and blackened, and they wore full riot gear. Each one had several weapons and they pointed their weapons at each of us. We were all sitting in mid ship. I remember looking up to the wheelhouse where Derek Graham stood alone, his hands up against the window, and I hoped he would be safe, remembering what happened to those on board the *Mavi Marmara*.

Both Derek and his wife Jenny have all our admiration and thanks, as it is due to their courage and calm that we all came through safely. They both are living examples of nonviolent love in action and we were all pleased to have them as leaders on the *Rachel Corrie*'s journey to Gaza.

We were all searched and all passports, mobiles, computers, cameras, etc., were taken from us. Some soldiers took the Chief Engineer below to the Engine Room. Derek was up in the wheelhouse and six soldiers went up and commandeered that part of the ship. Derek had his hands tied behind his back and made to kneel for forty-five minutes before being taken to join the crew. We sat for several hours in the hot sun, while the soldiers searched the ship. Eventually the passengers were taken below to the captain's office, where we sat for three hours during the sailing to Ashdod. We had nothing to eat but we were allowed to drink water. There was no shouting, no violence, and everyone remained very calm and orderly.

All the security tags were still intact on the cargo in the hatches, when the Israeli soldiers went below to search the ship. Jenny Graham was commanded to accompany the soldiers around the ship to open locked cabins.

The boat was then sailed to Ashdod Port in Israel. As we sailed into the port we saw the *Mavi Marmara* Turkish boat and all the other free Gaza boats docked. We descended the gang plank of the boat surrounded by Israeli soldiers and were taken off individually to be searched with our luggage. Jenny Graham was strip-searched at Ashdod Port. We were then driven by bus to a processing center, where we were each individually photographed, fingerprinted, and questioned by IOF.

They asked me why we did not accept agreement made between Irish and Israeli government for the *Rachel Corrie* to divert to Ashdod and the aid to be taken to Gaza. They also wanted to know who were in charge on the other Flotilla boats. I refused to answer any questions saying I wanted a lawyer.

A further interview took place with a female Israeli officer. When I refused to sign the forms she had, which were in Hebrew, stating that we had entered Israel illegally and asked for a lawyer, she became very angry and threatened me with prison if I did not sign the forms and cooperate. I refused and was returned to the main room to join the others.

Several hours later, after everyone was processed in a similar manner, we were bused to Ben Gurion Detention Center. It was midnight at this stage. Here, we were met by Ambassador O'Reilly, the Irish ambassador to Israel and the Irish consulate, Connor Long. They arranged for us to phone our families.

After some consultation and we got assurances that all passengers and crew would be released without charge and returned home the following day, the Irish passengers agreed to be repatriated to Ireland.

Sunday, 6 June 2010. Jenny Graham, Fiona Thompson, and I were taken to a cell-block together. We had a meeting with an Irish Consulate representative, who informed us of details regarding our flights.

At 8:00 P.M., we were taken to the airport, where our luggage was checked, and we were processed for flights. Here we saw the crew who were leaving for flights home to the Philippines, and Cuba. The captain had already flown home to Scotland and our five Malaysian friends had gone home via Jordan earlier that day. We were returned to Ben Gurion Detention Center, but this time to a different cell. It was the cell I had been in before last June 2009, when I was detained in this centre after being arrested, imprisoned for a week and finally deported from Israel.

Monday, 7 June: Early in the morning the Irish Group, Denis Halliday, Jenny and Derek Graham, Fiona Thompson and I were escorted to Ben Gurion Airport to fly via Frankfurt, to Dublin, Ireland. Our flights had been arranged and paid for by Irish Government.

During our entire captivity on the confiscated *Rachel Corrie*, our arrival in Ashdod, our illegal detention in Ben Gurion Detention Center, until we were eventually repatriated back to Ireland, there was huge military security around us and we were kept incommunicado for three days (apart from one phone call to our families arranged by our Irish Ambassador, and one meeting with the Irish consulate on Sunday).

The Irish Delegation arrived home to a great reception in Dublin from families and supporters of Palestine. The press release was organized by the Irish Palestine Solidarity Committee. Our thanks go to those who organized this and to the Irish Government for their help during our mission to Gaza.

To the people of Gaza, we are sorry we never got to you. Sorry to have raised your hopes and dashed them when we, yet again, were diverted against our will and wishes to Ashdod.

But the Freedom Flotilla will be back. Someday, God willing (*In-sha-illah*) Gaza's seaport (after more than forty-two years of forced closure by Israeli military occupation) will be open and Palestinians will have free access to their waters and the world. Some day too Gaza's airport will be reopened (after having been bombed by the Israeli military) and they will be free to cross and trade through the land crossings. All this will happen, not because the Free Gaza movement sails to Gaza (but this helps); but because the people of Gaza and Palestine have kept faithful to their nonviolent resistance to demand an end to the occupation and their right to self-determination and human dignity.

We also hope that the International independent enquiry into the massacre by Israeli soldiers of the nine peace activists on board the *Mavi Marmara* will bring forth the truth; and that justice will be done for those people who died needlessly as they tried to help those suffering in Gaza.

Salam,
Mairead Maguire
Nobel Peace Laureate
July 2010

Chapter 22:

Epilogue:

⌘ ⌘ ⌘

By Greta Berlin

30 April, 2011

The murder of human rights activist, Vittorio Arrigoni, is a tragedy for his family, for those of us who knew him, and for the Palestinians who loved and admired him. The Steering Committee of Freedom Flotilla 2 condemns this senseless murder and the people who are behind it. They took the life of one of the most passionate supporters of justice for Palestine. This murder is damaging to the Palestinian struggle for freedom and justice as well as our work in support of that struggle.

In his honor, we are naming our next voyage, FREEDOM FLOTILLA – STAY HUMAN.

Nothing that we write can capture the man who was so full of the joy of life, a man with the pipe in his mouth and the captain's hat always tilted at an angle on his head. The man with the big smile and gentle nature, someone who used his physical strength to hold small children in his arms, sometimes several at a time. His laughter and his last comments every time we saw him will ring in all of our ears as we board the boats to return to Gaza in June 2011.

"Stay Human," he would say, then grin and clench his pipe in his teeth.

Vittorio had sailed with us from Greece on the first small fishing boat to enter Gaza in the summer of 2008, one of 44 activists sailing to protest the illegal blockade imposed by Israel against the 1.5 million Palestinians living in Gaza. We will do our best, Vik, to carry on the work you have done. The flotilla will return to Gaza in your honor.

Notes:

⌘   ⌘   ⌘

From Chapter 1: All Aboard to Gaza

1. *Middle East Report*, 152, <u>The Uprising</u> (1988): 52-53.

From Chapter 7: Gaza Is Not A Prison

Reference notes regarding internment camp and concentration camp:
Internment Camp (n)
　A camp where prisoners of war and hostile aliens are kept during a time of war.
http://www.thefreedictionary.com/internment+camp
Concentration Camp (n) http://www.thefreedictionary.com/concentration+camp

1. A camp, where civilians, political prisoners, and sometimes prisoners of war are detained and confined, typically under harsh conditions.

2. A place or situation characterized by extremely harsh conditions.

Civilian internee is a special status of a prisoner under the Fourth Geneva Convention. Civilian internees are civilians who are detained by a party to a war for security reasons.

The Fourth Geneva Convention relates to the protection of civilians during times of war. It specifies that those "in the hands" of an enemy and under any military occupation by a foreign power may not be punished for an offense he or she has not

personally committed. Reprisals against protected persons and their property are prohibited.
http://www.icrc.org/ihl.nsf/385ec082b509e76c44256739003e636d/6756482d861 46898c125644e004aa3c5

From Chapter 18: Stealing Gaza's Gas
David Schermerhorn, page 187

1 Andrew Muncie's Video
http://www.youtube.com/watch?v=PAUzugKX1AE
2 Gaza-Jericho Agreement May 4, 1994, Bloomberg.com
http://www.bloomberg.com/apps/news?pid=newsarchive&sid=aUNII FwH22dU
3 UN Convention on the Law of the Sea Part V
4 Peter Eyre interview on Energy World http://www.presstv.ir/Programs/player/?id=84338
5 New York Times 9/28/2000
6 Wikipedia Camp David Accord
7 Peter Eyre interview on Energy World
http://www.presstv.ir/Programs/player/?id=84338
8 Times On-Line 5/23/07
9 Wikipedia Second Intifada
10 Interviews with Gazan fishermen.
11 Wikipedia Directional Drilling
12 United Nations Mission Report of Catherine Bertini.
13 Pepijn Koster 7/1/07
http://www.myfavouriteplaces.org/wl/pivot/entry.php?id=52
14 www.uruknet.info ISM Nov. 5, 2008
15 IMEC 4/9/2009
16 Ha'aretz 12/28/08
17 Michel Chossudovsky Global Research 1/8/09
18 New York Times 12/20/08
19 Israeli Intelligence and Terrorism Information Center
20 ibid
21 New York Times 11/18/08
22 Enrique Ferro blog 12/14/09
23 Globes online 4/16/2009
24 Haaretz.com Avi Bar-Eli 11/02/2009
25 1/8/09 NY Times Op-Ed by Rashid Khalidi Ha'aretz 4/13/2009 Amos Harel

Notes on Israel's Disinformation Campaign on Page 251

NOTES:

[1] Amnesty International, Annual Human Rights Report (26 May 2010); http://thereport.amnesty.org/

[2] "The pasta, paper and hearing aids that could threaten Israeli security," The Independent (2 March 2009)

[3] "Restrictions on the transfer of goods to Gaza: Obstruction and obfuscation," Gisha (January 2010)

[4] "Carter calls Gaza blockade 'a crime and atrocity," Haaretz (17 April 2008), http://www.haaretz.com/news/carter-calls-gaza-blockade-a-crime-and-atrocity-1.244476

[5] "Gaza aid convoy refuses to deliver package to Gilad Shalit," Haaretz (27 May 2010)

[6] "Comprehensive Report on Status of Palestinian Political Prisoners," Samoud (June 2004); Palestinian Children Political Prisoners, Addameer, http://www.addameer.org/detention/children.html

[7] Article 42 of the Hague Regulations stipulates, a "territory is considered occupied when it is actually placed under the authority of the hostile army," and that the occupation extends "to the territory where such authority has been established and can be exercised." Similarly, in the Hostage Case, the Nuremburg Tribunal held that, "the test for application of the legal regime of occupation is not whether the occupying power fails to exercise effective control over the territory, but whether it has the ability to exercise such power." Palestinians living in the Gaza Strip, like those in the West Bank, continue to be subject to Israeli control. For example, Israel controls Gaza's air space, territorial waters, and all border crossings. Palestinians in Gaza require Israel's consent to travel to and from Gaza, to take their goods to Palestinian and foreign markets, to acquire food and medicine, and to access water and electricity. Without Israel's permission, the Palestinian Authority (PA) cannot perform such basic functions of government as providing social, health, security and utility services, developing the Palestinian economy and allocating resources.

[8] John Holmes, Briefing to the U Security Council on the Situation in the Middle East, including the Palestinian Question, 27 January 2009.

[9] Convention (IV) relative to the Protection of Civilian Persons in Time of War. Geneva, 12 August 1949, Article I stating, "The High Contracting Parties undertake to respect and to ensure respect for the present Convention in all circumstances." See also, Legal Consequences of the Construction of a Wall in the Occupied Palestinian Territory, Advisory Opinion, I. C. J. Reports 2004, p. 136 at 138;

http://www.icj-cij.org/docket/files/131/1671.pdf.

All other footnotes are in the body of the chapters, including videos from YouTube.

Appendix A
GAZA CHRONOLOGY June 19 – Dec. 27, 2008

⌘ ⌘ ⌘

Anis Hamadeh, Iveseh Lubben, Guzin Bilgi, Suzanne Shuster, and Paul Larudee

19th June:
Cease fire agreement between Israel and the Hamas government comes into force for six months. Israel insisted on a verbal agreement. It stated: cessation of all military hostilities on both sides, opening of Gaza's borders after seventy-two hours for 30 percent more trade and unrestricted trade after ten days. Egypt supported the extension of the agreement to the West Bank. (Source: International Crisis Group: Ending the War in Gaza. Middle East Briefing No. 26, 5.1.2009, 3)

19th June:
Israeli warships fire four rockets at Palestinian fishermen in Palestinian waters. On the same day, aircraft circling over Gaza City break the sound barrier near the ground and trigger a panic among the people. In the area of Khan Younis, Israeli patrols shoot over the border fence at farmers, who work on their fields on the other side of the border. (Source: Ma'an, 26.06.2008). This scenario is repeated almost daily.

24th June:
Two young officials of Jihad are murdered in their homes in Nablus by units of the IOF (Israeli Occupation Forces). On the same day, the al-Quds Brigades fire three

rockets at Sderot in retaliation. (Source: Ma'an 24.06.2008) The Israeli side uses the action of Jihad as an excuse to close the border crossings again.

26th June:

The al-Aqsa Brigades fire a rocket on Sderot after many Fatah members have been arrested in raids by the Israeli army. With this the al-Aqsa Brigades want to force the extension of the cease fire to the West Bank. The spokesman of the Hamas government in Gaza warns the al-Aqsa Brigades that their actions would prevent the lifting of the blockade and favor instead the narrower interests of an organizational and political nature.

29th June:

A delegation of farmers complains to the Hamas Ministry of Agriculture that because of the Israeli bombardment they can no longer cultivate their fields along the border fence.

4th August:

During a meeting of the Israeli labor party the minister of defense, Ehud Barak, threatens a ground invasion into the Gaza strip, despite Hamas' adherence to the cease fire.

8th August:

The director of the secret service Shin Bet, Yuval Diskin, thinks that a cease fire would reduce the pressure on Hamas to release Shalit. He calls on the army to prepare for a major military offensive. (Source: Ma'an 8.8.2008) These statements reinforce the impression among Palestinians that as far as the Israeli military leadership is concerned the purpose of the ceasefire is to gain time in order to prepare an offensive.

29th September:

The Israeli Navy sinks a fishing boat after fishing boats were shot at and rammed several times. Source: http://www.btselem.org/english/testimonies/20080910_israeli_navy_boat_charges_into_a_fishing_boat_witness_al_hasi.asp.

4th November:

Israeli troops enter into Khan Younis. Deliberately targeted projectiles kill six Hamas members and injure several people, including one woman. In Deir al-Balah several rockets are fired at residential areas. Near Wadi Salqa two houses of the Hawaidi family are destroyed and seven family members, three of them women, are kidnapped and taken to Israel. The same day Israeli border guards prevent French consular officials, who want to get a picture of the situation, from entering the Gaza strip. (Some background information: the dubious tunnelers Abu Dawabah is arrested and claims during interrogation that both Hamas and al-Aqsa brigades had offered him money for kidnapping an Israeli soldier. (Source: Ma'an 3.11.2008) One day later the Hamas Ministry of Internal Affairs issues a denial. (See also International Crisis Group: Ending the War in Gaza. Middle East Briefing No. 26, 5.1.2009, p.5)

5th November:

Residential areas in the north of the Gaza strip and Khan Younis are bombarded. Israeli troops kill a leader of Jihad and six Hamas officials. Because of this, Hamas, the al-Aqsa Brigades and Jihad fire rockets into Israel. Until then Hamas fully observed the ceasefire. Jihad and the al-Aqsa Brigades state that the ceasefire will not prevent them from reacting to Israeli violations of the agreement. In spite of this, Hamas wants to continue the ceasefire and ask Egypt for mediation.

5th November:

The Gaza Strip is completely sealed off. Even food, medicine, fuel, spare parts for generators and water pumps, paper, telephones and shoes can no longer or only in minimal amounts enter the Gaza Strip.

8th November:

Israeli bulldozers enter into the strip at several points. This leads to armed clashes with the units of the Democratic Front for the Liberation of Palestine (DFLP).

9th November:

Hamas Chief Ismail Haniyeh declares to European delegates, who had broken through the sea blockade with a boat of the Free Gaza movement and visited Gaza, that Hamas could live with a solution of the Palestine problem on the basis of UN Resolutions. (Source: Ma'an 9.11.2008)

12th November:

A further four Hamas members are killed. Israeli airplanes fire rockets at residential areas. The Palestinian factions are getting ever more skeptical about the ceasefire. Israeli bulldozers cut a 150-meter swath into an area in the Gaza Strip for military patrols, destroying about 750 hectares of agrarian land. (Source: Ma'an 21.11.2008)

13th November:

Israeli border patrols bar a UN food convoy from passing the border. The DFLP claims that for Israel this was not about the ceasefire, but about breaking

resistance to the occupation. In the following days the Popular Front for the Liberation of Palestine (PFLP), the DFLP, the Popular Committees and Hamas fire projectiles at Israeli places while Israeli airplanes bomb the north of the Gaza Strip.

16th November:
The Israeli Minister of Transport calls for killing the whole Hamas leadership. During new attacks another four members of the Popular Committees are killed. By
now fifteen people have been killed during the air strikes in recent days. The Popular Committees declare the end of the cease fire. Their spokesperson blames Israel.

17th November:
The DLFP and Jihad fire rockets into Israel.

18th November:
The food crisis gets worse and worse. Fifty percent of the bakeries cannot operate
anymore due of lack of flour. Others use animal feed to bake bread. Israeli tanks
enter the strip; there are armed clashes with the PFLP and the mujahaddin, another resistance group of Fatah. The Israeli Navy arrest fifteen fishermen and three
foreign solidarity activists off the coast of Gaza. The "Internationals" accompanied
the fishermen in the hope that their presence would guarantee a minimum of protection. They are taken to Israel and get expelled after six days of solitary confinement. (Source Ma'an 18.11.2008). The three fishing boats were given back after
nine days, but one boat was damaged, the GPS device was missing. During their
days in prison, the solidarity workers were barred from contacting their lawyers
and their embassies. Source:
 http://www.freegaza.org/de/home/547-three-palestinian-fishing-boats-returned
and http://www.freegaza.org/de/home/558-kidnapped-in-gaza

20th November:
Yet again a Hamas member is killed by targeted rocket strikes. Hamas increasingly
comes under pressure from the other groups as well as their own base, who demand they force Israel to keep to the ceasefire. But how?

23rd November
Diplomatic sources claim that the Egyptians stepped in and got Hamas and the
Israeli government to agree to resume the ceasefire according to the conditions
originally negotiated. This is confirmed by Hamas. Hamas spokesman Ayman Taha
furthermore states that the other resistance groups also agree to the continuation

of the cease fire on the condition that the blockade is lifted. Israel does not comment on this.

24th November:
A member of the Popular Committee is killed by an Israeli rocket after Israeli claims that rockets were fired, but no one claimed responsibility for that; the Israeli Minister of Defense, Ehud Barak, retracts the order to open the border for urgently needed food deliveries. As far back as August, rockets had been fired on several occasions from the Gaza Strip to the Negev desert, without claim of responsibility. This led to the closure of the border each time. At the time Hamas, leader Mahmud al-Zahhar accused Israeli agents of creating a pretext for a land invasion. (Source Ma'an 12.9.2008). Also at the time, the names of groups nobody in Gaza had heard of before and knew anything about crop up such as: Ahrar al-Jalil, Tawhid Brigades or Hisb Allah. Some believe they are collaborators wanting to corrupt the ceasefire. Other voices believe they are small radical cells that think Hamas have made too many concessions.

28th November:
The Israeli army kills a man from Khan Younis, who doesn't belong to any organization. On the same day eight Israeli soldiers are injured at a boarder border post through attacks by the mujahaddin.

30th November:
Jihad declares they no longer feel bound by the ceasefire. The al-Aqsa Brigades fire projectiles at Sderot again. Hamas and Jihad are warned by mediators from Qatar that Israel plans a major military offensive in the Gaza Strip. The political leadership of Hamas issues an urgent appeal to armed groups including their own al-Qassam Brigades to stop firing rockets into Israel.

2nd December:
Israeli tanks enter the Gaza Strip again. Two teenagers are killed in air strikes.

4th December:
Al-Aqsa Brigades fire rockets at Ashkelon.

5th December:
Massive assaults by Jewish settlers on Palestinians in Hebron. While the al-Aqsa Brigades, the DFLP and the al-Quds Brigades of the Jihad fire rockets at Israeli

places as a reaction to the events in the West Bank, Hamas organizes solidarity demonstrations with Palestinians in Hebron to rescue what is left of the ceasefire agreement.

7th December:
The blockade in the Gaza Strip is getting more severe. A boat from Israel with peace activists wanting to bring food and gifts for children to Gaza on the occasion of the feast of sacrifice is forced to turn back by Israeli warships. The same fate befalls a boat from Qatar and another one from Libya, both of which want to deliver food to Gaza.

13th December:
Tzipi Livni states that in case a Palestinian state is set up, the Palestinian people living in Israel would be expatriated. By now, no organization thinks there is any purpose in extending the ceasefire. Brigades of the DFLP, al-Aqsa, the Popular Committees and Jihad fire at Israeli places on a regular basis. The political leadership of Hamas in Gaza, especially the de facto president Haniyeh, has no means of preventing this, because even their own armed faction, the al-Qassam Brigades, no longer see any sense in the ceasefire.

14th December:
The Hamas leadership abroad states through Khaled Mashaal that Hamas rejects an extension of the ceasefire, whereas Haniyeh still hopes that Egyptian mediation will help achieve an extension.

19th December:
On the same day the six-month-ceasefire ends all factions declare at separate mass events that they consider the ceasefire to be finished—even Fatah.

20th December:
Fawzi Barhum, the spokesman of Hamas, calls on all factions to form a common resistance front. His acerbic reply to the Russian demand that Hamas should consider the extension of the ceasefire is that the onus was now on the international community to put pressure on Israel to cease the attacks on the Palestinian people, instead of blaming the victims of these attacks. (Source: Ma'an 21.12.2008) But the Egyptians do not react.

23rd December:
The former Minister of Foreign Affairs of the Hamas government, Mahmud al-Zahhar, declares once again that Hamas is prepared to continue with the ceasefire

agreement, provided Israel adheres to the conditions agreed in June, in particular the lifting of the blockade. But the discourse of al-Qassam Brigades is more subdued. Abu Ubaida, spokesman of al-Qassam Brigades, speaks only about the possibility of suspending the military action and no longer about a ceasefire and does not exclude any military action in Israel if Israel does not stop its aggression against Gaza. (Source: Ma'an 23.12.2008)

27th December:
The Israeli military attacks the Gaza Strip, killing about 1,360 people, mostly civilians including more than 400 children, by 18 January 2009. Many thousands are injured and made homeless. Israel uses phosphorus as a weapon, turns over a cemetery, shoots at the UN, schools, mosques etc. About thirteen people die on the Israeli side; some of them are killed by their own soldiers. The West puts the whole blame for the catastrophe on Hamas.

Appendix B:
Free Gaza Related Books, DVDs and Web Sites

⌘ ⌘ ⌘

Books:

Arrigoni , Vittorio, *Gaza Ratiamo Umani, Il Manifesto-Manifestolibri, 2009* - **Gaza: Stay Human**, New York, Kube Publishing Ltd, 2010; (Available in Italian and in English)

Bayoumi, Moustafa, editor, **Midnight on the Mavi Marmara**, New York, O/R Books, 2010; www.**orbooks**.com/our-books/midnight;

Goffeng, Espen, *Doedelig Farvann* **(Deadly Seas)**, Manifest Publishing, Due out November 2010 by (available in Norwegian)

Jasiewicz, Ewa, *Gaza Getto Nieujarzmione*, WAB Press; Due to be published, Autumn, 2010 (Available in Polish)

Lock, Sharyn and Sarah Irving, **Gaza Beneath the Bombs**, London, Pluto Press, 2010.

Wright, Col. Ann and Susan Dixon, **Dissent: Voices of Conscience-Government Insiders Speak Out Against the War in Iraq**, Maui, Hawaii, Koa Books, 2010

DVDs:

To Gaza with Love: A Film by Aki Nawaz, www.PalestineOnlineStore.com

Gaza: We are Coming, Directed by: Yorgos Avgeropoulos, Yiannis Karipidis. A Small Planet production for Al Jazeera Satellite Network © 2009 / World Sales: Anastasia Skoubri info@smallplanet.gr; Winner of the 12th Thessaloniki Documentary Film Festival; available in Greek, English or Arabic

To Shoot an Elephant: A documentary by Alberto Acre and Mohammad Rujailah, http://toshootanelephant.com/node

Web Sites:

www.palsolidrity.org, www.freegaza.org, www.witnessgaza.com, www.electronicintifada.net, www.palestinechronicle.com www.paltelegraph.com, www.goldstone-report.org

Made in the USA
Charleston, SC
26 January 2012